VALIDITY in ED &
PSYCHOLOGICAL T

VALIDITY in EDUCATIONAL & PSYCHOLOGICAL ASSESSMENT

PAUL E. NEWTON & STUART D. SHAW

CAMBRIDGE ASSESSMENT

Los Angeles | London | New Delhi
Singapore | Washington DC

CAMBRIDGE ASSESSMENT

Established over 150 years ago, Cambridge Assessment operates and manages the University's three exam boards and carries out leading-edge academic and operational research on assessment in education. It is a not-for-profit organisation developing and delivering educational assessment to eight million candidates in 170 countries every year.

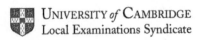

UNIVERSITY *of* CAMBRIDGE
Local Examinations Syndicate

Cambridge Assessment is the brand name of the University of Cambridge Local Examinations Syndicate, a department of the University of Cambridge. Cambridge Assessment is a not-for-profit organisation.

Los Angeles | London | New Delhi
Singapore | Washington DC

SAGE Publications Ltd
1 Oliver's Yard
55 City Road
London EC1Y 1SP

SAGE Publications Inc.
2455 Teller Road
Thousand Oaks, California 91320

SAGE Publications India Pvt Ltd
B 1/I 1 Mohan Cooperative Industrial Area
Mathura Road
New Delhi 110 044

SAGE Publications Asia-Pacific Pte Ltd
3 Church Street
#10-04 Samsung Hub
Singapore 049483

Published in association with:
Cambridge Assessment
1 Hills Road
Cambridge
CB1 2EU

Editor: Marianne Lagrange
Editorial assistant: Rachael Plant
Project manager: Sharon Cawood
Production editor: Thea Watson
Copyeditor: Lisa Cordaro
Proofreader: Jill Birch
Indexer: Avril Ehrlich
Marketing manager: Catherine Slinn
Cover designer: Naomi Robinson
Typeset by: C&M Digitals (P) Ltd, Chennai, India
Printed in India by Replika Press Pvt Ltd

Library of Congress Control Number: 2013946019

British Library Cataloguing in Publication data

A catalogue record for this book is available from the British Library

ISBN 978-1-4462-5322-9
ISBN 978-1-4462-5323-6

CONTENTS

ABOUT THE AUTHORS

Paul E. Newton is Professor of Educational Assessment at the Institute of Education, University of London. His research focuses primarily on issues related to the evaluation of large-scale educational assessment systems, and he is particularly interested in theories of validity for educational and psychological measurement, past and present. He has published on a range of assessment topics including validity, comparability, assessment purposes, national curriculum test reliability and public understanding of measurement inaccuracy.

Having obtained a PhD in developmental psychology, Paul moved into educational assessment and has spent most of his career as a researcher within a range of assessment agencies, including the Associated Examining Board, National Foundation for Educational Research, Qualifications and Curriculum Authority, Ofqual and Cambridge Assessment.

Paul is a member of the Editorial Board of the international journal *Assessment in Education: Policy, Principles and Practice*, and has served on a variety of national and international committees including the Executive Committee of the International Association for Educational Assessment. He was a member of the Assessment Reform Group until its retirement in 2010, and is a Fellow of the Association for Educational Assessment in Europe.

Stuart D. Shaw has worked for Cambridge Assessment since January 2001, where he is particularly interested in demonstrating how Cambridge Assessment seeks to meet the demands of validity in its assessments. Before leading a research team in the area of mainstream international examinations, Stuart worked on a range of Cambridge English products with specific skill responsibilities for assessing writing. He has experience in the areas of researching and managing English second language writing assessment; developing, revising and introducing assessment procedures for new testing scenarios, and disseminating good practice to others through mentoring, lecturing and informal advice; and establishing criteria for good practice in the type of public examination offered by Cambridge English and Cambridge International Examinations.

Stuart has a wide range of publications in English second language assessment and educational research journals. He is a Fellow of the Association for Educational Assessment in Europe, and a Fellow of the Chartered Institute of Educational Assessors.

ACKNOWLEDGEMENTS

In bringing this book to completion, we were reminded constantly of our indebtedness to a great many individuals. Their encouragement, forbearance and expert engagement undoubtedly has contributed to the quality and value of the work. In the course of researching and writing the book, we engaged with numerous measurement and assessment specialists and although on occasions we have contended with them, we hope we have done so without being unduly contentious.

Our first debt of gratitude is to Val Klenowski (Queensland University of Technology) and Constant Leung (King's College London) for their insightful and encouraging reviews of the manuscript.

We owe an equal debt to a number of specialists in the field of educational and psychological testing who provided expert input and reflection on individual chapters: Paul Warwick (University of Cambridge) and Isabel Nisbet (Cambridge International Examinations) who reviewed Chapter 1; Howard Everson (City University of New York) who reviewed Chapter 3; Dylan Wiliam (Institute of Education, University of London) who reviewed Chapter 4; Andrew Maul and Derek Briggs (University of Colorado, Boulder) who reviewed Chapter 5; and Helen Patrick (independent consultant) who reviewed Chapter 6; and Gordon Stobart (Institute of Education, University of London) who reviewed a number of chapters. We gladly acknowledge our gratitude to them for their universally insightful and useful comments.

We are particularly indebted to the Validity Advisory Group, which was established with the support of the business streams that comprise Cambridge Assessment, for supporting the development of the text and reviewing chapters: Tim Oates (Chair, Cambridge Assessment), Beth Black (Oxford Cambridge and RSA Examinations), Neil Jones (Cambridge English), Paul Beedle (Cambridge International Examinations) and Victoria Crisp (Cambridge Assessment).

We are also indebted to the decision-makers within Cambridge Assessment, particularly Tim Oates, who supported the project and allowed time to be committed to it. In addition, as the first author relocated during the writing of the book, we are similarly indebted to those at the Institute of Education who supported its completion.

The academic research community in Cambridge Assessment has been a source of great support and intellectual invigoration. Many colleagues have contributed to the book by sharing their time, resources and knowledge. We extend special thanks to Anthony Dawson (Cambridge International Examinations), Nick Saville (Cambridge English), Phineas Hodson (Cambridge International Examinations) and Tom Bramley (Cambridge Assessment) for their judicious and perceptive observations and analyses. The book is considerably stronger in light of their skills and expertise.

We have benefited greatly from conversations with experts from the academic research community beyond Cambridge Assessment, particularly Mike Kane (Educational Testing Service), Keith Markus (John Jay College of Criminal Justice, City University of New York), Denny Borsboom (University of Amsterdam), Alastair Pollitt (independent consultant), Ayesha Ahmed (University of Cambridge), Alison Wood (Assessment and Qualifications Alliance) and Jo-Anne Baird (University of Oxford).

Numerous others have played a part along the way, to whom we owe great thanks. In particular, we are especially fortunate to have worked with Fiona Beedle (Librarian, Cambridge Assessment). We would like to acknowledge her unrelenting enthusiasm and extraordinary ability to locate the most obscure and archaic materials in support of our research.

Finally, we recognize that this book could not have reached publication without the professional contribution and flexibility of the administrators and editors at Sage, particularly Marianne Lagrange. We thank them for their reassuring sagacity and patience.

LIST OF TABLES AND FIGURES

FOREWORD

In developing, administering and evaluating assessments, what possibly could be more important than validity? Surely clarity regarding purpose, impact and whether each assessment actually assesses what it claims to assess should be a pre-eminent concern of both developers and users? However, in England – the home country of the authors – discourse around assessment has been dominated by issues of 'standards', assessment load, washback of assessment into pedagogy, and balance of assessment forms. It can readily be argued that although various assumptions regarding validity are embedded in these matters, illuminating discussion of validity and coherent effort devoted to validation has assumed too low a profile.

Over the past 30 years, assessment arrangements in England have seen huge reversals in policy. Contrary positions have emerged on the balance of forms of assessment; subtle yet important shifts have arisen regarding the purposes and uses of qualifications; and pendulum swings have occurred in both surface and fundamental matters. My long view on this is that an absence of clarity regarding validity has both permitted and fuelled this intensely dynamic history. Elsewhere across the globe, debates over validity frequently are subordinated to (undeniably important) concerns such as the development of entitlement to universal education, improving equity and quality in education and training, and tackling maladministration in assessment. However, confusion regarding validity, or simply the neglect of it, is a serious matter. Instances of deleterious washback from assessment into learning, misclassification of individuals and groups, and waste of resources can emerge as immediate consequences. Neglect of validity denies to society, policymakers and assessment professionals key anchor points regarding quality and practice.

In order to trace better the form of these possible anchor points, the authors of this book have turned to the most prominent discourse on validity – the US-led debate – and have examined both the quality and nature of the debate. If neglecting validity carries risk, is tackling it head-on productive and helpful? The authors observe that even where validity has been an explicit concern of both the education establishment and the assessment community, there has been scant consensus. Their meticulous examination of the unfolding construction of competing perspectives tells a story of seismic paradigm shifts, misconstruals and misunderstandings. In tracing the winding paths of reasoning and assertion, they explore the extent to which the *form* of the debate has conditioned the substantive *content* of the debate.

While among theorists and developers the skirmishing and trench warfare of paradigm wars unfolds, the practical task of delivering dependable assessment in schools, universities and workplaces continues to be essential to creating both individual and social good. The analysis in this book steers a careful pathway between validity scholars' tendency to myopia – created by applying tight analytic attention to the arguments of specific theorists and practitioners – and the reverse tendency towards unconstrained expansion of concern and focus. What I find particularly attractive about the authors' approach is the combination of forensic analysis of leading thinkers' theses (and thus frequently putting the record straight), with a pragmatic, wide-ranging overview of ambitious assessment policies. Their analysis culminates in a compelling drive towards 'locating assessment within complex systems'. This takes us through a consideration not only of the essential characteristics of assessment instruments, but also of human intentions regarding assessment, the fallibilities and triumphs of design, and the uses and abuses of outcomes.

This wider analysis immediately contextualizes the 'extractions' from the validity debates represented by reference points such as the American Educational Research Association (AERA), American Psychological Association (APA) and National Council on Measurement in Education (NCME) standards, the Cambridge Approach and the Cambridge English 'Validity, Reliability, Impact, Practicability and Quality' model. These have led to a material improvement in design, administration and evaluation – they have stimulated greater attention to purpose, the construct base of assessment, the responsible use of outcomes and impact.

Newton's and Shaw's exploration of impact and utility – which remains a key matter, whether or not it is included in more restricted definitions of 'validity' – highlights the important insights and methodological lessons emerging from extended validation programmes. Valuable practical experience of the resource-hungry nature of these studies, and the moral impetus behind them, is emerging from studies in train as this volume goes to print. While the authors identify the very real defects in both the manner and content of the last 100 years of analytic work on validity, the scholarly deconstruction of thinking provides a key means of moving to a revised theoretical base which better underpins practical action: a pathway to better instruments and better policy.

Tim Oates

PREFACE

The concept of validity was introduced formally to measurement professionals within education and psychology during the 1920s. It is now widely accepted as the most fundamental of all testing concepts. Yet, excluding a small number of edited collections, almost no books are entirely devoted to the topic. This led us to think that we might be able to make a useful contribution to the field by writing a book on validity, given that it was a topic that we had been interested in for some time, and that we wanted to explore in far more depth. We did not think that this would be easy. We did not think that we would necessarily be able to make sense of all of the subtle intricacies of a concept that has challenged measurement specialists for the best part of a century – but we decided to do it anyway. Having now completed the book, we can safely say that it was not at all easy; we should admit also that we did not manage to make sense of all of the subtle intricacies either, but we have learned a lot, and hope that what we have written may help others to find their own way through the nuanced, abstract and often confusing maze of ideas on validity theory and validation practice.

Originally we envisaged this book as a resource for master's level courses in educational and psychological measurement and assessment, and as a resource for measurement scientists and practitioners who wish to gain a deeper understanding of validity and validation. Therefore, we tried to make it as accessible as possible: for example, by avoiding the use of statistical formulae, and by addressing the underlying philosophical issues in a straightforward manner. Where we have ventured into philosophical territories, we hope to have done so as lucidly as possible without having oversimplified what ultimately are quite complicated debates. For those of our readers who wish to explore the technical and philosophical foundations of validity in more detail, we can recommend a text that has been recently published, and which therefore only features in this Preface: Markus, K.A. and Borsboom, D. (2013) *Frontiers of Test Validity Theory: Measurement, Causation and Meaning*. New York: Routledge.

We hope that we have written with sufficient clarity that even a validity novice might be able to benefit from reading it. Having said that, anyone who is unfamiliar with the concept might benefit even more if they were to begin by reading one or two of the more accessible overview articles that can be found in the literature. This will help to set the scene and contextualize the debates with which we engage. We have found the following articles useful:

- Brown, T. (2010) 'Construct validity: A unitary concept for occupational therapy assessment and measurement', *Hong Kong Journal of Occupational Therapy*, 20 (1): 30–42.
- Crooks, T.J., Kane, M.T. and Cohen, A.S. (1996) 'Threats to the valid use of assessments', *Assessment in Education: Principles, Policy and Practice*, 3 (3): 265–85.
- Downing, S.M. (2003) 'Validity: on the meaningful interpretation of assessment data', *Medical Education*, 37 (9): 830–7.
- Haladyna, T.M. (2006) 'Roles and importance of validity studies in test development', in S.M. Downing and T.M. Haladyna (eds), *Handbook of Test Development*. Mahwah, NJ: Lawrence Erlbaum Associates, pp. 739–55.
- Kane, M.T. (2001) 'Current concerns in validity theory', *Journal of Educational Measurement*, 38 (4): 319–42.
- Sireci, S.G. (2009) 'Packing and unpacking sources of validity evidence: history repeats itself again', in R.W. Lissitz (ed.), *The Concept of Validity: Revisions, New Directions and Applications*. Charlotte, NC: Information Age Publishing, pp. 19–37.
- Wiliam, D. (2008) 'Quality in assessment', in S. Swaffield (ed.), *Unlocking Assessment: Understanding for Reflection and Application*. Oxford: Routledge, pp. 123–37.

We should state from the outset that this is not a 'how to' guide to validation. There is definitely a gap in the market for a book like that, but our book is more of a 'how to understand' guide to validity and validation. We think that it is important to understand validity and validation before embarking on validation research. As we see it, the purpose of validation is to provide empirical evidence and logical analysis in support of an argument which concludes in a validity claim. Put simply, if you do not understand what you are trying to claim, then you will not be able to develop a strong validity argument.

One of the hardest nuts to crack was the title for this book. Validity in educational and psychological *assessment*, or validity in educational and psychological *measurement*? *Education* and *psychology*? *Validity* or perhaps simply *evaluation*? First, we work in education, and our interest in validity relates particularly to curriculum-embedded school examinations. Inevitably, this will have shaped the range of issues and authors whose work we have engaged with most deeply. However, it is simply not possible to understand the history of ideas on validity without adopting a far broader perspective, since the concept has been honed collectively by the various communities that together comprise the field of educational and psychological measurement. So, we have made an effort to engage with the most important of contributions, from whichever subdomain they might have emerged (personnel psychology, educational psychology, educational testing, clinical psychology, etc.).

Second, one of the more recent and most damning criticisms of validity theory is that it has failed to scrutinize in sufficient detail its central idea: measurement. Some would say that the attributes of educational and psychological measurement – intelligence, aptitude, proficiency, etc. – simply are not the kind of things that can be *measured*. They might still be *assessed*, because the idea of assessment is far looser than the concept of measurement, so all is not lost; but the idea of measurement carries connotations of structure that the attributes of education and psychology may not possess. Because we do not have a strong attachment to the term 'measurement' as opposed to 'assessment' – and because validity theory has been developed to embrace any kind of structured assessment – we could have avoided talk of measurement entirely. In fact, we chose to do the reverse, for the simple reason that our account is essentially historical, and that the validity literature has tended to be couched in terms of 'measurement' talk within the 'educational and psychological measurement' literature. Ostensibly, then, the title of our book is out-of-kilter with the terminology that we use within it. In fact, our use of 'assessment' in the title is a very useful reminder that the concept of validity that we discuss is intended to embrace anything from multiple-choice tests to personality inventories, clinical interviews and performance assessments. The use of 'assessment' is also a useful reminder that 'measurement' might be too strong a concept to apply to the attributes of education and psychology.

Third, validity or evaluation? One of the thorniest problems in the literature of the 21st century is the extent to which validity covers the many aspects of an assessment's wider context. Some validity theorists adopt a very liberal definition, which stretches to include the evaluation of just about anything to do with a testing policy. Others adopt a very conservative definition, which does not even embrace everything to do with a test. In Chapter 6, we attempt to sidestep this lexical dispute over the scope of the term 'validity' by choosing not to affiliate with either of these camps, nor with any of the camps in-between. Instead, we choose to describe in some detail the ingredients of comprehensive 'evaluation' interpreted broadly. We contemplated adopting the same strategy in our title by not referring to 'validity' at all, but that would have given the wrong message. The term 'validity' is certainly problematic, but a key objective of the text is to help to explain *why* it is problematic, by exploring the history of its many different uses and incarnations.

Finally, a number of reviewers suggested that we might introduce chapters with abstracts or summaries of key points, and conclude chapters with key readings and questions for further contemplation. We thought that these were excellent suggestions – but deadlines got the better of us! However, we vowed to put this right by developing a number of learning resources to accompany the book. You should be able to find information on these resources on the Cambridge Assessment website (www.cambridgeassessment.org.uk).

Paul E. Newton
Stuart D. Shaw

CHAPTER 1

VALIDITY AND VALIDATION

Validity is the hallmark of quality as far as testing is concerned, being the 'single most important criterion' for evaluating a test (Koretz, 2008: 215). At this level of generality, the many sub-communities of scientists and practitioners that comprise the field of educational and psychological measurement are probably in agreement. However, when interrogated further, this relatively bland consensus can be shown to conceal many different perspectives on the meaning of validity, reflecting claims at a variety of levels, for example, that:

1 it is possible to measure an attribute accurately using test scores (validity as a measurement concept); or
2 it is possible to make accurate and useful decisions on the basis of test scores (validity as a measurement and decision-making concept); or
3 it is acceptable to implement a testing policy (validity as a concept spanning measurement, decision-making and broader impacts and side-effects).

The first of these alternatives is essentially a technical or scientific claim concerning test score meaning: it was how validity was originally defined in the 1920s. The third is ultimately a social or ethical claim concerning test score use. Plenty of debate in recent years has focused on whether or not ethical concerns have anything to do with validity. The second alternative lies somewhere in-between these extremes, having dimensions that are essentially scientific (accuracy) and essentially ethical (usefulness). We begin this book with these three alternatives simply to highlight the fact that the very nature of validity is heavily contested within the field of educational and psychological measurement, despite nearly 100 years of debate on the topic. Part of our intention is to explain why it remains so contested. Not only is the concept heavily contested, but it also can be very confusing to understand for both novice and expert alike. There are many reasons for this:

- There is a very large, disparate literature on validity within educational and psychological measurement, spanning the best part of a century.
- There are large, disparate literatures on validity within other disciplines that are related only tangentially to the testing concept.
- The 'official' meaning of validity among measurement professionals has evolved over time.
- The concept has gained stature over the decades and expanded correspondingly.
- Some of the most important accounts are extremely hard to read (e.g. Messick, 1989a).
- The term 'validity' is employed in so many different ways, in so many different contexts, that often it is entirely unclear what the speaker intends to convey.

The final point is crucial. It is often unclear whether or not the term is being used in a technical sense; and, if it is being used in this way, whether this is the technical sense of educational and psychological measurement, or of another discipline entirely. So this chapter begins by exploring a range of everyday and technical meanings to help set the scene for the account that follows.

What do *we* mean by validity?

When we (the authors) refer to validity, we are referring to a technical term of educational and psychological measurement which relates to the idea of validation. Validity and validation are two sides of the same coin. Validation is an investigation into validity, so validity is the property that is to be investigated; and validation is the process by which it is investigated. *Validity theory* provides a conceptual framework to guide *validation practice*. The main chapters of this book will demonstrate how even this technical meaning of validity has proved to be highly controversial and continually resisted precise definition.

In everyday life, validity is the quality or state of being valid, where this can mean anything from being true, to being cogent to being legally acceptable. It derives from the Latin word *validus*, meaning 'strong', 'healthy' or 'worthy' (Wiktionary, 2013). The technical concept of validity, as it has evolved within educational and psychological measurement, has been associated with all of these different meanings at one point or another, as we shall see as the chapters unfold. First, we consider how validity has evolved within other contexts and disciplines.

Validity across disciplines

Validity has a well-established and very specific meaning in philosophy in the sub-discipline of logic, where it applies to deductive arguments. Fogelin and Sinnott-Armstrong (2001), for instance, defined validity as follows: 'An argument is *valid* if and only if it is not possible for all of its premises to be true when its conclusion is false' (p. 36, italics in original). This is an example of a valid deductive argument:

all men are mortal, Samuel Messick was a man, therefore Samuel Messick was mortal. The following argument would be equally valid: all men are immortal, Samuel Messick was a man, therefore Samuel Messick was immortal. In the terminology of deductive argument, the second of these examples is a valid argument, given its logical structure, but it is not a sound argument because one of its premises is untrue.

Over the past couple of decades, an argument-based approach to validation has become popular (see Chapter 5). From this perspective, validation is seen as the process of developing and appraising the strength of an argument concerning the interpretation and use of test scores. The formal, deductive arguments of philosophy are not actually that relevant to validation which, instead, tends to involve informal, largely inductive arguments. Many informal logicians explicitly avoid using the term 'validity' to describe inductive arguments, since it implies too high a standard. Instead of judging them according to the standard of validity, they are judged according to the standard of *strength* (see Fogelin and Sinnott-Armstrong, 2001). Therefore, we might legitimately refer to the strength of a validity argument, but not to the validity of a validity argument. This is a good thing, because having to refer to the validity of validity arguments is potentially very confusing.

Just as validity has a distinctive meaning in philosophy, it also has distinctive meanings across other academic disciplines (Newton and Shaw, 2013). The concept appears in fields as disparate as law (e.g. Austin, 1995[1832]; Waluchow, 2009), economics (e.g. MacPhail, 1998) and pattern recognition (e.g. Halkidi et al., 2002). It appears in disciplines that are quite distant from educational and psychological measurement and, more confusingly, in disciplines that lie right on its borders, such as genetic testing (e.g. Holtzman and Watson, 1997) and management (e.g. Markus and Robey, 1980).

Validity for research

Perhaps most confusing of all, validity appears as a concept within education and psychology, but without connotations specific to measurement. This is to draw a distinction between *validity for research* and *validity for measurement*. Validity for research is relevant whenever conclusions are to be drawn on the basis of research evidence. Validity for measurement is relevant only for conclusions that relate specifically to measurement.

A particularly important contribution to the literature on validity for research was made by Campbell (1957), who drew a distinction between internal validity and external validity in relation to the design of social science experiments. On the one hand, internal validity concerned the degree of confidence that could be placed in the conclusion that an observed effect was genuine for the experimental group. Confidence in this conclusion could be increased by designs which enabled alternative explanations to be ruled out: for example, the addition of a 'no treatment' control group to a pre-test/post-test design, which enabled the researcher to rule out explanations such as the effect simply being one of maturation between pre-test and post-test. On the other hand, external validity concerned the degree of confidence that could be placed in the conclusion that the observed effect would generalize from the experimental group to the population from which the group was drawn, or to other populations, settings or variables. Confidence in this conclusion would decrease with biased sampling procedures, or if evidence accrued that the very process of experimentation or observation seemed to be causing the effect.

These ideas were developed by Bracht and Glass (1968), who subdivided external validity into two sub-categories: population validity and ecological validity. Population validity concerned confidence in the generalization of conclusions across populations. Ecological validity concerned confidence in the generalization of conclusions across conditions: for example, settings, treatments, researchers and dependent variables. Over the years, the concept of ecological validity was subdivided further: outcome validity concerned generalization across dependent variables; temporal validity concerned generalization across time; and treatment variation validity concerned generalization across treatment variations.

Campbell also developed his thesis (Campbell and Stanley, 1966[1963]; Cook and Campbell, 1979). Cook and Campbell (1979) divided internal validity into statistical conclusion validity plus internal validity, and divided external validity into construct validity plus external validity, thus deriving a four-way classification which corresponded to the four major decisions facing researchers.

Concepts of validity for research have been developed in different directions by researchers within qualitative traditions, including Lather (1986, 1993), Maxwell (1992), Kvale (1995) and others. In these contexts, validity often has been interpreted to mean confidence in the trustworthiness or credibility of description and interpretation: that is, the legitimacy of the knowledge produced. It also has been extended to embrace the social consequences of qualitative research. Lather (1986) proposed three main conceptions of validity:

1   face validity, which elevated the importance of member-checking – i.e. playing researcher accounts back to participants;
2   construct validity, which stressed systematized reflexivity, exploring how the researcher's theory had changed in response to the data; and
3   catalytic validity, which referred to the degree to which the research process facilitated the transformation of reality by participants, reorienting, focusing and energizing them.

Although it is important not to confuse validity for measurement with validity for research, it is very easy to do so for all sorts of reasons. First, some of the key contributors theorized validity in both contexts – most notably, Campbell. Having said that, even he kept his discussion of validity for measurement (Campbell and Fiske, 1959; Campbell, 1960) quite distinct from his discussion of validity for research (Campbell, 1957; Campbell and Stanley, 1966[1963]; Cook and Campbell, 1979). Second, many of those who theorized validity for research borrowed ideas from the existing literature on validity for measurement. For example, both Cook and Campbell

(1979) and Lather (1986) proposed versions of construct validity which had been originally theorized for measurement by Cronbach and Meehl (1955). Third, quite a few terms are common to both the research and measurement literatures, sometimes with quite different meanings attached. For example, the distinction between internal validity and external validity drawn by Campbell (1957) in the context of research was quite different from the distinction drawn seven years earlier, in the context of measurement, by Guttman (1950), using exactly the same terminology. Finally, it is easy to confuse the two because validation inevitably involves research, which means that validity for research is relevant whenever validity for measurement is being investigated; whereas the converse is not true.

In short, if you want to understand validity for measurement, first you need to appreciate that it is not the same as everyday validity, it is not the same as academic validity across different disciplines, and it is not the same as validity for research. Validity for measurement may resonate with many of these alternative ideas, occasionally share their nomenclature and even have inspired them, but ultimately it is different. Bear this in mind when you are searching for 'validity' on the internet.

Validity for measurement: attributes and decisions

When we (the authors) refer to 'validity', we mean validity for educational and psychological measurement. At the risk of over-generalizing, we might be persuaded to extend this conception to social measurement more broadly, but educational and psychological measurement is our central concern. This is a very broad discipline; in fact, perhaps it is better described as a group of disciplines, some more educational and some more psychological. As we will discuss in Chapter 2, the field coalesced around the turn of the 20th century, as measurement movements united interests as disparate as those of academic psychologists who wished to tap the essence of the human mind, and practising educationalists who wished to hold schools to account for the quality of education delivered.

Educational and psychological measurement, like engineering, is a group of disciplines with a very practical side to it. Generally speaking, individuals are measured in order to make decisions. Thus, measurement and decision-making are intimately linked on the assumption that the more accurate the measurement, the better the decision that ultimately can be taken. The various professions can be characterized very roughly in terms of the most significant decisions that they need to make, and the different attributes that they need to measure in order to make those decisions. Table 1.1 illustrates a range of decisions and attributes for a variety of measurement professionals. It should be read as follows: a clinical psychologist might be interested in diagnosing a personality disorder, for example manic depression, to help them to decide on a treatment for a client. Although the table makes a useful point, the dividing lines between professions are not actually that easy to draw, since many different types of decision are made by professionals working in all of these fields.

Sometimes test scores are aggregated across individuals to provide composite measures of higher-level attributes. This is particularly common in education, when

Table 1.1   Examples of attributes measured to make decisions

Measurement professional	Attribute (example)	Decision
Clinical psychologist	Manic depression	What treatment to prescribe
Vocational counsellor	Compassion	Vocational guidance for a student
Educational psychologist	Dyslexia	What intervention to offer a family
Teacher	Mathematical attainment	The set or stream in which to place a student
Personnel psychologist	Aptitude for clerical work	Whether to select a candidate for a job

results are aggregated across students to provide composite measures of educational effectiveness for teachers, schools, regions or even the nation. For example, test results aggregated to the class level might be used to judge whether one teacher has taught more effectively than another. (For an extended discussion of how test scores are used to make all sorts of decisions within educational settings, see Newton, 2007 or Newton, 2010.)

Validity for measurement is intimately concerned with the accuracy with which it is possible to measure an attribute by using a test; however, historically it has equally concerned the potential to make correct decisions based on those measurements. In this sense, the ultimate purpose of measurement is to improve the ratio of correct-to-incorrect decisions. If we measure in order to make decisions, then the first thing that we need to consider, both when designing and when evaluating tests, is the use to which those test scores will be put: that is, the decisions that will be made on their basis. Ultimately, so the argument goes, it is the decision that determines which attribute needs to be measured. If, for example, we needed to decide which children were ready to start formal schooling, then we would need to find a way of measuring an attribute such as 'readiness for formal schooling'. If, instead, we needed to decide which of 20 candidates to appoint to a clerical post, we would need to find a way of measuring an attribute such as 'aptitude for clerical work'. In the professions of educational and psychological measurement, measurement is the handmaiden of decision-making. This is why many, if not the largest majority of, measurement professionals would insist that validity for measurement is inseparable from – if not tantamount to – validity for decision-making. This is a highly contested area, and one that we shall return to throughout the book.

There is one peculiarity of validity for measurement related to its role in decision-making that is worth emphasizing from the outset. It is of particular importance in educational settings, where often results from a single test are used for multiple purposes. The idea that results from a single test might be interpreted in terms of a variety of different attributes has been part of the received wisdom of the measurement professions since the early days of the 20th century (Table 1.2).

The principle implicit in Table 1.2 is that results from a single arithmetic test might be used to measure, in this case, four qualitatively distinct attributes: achievement, aptitude, dyscalculia and general intelligence. Although the test might have been originally designed to assess nothing more than achievement in arithmetic, it has the

Table 1.2   Validation of a single arithmetic test for different purposes

Testing purpose (decision to be made)	Kind of attribute that might be implicated by the decision
Is the student ready to begin the next instructional sequence?	Achievement in arithmetic, i.e. mastery of the programme that has been taught so far
Should the student be enrolled in a higher-level mathematics class?	Aptitude for higher-level mathematics, i.e. potential to master a higher-level programme
Should certain low-performing students be segregated from others, requiring special intervention?	Specific learning difficulty, e.g. dyscalculia
Should certain high-performing students be placed in a stream for the exceptionally talented?	General intelligence

Adapted from Anastasi (1976), Table 13

potential to be used for measuring other attributes as well. Therefore, the question for the evaluator is whether or not it is possible to defend the use of results from the arithmetic test as measures of each of the attributes in turn.

For some academically-minded psychologists, questions such as this stretch the concept of validity too far. For them, validity is a concept more like truth, so the truth about what a valid arithmetic test measures is simply 'achievement in arithmetic'. However, for many practitioners, especially those in educational settings, validity is less like truth and more like plausibility, and they are willing to embrace the principle that a single test might be used to measure a range of attributes. Again, the issue for the practitioner is whether each attribute can be measured with *sufficient accuracy* to support a claim to validity. The arithmetic test might support an accurate assessment of achievement in arithmetic, but how accurate an assessment of general intelligence does it provide? This is certainly a slightly quirky extension of the basic validity question, but it has been fundamental in shaping thinking on validity and validation since the very early years of the 20th century.

Kinds of validity for measurement

If you want to understand validity for measurement, then trawl the internet at your peril! Not only will you be overwhelmed by a plethora of validities that are not fundamental to measurement, you also may be overwhelmed by the volume of validities that have been theorized specifically for it. It has been observed already that validity for research has been subdivided into many different 'kinds' over the years: internal, external, statistical conclusion, outcome, and so on. Over the decades, validity for measurement has been subdivided into many more. Table 1.3 presents a list of 151 such validities that we have found in the literature while researching this book. Somewhere in the region of 28 are mere synonyms of others in the list. Although quite a few of the terms have been given different meanings by different authors, there is actually quite a lot of overlap in the meanings associated with most of the terms.

People began to divide validity into 'types' or 'kinds' back in the 1940s, generally to classify different approaches to establishing validity for measurement. The most fundamental distinction was captured by Cronbach (1949), in his distinction between:

- *logical validity* – a category for grouping approaches based on logical analysis, typically of test content; and
- *empirical validity* – a category for grouping approaches based on empirical evidence, typically involving the correlation of test scores between tests.

Table 1.3   Kinds of validity that have been proposed over the decades

Abstract	Content sampling	Divergent	Incremental	Nomological	Scoring
Administrative	Context	Domain	Indirect	Occupational	Self-defining
Aetiological	Contextual	Domain-selection	Inferential	Operational	Semantic
Artifactual	Convergent	Edumetric	Instructional	Particular	Single-group
Behavior domain	Correlational	Elaborative	Internal	Performance	Site
Cash	Criteria	Elemental	Internal test	Postdictive	Situational
Circumstantial	Criterion	Empirical	Interpretative	Practical	Specific
Cluster domain	Criterion-oriented	Empirical-judgemental	Interpretive	Predictive	Statistical
Cognitive	Criterion-related	Essential	Intervention	Predictive criterion	Status
Common sense	Criterion-relevant	Etiological	Intrinsic	Predictor	Structural
Communication	Cross-age	External	Intrinsic content	Prima Facie	Substantive
Concept	Cross-cultural	External test	Intrinsic correlational	Procedural	Summative
Conceptual	Cross-sectional	Extratest	Intrinsic rational	Prospective	Symptom
Concrete	Cultural	Face	Item	Psychological & logical	Synthetic
Concurrent	Curricular	Factorial	Job analytic	Psychometric	System
Concurrent Criterion	Decision	Faith	Job component	Quantitative face	Systemic
Concurrent Criterion-related	Definitional	Fiat	Judgemental	Rational	Theoretical
Concurrent true	Derived	Forecast true	Known-groups	Raw	Theory-based
Congruent	Descriptive	Formative	Linguistic	Relational	Trait
Consensual	Design	Functional	Local	Relevant	Translation
Consequential	Diagnostic	General	Logical	Representational	Translational
Construct	Differential	Generalized	Longitudinal	Response	Treatment
Constructor	Direct	Generic	Lower-order	Retrospective	True
Construct-related	Discriminant	Higher-order	Manifest	Sampling	User
Content	Discriminative	In situ	Natural	Scientific	Washback
Content-related					

Over the decades, the validity 'cake' has been sliced in many ways, by many scholars. Some degree of consensus over how best to subdivide the concept has been achieved through official statements issued by joint committees of the North American educational and psychological measurement professions (e.g. American Psychological Association (APA) et al., 1954, 1966, 1974; American Educational Research Association (AERA) et al., 1985, 1999).

Largely influenced by these statements, terms that seemed originally to have been used to describe different *approaches to investigating validity* came to be seen increasingly as terms for describing different *kinds of validity*. Thus, from the 1950s to the 1970s, the concept of validity split along the following lines:

1   *content validity* – a narrowed derivative of logical validity;
2   *criterion validity* – a narrowed derivative of empirical validity; and
3   *construct validity* – a more 'scientific' conception originally theorized as though it were the validity of last resort, when neither content validity nor criterion validity could be relied on.

Oddly, although these three kinds of validity were widely accepted to be conceptually fundamental, all sorts of other kinds of validity continued to be proposed in the literature (e.g. convergent, discriminant, trait, nomological and many more). New kinds of validity continue to be proposed even to the present day (e.g. representational, elaborative, formative, summative and many more). This is all the more bizarre because, since the mid-1980s, the educational and psychological measurement professions have recognized officially that validity is a *unitary concept*. This position was recommended to the professions most forcefully by Samuel Messick, who insisted that it was simply not appropriate to divide validity into different kinds because there was really only one *kind* of validity: *construct validity* (Messick, 1980).

Because the term 'validity' is used in so many different ways, and because so many different 'kinds' of validity have been proposed, even within the field of educational and psychological measurement, it is very easy to become very confused when trying to get to grips with the concept. The following chapters will help to explain how the idea of kinds of validity came into fashion and then went out again. For this purpose, the only three 'kinds' that you really need to worry about are content, criterion and construct (with criterion validity sometimes subdivided into predictive validity and concurrent validity). You will see others referred to at various points throughout the book, and no doubt you already will be familiar with yet others. However, content, criterion and construct validity are the ones that really matter to the historical narrative.

Finally, whenever you read and think about validity, be sure that you are reflecting on validity for *measurement*, rather than validity for *research*. Validation is based on research, of course, so considerations of validity for research always need to be borne in mind. However, they are secondary considerations. They concern the validity of validation research conclusions, as opposed to the validity of measurement conclusions, based on validation research. (Hereafter we shall no longer speak of 'validity for measurement', and simply refer to 'validity'.)

Conventions used in the book

If you are happy to go with the flow of the terminology that we will routinely employ throughout this book, then feel free to skip this section. However, if for example you have felt increasingly disenfranchised with each new mention of tests, scores or measurement, then please read on.

Educational and psychological measurement

We describe our discipline as *educational and psychological* to emphasize, first and foremost, that it spans both education and psychology. This is more important than it initially might appear, due to the disparity of interests and professions within this broad group. Despite substantial differences of perspective, the measurement professions within both education and psychology have strived to maintain a common understanding of validity. This need not have been the case and, had it not been so, our understanding of validity might well have been all the poorer for it.

We use the term *measurement* in a generic sense, aware that it carries both technical and emotional baggage. We certainly do not intend to ostracize those within education and psychology who prefer to call their enterprise 'assessment', 'performance evaluation' or even 'diagnosis' – our use of measurement is intended to embrace each one of these possibilities. In addition, when we refer to measurement, we are not invoking a continuum which has 'real' measurement at one end, and 'faux' measurement at the other end. We are not trying to invoke the idea of measurement scales (cf. Stevens, 1951); neither are we taking a position on the possibility of 'genuine' measurement in the social sciences (cf. Michell, 1999). We use the term in its loosest sense, to embrace even 'nominal' measurement: for example, the binary diagnosis of disordered versus not disordered. Similarly, when we speak of measurement professionals, we are not meaning to imply a group of particularly hardcore quantitative statisticians. We use the term to embrace anyone with a professional remit for any aspect of educational or psychological measurement, assessment, performance evaluation or diagnosis.

In exactly the same way, when we refer to *tests* and *scores*, we in no way mean to ostracize those who prefer to describe their tools in terms of examinations, tasks, performances, questionnaires, marks, judgements, outcomes or suchlike. We use the term 'test' in a generic sense to embrace any structured assessment of behaviour: that is, any measurement *procedure*. This is standard practice in the academic literature on validity. Common to all such procedures will be a set of operations in which behaviour is elicited, evaluated and interpreted; often, the outcome also will be summarized as a score, result or profile report, which is intended to characterize the individual (or higher-level entity, e.g. school) in terms of the attribute being measured.

Traditionally, the concept of validity has referred to the quality or potential of a measurement procedure. For this reason, it is quite hard to discuss validity in the absence of a procedure: that is, in the absence of something that can be replicated. The claim that a measurement procedure is valid is often tantamount to giving it the 'thumbs up' or a 'green light' or a 'stamp of approval'. In other words, to claim that it is valid is to sanction its use for measuring a certain kind of attribute and, therefore, for making a certain kind of decision. From this perspective, we are actually talking *hypothetically* about a *generic procedure* and its *potential* to support good measurement and decision-making in the future. The claim to validity might well have been based on evidence of how it actually had resulted in good or bad measurement or decision-making in the past. However, *in declaring the measurement procedure valid*, we would be making a claim about its potential to support good measurement and decision-making in the future.

On occasion throughout this book, we may use a range of different terms from 'measurement' to 'assessment', 'test' to 'questionnaire' and 'score' to 'outcome'. However, typically we will not be highlighting significant distinctions between connotations of alternative terms. Thus, for consistency and ease of communication alone, we will tend to default to 'measurement', 'test' and 'score'. The important point to note is that the concept of validity is not specific to any one branch of measurement, assessment, performance evaluation or whatever. It is generic, and applies across the full range of contexts.

Finally, there is a sense in which this book, despite having been written by two British people, may have a whiff of North America about it. This is an inevitable consequence of the majority of the academic literature on validity having been published in the USA. Despite this, we are convinced that lessons learned from the North American literature – situated as they are against a backdrop of large-scale, commercially-produced, standardized tests – are universally relevant. It may well be that hard-fought battles to seek consensus across the very disparate professions of educational and psychological measurement within the USA has helped to ensure an international currency for the concepts of validity and validation.

In theory, just about anything written about quality in educational or psychological measurement could be taken as saying something important about validity. However, to do justice to the explicit literature on validity and validation is hard enough; to try to embrace the implicit literature as well would be impossible for us. This is why we have restricted our discussion to the mainstream literature and, again, why the book has a slightly North American lilt to it.

Attributes or constructs?

There is substantial confusion in the literature over how to refer to the characteristics that we are trying to measure. In particular, it is just not clear what name we ought to give to the category that includes 'things' such as achievement, attainment, aptitude, disorder, learning difficulty, attitude, proficiency, competence, etc. There are a number of obvious contenders, perhaps the most obvious of which is the word 'characteristic' itself. Other contenders include 'trait' or 'disposition', although both of these tend to suggest human characteristics, whereas we sometimes wish to measure different sorts of 'things' such as school effectiveness. Currently, the two main contenders within the literature are *construct* and *attribute*. It is probably fair to say that for now, 'construct' tends to be used more frequently than 'attribute'.

Unfortunately, plenty of philosophical baggage is associated with both of these terms. Having said that, there is probably more baggage associated with construct than with attribute. There is also a large amount of baggage associated with the word 'construct' that is specific to educational and psychological measurement. The term 'construct validity' came into widespread use during the mid-1950s. Since then its meaning has evolved substantially, transforming from just one kind of validity alongside others to the whole of validity (see Chapters 3 to 5). As it happens, if all of validity is supposed now to be construct validity, then the modifier label, 'construct', is actually redundant. More recently still, various scholars have concluded that the label 'construct' is not simply redundant but misleading, since it implies a philosophical tradition that is no longer considered credible in the 21st century (e.g. Borsboom et al., 2004, 2009).

Although there could be no straightforward resolution of this terminological conundrum, the convention that we will adopt is to use 'attribute' rather than 'construct'. Sometimes we will revert to using the term 'construct' if it is important to follow the exact terminology of the position that we are discussing (e.g. when discussing the genesis of construct validity, or the distinction between 'theoretical constructs' and 'observable attributes'). However, in the main we will refer to 'attributes'. Although there are various reasons why we might choose to do so, our principal reason is to minimize the risks associated with excess baggage; our secondary reason is to be able to reserve the term 'construct' for talk about construct validity.

Particular kinds of attribute

We have identified already certain kinds of attribute of particular significance to educational and psychological measurement, including achievement, aptitude and intelligence. Attribute names fall both in and out of fashion, and rightly too: the everyday meanings of terms such as these can, and do, change over time. Alternatively, the everyday connotations may stay the same while scientific understandings change; or alternative names may be chosen in order to foreground particular implications.

The history of the USA College Board SAT illustrates this case very well. The SAT is designed to assess academic readiness for university (College Board, 2013a). When it was first introduced in 1926, it was known as the 'Scholastic Aptitude Test' and abbreviated to SAT (College Board, 2013b). Particularly then, but even now, the term 'aptitude' had connotations of an innate and largely fixed ability akin to intelligence. Following a long period of academic debate over the nature of intelligence and aptitude, and growing concern that what was measured by the SAT was not well described by a word that had connotations of innateness, the name was changed to 'Scholastic Assessment Test' in 1990. However, just a few years later the name was changed once again, and only the letters 'SAT' were retained: it was no longer an acronym but a name in its own right (Wikipedia, 2013). That which is measured by curriculum-based, end-of-course tests or examinations is also known by a variety of names, including 'achievement', 'attainment', 'proficiency', 'competence', etc. Each of these may have slightly different connotations: for example, 'achievement' may be considered to have evaluative overtones, suggesting an accomplishment, especially after having followed a course of instruction. In fact, some prefer the more neutral term 'attainment' for the simple reason that from a value perspective, mastering the same learning objectives may be more or less of an achievement for one learner in comparison with another. Even attainment is not entirely neutral, since it tends to imply that an attempt has been made to master a particular set of learning outcomes, some of which will have been attained, others not. When the intention is simply to certify the capacity to do x, y or z – regardless of whether or not the test-taker has followed a particular course of learning or instruction – the term 'competence' or 'proficiency' is often preferred (see Messick, 1989a: 68).

The fact that different names (for essentially the same, or very similar, attributes) are associated with different contexts and periods in time, presents a challenge for any historical account. This book tends to default to the names that were most prevalent during the early years of validity theory and validation practice: in particular, *achievement*, *aptitude* and *intelligence*. Of course, it is important how the meanings of these words have changed over time. Even today there is no universal agreement on their precise connotations. However, for the sake of a coherent narrative, it is important to have some consistency across chapters. Incidentally, although evaluative overtones would seem to attach to the term 'achievement', the technical usage has never really carried this implication, so a more neutral reading would be appropriate. Equally, while connotations of innateness often were associated with the term 'aptitude' during the early years, the term should be read more agnostically when it appears in the following chapters.

Reliability and validity

Finally, it is worth saying just a few words about reliability and its relationship with validity. This relationship always has been awkward to express. As we shall see, the earliest definitions of validity were framed in terms of the degree to which a test measures what it is supposed to measure. Reliability was, and always has been, defined more specifically in terms of consistency of outcome.

It is useful to contrast consistency with accuracy. If scores from a test were very inconsistent, then we could stake no claim to accurate measurement at all. For example, a ruler that expands and contracts substantially throughout the course of a day returns very inconsistent readings of the same object from one hour to the next. Although it might happen to record an accurate measurement every so often, we certainly could not rely on it to do so. If we cannot rely upon it to reproduce any particular measurement, then we certainly cannot rely upon it to reproduce the correct measurement. When we need to be able to rely upon each and every measurement that we make, we need to be able to demonstrate a high level of consistency.[1] In the absence of evidence of consistency, any claim to be able to measure accurately (using a particular measurement procedure) would be indefensible.

However, consistency is not enough. For example, two watches can be consistent with each other, yet both be six hours slow. If a ruler has been calibrated incorrectly it will be consistent but inaccurate: that is, it will always return the same reading for objects of the same length, but those readings will never be accurate. In exactly the same way, a test might lead us to rate certain people intelligent and others unintelligent and consistently so, but we might still be consistently wrong in those ratings. Thus, consistency – that is, reliability – is a necessary condition for ensuring high measurement quality, but it is not a sufficient one. Consequently, if validity is to be understood in terms of measurement quality, then reliability is just one facet of it, and a rather abstract, technical facet at that. The remainder of this book will have relatively little to say about reliability specifically.

An outline of the history of validity

The historical account that follows is our attempt to describe and explain how conceptions of validity have evolved within the field of educational and psychological measurement. It explores answers that have been provided down the ages in response to two fundamental questions: the first concerning validity theory, and the second concerning validation practice.

1   What does it mean to claim validity?
2   How can a validity claim be substantiated?

The narrative that we present may seem occasionally to focus more heavily on the first question than the second. To the extent that this is true, it is because answers to the first question need to be provided before the second can be addressed; yet, as we will see, answers to the first are still hotly debated. Having said that, as we discuss each new contribution to validity theory, their implications for validation practice should become fairly clear. Indeed, a key driver of change in validity theory over the years has been the desire to improve validation practice.

We note that there have been few, if any, comprehensive, coherent and clear accounts of validity theory. The literature is characterized better as a compendium of piecemeal insights, concepts and arguments in search of the holy grail: consensus over a generally accepted theory. The measurement community seemed to be getting close to this holy grail through the pioneering scholarship of Samuel Messick, from the 1970s to the 1990s. Yet while his theory of validity was undeniably comprehensive, it tended to lack clarity. Not only was his magnum opus (Messick, 1989a) long and dense, attempting to draw together a vast body of work on validity and validation, it was also philosophically challenging: one eminent reviewer described it as 'viscous' (Cronbach, 1989c: 24). In addition, we believe that his position on certain key issues changed gradually over the years, without this being acknowledged explicitly (as will be discussed in Chapter 4). The lack of clarity in his presentation makes it much harder to pass judgement on the coherence of his theory.

Over the years, documents intended to encapsulate professional standards – official statements from the professions – have functioned as a surrogate for a generally accepted theory of validity. Without a shadow of doubt, paramount among these have been successive editions of documents prepared since the mid-1950s by committees of measurement professionals from North America. These were originally presented as *Technical recommendations* (e.g. APA et al., 1954; AERA and National Council on Measurements Used in Education (NCMUE), 1955), but are now described as *Standards* (e.g. AERA et al., 1999), with the sixth edition scheduled for release during 2013, at the time of writing. Throughout this book they will be referred to as successive editions of the *Standards*.

Each edition of the *Standards* has provided succinct guidance on validation, preceded by similarly succinct consensus statements on the meaning of validity. These consensus statements are the nearest that we have come to generally accepted definitions of validity, yet their very succinctness reveals that they are not well-developed theoretical accounts. Moreover, as we shall see, neither are they free from ambiguity, if not occasional contradiction, which further emphasizes that they probably are best viewed as heuristic principles, born as a product of compromise rather than universal satisfaction. We will refer to the conception of validity sketched by successive editions of the *Standards* as the *consensus definition* of the measurement professions (Newton, 2012a). Although these definitions were the product of North American committees, attuned to North American concerns, the principles outlined in the *Standards* have been appropriated internationally. Thus, terms such as 'content validity', 'criterion validity' and 'construct validity' have come to provide a lingua franca for measurement professionals the world over. Successive versions of the consensus definition indubitably have provided an international reference point for understanding validity and validation within the field of educational and psychological measurement.

The fact that successive editions of the *Standards* were never intended as definitive accounts of validity theory may help to explain why their descriptions have sometimes resulted in confusion, over-simplification and poor validation practice (Dunnette and Borman, 1979; Guion, 1980). Indeed, widespread evidence of poor validation practice is the principal reason why the consensus definition has needed to be revised significantly from time to time (see Chapter 4 in particular). This has established an increasingly explicit challenge for generations of validity theorists: to move beyond the disparate heuristic principles of the *Standards* towards a comprehensive, coherent and clear account of validity theory. However, few have been prepared to rise to this challenge. In retrospect, it is clear that successive editions of the textbook that many refer to as the 'holy book' of its field, *Educational Measurement*, have repeatedly stimulated the most definitive accounts of validity and validation of their generations. It is interesting to note that only two of these accounts were entitled 'Validity' (Cureton, 1951; Messick, 1989a), while the other two were entitled 'Test validation' (Cronbach, 1971) and 'Validation' (Kane, 2006), respectively.

The remainder of this chapter explains the structure of the book, which is divided into four main chapters concerning five key phases in the history of validity theory. These are followed by a concluding chapter. The partition into five key phases is broadly consistent with previous accounts which tend to carve the history of validity into three phases: 'pre-trinitarian', 'trinitarian' and 'unitarian'. This terminology comes from Robert Guion (1980), who described the concept of validity, from the mid-1950s to the 1970s, as a 'holy trinity' comprising content validity, criterion validity and construct validity. We make more than previous accounts of advances in recent years, which we describe as a brand new phase, and we discuss the early years in more detail than is common and with a different emphasis. We believe that the history of validity theory can be usefully mapped to the periods between:

1   the mid-1800s and 1920: a gestational period
2   1921 and 1951: a period of crystallization
3   1952 and 1974: a period of fragmentation
4   1975 and 1999: a period of (re)unification
5   2000 and 2012: a period of deconstruction.

Of course, there are no sharp dividing lines between these phases. They represent a crude attempt to add some structure to a far more rambling, diverse and complex evolutionary course. However, they do seem to capture something important about differences in the zeitgeist between eras, and it is no coincidence that many of the transition points correspond to the publication of revised editions of the *Standards*.[2]

Before introducing each of these five phases, it is worth emphasizing that our historical account focuses primarily on changes in conceptions of validity rather than advances in techniques for validation. In fact many, if not most, of the techniques that we rely upon today, both logical and empirical, were developed in at least a primitive form before the 1950s (as we explain in Chapter 2). Over the decades, debate has focused primarily on how and when to employ these techniques. Therefore, different phases can be characterized by different kinds of answer to a central question: how much of what kind of logical analysis and empirical evidence is required in order to substantiate a claim to validity?

The genesis of validity (mid-1800s–1951)

Chapter 2 covers the first two phases: a gestational period from the mid-1800s to 1920, and a period of crystallization from 1921–1951. It is heavily skewed towards the crystallization period, during which the concept of validity developed an explicit identity – or perhaps more correctly, a range of different identities.

A gestational period (mid-1800s–1920)

Although the examination was not a product of the 19th century, many countries became increasingly reliant on structured assessments during this period as a basis for making complex decisions about individuals and institutions, especially in Europe and North America. The middle of the century witnessed the introduction of the written examination for schools in the USA (by Horace Mann) and the launch of Local Examinations for schools in England (by the universities of Oxford and Cambridge). Structure, it was assumed, was the key to increased accuracy of assessment, and therefore to better decision-making, facilitating outcomes that were fairer for individuals and more useful for society.

By the end of the 19th century, belief in the potential of structured assessment was high, and results from written examinations were used for all sorts of different purposes, from selecting individuals for jobs in the Civil Service to holding schools to account for the quality of their education. However, the prominence of the written examination was not unquestioned, and many were beginning to wonder whether results from examinations were quite as accurate as they often were assumed to be, particularly given the inevitable element of subjectivity involved in judging them. Attention turned to the development of instruments with more structure and less subjectivity: true/false tests, multiple choice tests, sentence completion tests and the like. The idea of the standardized test was born.

While the more practically-minded professionals were busy developing fairer and more effective techniques for structured assessment, the more academically-minded scientists were busy developing ways of probing the very nature of the human mind. Advances in statistical methodology greatly accelerated this work: in particular, the invention of the correlation coefficient, which enabled the statistical patterns inherent in results from examinations and tests to be quantified and interpreted. The fact that certain individuals tended to score high across a range of assessments, while others tended to score low, was treated as indicative of important differences between them. Instruments designed to investigate such differences increasingly came to be seen as tests of mental capacities. The idea of the mental test was born.

These practical and scientific concerns coalesced within what became known as the measurement movement, which flourished during the early years of the 20th century, particularly in North America, but also in Europe and other parts of the world. A huge industry emerged, which churned out tests of all sorts of attributes (general intelligence, specific aptitudes, educational achievement, etc.) in all sorts of formats. This industry burgeoned in the USA following the success of testing for placement and selection during the First World War, but how was this new industry to be controlled or regulated, if at all, and how were consumers to judge the quality of these new tests?

A period of crystallization (1921–1951)

Education provided a home for many of the uses to which tests increasingly were being put. Tests of educational achievement were used to judge students as well as their schools; tests of general intelligence were used to diagnose 'backwardness' and 'excellence'; and tests of specific aptitudes were used as the basis for vocational guidance. Therefore, it is not surprising that issues of quality and control were hotly debated among members of the educational research community. In 1921, the North American National Association of Directors of Educational Research publicized its intention to seek consensus on the meaning of the terms and procedures that were becoming the stock-in-trade of the measurement movement. At the end of a list of key terms, validity was defined as the degree to which a test measures what it is supposed to measure (cf. reliability, defined in terms of consistency). This provided the foundation for all subsequent thinking on validity.

If validity was to be defined as the degree to which a test measured what it was supposed to measure, then how might a claim to validity be established? Two basic approaches to answering this question were honed during the early years: one based primarily on the logical analysis of test content; and the other based primarily on empirical evidence of correlation. Many believed that the best approach to establishing validity was to gather empirical evidence of correlation between the test and what it was supposed to measure. Evidence of high correlation would support the use of test results for measuring the attribute in question. According to proponents of this approach, the correlation coefficient – or the 'validity coefficient' as it came to be known – provided definitive evidence of validity, even when the content of a test appeared to be quite far removed from the attribute that was supposedly being measured. This was not uncommon for the new-style standardized tests, owing to their brevity and structured formats, making the empirical approach seem all the more attractive.

The key question, from this perspective, was what the test results ought to be correlated against: what should be used as a *criterion* against which to judge the accuracy of results? Often, the judgement of expert practitioners – for example, teachers – was used for this purpose. For example, a teacher might be asked to rank their class in terms of intelligence – thereby constructing a *criterion measure* of intelligence – against which the results from a novel test of intelligence would be correlated. Empirical evidence of high correlation would validate the standardized test as a measure of intelligence. However, there were many other ways of constructing a criterion. For example, one way to validate a (short) standardized test of achievement, which sampled the domain only selectively, was to correlate it against a (long) comprehensive assessment of achievement: i.e. a battery of assessments that sampled the domain in full. While the short test might not actually cover the full range of learning outcomes associated with the long assessment, evidence of high correlation with the long assessment would validate the test as a measure of the full domain.

Although it was quite possible to validate educational achievement tests using empirical evidence, some believed that this was not at all the best approach. Their argument went that if a test of educational achievement had been adequately designed, then it ought to be its own best criterion. That is, it ought to be obvious, from logical analysis of the test content alone, whether it measured what it was supposed to measure. If a group of expert practitioners scrutinized the content of the test and judged that it matched the content of its curriculum, then the test was valid, period.

As time went by, different communities moulded the classic definition in different ways. Ultimately, many whose interests lay mainly in measuring aptitudes (e.g. certain personnel psychologists) tended to prioritize empirical evidence of correlation. Ultimately, many whose interests lay mainly in measuring achievement (e.g. certain educators) tended to prioritize logical analysis of content. These dividing lines were not absolute by any means, but they certainly were becoming more pronounced. Naturally, the different ways of interpreting validity fed back into different priorities for test development. Aptitude testers developed tests to optimize correlation against criterion measures. Achievement testers developed tests to optimize the sampling of criterion content. Yet aptitude testers could not ignore issues of content, especially the content of the criterion measure; neither could achievement testers ignore issues of correlation, especially the part–whole correlation of question-to-test. Tensions within both camps were substantial and uncomfortable.

The fragmentation of validity (1952–1974)

At the beginning of the 1950s, a committee of the APA, chaired by Lee Cronbach, was given a remit to develop professional standards to govern the information that test producers ought to provide on their tests, to allow users of those tests to judge their quality. An early draft of the very first *Standards* document was published for discussion in 1952 (APA, 1952).

The 1952 draft had a section on validity, which followed the lead of a number of earlier textbooks by classifying validity into 'types' or 'aspects', according to the approach employed to establish it. The most fundamental of distinctions had been captured by Cronbach (1949) in his contrast between logical validity and empirical validity. A few years earlier, Greene et al. (1943) had drawn a similar distinction between curricular validity and statistical validity; although they had added a third type, which they called 'psychological and logical validity'. The 1952 draft went a step further by distinguishing four types of validity: content, predictive, status and congruent. By the time of the final publication in 1954, these types of validity were known as content, predictive, concurrent (previously status) and construct (previously congruent). Greene et al. (1943) had introduced psychological and logical validity to deal with school subjects for which neither curricular methods nor statistical methods could be applied. They described this approach to validation as 'a sort of arm-chair psychological dissection of the total process' (1943: 60). In proposing construct validity, the APA committee's intention was similar: that is, to describe an approach to validation which could be employed when neither logical analysis nor empirical evidence were deemed to be sufficient.

The idea of construct validity had been first proposed by a subcommittee comprising Paul Meehl and Robert Challman. It was later modified and clarified by the entire committee. Two of the committee members, Cronbach and Meehl, subsequently elaborated its principles within what was to become a landmark paper, 'Construct validity in psychological tests' (Cronbach and Meehl, 1955). They framed their problem as follows. Certain kinds of test (e.g. achievement tests) are evaluated in relation to a universe of content (hence, content validity). Other kinds of test (e.g. aptitude tests) are evaluated in relation to a criterion measure (hence, criterion-related validity, which subsumed predictive and concurrent validity). However, for a substantial number of tests there was no such yardstick, and validation needed to proceed differently. For tests such as these, including many personality tests, it needed to be determined which psychological 'construct' accounted for test performance. By 'construct', they meant the 'postulated attribute' which was presumed to be manifest in test performance. According to Cronbach and Meehl, this new approach subsumed both logical analysis and empirical evidence. Indeed, it embraced any form of evidence or analysis which could be brought to bear on the psychological meaning of test scores. Therefore, construct validation was neither quintessentially logical, nor quintessentially empirical, but quintessentially scientific. It rested on a theory from which predictions were generated and tested out.

The *Standards* was revised in 1966, which resulted in the four types of validity being collapsed into three: content, criterion-related and construct. However, the discussion of validity and validation remained essentially the same, and continued as such into the third edition, which was published in 1974. Although all three editions of the *Standards* from 1954 to 1974 insisted that the three types of validity should not be considered mutually exclusive, the way in which they were presented seemed to suggest otherwise. Thus, content validity tended to be seen as the specialized form of validity for achievement tests, criterion validity for aptitude tests, and construct validity for personality tests. Validity theory and validation practice became fragmented along these lines. Although the nomenclature of validity 'types' had been originally introduced to mark alternative approaches to validation, it increasingly came to be seen as marking alternative conceptions of validity.

This fragmentation was especially pronounced for criterion validity. The classic definition could still be reconciled with content validity and construct validity: achievement tests purported to measure achievement, as defined by curriculum content; while personality tests purported to measure personality, as defined by a theory of the construct in question. However, it was far harder to reconcile the classic definition with criterion validity. Predictor tests were viewed typically as 'black boxes', and whatever they might measure, if anything, was considered to be largely irrelevant – just as long as they were able to predict a criterion measure with some degree of accuracy.

The (re)unification of validity (1974–1999)

Cronbach and Meehl (1955) opened the final paragraph of their treatise on construct validity by insisting that in no way did they advocate it as preferable to either content validity or criterion validity. However, even as early as their landmark paper there were indications that at the very least, construct validity might be considered first among equals. For example, they had stated explicitly that construct validation was important at times for every sort of test, including both aptitude tests and achievement tests. Cronbach later came to emphasize the relevance of constructs to all educational and psychological testing (Cronbach, 1971), which helped to pave the way to the next phase in the history of validity theory.

We describe the period between 1974 and 1999 as the 'Messick years', because his conception on validity had come to dominate the world of educational and psychological measurement by the latter part of it. Developing ideas from Harold Gulliksen and Jane Loevinger, and with the support of allies including Robert Guion, he appeared to bring the majority of measurement professionals of his generation around to the viewpoint that all validity ought to be understood as construct validity.

Although it is not obvious from his complex presentation of validity theory, perhaps the most significant contribution that Messick made during this period was to reclaim measurement as the focus of validation in all contexts. You will recall that the classic definition of validity was framed explicitly in terms of measurement: that is, the degree to which a test measured what it was supposed to measure. However, as time went by, it became commonplace to distinguish between validity for measurement and validity for prediction. Messick demolished this distinction by insisting, along with Guion, that in the absence of a clear understanding of what was being measured, prediction was indefensible. As far as aptitude tests were concerned, there were now three fundamental imperatives for validation:

1   to establish that the criterion measure measured what it was supposed to measure;
2   to establish that the aptitude test measured what it was supposed to measure; and
3   to establish a theoretical rationale for why the aptitude test should predict the criterion measure, in addition to presenting evidence that it actually did.

This was nothing like the 'blind empiricism' that had characterized practice within personnel settings (and elsewhere) for decades prior to the 1970s; neither was this any longer simply criterion validation, but construct validation writ large.

In exactly the same way, Messick upped the ante for the validation of achievement tests. No longer was it sufficient for subject matter experts to claim validity purely on the basis of a logical analysis of test content. Fundamentally, it was not test *content* that needed to be representative of curriculum content, but test *performances* that needed to be representative of the full set of learning outcomes defined by the curriculum. Therefore, validation needed to demonstrate that the proficiency that each question was presumed to tap was actually tapped: that is, that performances were neither inflated nor deflated by factors irrelevant to what the test was supposed to measure. In exactly the same manner, it needed to be established that the scores awarded by those who marked the test performances were neither inflated nor deflated by construct-irrelevant factors. In short, the evaluator needed to be confident that the variance observed in a set of test scores (i.e. the fact that certain test-takers scored high, while others scored low) was attributable to construct-relevant factors, and not to construct-irrelevant ones. Thus, Messick emphasized the importance of discounting plausible threats to the valid interpretation of test scores: specifically, the twin threats of construct under-representation and construct-irrelevant variance.

In presenting these arguments, Messick promoted a new science of validity to be understood along the lines of construct validity. Validation involved the integration of logical analysis and empirical evidence to substantiate the claim that the test measured what it was supposed to measure, and therefore that it could be used for its intended purpose(s). Messick recast all validation as laborious scientific enquiry into score meaning, encouraging evaluators to accumulate as much evidence and analysis as they could lay their hands on, rather than assuming that they could stake a claim to validity on the basis of a single analytical or empirical study in isolation. This reunification of validity was Messick's triumph.

In addition to providing a comprehensive account of the science of validity, Messick undertook an even bigger challenge: to locate ethics at the heart of validity theory. Ultimately, this proved to be Messick's tribulation. His thesis was very confusing, if not ultimately confused. For example, although he located the consideration of values in the ethical row of his progressive matrix, his discussion seemed to overemphasize the scientific evaluation of values (e.g. investigating consistency between trait implications and the evaluative implications of construct labels), and downplay genuinely ethical evaluation (e.g. representing conflicting theories or ideologies within an overall evaluative argument). Similarly, he stressed the importance of investigating consequences from testing. Yet once again, he ultimately came to treat the evaluation of consequences far more scientifically than ethically. That is, as time went by, he became far more focused on how consequences informed the evaluation of test score meaning, and far less focused on evaluating, for its own sake, the positive or negative social value that attached to consequences from testing, including test misuse.

Messick provided important insights into how values and consequences ought to be included in the science of validity. However, ultimately he failed to provide a persuasive synthesis of science and ethics within validity theory. In doing so, it is fair to say that he confused many within the measurement professions, and left a legacy of a rift between those who continued to exclude ethical analysis, and those who made a point of including it.

The deconstruction of validity (2000–2012)

During the 1990s, work on validity and validation was influenced heavily by Messick. Indeed, while the fourth edition of the *Standards*, published in 1985, showed clear evidence of his impact, the fifth edition published in 1999 was essentially a consensus interpretation of his position. These were truly the Messick years. Yet with the turn of the millennium, things began to change.

For some time, Michael Kane had been developing a methodology to support validation practice grounded in argumentation (e.g. Kane, 1992). This provided a framework or scaffold for constructing and defending validity claims. Thus, while Messick defined the claim to validity in terms of an overall evaluative judgement, Kane explained how that claim to validity could be constructed and defended. Similarly, whereas Messick and the *Standards* directed evaluators towards the sources of evidence which ought to be used when staking a claim to validity, Kane indicated how those sources ought be integrated within an overall validity argument. Argument provided evaluators with a methodology for subdividing the big question of validity into manageable chunks. It clarified where to begin (with the intended interpretation and use of test scores), how to proceed (by making explicit the claims that would support that interpretation and use in the form of an argument, and by testing their assumptions), and when to stop (when the argument was judged to be coherent and complete, and when its inferences and assumptions were judged to be plausible). The argument-based approach better equipped evaluators to identify the full range of issues that need to be addressed, as well as the issues that required most attention: the weakest links in the argument chain.

With the turn of the millennium, Kane began to commit more of his energy to the development of validity theory, which involved an increasingly trenchant rejection of Messick's very stringent requirements for staking a claim to validity. He was concerned that the new version of construct validity theory bought too heavily into the philosophical baggage associated with Cronbach and Meehl (1955). Indeed, the perspective that Cronbach and Meehl had advocated was immersed in a particular philosophical tradition which, at the dawn of the 21st century, might well be considered at least a little outdated. It was based on the principle that the meaning of a theoretical construct was given by its association with other theoretical constructs within a grand scientific theory. If validation was tantamount to scientific enquiry into score meaning, and the meaning of a score was dependent on the development of a theory relating one theoretical construct to others within a large network of theoretical constructs, then validation would become a truly epic, never-ending quest. It is fair to say that both Cronbach and Messick tended to characterize validation in these 'never-ending' terms. Yet according to Kane, this was unduly complex as a general account of validity, and it was unnecessary to portray validation as quite such a laborious and interminable undertaking.

Whereas Messick gave the impression that validation always ought to require the integration of all sorts of empirical evidence and logical analysis, Kane stated clearly that validation requirements were entirely dependent on the particular interpretation and use of results that the test user had in mind. If the interpretation of results was not especially 'ambitious' – for example, if it involved a fairly simple attribute – then only a small amount of evidence and analysis would be required to substantiate it. In particular, Kane drew a distinction between observable attributes and theoretical constructs. He implied that interpretations drawn in terms of theoretical constructs might well require the kind of laborious scientific enquiry into score meaning that is characteristic of traditional construct validation; whereas he argued that interpretations drawn in terms of observable attributes did not. Observable attributes – literacy or proficiency in algebra, vocabulary knowledge, achievement in arithmetic, skill in solving quadratic equations, etc. – were far easier to validate than theoretical constructs. Not only did Kane's methodology help to simplify the process of validation, his new theory of validity appeared to reduce the evidential burden, at least for many of the attributes at the heart of educational and psychological measurement. Incidentally, this was not simply a deconstruction of validity in the sense of decomposition and simplification; but also a deconstruction in the sense of downplaying the significance of theoretical constructs.

Kane is not the only theorist of recent years to propose a deconstruction of construct validity theory, since challenges have been mounted on various fronts. In particular, Messick has been repeatedly challenged for attempting to provide an integration of ethics and science within validity theory. Particularly prominent in recent years has been the critique mounted by Gregory Cizek, who has insisted that there can be no integration of scientific and ethical analysis, since the two are mutually incompatible arguments. According to Cizek, it is no coincidence that there is a now a significant disjunction between the theory of validity and the practice of validation: the kind of validation envisaged by Messick – that genuinely integrates ethical and scientific analysis – is simply not feasible.

Others have taken the critique of construct validity theory even further: notably, the research partnerships led by Denny Borsboom, which have argued – contrary to a principle that has been fundamental to educational and psychological measurement for decades – that validity is not a property of the interpretation of test scores after all, but a property of tests. In making this claim, they wished to reinstate the classic definition of validity with no additional baggage, and to take it very literally indeed. New and challenging perspectives on validity also have been championed by Joel Michell, Pamela Moss and Susan Embretson, to name but a few.

Since this chapter is less an account of the history of validity, and more an account of validity-in-the-making, we engage more critically with the literature of this phase.

Twenty-first-century evaluation

In Chapter 6 we bring together insights from the preceding chapters to help identify a full range of issues that need to be taken into account when aspects of testing are to be evaluated, including measurement objectives, decision-making objectives and broader policy objectives. The framework at the heart of Messick's account has been the source of much confusion over the years, and much maligned. However, we think that its underlying logic was basically right, so we end the book by proposing a new framework for the evaluation of testing policy, which is our reinterpretation of the original progressive matrix.

Notes

1 When measurement professionals within education and psychology make decisions, they often rely on single measurements: for example, results from a single
   achievement test. In fact, it is good practice to triangulate evidence across multiple measurements, but even this is likely to involve just a few measurements
   from related tests.
2 Work on the first *Standards* began in 1952, the third edition was published in
   1974 and the fifth edition was published in 1999. Of course, there is no significance in the final date, 2012, other than it marks the year during which the
   majority of this book was written.

CHAPTER 2

THE GENESIS OF VALIDITY: MID-1800s–1951

This chapter explores the period that we describe as the 'early years' as far as validity is concerned, which can be divided into a gestational period from the mid-1800s–1920, and a period of crystallization from 1921–1951.

A gestational period (pre-1921)

The emergence of validity as a formal concept of educational and psychological measurement can only be understood in the context of major developments in testing for educational, clinical, occupational and scientific purposes which occurred during the second half of the 19th century, and the first half of the 20th century, particularly in England, France, Germany and the USA.

The second half of the 19th century was a period during which school and university entrance examinations blossomed. The University of London was established in 1836 to set and regulate examinations, which included matriculation examinations: that is, entrance examinations for its federated colleges. In 1871, the university announced that matriculation would provide exemption from the entrance examinations of other institutions, including the Royal Military College and the Royal College of Surgeons (Cain, 1982). The establishment of Local Examinations by the universities of Oxford and Cambridge in 1857 and 1858, respectively, paved the way to the improvement of education in secondary schools (Roach, 1971). Similarly, the India Act 1853 led to the establishment of examinations as a mechanism for impartial selection within the Indian and home civil services (Montgomery, 1965; Sutherland, 1984). In the USA, Horace Mann promoted the virtues of the written examination, claiming their superiority over older methods such as the oral quiz on the basis of their impartiality (given that the same questions were submitted to all scholars of the same grade in all schools), but also on the basis of their reliability, economy and practicality (Ruch, 1929). Influenced by Mann, the first written examinations in the USA were introduced by school examining committees in Massachusetts in 1845, and used to determine high school graduation (Linden and Linden, 1968).

Shortly after his half-cousin Charles Darwin had published *The Origin of Species*, Francis Galton published *Hereditary Genius* (1869). He developed and pioneered the use of new statistical techniques which he applied to the study of heredity, laying a foundation for the study of individual differences as a discipline in its own right. In a commentary appended to Cattell (1890), Galton prefigured what would become known as the empirical approach to validation, proposing that 'the sets of measures should be compared with an independent estimate of the man's powers' to determine which were the most instructive (Galton, 1890: 380). Numerous British psychometric pioneers developed Galton's statistical approach, including Karl Pearson, Charles Spearman, William Brown, Cyril Burt and Godfrey Thomson. Spearman was particularly influential in applying the method of correlation to psychological data (e.g. Spearman, 1904), and his simplification of the technique made it accessible to the run-of-the-mill psychologist and educationist (Burt, 1924).

In France, during 1904, Alfred Binet had been approached by the French Ministry of Public Instruction to serve on a committee tasked with the problem of 'backward children'. With Herbert Simon, he devised a series of tests of increasing difficulty, designed to discriminate between unmotivated and incapable children, for placement of the incapable into special classes for the 'mentally deficient'. The first scale was released in 1905, with revisions published in 1908 and 1911 (Burt, 1924; Sutherland, 1984). The Binet-Simon tests were translated and adapted by enthusiastic psychologists across the world, including: Henry Goddard, Robert Yerkes, Lewis Terman and Arthur Sinton Otis in the USA; Cyril Burt in England; Zaccaria Treves and Umberto Saffiotti in Italy; and William Stern in Germany. Under the guidance of Yerkes, related tests of intelligence were developed for use in the selection of army recruits, and were administered to more than 1.5 million North Americans during the First World War. The success of this initiative was such that group tests were rapidly introduced into many North American universities and schools, typically being administered at entrance or at times of promotion. It also stimulated the growth of vocational testing internationally such that in 1924, Burt observed that most of the civilized countries of the world now possessed institutes of vocational guidance in which trained psychologists carried out vocational tests and offered vocational guidance.

Toward the end of the 19th century, the foundations of the measurement movement were being laid in the USA by James McKeen Cattell, following in the tradition of Galton (Linden and Linden, 1968), as well as by researchers such as Herbert Rice, who wished to bring scientific methods based on the use of achievement tests to the study of education (Scates, 1947). It was Cattell (1890) who introduced the term 'mental test'. Shortly after the turn of the century, Edward Thorndike helped to establish the sub-discipline of educational psychology, with the publication of a textbook describing the development of tests for the prediction of educational success (Thorndike, 1903) and a textbook on the theory of mental and social measurements (Thorndike, 1904). Following Thorndike's lead, educational researchers including Calvin Stone, Stuart Courtis, Burdette Ross Buckingham, Leonard Ayers, Guy Montrose Whipple and many others turned their hands to the construction of tests designed to support instructional processes. As these tests became increasingly accessible to teachers, their sale and use grew to unprecedented proportions.

Of particular significance to the birth of the concept of validity was growing discontent with the traditional school achievement examination. The seeds of this discontent had been sown in North America by researchers such as Meyer (1908), who demonstrated the unreliability of marks from written examinations, and Starch and Elliott (1912, 1913), who followed in his wake. Many believed that the written examination suffered from a major defect: its results could not be evaluated fairly by human minds. In contrast, new-style tests – based on simple recall, sentence completion, true/false or multiple-choice selection and suchlike – were freed from this 'personal equation' (Ruch, 1929).

Concern over the personal equation focused the minds of educational assessors, psychological investigators and personnel selectors on developing more objective methods of assessment. The measurement movement was really beginning to take root now. Although the movement had an international following, its impact was particularly pronounced in the USA, which might help to explain why validity theory began (and largely remained) a product of North America. The movement fostered an industry committed to the development and publication of standard(ized), tests and to the promotion of new-style objective tests. As Ruch explained in 1929, objective tests were basically standard tests without the refinements of experimental study and standardization. (His ambition was to bring the technology of objective testing to the teaching profession, in order to help overcome what he judged to be a fundamental limitation of standard tests: their lack of alignment with local curricula.) As the movement progressed, often the terms 'standard test' and 'objective test' were used interchangeably.

During the second decade of the 20th century, the publication of standard tests mushroomed. In a collection of reports from the Committee on Standards and Tests of the National Council of Education, Courtis (1916) reported a remarkable growth in interest in the measurement movement, indexed by the expansion in use of his standard research tests (mainly his arithmetic tests) from one school in 1909 to a despatch of 455,007 to instructors in 42 states between August 1914 and August 1915. Not only were tests and testing mushrooming; research into tests and testing expanded similarly. In a review of Whipple (1915), a new edition of the *Manual of Mental and Physical Tests*, Freeman (1917) observed that in the five-year period between its publication and revision, the number of references reporting experimental research into the focal tests had more than doubled, from 190 to 390. Therefore, the period from 1910 to 1920 was a decade of increasing focus on the validity of mental measurement, although not necessarily described as such.

To summarize the state of play by the end of the gestational period, interest in structured assessment had grown exponentially and already had evolved substantially;

and quite distinct sub-domains of educational and psychological measurement had begun to establish. These included:

- *professional communities* – where written examinations and tests were used for clinical diagnosis, assessing educational achievement and occupational guidance and selection; and
- *scientific communities* – where tests were devised to explore the very structure of ability, intelligence and other such personality characteristics, in terms of which individuals were supposed to differ, often on the assumption that such differences might be innate.

In addition to distinctions that were emerging between sub-domains, distinctions had been drawn between different kinds of test: for example, between linguistic tests and performance tests, individual tests and group tests, written examinations and standardized tests. Perhaps most importantly, the correlation coefficient had become very widely recognized, and was beginning to be used as a tool for judging the quality of tests.

A period of crystallization (post-1921)

It is unclear when or how the term 'validity' began to acquire special significance among measurement specialists. Early examples of its use can be identified as far back as the 19th century (see Cattell and Farrand, 1896, in von Mayrhauser, 1992), but it seems likely that it was not until the second decade of the 20th century that the term began to take root in the lexicon of researchers and practitioners. Even then, authors seemed to be using it in different ways. For example, in 1914 Frank Freeman, who since 1911 had contributed an annual report on tests to the *Psychological Bulletin*, referred to 'the technique and validity of test methods' (Freeman, 1914: 253; see Schouwstra, 2000). The following year, Terman et al. evaluated 'the validity of the intelligence test' (1915: 562) and 'the validity of the IQ' (1915: 557). The year after, Starch (1916) referred to 'the validity or the fairness of these measurements' (1915: 3), and Thorndike discussed 'the essentials of a valid scale' (1916: 11).

In 1921, in the USA, the National Association of Directors of Educational Research established and promoted an intention to formalize and standardize both the procedures and the concepts of educational measurement. Their problem was not a lack of concepts and procedures, but a lack of consistency in their application. They were not the first to attempt to bring an element of standardization to testing practice in the USA. The American Psychological Association (APA) had established committees to achieve similar goals twice previously: first in 1895, under Cattell; and second in 1906, under James Rowland Angell. These committees sought to improve standardization through establishing norms and identifying and promoting the 'best' tests and procedures. In 1919, the APA appointed a qualifications committee to explore the potential for professional certification, in response to concerns that mental tests were being widely used for psychological diagnosis by individuals unqualified to do so. Reflecting on these various attempts at standardization and control, Fernberger (1932) concluded that they had all resulted more or less in total failure. He concluded that the APA saw itself as an organization of scientists, not professionals, and lacked the will, let alone the ability, to control its members.

In a 'Report of the Standardization Committee' of the National Association of Directors of Educational Research, the returns from a questionnaire to members were discussed, which revealed 'a practically unanimous sentiment in favour of the publication of an official list of terms, procedures, etc.' (Buckingham et al., 1921: 78). In response, the committee proposed definitions for terms including 'scale', 'standard scores', 'average', 'achievement', 'capacity' and suchlike. The goal of the committee and membership was for uniformity and certainty of interpretation in relation to these technical terms. Indeed, members were asked explicitly to try to conform to these regulations when preparing material for publication, or else to provide (in a footnote) the reason why they had chosen to use an alternative form. In addition, the committee recommended that makers of tests should be careful to investigate the effect of every factor involved in standardization, specifying the following component operations:

1   preparation and selection of test material
2   experimental organization of the test and instructions for giving the test
3   trial of a tentative test to determine value of elements, gross validity, reliability and optimum conditions of giving, scoring, etc.
4   final organization of the test
5   final formulation of conditions under which the test is to be given, scored, tabulated and interpreted
6   official determination of validity
7   official determination of reliability
8   official determination of norms.

In a subsequent section headed 'Problems', the committee recommended as follows:

> Two of the most important types of problems in measurement are those connected with the determination of what a test measures and of how consistently it measures. The first should be called the problem of validity, the second, the problem of reliability.
>
> Members are urged to devise and publish means of determining the relation between the scores made in a test and other measures of the same ability; in other words, to try to solve the problem of determining the validity of a test. (Buckingham et al., 1921: 80)

Thus, it would seem, the very first official definition of validity was proposed; and members of the National Association of Directors of Educational Research were challenged to develop and promote new methods of validation. Within a few years the early formulation had been modified slightly, to become what might be described as the *classic definition* of validity:

> By validity is meant the degree to which a test or examination measures what it purports to measure. (Ruch, 1924: 13)

That concepts for theorizing the evaluation of measurement quality should come to the fore during the 1920s was not incidental. This was a direct response to the rapid expansion of tests and testing in the hands of converts to the new style. Ruch observed that 'an already bewildering situation is daily becoming more aggravated' (1925: 349), referring to the challenge routinely faced by school superintendents, directors of research and so on, of selecting the 'best' tests to use. Unfortunately, often the enthusiasts creating these new tests were disinclined to be critical of their instruments or the interpretation of their results. Thorndike and Hagen characterized the years between 1915 and 1930 as a 'boom' period, during which new tests 'multiplied like rabbits', and '[m]any sins were committed in the name of measurement by uncritical test users' (Thorndike and Hagen, 1969: 6).

Existing accounts of the early years

Although there are plenty of accounts of the history of validity (e.g. Geisinger, 1992; Shepard, 1993; Kane, 2001) descriptions of the early years tend either to be omitted entirely, or presented in a manner that seems a little over-simplistic. In many accounts, the early years hardly figure at all (e.g. Langenfeld and Crocker, 1994; Hubley and Zumbo, 1996; Gray, 1997; Jonson and Plake, 1998). In fact, it is not at all uncommon for historical accounts (e.g. Moss et al., 2006) to give the impression (at least) that all of the important developments are traceable through successive editions of *Educational Measurement* (beginning with Lindquist, 1951) and the *Standards* (beginning with APA et al., 1954). When the true diversity and sophistication of the early years becomes apparent, this impression seems implausible. In many ways, developments in validity theory and validation practice from the middle of the 20th century onwards are simply elaborations of insights that had been established far earlier.

When the early years do figure in historical accounts, they are often a little oversimplified in the sense of focusing on certain, apparently unsophisticated features at the expense of many other, more sophisticated ones. Geisinger (1992) emphasized the relationship between validity and correlation in the period prior to the 1950s and linked this to the idea of 'dust-bowl empiricism': the elevation of empirical evidence at the expense of logical analysis. Shepard (1993) characterized the 1920s to the 1950s as a period of deference to test-criterion correlations, typically judged in terms of a single coefficient. During the 1940s, she observed, the concept of validity came to be synonymous with the predictive correlation coefficient. Similarly, Kane (2001) characterized the early years as the 'criterion' phase, stressing the dominance of test-criterion correlations, and suggesting that the criterion was basi-cally taken for granted during this period. Cronbach (1971: 443) observed that the theory of prediction was very nearly the whole of validity theory until about 1950, arguing that only recently had researchers relegated the theory of prediction and elevated descriptive and explanatory investigations – a point that was echoed recently by Brennan (2006). Messick (1989a: 18) also claimed that thinking on valid-ity shifted fundamentally from prediction, during the early years, to explanation. Our own research, based on early textbooks and journal articles of the period, has uncovered a more subtle and interesting story. There is undoubtedly a sense in which the 'criterion phase' captures something very important about the early years; yet at the same time it is indeed an over-simplification, and to characterize this period simply as the 'prediction phase' is worse still.

The first official definition of validity – the degree to which a test measures what it purports to (i.e. is supposed to) measure – needed to be operationalized for validation purposes. This required a criterion by which validity could be judged, therefore the idea of a criterion was central to early accounts. Yet the criteria in question were many and varied, and approaches to establishing validity equally diverse and numerous. This was not exclusively a period of 'criterion-oriented validation', as that term came to be understood from the mid-1950s (Cronbach and Meehl, 1955): that is, a period during which only predictive or concurrent approaches to validation were utilized. For example, it is not true that issues of 'content validity' were rarely, if ever, considered during this period, although the term was not invented until much later.

In fact, content considerations were always fundamental to the design and evaluation of all tests (all tests need content), although content considerations were particularly significant for achievement tests. Admittedly, often the logical analysis of content was supplemented by empirical evidence of correlation – and content considerations were not as robust as they ought to have been in certain quarters – but content considerations always came first. Furthermore, although there is certainly an interesting tale to be told about the reconceptualization of content sampling theory under the influence of the measurement movement, and although there were other ways in which the technology of mental testing com-promised the content sampling ideal, this does not mean that the principle of content sampling was somehow absent from early debate over the design and evaluation of tests. If reference to the 'criterion' or 'predictive' phase should give the impression that content concerns were universally trivialized during the early years, this is not true, certainly not as far as mainstream educational assessment was concerned. We should recall that the concept of validity was born to, and moulded by, the National Association of Directors of Educational Research.

If the concept of validity was not quite so narrow and unsophisticated during the early years, then why might such giants of validity theory as Cronbach, Messick, Kane and Shepard seem to suggest otherwise? For example, Cronbach not only lived through, but even worked through, a substantial chunk of the early years, studying full-time on his PhD in education from 1938 and subsequently working as an assistant to Ralph Tyler in his landmark Eight-Year Study (Cronbach, 1989b) – the significance of which will become clear shortly. Messick, too, studied for his PhD toward the end of the early years. We can only speculate as to why the more interesting story has not been conveyed through existing historical accounts, so here are a few speculations.

First, many accounts of the history of validity have been written during the past 20 years or so, to make sense of the transition from a trinitarian conception of validity (in which content, criterion and construct validity stood alongside each other) to a unitarian one (whereby construct validity came to subsume the other two). As mentioned previously, the trinitarian conception had its roots in the very first *Standards* document (APA et al., 1954). As such, 1954 makes an obvious starting point for a history of validity, and successive editions of this publication, alongside successive editions of the text that many measurement specialists think of as the 'holy book' of their field, *Educational Measurement*, certainly mark crucial watersheds. Unfortunately, the omission of any discussion of the early years is counterproductive, since any sense of continuity between classical and current conceptions of validity is lost. For example, the maxim that 'all validity is construct validity' is not too dissimilar from the earliest definition of validity as the degree to which a test measures what it is supposed to measure (Newton, 2012a). In short, 1954 does not mark the beginning of validity theory, but an unhelpful detour from a journey that began on a promising path many decades earlier. Teaching validity from a baseline of 1921 makes far more sense of present-day theory and practice than starting from a baseline of 1954. Only with reference to developments during the early years can the trinitarian characterization of validity and validation be really understood.

Second, there were no seminal reference works on validity theory between 1921 and 1951. More precisely, there were many seminal works, but none which seem to have resulted in early consensus, and therefore none which acted as a true reference point for educational and psychological measurement. This was not true of later years, whereby each new generation of professionals could refer to a revised section on validity within successive editions of the *Standards*, or to a new section on validity or validation within successive editions of *Educational Measurement*.[1] Perhaps there were too many seminal works during the early years for a coherent tradition to emerge, with each new theorist promoting a slightly different perspective. The 1920s was particularly prolific for educational measurement, witnessing the publication of numerous important and influential textbooks (e.g. McCall, 1922; Monroe, 1923; Ruch, 1924; Kelley, 1927; Ruch and Stoddard, 1927; Ruch, 1929). Perhaps more importantly, in addition to differences in perspective between authors working *within* sub-domains, larger differences were beginning to emerge between authors working in *different* sub-domains. Thus, accounts written in the context of aptitude testing within organizations (e.g. Hull, 1928; Bingham, 1937) had a somewhat different emphasis from those written in the context of achievement testing within schools. Accounts written from a more academic perspective, with an emphasis on psychology and psychometrics, again had a somewhat different feel (e.g. Thurstone, 1931; Guilford, 1936). However, this did not reflect the emergence of sharp dividing lines between sub-professions of educational and psychological measurement: for example, directors of education had just as much interest in intelligence tests as they did in special aptitude tests or school achievement tests. Had types of test clustered more clearly within sub-domains of professional practice, then validity theory might have developed a clearer identity right from the outset – or more likely still, a number of different identities. In short, there were differences of emphasis during the early years but no dominant approach, so it is actually quite hard to characterize the period.

Third, the sub-domains of professional practice tugged validity theory in different ways during different phases, and the 1940s were particularly dominated by the war effort. In fact, both world wars had a major impact on the perception of testing and validation. The large-scale implementation of mental testing during the First World War was facilitated by Otis, who had developed the technique of group testing: the administration of a single test to a large number of people at the same time, in contrast with the traditional approach of administering tests individually, person by person. He also had devised a method of scoring by stencil, which meant that tests could be marked very rapidly. Under the direction of Yerkes, group tests for military aptitude were developed: the Army Alpha and Beta. Their widespread adoption gave the technology of mental testing such enormous publicity and prestige, that following the war there was a mad rush to transfer the methods to other occupational settings. According to Osburn (1933), the First World War not only brought the word 'criterion' into more general use, it also led to the widespread perception of test construction as a process that was far more empirical than logical, as tests often came to be mechanically constructed to optimize the prediction of criterion measures. Taken to an extreme, this approach to test construction came to be much maligned, being described as 'blindly empirical' (Peak, 1953: 288). The adoption of this empirical approach by many test developers during the early years helps to explain why commentators often have emphasized the dominance of 'prediction' theory. Yet, to characterize everything that happened prior to 1952 in this manner would be misleading, since it would tell only one side of a far more complex and fascinating story.

Given the vast literature on test theory and practice from the middle of the 19th century to the middle of the 20th century, and given the range of professional and academic perspectives that it embraces, it might seem impossible to construct a plausible, comprehensive and even moderately objective report on the history of validity during the early years. We fully acknowledge the scale of this challenge. Expressing similar sentiments, Tim Rogers observed that:

> Trying to piece together exactly how validity emerged in the testing enterprise is like an archaeologist [sic] trying to construct a dinosaur from a few bones. Much of the critical information is not readily available and has to be filled in by guesswork. (Rogers, 1995: 245)

The following account is our reconstruction of a long and productive period that we cannot claim to know well, and have glimpsed only partially through the literature that we have managed to track down. We admit that our narrative may be slightly nuanced because we wish to tell a slightly different story from the one that is often told, and want to highlight synergies with our account of subsequent periods.

Explaining the caricature

Before exploring the evidence which is suggestive of greater diversity and sophistication during the early years, it is worth pausing to reflect further why it might have become known as the 'prediction' phase. There are at least two major factors that, in combination, might help to explain this caricature: first, the widespread adoption of blindly empirical methods, particularly for the purpose of aptitude testing; second, a degradation of the classic definition over time, as the preferred *method* for investigating validity came to be mistaken for a *definition* of validity in its own right. The second factor appears to involve a three-stage deterioration from:

1 quality of measurement supported by the test, to
2 degree of correlation between the test and its criterion, to
3 coefficient of correlation between the test and a criterion measure.

The following sections attempt to illustrate how this definitional degradation might have occurred over time, while the adoption of blindly empirical methods will be discussed subsequently in the section 'Validity and special aptitude tests'.

From quality of measurement to degree of correlation

In one of the first textbooks of its kind, *How to Measure in Education*, McCall (1922) reflected on the earliest formal definition of validity. Asking his reader how we might know whether a test measures what it purports to measure, he responded that we can know what it measures 'only by its correlations' (McCall, 1922: 204). McCall identified two methods for determining this correspondence for achievement tests:

1 follow up the testing with prolonged careful observation of how pupils demonstrate the proficiency in everyday life – that is, rank them first on the test, and then in real life, and correlate the ranks
2 test a population of pupils whose proficiency is already known – that is, rank them first on the proficiency, and then on the test, and correlate the ranks.

In both cases, the criterion against which the validity of the test was to be judged was the pupil's actual, real-life proficiency. If the ranking given by the test agreed with the actual, real-life ranking, then the test was valid for measuring that ability. McCall's *degree of correlation* elaboration of the classic definition was essentially a conceptual abstraction. It envisaged a hypothetical, true proficiency rank as the absolute criterion against which, in theory, the actual, observed proficiency rank from the test ought to be judged. In fact, even McCall was prepared to accept that there was probably no such thing as a single true proficiency rank, and he preferred to think in terms of a range of true proficiency ranks across a family of similar real-world situations (McCall, 1922: 209). Yet the abstraction provided a useful heuristic to guide validation.

The degree of correlation conception naturally recommended a particular approach to validation: the careful construction of a comprehensive criterion measure according to which the shorter, more practical test could be judged. Thus, McCall introduced the idea of prolonged careful observation of pupils in real-life situations, to determine their true proficiency as precisely as possible. This more comprehensive judgement of proficiency then could be used as a criterion measure for test validation purposes. Importantly, even this comprehensive judgement was still only a measure of the criterion – a measure of the pupil's actual, real-life proficiency – and not the criterion itself. Ultimately, the criterion was more of a conceptual abstraction than an empirical operationalization, yet the criterion measure was as faithful a representation of the criterion as could be realistically achieved.

During the early years, different approaches to the development of criterion measures were proposed and utilized. Results from tests to be validated came to be correlated against:

- the judgement of suitably qualified experts, especially teachers
- results aggregated across multiple existing tests purporting to measure the same thing
- results from specific tests that commanded particular respect with the passage of time.

In relation to studies such as these, during the 1920s the elaboration of the classic definition of validity still seemed to be conceptual. That is, although correlation was central to the process of validation, the definition of validity and the method of validation were discrete. Importantly, validity was not framed in terms of prediction, in the sense of predicting future proficiencies, but in terms of correlation: that is, the correlation between actual test result and hypothetical true proficiency.

From degree of correlation to coefficient of validity

As time went by, textbook authors restated the degree of correlation definition in their own words, influenced by their own interests and settings. As these proliferated, sometimes the subtlety of the classic definition was lost, as criteria came to be described less as conceptual abstractions, and more as concrete measures. For example:

> The *validity* of a test is the closeness of agreement between the scores and some other objective measure of that which the test is used to measure. The other measure is called the *criterion*. The coefficient of validity of a test is the coefficient of correlation between test scores and criterion scores. (Bingham, 1937: 214, italics in original)

Thus, within a number of prominent texts, validity came to be defined in terms of *observed* agreement between test scores and scores from a criterion measure, rather than in terms of *hypothetical* agreement between test scores and true proficiency. Understood in this manner, validity was reduced to no more nor less than an empirical correlation: the *coefficient of validity*. This was problematic as a definition, since it relied on there being no question as to the validity of criterion scores as measures of true proficiency – which, of course, could never be assumed.

The fusion between method and definition was very pragmatic and functional, in the sense of emphasizing the use to which test results would be put. The size of the correlation coefficient was assumed to indicate the degree of validity of the use, therefore, a test would have very many different validities, depending on the particular use in question, and the particular criterion chosen. This seemingly atheoretical definition of validity was to be epitomized later in a famous quotation from Guilford: 'a test is valid for anything with which it correlates' (1946: 429). In making this point, Guilford was contrasting explicitly this atheoretical conception ('practical validity') with a genuinely theoretical one ('factorial validity'). According to Guilford, validity came in two kinds, and only the second addressed the more fundamental question of whether the test measured what it was supposed to measure.

Even during the 1930s and into the 1940s, degradation of the classic definition – from conceptual to pragmatic – was not universal. For example, 10 years before he distinguished between practical and factorial validity, Guilford had defined the 'coefficient of validity' as 'the correlation between a test and some better established measure of the same trait which the test was designed to measure' (1936: 364). This was clearly a conceptual definition, not a pragmatic one, and therefore one that admitted the possibility that the criterion measure might be inadequate. As we will discuss further in Chapter 3, although there are parallels between the rise of operationist thinking in psychology and degradation of the classic definition – in the sense that both elevated the observable and relegated the unobservable – it may be unwise to overestimate the impact of this zeitgeist on validity theory during the early years.

Although many accounts of the early years imply that an atheoretical conception was dominant, emphasizing how validators placed undue (if not exclusive) emphasis on empirical evidence of potential to predict, this would seem to be an oversimplification. Admittedly, degradation of the classic definition may not have been uncommon, particularly in contexts dominated by selection and guidance functions. Yet atheoretical conceptions were far from universal (as will be explained in more depth in the remainder of this chapter). Moreover, even within personnel settings, recognition of the inadequacy of the degraded definition became widespread during the 1940s, as a subsequent section, 'The criterion problem', will explain.

Validating tests for different purposes

In his preface to *Aptitude Testing* (Hull, 1928), Terman usefully distinguished between the three primary concerns of educational and psychological measurement during the early years:

1   school achievement
2   general intelligence
3   special aptitudes.

He observed that for the most part, the principles and techniques are the same in each of these three fields, thereby recommending Hull's textbook to all students as unquestionably one of the most significant. The similarities noted by Terman help to explain why there was so much cross-fertilization between the sub-professions during the early years, and why a concept of validity proposed in the context of educational research was generalized so readily.

In the following sections, conceptions of validity within the three fields are discussed separately in order to foreground certain of their peculiarities. This is to help convey the diversity of validity theory and validation practice during the early years, and to help explain why the concept of validity fragmented from the mid-1950s onwards. A final section on challenges for clinical and personality testing paves a way to the key development of the 1950s: the notion of construct validity.

Validity and school achievement tests

Walter Monroe was Professor of Education (from 1919 to 1950) and Director of the Bureau of Educational Research (from 1921 to 1947) (University of Illinois, 2011). He is not credited often as a pioneer of validity theory, but his early contributions were substantial, and his later reflections on the evolution of validity theory during the early years are very informative. In 1923, he expressed the classic definition slightly differently from McCall:

> Under the head of validity we inquire into the degree of constancy of the functional relation existing between the scores yielded by the test and the abilities specified as being measured in the statement of that function. (Monroe, 1923: 188)

Clearly, his definition is based on correlation and, once again, is more conceptual than pragmatic. However, it should not be assumed that Monroe reduced validation to empirical correlation. Quite the reverse; he described validity as a multifaceted concept that he subdivided as follows:

1   Objectivity in describing performances
2   Reliability:

    a.   coefficient of reliability
    b.   index of reliability
    c.   probable error of measurement
    d.   coefficient of correspondence
    e.   overlapping of successive grade groups

3   Discrimination:

    f.   does the distribution of measures agree with the normal curve?
    g.   are differences shown between groups which are known to differ in ability?

h. into how many groups is a typical class divided? Is this sufficient to discriminate properly between the members of a class?

4 Comparison with criterion measures:

i.   teachers' marks
j.   measures yielded by other tests
k.   composite test scores

5 Inferences concerning validity, based upon the structure of the test and its administration:

l.   do the content of the exercises and the structure of the test appear to be consistent with its function?
m. do all pupils have an opportunity to demonstrate their abilities?
n.   to what extent are testing conditions controlled?
o.   is the variation of abilities, other than those being measured, reduced to a minimum? (Monroe, 1923: 183–4)

The sub-headings within these five sections indicate clearly the breadth of the concept of validity envisaged by Monroe. It included a full range of approaches to establishing both reliability and discrimination, alongside coefficients of correlation with criterion measures. Under 'Objectivity in describing performances', Monroe noted the challenge of the 'personal equation' in rating examination performances, citing the examiner as a source of divergence between test score and true ability, introducing either constant (systematic) or variable (random) error. He observed that objectivity might be increased by the use of questions that admit only straightforwardly right or wrong answers, or by training examiners in how to rate answers to more complicated questions. Under 'Inferences concerning validity', he identified evidence based on the analysis of test content and response processes, highlighting threats that would be described later using the terms 'content under-representation' and 'construct-irrelevant test variance' (e.g. Messick, 1989a). Six threats to valid inference were identified through the following questions.

1 Do the tasks within the test require abilities other than those supposedly being assessed, where those abilities cannot be presumed constant across pupils?
2 Can the tasks be answered in a variety of different methods, where the intended method is not specified?
3 Is the test administered under a variety of conditions, where those conditions might impact differently on pupils?
4 Do students continue to exercise their ability for the duration of the test, across all tasks?
5 Are the tasks representative of the field of ability being tested?
6 Are all pupils given the opportunity to demonstrate their ability?

This was a truly unitary conception of validity, requiring the integration of multiple sources of empirical evidence and logical analysis:

> Our final estimate of the validity of a test should be the consensus of information secured under the head of objectivity, reliability, discrimination, and comparison with criterion measures, plus such inferences as we are able to make. (Monroe, 1923: 227)

Subsequent writers adopted similarly unified accounts, requiring the integration of arguments based on logical analysis and empirical evidence, typically categorizing sources of evidence into one of two primary categories, for example: 'the opinion of competent judges' versus 'correlation' (Kelley, 1927); 'expert opinion' versus 'experimental' (Ruch, 1929) and 'curricular' versus 'statistical' (Ruch, 1933).

Perhaps the most important point to emphasize is the centrality of logical analysis to the concept of validity, even within the earliest accounts. Clearly, empirical correlation was only part of the story of validation during the early years. As far as achievement tests were concerned, logical analysis assumed a fundamental role right from the outset. Ruch (1929) identified three different approaches to the logical analysis of tests:

1   judgement of competent persons on the appropriateness of content
2   alignment of content with courses of study or textbooks
3   alignment of content with recommendations from national educational committees.

For teachers who needed to tailor tests to their own curricula, Ruch claimed that the guiding principle in validation ought to be that the test parallels the actual teaching: that is, the test represents an extensive sampling of the materials of instruction (Ruch, 1929: 30). The concept of extensive sampling was fundamental to early views of validity, particularly for school achievement tests; yet it was soon to become a site of conflict, and one that would remain so for decades to come.

Sampling theory versus test construction practice

Monroe (1923) emphasized that, in theory, exercises in an achievement test ought to be limited to the field of study and representative of it. This promoted the idea of test construction as a form of *random sampling* from that field. Where this was not feasible, the test ought to be at least representative of the most important elements of the field: for example, a spelling test ought to sample from the most frequently used words of the English language.

However, right from the outset, Monroe (1923) recognized how new approaches to test development presented a threat to effective sampling. One of the major innovations and triumphs of the early years was the technique of scaling, which resulted in a series of tests of differing levels of difficulty: for example, tests designed to be appropriate for students in different grade levels. Test development involved experimental trialling of a large pool of items, which *as a set* were supposed to be representative of the field in question, followed by allocating items to tests within the series on the basis of their difficulty. Thus, *for each individual test*, items were not selected on the basis of content, and therefore no individual test would represent the field effectively.

The logic of scaling also encouraged test developers to seek out items with particularly useful statistical properties. From this perspective, there was no point in a test including items that all students at a particular grade would answer correctly or incorrectly, because this would add no information concerning individual differences. Furthermore, there was good reason to include items that were particularly sensitive to differences between grades: that best discriminated between students in different grades. This established a fundamental tension between statisticians who were driven by concern for discrimination, and teachers who were driven by concern for sampling what had been actually taught (Osburn, 1933).

Measurement versus evaluation

Ralph Tyler, one of the foremost educationists of the 20th century, was awarded his PhD by the University of Chicago in 1927, moved to Ohio State University in 1929 and, in 1934, was appointed research director of the evaluation staff for what became known as the Eight-Year Study of student learning processes. The period between 1929 and 1934 is of particular relevance to our discussion of validity. During this time Tyler published regularly in the journal *Educational Research Bulletin*, writing regular reviews of 'new tests' and a series of articles on issues related to the validity of achievement tests.[2]

Tyler was not impressed by the use of teachers' marks as an empirical criterion for judging validity, and proposed an alternative approach based on the construction of better criterion measures (Tyler, 1931a). Assuming that valid criterion measures needed to sample the full range of important educational objectives, he defined validity in terms of 'the usefulness of the test in measuring the degree to which the pupils have attained the objectives which are the true goals of the subject' (Tyler, 1932a: 374). He was not opposed to the empirical approach to validation per se. Indeed, he proposed that test development should begin with the development of 'preliminary tests' for each of the course objectives (thereby creating comprehensive criterion measures), but then should continue with the preparation of more practicable tests which could be validated by correlating their results against the criterion measures. Developing separate tests for each of the course objectives also helped for diagnostic purposes.

Sampling a full range of objectives was fundamental to Tyler, in relation to both test construction and validity. However, this was not the narrow view of content that had been associated with the analysis of textbooks, since ultimately Tyler was interested in *mental processes*. He bemoaned the common failure to distinguish between the content of a subject, and the mental processes which a student of that subject was expected to exhibit (Tyler, 1932b). This led him to the conclusion that truly representative sampling would require the development of broader equipment than currently available for those who wished to evaluate school achievement, particularly if the 'intangibles' were to be adequately appraised: art appreciation, attitudes, interests, etc. (Tyler, 1932b, 1934, 1936).

Tyler was particularly concerned with the potential for negative impacts on instruction caused by the omission of important objectives from standardized tests. In a review of *A Test Book to Accompany Introduction to Science*, produced by Caldwell and Curtis to accompany their textbook of the same name, he observed that most of the items tested information, and very few tested the interpretation of scientific data or the application of scientific principles. Since these were vital objectives, the test book was likely to be a danger to students or teachers who adapted their studying or teaching to the emphasis of the test (Tyler, 1931b). The effects of measurement on instruction were also the focus of a symposium organized by Woody and others (1935). Monroe, who was one of the contributors, observed that 'the test makers of the country have been the real curriculum-makers' (Monroe, 1935: 496). Over a quarter of a century he had become convinced that the use of objective tests was nullifying attempts to reform the curriculum.

Sampling theory versus test construction theory

Although random sampling was supposedly the ideal for test development, as far as achievement tests were concerned, this was obviously never a practicable solution. An alternative approach became increasingly popular from the mid-1920s, initially borrowed from the field of intelligence testing (Osburn, 1933). For many years validity had been investigated by correlating *test* scores against criterion measures. The new approach involved correlating *item* scores against criterion measures. This seemed to assume implicitly that test performance ultimately ought to be determined by a single attribute (e.g. intelligence), which each item tapped to a greater or lesser extent. If so, then in theory, each item ought to be measuring the essentially the same thing: i.e. the same attribute. If this were true, then items that correlated highest with the criterion measure (e.g. the established intelligence test) ought to be selected preferentially for the new test.

In an exposition of the theory of test construction, Lindquist (1936) applied this principle to the development of achievement examinations. He began by noting that the logic of deriving a single score to represent achievement in a field only really made sense for homogeneous fields. So, if different components of a field failed to correlate to an appreciable degree, then they ought to be assessed and reported on separately. Having said that, he acknowledged that no fields are perfectly homogeneous, so there would always be a certain degree of compromise. He suggested that where tests were needed for diagnostic purposes, there was less justification for compromising, and separable components ought to be assessed and reported separately. Yet at the same time, he recognized the many uses of results that depended on aggregating to a single score, even when faced with somewhat heterogeneous fields:

> The general achievement test, then, is in a sense simply a device for securing con-
> veniently and on a *comparable* basis for all students, a composite description of total
> achievement in those situations where a composite type of interpretation must in any
> event be made. (Lindquist, 1936: 28, italics in original)

Because it simply was not possible to construct a robust measure of overall
achievement on the basis of an appropriately weighted sample of behaviour from
across the entire achievement domain, the task of test development needed to be
reconceptualized. Lindquist recast it as an exercise in *restricted sampling*, where
the intention was to tap the essence of general achievement rather than to sample
the achievement domain representatively. Extrapolating from early elaboration of
the classic definition – the degree of correlation of a test with its criterion – he
reasoned that item validity could be defined in the same way as test validity: that
is, as the degree of correlation of an item with its criterion. Indeed, the criterion
would be the same in both cases: the true level of general achievement of candidates. Theorizing item validity in this way led to the principle that items which
correlated highest with general achievement ought (within limits) to be selected
preferentially. Therefore, the theory of test development changed subtly from
random (or representative) sampling of the overall achievement domain, to
restricted sampling of the general achievement attribute. The rationale seems to
go something like this: if we were able to sample randomly, such as to represent
the domain in its entirety, then each item would play its own role in contributing
to the aggregate measure of overall achievement. However, since we are not able
to sample on this scale, each item is forced to play essentially the same role in
contributing to the aggregate measure – this time by tapping the essence of general achievement.

According to this thesis, items that failed to correlate with the general achievement criterion – that failed to discriminate between students who were high or low
in terms of general achievement – would contribute nothing to the test, regardless
of whether or not they sampled important content. Similarly, when forced to choose
between items of equivalent logical relevance, from a content perspective, those
with higher item validity coefficients would be selected preferentially. Moreover,
items would be needed that discriminated well for students across the full ability
range, which would compromise the content sampling ideal further. Of course, the
content sampling ideal would still guide the initial development of items prior to
item trialling; however, the rationale for selecting and de-selecting items for the final
test form would be to tap the essence of the general achievement attribute, rather
than to sample the domain representatively.

Adopting this theoretical perspective, the challenge then became one of identifying
appropriate criterion measures. Lindquist (1936) noted that one of the most frequently
used measures was the test itself: the correlation between the item and the aggregate
of all other items from the item pool, which blurred the traditional distinction between
reliability and validity (Buros, 1977, attributed the method of correlating item scores
against the item pool aggregate score to Ruch and Stoddard, 1927). Of course, this
could prove problematic, since if the aggregate of all other items was not actually a

strong criterion measure after all, then the selection of items that correlated with it would make the test more reliable, but not necessarily more valid. Buros had criticized this approach to test development and validation as early as 1935, and remained strongly opposed to it for the remainder of his career (Buros, 1977).

Proponents of the approach were not unaware of the tensions that this raised. Wood et al. (1933) contrasted validity from the curriculum viewpoint with validity from the general achievement testing perspective, proposing that both needed to be considered in arriving at a compromise. However, at the same time they concluded that since the content of achievement tests could not be expected to parallel any course of study exactly, the task of selecting items could not be left to subject matter experts, and was instead primarily a technical problem. This was an uncomfortable conclusion. Indeed, a largely unresolved tension between logical and empirical considerations can be detected running throughout the chapter by Lindquist (1936): he strongly recommended the use of empirical methods while simultaneously admitting the danger of eliminating logically relevant items on purely empirical grounds.

The ongoing tension between empirical and logical

The tension between empirical and logical considerations continued throughout the 1930s and into the 1940s. Critics of over-reliance on empirical considerations emphasized the inadequacy of criteria for establishing validity, and the backwash on teaching and learning from the omission of important educational objectives. They stressed the need to develop new forms of assessment to deal with the full range of educational objectives that needed to be evaluated. Advocates of empirical approaches emphasized the impossibility of sampling the full range of important educational objectives, and the fallibility of human judgement in the absence of standardized tests.

It would be very hard to reach a definitive conclusion over which perspective ultimately won out in the context of school achievement testing, although there are hints that the pendulum was beginning to swing against the measurement movement and the dominance of empirical considerations. For example, an editorial note to the article 'Evaluating evaluation' (Orata, 1940) noted the rise of newer methods of measurement and the shift in emphasis from measurement to evaluation, influenced particularly by the work of Tyler. In an article advocating the approach of the scientist (rational) over the approach of the technician (empirical), 'Rational hypotheses in the construction of tests', Travers (1951) also emphasized the importance of Tyler and his students in shifting opinion back toward the rational, from a period dominated by the technician. Similarly, in an article 'Educational measurement in 1920 and in 1945', Monroe (1945) observed that while curriculum content was considered a secondary concern in 1920, it was now a major one. He also recognized the growth of the *evaluation movement* and its desire to appraise a much broader range of educational objectives; sentiments echoed subsequently by Rulon (1946). The evaluation movement emphasized two key principles:

1   that evaluation could not begin until the curriculum had been defined in terms
    of behavioural objectives; and
2   that *any* useful measuring device might be employed in the production of a
    comprehensive account of pupil growth – be that an objective test, essay exam-
    ination, teacher judgement or whatever.

Validity and general intelligence tests

As for achievement testing, both logical and empirical considerations were relevant
to intelligence testing, during test development and validation.

A logical approach to test development

Terman and colleagues in Stanford, California, revised and extended the Binet-
Simon scales. Terman (1918) viewed intelligence differently from school achievement, characterizing it as raw brain power. He eloquently described the logic of
intelligence testing by analogy, describing the process of assaying the value of gold
within a vein of quartz on the basis of a few random samples of ore. An extended
quotation is useful to illustrate his claim:

> *Collecting Samples for Assaying.*—In ascertaining the value of the gold deposit would
> it be safe to take all the assayer's samples from a single part of the quartz vein?
> Common sense would of course suggest the precaution of taking samples from many
> places and of estimating the gold content in terms of average richness. Similarly in
> testing intelligence the subject is not asked to perform one intellectual 'stunt,' but many.
> He may be given tests of memory, of language comprehension, of vocabulary, of ori-
> entation in time and space, of ability to follow directions, of knowledge about familiar
> things, of judgment, of ability to find likeness and differences between common
> objects, of arithmetical reasoning, of resourcefulness and ingenuity in practical situa-
> tions, of ability to detect the nonsense in absurd statements, of speed and richness of
> mental associations, of power to combine related ideas into a logical whole, of ability
> to generalize from particulars, etc. The average of a large number of performances thus
> gives a kind of composite picture of the subject's *general intelligence*. (Terman, 1918:
> 163–4, italics in original)

In a sense this early conception of intelligence testing was similar to the early conception of achievement testing, with both appearing to invoke the concept of random sampling.[3] At least in theory, then, the intelligence test was open to validation
on the basis of logical analysis, in much the same way as school achievement tests
were. Of course, this would require a thorough description of the universe of intel-
ligent behaviours that comprised intelligence, just as the logical analysis of school
achievement tests required a thorough description of the universe of learned behaviours (educational objectives) that comprised the curriculum.

Unfortunately, the task of defining a universe of intelligent behaviours was not
at all straightforward. Indeed, the lack of a clear definition of intelligence was a

major theme in one of the most influential of early criticisms of intelligence testing from the public intellectual and political commentator, Walter Lippmann, in a series of six articles in the *New Republic* in 1922. This lack of adequate definition recommended alternative approaches to validation, as we describe below.

As illustrated by passages quoted in Burt (1924: 24), Binet believed that nearly all of the phenomena with which psychology concerned itself were phenomena of intelligence: meaning that a test of any faculty was in a sense a test of intelligence. (According to Gould, 1981, unlike many who followed in his footsteps, Binet was careful not to reify the concept of general intelligence, and actually resisted the idea that this was what his scale measured.) The many possible manifestations of intelligence led to the principle that tests needed to be manifold and heterogeneous. Developing Binet's distinction between faculties and general intelligence, Burt (1924) noted that performance on any test would necessarily be a product of both general intelligence and specific capacities. As such, it seemed that a cardinal principle of intelligence testing, post-Binet, was never to employ a single test, but always to combine tests of different types into an average measure. The purpose of averaging, he observed, was to eliminate the varying influences of specific capacities.

Once again, it is worth drawing attention to the parallel between general intelligence and general achievement during the early years. For both attributes, there seemed to be a desire to capture the essence of their respective domains under circumstances that prevented representative sampling. In the case of achievement testing, the limitation seemed to be primarily practical: it was not possible to compose a test that effectively represented the domain. In the case of intelligence testing, the limitation seemed to be primarily conceptual: it was not possible to define the domain with sufficient clarity. Lindquist (1936) and Burt (1924) described completely different ways of overcoming what seems to be a very similar problem. Lindquist emphasized restrictive sampling, which involved attempting to assess only the essence of achievement. In effect, he assumed that validity could be maximized by intentional construct-underrepresentation. Burt emphasized permissive sampling, which involved attempting to assess considerably more than the essence of intelligence. In effect, he assumed that validity could be maximized by intentional construct-irrelevance, on the assumption that random irrelevant item variance would cancel out (i.e. disappear) in the test score, given the law of averages.

An empirical approach to validation

For McCall, the question of validity for general intelligence tests, as for school achievement tests, was a matter of correlation: 'The closeness of a test's correlation with what constitutes intelligence is a measure of its excellence as an intelligence test' (1922: 210). Of course, to investigate validity would require a criterion measure of intelligence against which to correlate results from the test, and this was no mean feat. The earliest studies relied primarily on the judgement of suitably qualified experts, often school teachers. Subsequently, following the First World War, a large number of general intelligence tests were produced, which meant that their aggregate could be used as a practical criterion of intelligence. Finally, over time, certain intelligence tests acquired the reputation of higher quality than others, and therefore came to be adopted as yardstick criterion measures for the evaluation of new intelligence tests.

A study by Jordan (1923a, 1923b) illustrated the use of all three of these approaches. He was interested to determine which of four group tests of intelligence was the most valid: Army Alpha, Miller Group Test, Otis Group Test or Terman Group Test. He administered each of these tests to 64 pupils of high-school age, and compared the results against the following criteria:

1   an intelligence rating from four teachers, averaged
2   the Stanford-Binet intelligence test
3   a Learning Test
4   the composite of all four tests.

Jordan took unusually robust precautions when eliciting teacher ratings, ensuring that the teachers only rated students whom they knew well, and providing them with the following instructions to guide their ratings:

> Rate for general intelligence, by which is meant: (a) tendency to take and maintain a definite direction in thinking; (b) the capacity for making adaptations for the purpose of obtaining the desired end; (c) the power of self-criticism. (Jordan, 1923a: 351)

The correlation coefficients arising from Jordan's (1923a) research are reproduced in Table 2.1.

From these results, Jordan (1923a) concluded that the Otis test was the most valid for testing intelligence at the high-school age, and the Miller test the least valid. Although admitting that his research could not answer definitively what the tests actually measured, he felt that the lack of correlation with the Learning Test suggested that existing 'capacity to learn' definitions were challenged. So, he proposed a revised definition along the lines of capacity to learn, when the material learned is difficult for the learner.[4] Jordan (1923a) admitted that nobody could say which of the four criteria really ought to have the most weight in judging validity, although personally he believed his teacher ratings to be superior to results from the Stanford-Binet test.

Table 2.1   Validity coefficient summary table

	Learning Test	Stanford-Binet	Teacher Rating	Composite
Otis	0.23	0.66	0.73	0.93
Army Alpha	0.21	0.69	0.61	0.91
Miller	0.17	0.53	0.68	0.90
Terman	0.21	0.68	0.66	0.91

Source: Jordan, 1923a: 361, Table XI

Beyond correlation with criterion measures

Lamenting a lack of sophistication in the measurement of adult intelligence despite 40 years of development within the field, Cattell (1943) decided to subject 44 published tests of intelligence to scrutiny. Based on a review of the literature, he identified four approaches to validation that appeared to be equally distributed among them:

1   correlation with other intelligence tests or subjective ratings of intelligence
2   inspection for increase of score with age
3   estimation of efficiency of prediction of scholastic or social and/or occupational achievement
4   inspection for decrease of score for 'mental defectives'.

Less common methods included:

- examination of normality of score distribution
- examination of internal consistency via subtest inter-correlations or item analysis.

Cattell roundly criticized each of these methods, and he was particularly sceptical about methods which judged the validity of newer tests in terms of older ones or the preconceptions of judges. He dismissed this methodology as based on the logic of 'holy apostolic succession': the view of a theologian, not a scientist. He concluded that no more progress had been made in validating intelligence tests over the previous two decades than in theorizing intelligence: that is, very little indeed. He could not understand why psychologists continued to use these approaches when the 'way out of this bankruptcy' had been indicated by Galton, Spearman, Thurstone, Burt, Thomson and others a generation ago. The answer, according to Cattell, was factor analysis, with the potential to transform validation from a lay activity to a genuinely scientific practice. Only factor analysis could enable the researcher to explore the fundamental question of the degree to which a test measured what it was supposed to measure. Cattell was not alone in promoting factor analysis as a fundamentally important validation technique (see also Guilford, 1946), but not everyone was quite so intolerant of alternative approaches. Many considered factor analysis to be just one weapon within the overall validation armoury (e.g. Ryan, 1939; Gulliksen, 1950).

Validity and special aptitude tests

By the end of the 1920s, the desire to measure general intelligence had waned, while the desire to measure special aptitudes had increased substantially, especially for the purposes of vocational guidance and selection. As explained in one of the earliest textbooks devoted to the topic, the purpose of aptitude testing was to forecast individuals' aptitudes in advance of their vocational choices, to ensure that career paths were able to maximize potentialities (Hull, 1928). Therefore, the practice of testing for special aptitudes assumed, first, that aptitudes were stable, if not innate; and second, that aptitudes differed both across individuals and within individuals, typically along continua.

An empirical approach to validation

Testing for vocational guidance and selection presented a challenge that was quite distinct from that of testing for achievement or intelligence. For achievement testing and intelligence testing, the criterion – achievement or intelligence – was a thing of the present. That is, each student to be tested had a certain level of intelligence or attainment, and the test was used to determine how much of it each individual possessed. When it came to guidance and selection, the criterion appeared to be a thing of the future: successful performance within the vocation in question, involving the exercise of skills and abilities that had not yet been developed. Exactly what, then, should an aptitude test look like, and how should it be validated?

Obviously, if a proficiency has not yet been developed, the idea of sampling it through a test is meaningless. This appeared to rule out logical approaches to validation based on the scrutiny of test content, and therefore to elevate empirical approaches. Thus, the ideal approach appeared to involve a four-stage procedure:

1   Administer the aptitude test.
2   Wait until those tested had received an opportunity to develop the requisite skills and abilities required for successful job performance.
3   Assess job proficiency in situ.
4   Correlate results from the aptitude test against the assessment of job proficiency.

The description of the period between 1921 and 1951 as the 'prediction' phase is perhaps most appropriate in the context of vocational guidance and selection. Undoubtedly the empirical approach to validation, based on the prediction of future job proficiency, was dominant.

An empirical approach to test development

The adoption of a logical approach to test construction appeared to be no less problematic than the adoption of a logical approach to validation. In the absence of clear rational principles, many psychologists believed that purely empirical approaches held the most promise for constructing occupational tests. This reduced test development to a more or less haphazard, trial-and-error search for effective predictors (McCall, 1922: 198).

Item analysis played an important part in the construction of tests for vocational guidance and selection, but with a somewhat different emphasis than was evident in the construction of achievement tests. Clearly, the initial step in the development of *achievement* tests was rational, involving explicit sampling considerations. Item analysis then was employed to eliminate items with poor statistical properties. With an intention to elevate homogeneity, evidence of poor item-test correlation might well lead to the rejection of an item, even despite its logical relevance. Yet the first step in achievement test construction was still inherently rational, based on sampling principles.

As indicated by McCall (1922), the initial step in the construction of *aptitude* tests was often far less rational, with little idea of exactly what needed to be tested in order to predict accurately. According to Travers (1951), for example, the starting point for the development of the Strong Vocational Interest Blank was that of minimum rationality: a vague hypothesis that if a large enough list of preferences was prepared, then at least some of them would discriminate between the professions. From there onwards the procedure was basically empirical: the selection of items that, when assembled into a test, would ensure maximum correlation with the criterion. This was essentially a multiple regression challenge, for which a range of approximations were developed to make the task feasible in a pre-computerized age (e.g. Richardson and Adkins, 1938; Gleser and DuBois, 1951). One such approach began with selection of the item that correlated highest with the criterion; the next item to be selected would be the one that, when combined with the first, would correlate highest with the criterion, and so on until the addition of new items failed to improve the correlation appreciably.

Adoption of the regression model for item analysis marked another subtle point of departure from achievement testing. Regression models naturally favour items that correlate relatively poorly with each other, while correlating relatively well with the criterion. So, while achievement test construction considered inter-item correlation to be a virtue associated with the production of homogeneous tests, aptitude test construction sought to reduce inter-item correlation to a minimum.[5] Some came to see this as a severe weakness of aptitude tests, since it inevitably made them factorially complex, making them substantially less effective as ingredients for the construction of meaningful test batteries (Guilford, 1946). Guilford believed that the prediction of complex criteria was best achieved using batteries of factorially pure tests.

The criterion problem

The problem with a purely empirical approach to test construction and validation is that it can be no better than the criterion measure employed, since this is the yardstick against which all else is judged. As the early years progressed, it became increasingly clear that developing robust criterion measures was the Achilles' heel of aptitude testing. According to Jenkins (1946), little attention was paid to the *criterion problem* in the period between 1920 and 1940. Psychologists had become expert in techniques of item analysis, factor analysis and prediction of criteria, but had assumed tacitly that those criteria were either 'given of God or just to be found lying about' (Jenkins, 1946: 93). While the idea of validity for predictor tests was familiar, the idea of validity for criterion measures was fairly novel.

There were two major components of the criterion problem: the definition of the criterion, and the development of a procedure with which to measure the criterion. By the 1940s, particularly in the light of lessons learned from large-scale aptitude testing during the Second World War, such problems loomed large. Toops (1944) illustrated a range of related issues, with a particular focus on problems in defining the criterion. At a practical level, he noted the necessity of a single criterion score, but observed that job proficiency was not unitary. At a theoretical level, he noted the widespread lack of agreement over what should count as occupational success. Of course, in the absence of an adequate definition of the criterion there could be no hope of developing an adequate criterion measure. Even assuming the adequacy of a definition, often criterion measures were still very far from adequate in opera-tionalizing them. Where those measures involved the subjective judgement of job proficiency – as was often the case – the 'personal equation' loomed large.

The criterion problem was discussed in some depth by Thorndike (1949) in his textbook *Personnel Selection*, which grew out of his work in the US Army Air Forces during the Second World War. He identified three categories of criteria: ultimate, intermediate and immediate. He defined the ultimate criterion as the complete final goal of a particular type of selection or training: for example, the ability to drop bombs with maximum precision under combat conditions. Ultimate criteria were almost always multifaceted, and almost never available for direct study. This meant that validation research needed to fall back on intermediate or immediate criteria that were partial and somewhat removed: for example, supervisor rating of bomb dropping ability under non-combat conditions, or gunnery scores during a particu-lar phase of training.

Travers (1951) illustrated the fragility of the blindly empirical approach to test con-struction and validation – given the criterion problem – by using an imaginary tale of a personnel department that wished to discriminate between researchers who would stay in research, and those who would progress to high-level administrative work. It developed a test on regression principles to discriminate maximally between scientists who had stayed in research positions, and those who now worked in administration. Observing predictive efficacy over a number of years, the personnel department pub-lished their test as the *Scale of Administrative Ability*. However, when the items that carried the most impact were scrutinized subsequently, it seemed that actually the technicians responsible had developed a scale for discriminating between Jewish and non-Jewish backgrounds. This was the result of earlier selection procedures within the organization having been strongly anti-Semitic. This ever-present threat of replicating the inadequacies of the criterion measure led Travers to conclude that blind empiricism is a 'dangerous technique' (1951: 135). Messick was repeatedly to echo this conclusion from the 1970s to the 1990s.

Validity and personality tests

During the mid-1940s two researchers, Paul Meehl and Lee Cronbach, who were soon to publish a seminal paper on construct validity, were working independently on problems related to the valid interpretation of test scores. They were both trying to work out how to proceed when item responses could not be taken at face value.

Paul Meehl

Meehl (1945) was writing in the wake of considerable dissatisfaction with the kind of structured personality tests that were used often by clinical psychologists; tests that typically involved clients rating themselves. In clinical settings it was impractical or inappropriate to set up observations of everyday behaviour, so self-ratings had to do. Thus, for example, instead of observing samples of coyness in everyday life, a clinical psychologist would ask their clients whether or not they behaved coyly in one situation or another. Therefore, the self-rating functioned as a behaviour sample surrogate. The problem with this approach was that it appeared to require two things: an appropriate level of self-understanding, and a willingness to disclose. Particularly in clinical settings, neither of these could be guaranteed.

Meehl's response was to argue that self-rating should not be understood as a *direct sample* of behaviour per se, but as an *indirect sign* of something deeper. On the one hand, he accepted that self-ratings were no surrogate for sampling real-world behaviour. On the other hand, he proposed that such ratings could still be treated as signs of personality traits. For example, a psychopath might respond to a certain kind of self-rating item in a manner that was objectively false. Yet if psychopaths typically responded in this way, and this way of responding distinguished them from non-psychopaths, then the item was still informative – but as a sign, not as a surrogate sample.

A corollary of this reconceptualization of the structured personality test was that the developer could not rely on a logical approach to test construction based on sampling principles. In fact, Meehl (1945) recommended exactly the opposite approach, based on purely empirical methods – apparently consistent with the philosophy of operationism that was dominant within psychology at that time (see Chapter 3). On this basis, he claimed that discriminating items could be included within tests, regardless of whether there appeared to be any rational basis for their inclusion – in fact, he saw this as a virtue. If even the psychologist cannot see why an item is included, then it is unlikely that the test taker will be able to see the purpose behind it, and he/she will therefore be prevented from deliberately distorting the result of the test by providing 'fake' responses. Meehl later admitted that he considered his earlier position to have been unduly 'dustbowl empiricist', insufficiently theoretical and psychometrically simplistic (1971). His subsequent position was to emerge from an outstanding collaboration with Lee Cronbach.

Lee Cronbach

Cronbach (1946) was writing on a related issue, albeit from a different perspective. He too was concerned that test responses could not necessarily be taken at face value, which conflicted with the assumption that item content determines what the test measures: an assumption that he believed to be generally made at the time. However, unlike Meehl, who was mainly concerned with whether or not individuals had enough understanding or motivation to respond accurately, Cronbach was concerned mainly with the impact of item format (cf. content) on the ways in which individuals responded. He defined a 'response set' as the tendency to respond differently to items when presented in different ways, and identified six different kinds (including the tendency to give many responses, working for speed rather than accuracy and the tendency to gamble). The threat to validity was maximized when different individuals demonstrated different response sets on the same test: for example if, when faced with response categories such as 'true' versus 'false', certain individuals tended to use one category more than another, *just because that was how they tended to respond to items presented in that format* – not for any important reason to do with the attribute being measured. Cronbach (1946) believed that the best way to reduce this threat was to use item formats that were least susceptible to this phenomenon, particularly the multiple-choice format.

Alternative explanations

These two examples help to illustrate how a new way of thinking about validity and validation was foreshadowed in concerns to which both Cronbach and Meehl applied themselves toward the end of the 1940s. Whereas problems of unreliability, the unsystematic degradation of signal by noise, had been appreciated for many years, Cronbach and Meehl turned their attention to dealing with systematic error: error that lurked beneath the surface in otherwise reliable datasets. To put it slightly differently, they both developed the idea that there might be alternative explanations for consistent behaviour within testing situations; explanations which meant that the test was not necessarily measuring what it was presumed to measure. The idea of discounting plausible alternative explanations for consistent behaviour within testing situations was to be viewed later as the hallmark of the approach that they were soon to develop: construct validation (Messick, 1989a).

Validity and validation by the end of the 1940s

By the end of the early years, elements of consensus and areas of dispute were becoming increasingly evident within the burgeoning literature. Significantly, though, leading theorists were adopting quite different positions on the importance of logical and empirical considerations to the theory of validity and practice of validation. Indeed, it was precisely because the concept of validity was in such disarray at this point in time, that a committee of the APA was soon to be appointed in an attempt to instil 'a modicum of order' (Campbell, 1976: 202).

Divergent views

Rulon (1946) acknowledged that there were two basic approaches to the validation of achievement tests – logical and empirical – although he used the term 'obvious validity' rather than 'logical validity'. He emphasized the primacy of logical validation as the final proof of validity, characterizing empirical validation as a pragmatic fall-back option. On the one hand, according to Rulon (1946), a test was logically valid – that is, obviously valid – if it effectively sampled all of the instructional objectives in a domain. However, if the test did not sample all of the instructional objectives effectively, all was not lost, since validity still could be established empirically by correlating the test against a criterion measure, where that criterion measure *did* sample the instructional objectives effectively. This was the approach that had been recommended by Tyler. On the other hand, Cureton (1951) reversed this emphasis. He believed that logical analyses were beset by many pitfalls. The empirical approach to validation, which examined correlations between tests and criterion measures, was more direct, and therefore to be preferred wherever feasible. Logical analyses were particularly problematic for aptitude and personality tests, he believed.

Thorndike (1949) had worked on aptitude tests during the war, and was acutely aware of the criterion problem. For this reason, he emphasized that ultimate criteria could be determined *only* on logical (although he used the term 'rational') grounds; and that the relationship between immediate or intermediate criteria and the ultimate criterion also needed to be established very largely on logical grounds, with only limited help from empirical data.

Guilford (1946) had little faith in the logical evaluation of tests – which he discussed under the heading of 'face validity' – explaining that even sophisticated judgement often goes astray. As evidence of this he suggested that many a test deemed by judgement to measure one thing had been subsequently revealed, by factor analysis, to measure something else entirely. Therefore he concluded that logical validity may have nothing to do with 'actual validity', by which he appeared to mean a particular kind of empirical validity: 'factorial validity'.

Gulliksen (1950) also took exception to the elevation of logical analysis by Rulon (1946). His discussion focused on the idea of a criterion measure, proposing that its 'intrinsic validity' (its relationship to the criterion in question) could be effectively established only by employing multiple methods, including logical analysis, empirical relationships between items, and empirical relationships between the test and other tests. He explained how the same principle of adopting multiple validation approaches applied to tests of both achievement and aptitude. Thus, Gulliksen elevated the role of the scientist above that of the content expert, accepting that the content expert provided important evidence, but proposing that it was the scientist who ultimately passed judgement on validity, based on a variety of different sources of evidence. In adopting this position, Gulliksen echoed the unitary thesis presented by Monroe (1923), and prefigured the unitary thesis presented by Messick (1989a).

Finally, since Cronbach was not only responsible for authoring one of the most influential and enduring textbooks within the field of educational and psychological measurement, *Essentials of Psychological Testing* (1949), but was also the most influential figure of the next phase in the history of validity theory, we would do well to conclude by considering how he summarized the state of the art in validity theory within the first edition of his textbook, which was published toward the very end of the early years (Cronbach, 1949). He identified validity as the first of five technical criteria of a good test, which included:

- validity;
- reliability;
- objectivity;
- norms; and
- good items.

He distinguished between two different kinds of approach:

1 logical analysis – attempting to *judge* the degree to which the test measures what it is supposed to measure; and
2 empirical analysis – attempting to *investigate* the degree to which the test is correlated with some other variable, and therefore measures the same thing.

Logical analysis aimed at a psychological understanding of the processes affecting test scores, beginning with a clear definition of the attribute supposedly being assessed. Cronbach noted that validity could be established deductively by showing how the test corresponds to the definition of its attribute. Yet he was at pains to emphasize how even items that appeared to correspond to the definition may 'bring in irrelevant variables which make the test impure' (Cronbach, 1949: 49):

- items that different groups of test-taker answer using different methods;
- items that are accessible only to test-takers from certain cultural groups;
- items that are vulnerable to response sets;
- items that correspond to desired content, but fail to assess desired response processes, and so on.

Ultimately, Cronbach considered logical analysis far inferior to empirical: 'Over and over, it is found that tests which "ought to" predict some behavior do not. No test can be relied on for practical use until it has been validated empirically' (1949: 50). From an analysis of articles appearing in the *Journal of Applied Psychology* (1946–7), he observed that the most frequently-used criteria were ratings by instructors or supervisors, other tests of the same attribute, and school or training grades. However, again, he was guarded concerning the limits of empirical analysis, discussing the criterion problem in some depth. Finally, he noted the rise of a particular empirical approach to validation that seemed to be gathering considerable support, which he referred to as 'factorial validity': the degree to which a test could be considered a pure measure of just one type of ability.

A more interesting and nuanced story

Often, the early years of validity theory and validation practice are portrayed a little over-simplistically, as though they involved nothing more subtle than the correlation of test scores against criterion measures. In fact, the earliest definition of validity was far more sophisticated than this would imply, and the earliest approaches to validation far more elaborate and involved. Educationists took a lead in formally defining the concept, and the measurement movement – which embraced achievement testers, aptitude testers, intelligence testers and personality testers – united in an attempt to refine it and to develop new techniques for investigating it. The various professions of educational and psychological measurement took validity theory and validation practice in somewhat different directions; although, to be fair, there were differences between theorists and practitioners working within those sub-domains too. There were also trends within the sub-domains over time.

As conceptions of validity from the mid-1950s to the mid-1980s also tend to be viewed fairly simplistically – with boundaries drawn in terms of a small number of validity 'kinds' – it is natural to assume that the early years must have been even less sophisticated. The cursory treatment of the period between 1921 and 1951 in most historical accounts would seem to support this assumption, at least implicitly. In fact the reverse seems to be true. Many, if not most, of the important insights were apparent during the early years. This seems particularly true in relation to the range of validation methods developed during this period; often, even techniques that seem quite contemporary can be traced back this far. For example, it is tempting to think of the 'think aloud' technique as a product of recent interest in response processes and the contribution of cognitive psychology to validation practice, yet Cronbach extolled its virtues in the 1940s:

> One of the most valuable ways to understand any test is to administer it individually, requiring the subject to work the problem aloud … the tester learns just what mental processes are used in solving the exercises, and what mental and personality factors cause errors. (Cronbach, 1949: 54)

Since construct validity was not even invented until the early 1950s, we might be seduced into thinking that the methods of construct validation must have post-dated the early years. Of course, it is true that the quintessential methodological innovation of construct validation, the multitrait-multimethod (MTMM) technique, was not proposed until the late 1950s (Campbell and Fiske, 1959). Yet, construct validity was not really a new idea (Campbell, 1960), and many of the methods of construct validation – age differentiation, factor analysis, investigating the impact of experimental variables (such as practice) on test scores – had been reported in test manuals long before it was christened (Anastasi, 1963). Factor analysis in particular was well established by the end of the early years, and techniques that have become popular in recent years, grounded in item response theory, can be understood as conceptual descendants of this analytical procedure.

Other concepts closely allied to the social concerns of the late 20th century might be equally assumed not to have been considered during the early years: for example, concepts such as 'opportunity to learn', derived from the clash between testing practice and equality legislation during the 1960s and 1970s (see Chapter 6). In fact, it was widely accepted as early as the 1920s that even intelligence tests (in fact, particularly intelligence tests) should 'measure only those traits which every pupil has an equal opportunity to learn' (McCall, 1922: 220; see also Monroe, 1923: 23). Similarly, the elevation of consequences in the collective psyche of educational and psychological measurement during the 1990s might lead us to conclude that this is a fairly novel concern. Yet, washback on teaching and learning was a serious concern during the 1930s (e.g. Woody et al., 1935). Meyer (1934, 1935), for example, ran experiments to investigate how knowledge of the format through which students would be assessed (true/false, multiple-choice, completion and essay) impacted on their method of study and their memory for the material studied.

The plethora of approaches discussed within Monroe (1923) exemplifies the diversity and sophistication that can be found in accounts of validation during the early years. With the exception of evidence from consequences, they cover all of the remaining four categories of validation evidence from the fifth edition of the *Standards* (AERA et al., 1999): (1) test content and (2) response processes (see 'Inferences concerning validity'), (3) internal structure (see 'Objectivity in describing performances', 'Reliability and discrimination') and (4) relations to other variables (see 'Comparison with criterion measures').

In fact, there would seem to be very few major methodological innovations of validation that cannot be traced back to the early years, and it is hard to think of any that were not prefigured, at the very least, during this period.

In many of the seminal textbooks from the early years, distinctions between the concepts logical (rational, curricular, etc.) and empirical (statistical, correlational, etc.) were couched more in terms of *approaches to validation*, and less in terms of *kinds of validity*. It was only later that the terms 'content validity' and 'criterion validity' came to reify a distinction. Moreover, the 'criteria' of the early years were often more like the 'constructs' of the present day, in the sense of representing the attributes that tests were intended to measure. Thus, content considerations inevitably were apparent from the outset. Furthermore, theorists from Monroe and Tyler to Lindquist emphasized that the ultimate concern was not with test content per se, but with the mental processes that were required for successful performance. In many ways, then, the unitary conception that emerged during the 1980s was not so dissimilar from the unitary conception of the 1920s, which defined validity as the degree to which a test measured the attribute that it was supposed to measure. Indeed, we can recall how Monroe (1923: 227) described validity in terms of an overall evaluative judgement ('the consensus of information secured'), just as Cronbach (1971) and Messick (1989a) were later to define it.

Validity is sometimes seen as a post-hoc evaluative concept that comes into play only once a test has been developed. The true story is, and always has been, more complex, since validity needs to be built into a test from the earliest design decisions. With the advent of item analysis, validity came to be discussed at the item level, not simply at the test level. In achievement testing, items were selected preferentially if they correlated with the aggregate of scores from the item pool: that is, the item pool constituted the most plausible criterion measure. In aptitude testing, items were selected on the basis of their joint contribution to the prediction of external criterion measures, guided by multiple regression analyses. Thus, achievement testers verged towards the construction of homogeneous tests, while aptitude testers verged towards the construction of heterogeneous tests (Loevinger, 1947). In an important sense, then, the adoption of item analysis helped to 'guarantee' validity, by building it into the test construction process. (Although, technically speaking, each test still needed to be validated using a different sample of individuals from the one used as the basis for item analysis – a procedure known as cross-validation.) In another sense, item analysis was no guarantee at all, since it was entirely dependent on the validity of the criterion measure. The criterion problem was recognized by both achievement testers and aptitude testers, although its full significance took longer for personnel selectors to appreciate. However, by the beginning of the 1950s, the problems caused by blindly empirical approaches to test development were plain for all to see.

Test construction proved to be a site of uncomfortable tension for the measurement movement and, ultimately, a site of compromise. Nowhere was this more evident than in the tension between providing a practicable test of limited length, and providing a test that sampled the domain representatively. Pragmatists such as Lindquist simply gave up on the ideal of representative sampling, and opted instead for restricted sampling, using the machinery of item analysis to support this goal. Idealists such as Tyler roundly criticized the elimination of important objectives from standardized tests, emphasizing its inevitable impact on the taught curriculum. In fact, Tyler was something of an idealistic pragmatist, since he proposed the development of a multiplicity of comprehensive criterion measures against which more practicable tests could be validated. Yet the feasibility of his proposition appears not to have been demonstrated conclusively. As noted above, achievement testers frequently relied on the initial item pool as their best measure of the criterion, despite the fact that this was typically a highly restricted sample.

Toward the end of the 1940s and beginning of the 1950s, there was a clear tendency for theorists to take sides in a debate over logical versus empirical approaches to validation, tending to prioritize one at the expense of the other. Thus, Rulon and Thorndike ultimately emphasized logical over empirical; whereas Guilford and Cureton ultimately emphasized empirical over logical. Gulliksen was significant in emphasizing the need to adopt a scientific approach which embraced both logical analysis and empirical evidence in due proportion. It is not incidental that Messick's *magnum opus* (Messick, 1989a) was written in honour of Harold Gulliksen, with particular reference to insights contained in his 1950 paper. As we noted earlier, it is not that there were no seminal works during the early years. If anything, by the end of this period there were just too many seminal works, each tugging validity theory in different directions.

In the light of the foregoing account, how are we to interpret the claim that the transition from the early years to later phases represented a shift from prediction to explanation (Cronbach, 1971; Messick, 1989a)? Against the backdrop discussed so far, we must pay due credit to the picture painted by many whose careers began during the early years. In her review of the evolution of validation concepts, Anastasi (1986) explained that once the measurement movement had taken root, there was a tendency to 'veer away from theoretical rationale and construct formulation', such that the test manuals of the period 'created a general impression of almost blind empiricism' (1986: 6). It was some time before the centrality and utility of logical analysis became widely appreciated again. This seems to suggest that, for many test developers and publishers, the *practice* of test development and validation during the early years was dominated often by empirical procedures, despite the *theoretical landscape* of test development and validation being more sophisticated and diverse.

Having said that, the idea that validity and validation were cast primarily in terms of *prediction* during the early years is not quite right. It is more correct to say that they were framed in terms of *correlation*. Indeed, for tests that were designed primarily to measure rather than predict correlation (cf. prediction), this was not about predicting correlation, but about how correlation (not prediction) was the method of choice. In terms of the lexicon that was soon to be coined, this was essentially tantamount to *concurrent validation* (cf. predictive validation). Finally, many who wrote on validity and validation during the early years considered logical and empirical approaches to be complementary rather than mutually exclusive, even if they ultimately prioritized one over the other. In conclusion, the real insight of the prediction-to-explanation characterization lies on the explanation side of the equation. This is to highlight the invention and subsequent generalization of the concept of construct validity. Therefore, the transition is better described in terms of a shift from *logical analysis* and/or *empirical analysis* to *scientific analysis*.

Toward the end of the 1940s, the proliferation of labels with which to categorize different approaches to validation – logical validity, empirical validity, curricular validity, face validity, practical validity, factorial validity, etc. – was beginning to create the impression of fragmentation. Rather than different approaches to validation, the focus now seemed to be on different kinds of validity. Although Cronbach (1949), like many others, still seemed to emphasize approaches to validation rather than kinds of validity, his reference to logical validity, empirical validity and factorial validity seemed to be at least complicit with this shift in perspective.

Cronbach (1949) also drew a distinction between measurement and prediction, linked to a distinction between the diagnostic and predictive uses of results. For predictive uses, he argued, we do not need to know what test scores mean, just as long as we know that they predict – a sentiment which resonated with the blindly empirical approach to test development that had dominated personnel psychology up to that point. In fact, he went further still by refining the classic definition as follows: 'A test is valid to the degree that we know what it measures or predicts' (Cronbach, 1949: 48). Thus he drew a distinction that often was not drawn quite so explicitly between measurement and prediction. This distinction was to became even more pronounced during the next phase in the history of validity and validation.

Notes

1   The chapter on validity by Cureton (1951), in the very first edition of *Educational Measurement*, is an interesting anomaly in this respect because it did not have the kind of impact that later ones did. Although it is sometimes characterized as reflecting an emphasis on prediction (see Brennan, 2006), it is actually far more sophisticated and broad-ranging than this. Its discussion of validity is perhaps closer in spirit to the general holistic concept of recent years, than to the specialized fragmented one that was soon to be implied by the consensus definition within the very first *Standards* document (see Chapter 3). Rather than the culmination of the early years or the beginning of the next phase, it was almost ahead of its time.

2   Useful historical information can be found in Kral (2008) and University of Chicago Library (2008).

3   Incidentally, this was quite different from approaches that preceded it, including phrenology, which were based on the assumption that it was possible to determine defective intelligence on the basis of external signs, principally the size and shape of the head. As observed by Burt in 1924, when diagnosing mental characteristics, psychologists now relied on mental rather than physical criteria.

4   Cattell (1943) subsequently classified definitions of validity into three main categories: the capacity to think abstractly; the capacity to learn; and the capacity to adapt means to an end.

5   Having said this, even achievement test constructors sometimes elevated the importance of low inter-item correlation to avoid redundancy (e.g. Lindquist, 1936: 53). According to Monroe (1923), the procedure for developing general intelligence tests was closer to that for aptitude tests, albeit with a more rational point of departure. That is, the developer would begin with a very large battery of sub-tests, 'which, taken together, are considered to cover rather completely the field of general intelligence' (1923: 225). Then, in the interest of economy, an operational battery would be selected to comprise those sub-tests which, when aggregated, maximally predicted the full battery, with minimal inter-sub-test correlation.

CHAPTER 3

THE FRAGMENTATION OF VALIDITY: 1952–1974

The diversity of approaches to conceptualizing validity during the early years makes it hard to characterize the period succinctly. This resistance to characterization is likely to have been just as confusing for measurement professionals of the era as it is to us now. With such a variety of approaches to validation to choose from, and with even the experts valuing those approaches quite differently, how on earth were test developers and publishers to decide what information on test quality they needed to make available to consumers? More disconcertingly, in the absence of agreement on principles of best practice, how were test developers and publishers to be held to account?

Between 1950 and 1954, the American Psychological Association (APA) Committee on Test Standards, chaired by Lee Cronbach, undertook to specify what qualities should be investigated before a test was to be published, in order to produce an official statement of the profession to that effect. The 1940s had been a period of growing unease with testing practices: in personnel psychology, undue reliance on personality tests and logical approaches to validation had brought employment testing into disrepute; while in clinical psychology, ill-justified reliance on 'theoretical justifications' had done the same for clinical testing (Cronbach, 1983). The APA itself was somewhat divided on testing. Earlier dissatisfaction with an academic bias within the APA had led to the formation of breakaway societies, a situation that was ultimately judged to be contrary to the interests of psychology and broader national interests. In 1945, the American Association of Applied Psychology formally dissolved and became part of the APA (Wolfe, 1946). Therefore, within the new APA there were both optimistic practitioners expanding the variety and uses of tests, alongside more sceptical academics advising restraint (Cronbach, 1989a). One of the first activities of the new APA was to develop ethical standards for the distribution of psychological tests and diagnostic aids (APA, 1950). Yet, while the APA was keen to impose sanctions on those who violated the code, the boundaries of acceptable practice were not at all clear-cut, owing to a lack of consensus on how to characterize quality and best practice in educational and psychological measurement (Cronbach, 1989a). This context established a remit for the Committee on Test Standards.

The committee interpreted its remit not in terms of standards for test quality per se, but in terms of standards for the provision of information from which test quality could be judged by users in situ. This was based on the premise that quality was not an inherent property of a test but contingent on all sorts of things, particularly the use to which test scores would be put. Following the publication of a consultation draft (APA, 1952), their recommendations were modified and extended in cooperation with the American Educational Research Association (AERA) and the National Council on Measurements Used in Education (NCMUE). The first edition of the report of the Joint Committee, entitled *Technical Recommendations for Psychological Tests and Diagnostic Techniques*, was published in 1954 (APA et al., 1954). It included sections on dissemination, interpretation, validity, reliability, administration and scoring and scales and norms. The section on validity was by far the largest. Subsequent editions used the term 'standards' in their titles, and therefore we refer generically to these documents as successive editions of the *Standards*.

Although the first (and each successive) edition of the *Standards* was written from a very practical perspective, the 19 validity standards (pp. 18–28) were prefaced by an introductory section (pp. 13–18), which provided a theoretical grounding. Therefore, as a consensus statement of the professions, the report included both implicit standards for thinking about validity, and explicit standards for conducting and reporting validation research (Newton and Shaw, 2013). For many who were influenced by the *Standards* during the 1950s, 1960s and 1970s, they came to embody and cement a *fragmented* view of validity and validation, whereby the different uses that test scores were to be put to implied not simply different approaches to validation, but even different kinds of validity. Although written from a North American perspective and for a North American audience, many of the ideas presented in the *Standards* were appropriated internationally, and the content-criterion-construct conception became well known across the world.

Professional standards: edition 1

The first edition of the *Standards* adopted a very pragmatic view of validity. Instead of opening with the classic definition (e.g. Ruch, 1924) or a version thereof (e.g. Cronbach, 1949), it stated more generally that:

> Validity information indicates to the test user the degree to which the test is capable of achieving certain aims. (APA et al., 1954: 13)

In doing so, it followed the lead of Cureton (1951), who recently had opened his chapter on validity in the first edition of *Educational Measurement* (Lindquist, 1951), as follows:

The essential question of test validity is how well a test does the job it is employed to do. The same test may be used for several different purposes, and its validity may be high for one, moderate for another, and low for a third. (Cureton, 1951: 621)

Whereas Cureton (1951) went on to define validity more technically and holistically, the Joint Committee took an alternative approach. Instead of emphasizing the essential core features of validity and validation, it emphasized how validity and validation differed according to test score use. Different kinds of interpretation, it explained, required different approaches to validation. It identified four distinct kinds of interpretation related to four distinct aims of testing, implying four distinct approaches to validation.

By the early 1950s, it had become increasingly common for authors to group different approaches to validation using what might be termed 'validity modifier labels', for example:

- curricular validity vs. statistical validity vs. psychological and logical validity (Greene et al., 1943)
- factorial validity vs. practical validity (Guilford, 1946)
- logical validity vs. empirical validity vs. factorial validity (Cronbach, 1949)
- internal validity vs. external validity (Guttman, 1950).

The Joint Committee continued this tradition by labelling the four distinct approaches 'content validity', 'predictive validity', 'concurrent validity' and 'construct validity'. Their essential features are summarized in Table 3.1.

Different approaches to validation

Although the 19 validity standards were prefaced by an introductory section which outlined the underpinning theory, this really only provided a high-level sketch. In

Table 3.1 Four types of validity

Type of validity	Aim of testing (e.g. use of vocabulary test score)	Approach to validation	Presumed relation between test and criterion
Content validity	When trying to measure an attribute of the present (e.g. vocabulary)	Demonstrate how well the content of the test samples the criterion	The test is a sample of its criterion
Predictive validity	When trying to predict an attribute of the future (e.g. college success)	Demonstrate how well the test scores correspond to a (future) criterion	The test is a sign of its criterion
Concurrent validity	When trying to discriminate, or estimate, an attribute of the present (e.g. to discriminate schizophrenics from organics)	Demonstrate how well the test scores correspond to a (contemporary) criterion	The test is a sign of its criterion
Construct validity	When trying to infer an attribute of the present (e.g. intellectual capacity)	Demonstrate what psychological quality is measured by the test	There is no definitive criterion; the test is merely an indicator of its construct

fact, since there was no generally accepted definition for any of the terms adopted by the Joint Committee, it is perhaps surprising that the *Standards* did not go to greater lengths to explain them, and to delimit the breadth of validation inquiry that each was supposed to involve. Content validity clearly derived from earlier conceptions of logical validity, while predictive and concurrent validity clearly derived from earlier conceptions of empirical validity. Yet the range of techniques associated with each of the labels was not specified in as much detail as might have been expected, given the range of validity modifier labels already in circulation, and the diversity of approaches to validation potentially associated with each one. It is notable that the *Standards* contained no literature review (there was virtually no reference to the literature at all), neither were the positions adopted explicitly aligned to any prior theoretical perspective or theorist. As such, the views expressed were to be attributed exclusively to the contributing associations.

Content validity

According to the Joint Committee, *content validity* was said to be relevant when determining how an individual might be expected to perform in a given universe of situations, of which the test situation constituted a *sample*. Here, the idea was of a test designed to *measure* a particular criterion: for example, school-based learning objectives that a student had attempted previously to master. This criterion was to be measured directly. Therefore, the presumption was that the test behaviour directly sampled the criterion behaviour, and consequently that the test scores directly measured it. The conventional interpretation of achievement test scores would have typically fallen into this category.

According to the *Standards*, content validity was to be evaluated by showing how well the content of the test sampled the criterion behaviour. It noted that quantitative evidence of content validity was not generally feasible, explaining that judges' ratings of the appropriateness of items frequently was involved. A clear specification of the universe of items was required, as well as a description of the method by which items had been selected for the test, in order to judge the adequacy of the sampling. In addition to the judgement of experts, a coefficient of internal consistency was considered to be essential in order to demonstrate the extent to which test scores were saturated with common factors. The impact of any time limit also was deemed essential to investigate.

Predictive validity

Predictive validity was said to be relevant when determining how an individual might be expected to perform in a given universe of situations in the future, of which the test situation was merely a *sign*. Here, the idea was of a test designed to *predict* a particular criterion: for example, work-based skills that a potential employee had not yet even attempted to master. The criterion could not be measured directly, since it would not yet have reached maturity – if it had been developed at all – and therefore it only could be predicted. It was presumed that test behaviour indirectly signalled the criterion behaviour. The conventional interpretation of aptitude test scores would have typically fallen into this category.

Predictive validity was to be evaluated by showing how well predictions made from the test were confirmed by evidence gathered subsequently. Typically this was based on quantitative evidence, involving the correlation of test scores against criterion measures. Indeed, the correlation between test scores and the criterion measure was said to *establish* the predictive validity of a test. Importantly, though, a test would have as many predictive validities as the number of distinct criteria that it was used to predict. For example, an intelligence test might have simultaneously high predictive validity in relation to a subsequent science course, and low predictive validity in relation to a subsequent art course. According to the *Standards*, coefficients of predictive validity would need to be accompanied by estimates of probable error, including evidence of how the accuracy of prediction might differ across the score range. Similarly, if it seemed likely that validity coefficients would differ for identifiable subgroups, then these too should be investigated and reported. The potential unreliability of the criterion measure itself at least should be discussed, if not actually investigated.

Concurrent validity

Concurrent validity was said to be relevant when determining how an individual might be expected to perform in a given universe of situations in the present, of which the test situation was merely a *sign*. Here, the idea was of a test designed to *discriminate* or *estimate* a particular criterion: for example, to discriminate between clinically depressed and non-clinically depressed patients, where the criterion, depression, was already fully-fledged. Tests such as these often were developed as surrogate or substitute measures, when direct measurement was not feasible because it would cost too much, be too labour-intensive or dangerous. Once again, the presumption was that the test behaviour indirectly signalled the criterion behaviour. It often relied upon test developers being able to judge criterion membership independently of (i.e. prior to developing) the test, and therefore being able to construct the test primarily on the basis of predictive evidence. The conventional interpretation of diagnostic test scores would have typically fallen into this category.

A slightly different (and more conceptual) way of thinking about concurrent validity was in terms of the traditional practice of correlating scores on a test with a more direct, comprehensive and authentic criterion measure. In Chapter 2, we noted Tyler's belief that test development should begin with the construction of preliminary tests for each important course objective (providing comprehensive criterion measures), but then should continue by constructing more practicable (substitute) tests that were to be validated by correlating their results against their respective criterion measures. The more practicable tests could not be assumed to sample adequately, in the sense demanded by content validity; yet if they were still able to estimate the comprehensive criterion measures satisfactorily, then at the very least they could still be relied upon as signs, in the sense demanded by concurrent validity. Having identified this slightly different way of thinking about concurrent validity, we should stress that this was not how the *Standards* tended to characterize it. The *Standards* exemplified it very much in terms of the practical task of diagnosis and classification: that is, discrimination more than estimation.

Concurrent validity was to be evaluated by showing how well the conclusions drawn from the test were confirmed by evidence gathered concurrently: that is, how well test scores corresponded to, or correlated with, more definitive criterion measures. The *Standards* noted that almost all of the recommendations listed under predictive validity applied equally to reports of concurrent validity. However, it was emphasized that evidence of concurrent validity was not sufficient to establish predictive validity.

Construct validity

The story for *construct validity* was quite different. In fact, the very idea of construct validity was entirely new, having been invented to enable the committee to deal with the validation of interpretations drawn from personality tests, which it believed to have been inadequately theorized in the past. Cronbach (1989a) later explained that the impetus came from questionable practice among both counsellors and clinicians. For example, many counsellors were treating measures of vocational interests neither as direct predictors of future success in an occupation (implying predictive validity), nor as simple inventories to be interpreted directly in terms of content rubrics (implying content validity), but as indicative of psychological characteristics, e.g. 'physician interests'. What kind of validation, the Joint Committee pondered, would be required in order to defend an interpretation like this? The task of theorizing the validation of personality tests was given to a subcommittee, which comprised Paul Meehl and Robert Challman. Initially they came up with the idea of congruent validity, implying congruence between the interpretation and multiple lines of inquiry. This was modified and clarified later by the entire committee, and christened 'construct validity' (we will discuss the invention of construct validity in more detail below).

Construct validity was said to be relevant when none of the other approaches to validation could be relied upon. All of the other approaches required a clear criterion. For content validity, the criterion was defined in terms of a 'universe' of behaviour which was to be sampled by the test. In education, this was defined often in terms of the learning objectives that comprised a particular curriculum or syllabus. For predictive validity, the criterion was defined in terms of future behaviour: as judged, for example, by workplace supervisors. For concurrent validity, the criterion was defined in terms of contemporary behaviour: as judged, for example, by clinicians. For construct validity, so the story went, there simply was no definitive criterion that could be relied upon as a yardstick. In the absence of a gold standard for judging the validity of interpretations drawn from personality tests, validity would need to be evaluated differently.

Construct validity was to be evaluated by investigating what psychological quality – that is, what construct – was measured by the test. This presumed that the test was not a direct sample of its criterion, but merely a basis for *inferring* an underlying construct. Therefore, validation required 'both logical and empirical attack' (APA et al., 1954: 14). It meant first developing a theoretical model of the construct, then generating predictions from it, and finally gathering data in order to test those predictions. As such, construct validation meant validating both the test and the underlying theory simultaneously.

In summary, the Joint Committee theorized validity according to the relationship that appeared to obtain between a test and its criterion:

- an achievement test could be considered a *sample* of its criterion;
- an aptitude or diagnostic test could be considered a *sign* of its criterion; whereas
- a personality test, with no obvious criterion, should be considered an *indicator* of its construct.

Thus:

- logical approaches to validation were judged to be particularly suitable when test scores were to be interpreted in terms of achievement or proficiency, hence content validity;
- empirical approaches were deemed particularly suitable when test scores were to be interpreted in terms of aptitude or a disorder, hence predictive validity or concurrent validity; whereas
- both logical and empirical approaches were to be recommended when test scores were to be interpreted in terms of personality, hence construct validity.

Different kinds of validity

The first edition of the *Standards* presented mixed messages as to the extent to which validity ought to be considered a fragmented concept, tailored differently to different kinds of interpretation. On the one hand, its account was structured in terms of four different aims of testing. Each of these aims was associated with a different kind of interpretation of test scores, and involved 'a somewhat different type of validation' (APA et al., 1954: 13). It was emphasized further that, in order to determine the suitability of a test for each use, it was necessary to gather the appropriate sort of validity information. Therefore, the natural implication was that if you needed to validate a particular kind of interpretation (e.g. an interpretation drawn in terms of achievement), then you needed to adopt a particular approach to validation (content validation). Furthermore, not only did this represent a particular approach to validation, it also meant establishing a particular kind of validity (content validity). Therefore, content, predictive, concurrent and construct were intended as labels for different kinds of validity, as indicated by the heading 'Four types of validity' (APA et al., 1954: 13).

On the other hand, within just one sentence of this heading, they were referred to also as 'aspects'. Indeed, the *Standards* insisted that:

> It must be kept in mind that these four aspects of validity are not all discrete and that a complete presentation about a test may involve information about all types of validity. (APA et al., 1954: 16)

Now, this *might* have been taken to imply that scores from a single test can be interpreted in various ways, and that when more than one interpretation was intended, more than one kind of validity would need to be established. Indeed, this *would* have been implied. Yet, this very statement continued:

> A first step in the preparation of a predictive instrument may be to consider what constructs or predictive dimensions are likely to give the best prediction. Examining content validity may also be an early step in producing a test whose predictive validity is ultimately of major concern. Even after satisfactory predictive validity had been established, information relative to construct validity may make the test more useful. (APA et al., 1954: 16)

In short, according to the *Standards*, even when validating a particular kind of interpretation (e.g. a predictive inference), it might still be appropriate to adopt multiple approaches to validation (involving construct validity, content validity *and* predictive validity). How, then, were readers to interpret the guidance? At one extreme, the different kinds of validity were presented as though they were specialized to particular interpretations: the specialized validity for achievement inferences was content validity, the specialized validity for aptitude inferences was predictive validity, and so on. Thus, if scores from exactly the same test were to be interpreted in more than one way (e.g. in terms of achievement for one purpose, and aptitude for another), then more than one kind of validity would need to be established (both content validity and predictive validity). At the other extreme, the modifier labels merely described different aspects of a more general concept of validity: predictive, concurrent, content and construct concerns were presented as though potentially all of them were relevant to a whole range of interpretations.

Quite how readers were supposed to interpret this guidance was unclear. Perhaps the confusion evident within the text was an inevitable consequence of it having been written by committee (in fact, by committees), and therefore somehow having to accommodate a range of conflicting perspectives. However, it is certainly fair to say that the text *allowed* a fragmented reading, and perhaps even *encouraged* it, to the extent that it indicated how different kinds of validity needed to be established for different kinds of test. Indeed, it seemed to leave open the possibility that only one kind of validity needed to be established if a test was to be interpreted only in a certain way; which, in turn, seemed to license the presumption that content validity was the gold standard for achievement tests, while predictive validity was the gold standard for aptitude tests.

It is worth noting that two parallel Committees of Test Standards were appointed by AERA and NCMUE, respectively, with the former chaired by Jacob Orleans, and the latter chaired by Robert Ebel. Not only did they contribute to drafting the first edition of the *Standards*, they also jointly prepared an adaptation specific to the problems of achievement testing (AERA and NCMUE, 1955). The adapted report was fairly similar to the original. It explained how, even in the relatively narrow context of achievement testing, test scores could be interpreted in different ways to achieve different purposes. As such, all four types of validity were discussed. Once again, the document was somewhat ambiguous concerning the extent to which validity ought to be considered a fragmented, specialized concept. However, it did conclude that content validity was particularly important for instructional uses of achievement tests (e.g. evaluating achievement and planning remedial work), while concurrent and construct validity were particularly important for administrative uses of test scores (e.g. classifying pupils and promoting them). It also mentioned explicitly that content, concurrent and predictive validity could be thought of as specialized aspects of construct validity. However, that did not lead it to the conclusion that all validity was ultimately construct validity: that is, that construct validation was always required. Quite the contrary: it observed that construct validation was *only* required when the other three methods were judged to be insufficient.

In conclusion, while many who were influenced by this work came to see it as cementing a fragmented view of validity and validation – embodied in the idea of distinct kinds of validity – this was not necessarily how the text was originally intended. In fact, in some ways, the *Standards* expressed exactly the opposite sentiment. (We explore the entrenchment of a fragmented conception in more detail below.)

The invention of construct validity

As explained in Chapter 2, in his very first publication, Paul Meehl (1945) outlined an approach to understanding structured personality tests that differed significantly from earlier accounts. Instead of thinking of responses to self-rating questionnaires as surrogate samples (implying a logical approach to test construction and validation), he reconceptualized them as mere signs (implying an empirical approach). He later came to judge this reconceptualization 'overly "dust-bowl empiricist," insufficiently theoretical, and psychometrically simplistic' (Meehl, 1971: 245). A better way of thinking about such personality tests, he added, was soon to be elaborated by Cronbach and Meehl (1955).

The route to Cronbach and Meehl (1955) passed through another landmark paper, 'On a distinction between hypothetical constructs and intervening variables', by MacCorquodale and Meehl (1948). It involved a sophisticated analysis of language that was being used by some of the most prominent psychologists of the time, as the discipline was beginning to break free from the restrictions on which narrow behaviourism had insisted. MacCorquodale and Meehl wished to draw a clear distinction between two terms that often were being used inter-changeably: 'intervening variables', which they defined as constructs that merely abstracted empirical relationships; and 'hypothetical constructs', which they defined as constructs that referred to supposed (i.e. as-yet unobserved) entities or processes. They argued that the two terms had quite different meaning, and that using them interchangeably had led to fundamental confusion. Here, the detail of their analysis is less important than the recognition that Meehl was grap-pling with cutting-edge issues in the philosophy of science and the philosophy of psychology: most fundamentally, the challenge of escaping the straitjacket of operationism. His thinking on these matters came to underpin the notion of con-struct validity that soon he was jointly to pioneer.

As noted previously, early conceptions of construct validity were shaped initially by Meehl and Challman, before being moulded by the rest of the APA Committee on Test Standards. Given the novelty and significance of this new kind of validity, the committee encouraged Cronbach and Meehl to explain it in more detail, and to elaborate its implications. They developed their thesis in a paper, 'Construct validity in psychological tests' (Cronbach and Meehl, 1955) – note the focus on 'psycho-logical tests', incidentally – explicitly drawing on insights from many of the leading theorists of the previous decade, including Guildford (1946), Jenkins (1946), Mosier (1947), Cronbach (1949), Gulliksen (1950), Goodenough (1950) and Peak (1953). Cronbach (1971) later credited Cureton (1951) as having taken a lead in this direc-tion, and others including Tyler were acknowledged subsequently (see Cronbach, 1989a: 149). According to Cronbach (1992), Meehl contributed the philosophical base and much experience in personality measurement, while Cronbach brought a wealth of understanding of testing from across a range of educational and psycho-logical contexts. The authorship of Cronbach and Meehl (1955) ultimately was decided by the toss of a coin.

Underlying construct validation was the principle that certain tests (although only certain tests) were designed to measure attributes that could not be appre-hended straightforwardly. Therefore, the construct in construct validity was a postu-lated attribute, assumed to be reflected in test performance and inferred on the basis of test performance.[1] It might be qualitative (e.g. amnesia) or quantitative (e.g. cheerfulness), but it would always carry implications for future behaviour. Thus, knowing that a person was cheerful or had amnesia, was paranoid, anxious, intel-ligent or had a psychopathic personality, all enabled predictions about their future behaviour, including their behaviour in test situations. These were only probabilistic implications, of course, and relationships between unobservable constructs and observable behaviour were not presumed to be direct. In fact, the relationship between constructs and behaviour was presumed to be very complicated, due to the fact that behaviour always needed to be understood in terms of the interaction of multiple constructs.

The idea of an interaction of constructs implied that any particular instance of observable behaviour could be given a variety of quite different construct inter-pretations. For example, from one perspective, poor performance in a science practical examination might lead an observer to infer a low 'ability to plan experiments'. Yet from another perspective, exactly the same behaviour could be explained by inferring a high 'ability to plan experiments' interacting with low 'motivation to succeed' in the examination. The idea of interaction between postulated attributes also meant that validation could not focus on individual attributes or constructs in isolation. Instead, construct validation needed to be based on a whole theory of human behaviour within which to understand this interaction, and on which to base predictions of future behaviour. This would allow reasoning of the following kind: if a person had a certain level of construct x and a certain level of construct y, then in situation z we could expect them to behave in a particular way.

Therefore, construct validation was a matter of making predictions about how people would behave in various (test) situations, and then observing the extent to which those theory-based predictions held true. To the extent that those predictions held true, this provided support for the claims: that the test(s) measured the construct(s); that the construct(s) had been theorized plausibly; and that the broader theory within which the test(s) and construct(s) were situated was also plausible. Thus, construct validation involved, first, developing a theory with which to understand behaviour in the test situation; second, generating predictions from it; and finally, gathering data in order to test those predictions. Both the test and the underlying theory were to be evaluated simultaneously. As a later edition of the *Standards* put it:

> Through the process of successive verification, modification, or elimination of hypotheses, the investigator increases his understanding of the qualities measured by the test. Through the process of confirmation or disconfirmation, test revision, and new research on the revised instrument, he improves the usefulness of the test as a measure of a construct. (APA et al., 1974: 30)

Cronbach and Meehl (1955) called the underlying theory a *nomological network*. The network explained how unobservable constructs related to each other, and how they related to observable behaviour, including behaviour in test situations.

Construct validation was presented as scientific process, in which the plausibility of a proposed interpretation of test performance, framed in terms of a specified construct, was evaluated on the basis of a *programme of research* incorporating both logical analysis and empirical evidence.[2] Cronbach and Meehl (1955) highlighted the following techniques as particularly relevant:

- analysis of performance differences between groups, on the same test
- analysis of performance relationships across tests, based on test correlations and factor analysis
- analysis of performance relationships within tests, based on item correlations
- analysis of performance stability over time and under experimental manipulation, on the same test
- analysis of processes underlying performance on test items.

Critical to each of these analyses was not the *strength* of the observed relationship per se, but the *consistency* of the observed relationship with the underlying theory. Thus, high correlation and high stability might constitute either positive or negative evidence depending on the kind of relationship predicted from the theory.

Finally, according to Cronbach and Meehl (1955), when reporting the results of a research programme involving construct validation, the investigators would be obliged to make clear:

- what interpretation had been proposed, explaining the construct and its location within a broader theory;
- how adequately they believed it to have been substantiated; and
- what evidence and reasoning had led them to this conclusion.

These networks or theories were not always very precise and elaborate. Indeed, particularly during the early stages of research, they might well be quite vague and unelaborated. Ultimately, the entire nomological network was always open to question, which meant that there was always an onus of responsibility on the investigator to specify their network and/or theory with sufficient clarity for others to be able to pass their own judgement on its plausibility, and to decide for themselves how best to appropriate and use it.

In summary, construct validity was invented as a 'belt and braces' concept: a fallback option when neither logical (content) validation nor empirical (predictive or concurrent) validation sufficed. This new approach to validation, a more scientific approach, meant relying upon both empirical evidence and logical analysis. However, both the *Standards* and Cronbach and Meehl (1955) were clear that construct validity should not be seen as a competitor to content, predictive or concurrent validity. Therefore, the implication was that each of these three *could* be assumed to suffice under appropriate circumstances.[3]

Professional standards: editions 2 and 3

Between 1954 and 1974 the *Standards* was revised twice. The introductions to the revised editions explained that this was necessary in order to respond to constructive criticism, take account of progress in the science and practice of educational and psychological measurement, and respond to societal change. Preparation for the revision of the first edition began more than five years before the second edition was published (APA et al., 1966). The revision of the second edition began in 1971 and was published in 1974 (APA et al., 1974).

The more radical revision was the second, from 1966 to 1974, a period during which all sorts of testing problems had come to the fore: not simply technical ones, but also social and legal ones; in particular, problems related to the introduction of the Civil Rights Act of 1964 in the USA. In this context, concern over issues including invasion of privacy and discrimination against minority groups had been awakened.

Furthermore, serious misuses of testing had brought the professions into disrepute on numerous occasions. In an attempt to respond to concerns such as these, the third edition introduced a major new section, 'Standards for the use of tests'.

Although the validity section within the *Standards* did evolve over time, the differences between 1954 and 1974 did not appear to represent a sea change in the consensus position. The most obvious shift was from four basic kinds of validity to just three. It always was acknowledged that the differences between concurrent and predictive validity were small, amounting to little more than whether the criterion was measured contemporaneously or in the future. In fact, the only distinct standard recommended for concurrent validity was that it should not be described as though it was sufficient to establish predictive validity. Cronbach and Meehl (1955) had observed that the two approaches might be collapsed under the heading 'criterion-oriented' validation procedures. The second edition followed suit, by referring primarily to 'content validity', 'criterion-related validity' and 'construct validity'. This was revised very slightly in the third edition, which now referred to 'criterion-related validities' in the plural.

Although the *Standards* was written as the official position statement of the North American educational and psychological measurement communities, it was a while before the nomenclature of validity came to be appropriated widely, following a decade or so of debate over how best to characterize it. Some explicitly challenged the classification provided by the *Standards* and proposed entirely new schemes (e.g. Cattell, 1964), while others offered refinements and proposed subcategorizations (e.g. Campbell, 1960). Of particular significance were the classic textbooks of educational and psychological measurement, which evolved through multiple editions during this period, including Anastasi (1954, 1961, 1968, 1976), Cronbach (1949, 1960, 1970) and Thorndike and Hagen (1955, 1961, 1969, 1977). Both Anastasi and Cronbach changed their classification schemes significantly between their first and second edition, falling in line with the four-way classification of the 1954 *Standards*. As the 1966 *Standards* collapsed concurrent and predictive into criterion, so too did these two textbook authors. Anastasi (1968) adopted the 1966 terminology wholesale, referring to 'content validity', 'criterion-related validity' and 'construct validity'. Cronbach (1970) departed from it slightly, referring to 'content validation', 'criterion-oriented validation' and 'construct validation'. The second edition of Thorndike and Hagen (1961) followed the spirit of the *Standards* but not the letter, referring to:

- 'validity-as-representing' – rational, logical or content validity;
- 'validity-as-signifying' – construct validity; and
- 'validity-as-predicting' – empirical or statistical validity.

However, by their third edition in 1969, they were using exactly the same terminology as the 1966 *Standards*.

The remaining changes to the *Standards* between 1954 and 1974 seemed more to clarify than to correct earlier editions. It is interesting to note in this respect how the very first sentence of the 'Validity' section within the 1966 edition (which very closely followed the wording of the 1954 edition) was completely revised for the 1974 edition:

> Validity information indicates the degree to which the test is capable of achieving certain aims. (APA et al., 1966: 12)

> Questions of validity are questions of what may properly be inferred from a test score; validity refers to the appropriateness of inferences from test scores or other forms of assessment. (APA et al., 1974: 25)

Ostensibly, this transition might seem to have indicated a sea change in how validity was to be conceptualized, recommending that readers switch from a practical, use-based definition to a conceptual, interpretation-based one. However, although there may be a grain of truth in this perception, it seems likely that the change was initiated more as a matter of emphasis than substance. For example, it is certainly not the case that earlier editions eschewed talk of interpretation; in fact, almost the whole point of the original distinction between types of validity was to recognize the fact that a single test could be interpreted in many different ways, and that different approaches to validation were required to investigate those different interpretations. Furthermore, all three editions began with a standard that emphasized the importance of specifying the 'inference' for which the test was recommended: that is, the 'interpretation' that was to be investigated (standards C2, 1954; C1, 1966; E1, 1974).[4]

As the first edition clearly was ambiguous over whether validity ought to be considered a general holistic concept or a specialized fragmented one, we might have expected this to have been clarified in the second and third editions. However, in fact there was little, if any, clarification. All three referred both to 'types' and to 'aspects' when describing kinds of validity: the former suggesting fairly sharp dividing lines, and the latter suggesting the converse. It was almost as though recognition of ambiguity became *more* explicit from one edition to the next, without the authors being able to resolve it. Thus, the third edition claimed:

> The kinds of validity depend upon the kinds of inferences one might wish to draw from test scores. Four interdependent kinds of inferential interpretation are traditionally described to summarize most test use: the *criterion-related* validities (*predictive* and *concurrent*); *content* validity; and *construct* validity. (APA et al., 1974: 26–7, italics in original)

So, were these kinds of validity independent or interdependent? The very fact of identifying different kinds seemed to imply independence, but the *Standards* continued to insist on their interdependence:

> These aspects of validity can be discussed independently, but only for convenience. They are interrelated operationally and logically; only rarely is one of them alone important in a particular situation. A thorough study of a test may often involve information about all types of validity. (APA et al., 1974: 26)

As in the first edition, this passage was followed by the same example of a test used for predictive purposes being investigated from construct, content *and* criterion perspectives. In fact, whereas the first edition suggested that the first step 'may' be to consider constructs, the third edition stated that the first step 'should' be to consider them. Thus, on the one hand, the logic and nomenclature of validity types suggested independence; yet on the other, the *Standards* continued to insist on their interdependence. So, were they distinct or not?

Certainly, there was an effort to distinguish more clearly between construct validity and the other two, between the first and subsequent editions. Thus, the impact of speed on test scores was moved from content to construct validity; evidence of faking was moved from predictive to construct validity; evidence of internal consistency was removed from content validity; and it was further emphasized that item-test correlations were not evidence of criterion-related validity, although they might help to make a case for construct validity. The distinctions were quite stark by the third edition which, for example, now insisted that content validity was concerned only with sampling in an 'operational' sense, not in a 'theoretical' one (standard E12, 1974: 45). That is, it could not be concerned with sampling *processes*, since this was a matter of construct validity, not content validity. Thus, as more of the work of validation was judged to fall under the heading of construct validity, so content and criterion-related concerns became correspondingly narrower. In addition, the relevance of construct validity to all evaluations was demonstrated increasingly: in particular, the investigation of construct-irrelevant variance. In the second edition, for example, the importance of construct validation to achievement tests was illustrated in a discussion of how reading ability demands had the potential to undermine a science test (APA et al., 1966: 14).

We noted earlier the introduction of an entirely new section to the third edition, presenting standards for the use of tests, which was in direct response to public outcry over widespread test misuse. Misuse provided the backdrop against which Samuel Messick was to present his new theory of validity (e.g. Messick, 1975, 1980, 1989a). Indeed, it was an important impetus underlying his new theoretical position. However, within the third edition of the *Standards* the discussion of social consequences remained largely separate from the discussion of validity. Only a small number of changes to the validity section in the third edition reflected this new social and legal obligation on measurement professionals: for example, new standards for reporting evidence of bias or lack of bias, including differences in criterion-related validity for gender-based or ethnicity-based subsamples (standard E9, 1974).

Operationism

The philosophical notion of operationism provided background and context to debates over validity and validation during this phase, and during the later years of the one that preceded it. Although it may be unwise to overestimate its explicit impact, particularly during the early years, it would be equally unwise to underestimate its implicit influence. Operationism was a philosophy of science arising from concern over the collapse of Newtonian physics (Green, 1992). It represented an attempt to eliminate all metaphysics from the scientific method by requiring that all assumptions be grounded empirically. The physicist Percy Bridgman helped to give birth to this philosophy through his principle of operational analysis, which eliminated abstract concepts by reducing them to nothing more than sets of operations: that is, methods (Bridgman, 1927). Thus, for example, length was presumed to have no meaning other than the method by which it was operationalized: if a ruler had been used to operationalize length, then that ruler provided the operational definition of length. Operationism was introduced to psychology through the writing of Stanley Stevens (e.g. Stevens, 1935). It caught on almost immediately, resulting in the 'operational revolution' of the mid-1930s: a rapid and uncritical adoption by mainstream psychology within the USA (Rogers, 1989: 140).

Operationism was not without its critics (see Rogers, 1989; Green, 1992). Strict operationism seemed to imply that whenever a different method was employed, a different concept was defined. Thus, measurement by ruler vs. radar vs. trigonometry each represented a different concept of length. This would be true even for measurement operations as similar as ruler vs. tape measure. This was certainly a challenging idea – it seemed to imply that it was not even meaningful to compare measurements of the same object by different methods – and the implausibility of implications like this ultimately undermined operationism. Many of the early logical positivists initially embraced Bridgman's operationism, but later came to reject it. In fact, it was not long before operationism was rejected by mainstream philosophy in general. However, the same was not true for mainstream psychology, within which operationism lingered for far longer. Indeed, the idea of 'operationally defining' concepts remained commonplace within psychology throughout the 20th century (Rogers, 1989; Green, 1992).

It is hard to be definitive about the impact and influence of operationism on the concept of validity. For a start, the basic principles and practices of validity and validation were laid down long before operationism took root in academic psychology. Furthermore, in an important sense, the very concept of validity is antithetical to strict operationism. Under strict operationism, that which is measured by the test is simply that which is measured by the test. This would seem to make the very idea of validity – which questions what the test *really* measures – redundant. In addition, operationism was a complex abstract philosophy, whereas validity and validation were typically the prerogative of applied practitioners, whose concern for abstruse ideas such as these was likely to have been limited. Moreover, by the middle of the 1940s, it was clear that even the leading proponents of operationism within psychology had quite different conceptions of it (Green, 1992). In the absence of consensus over the meaning of operationism during this period, it is even harder to speculate over what its impact might have been.

Rogers (1989) put forward a very interesting hypothesis: that the appropriation of operationism by psychology was less philosophical and scientific than it was political and opportunistic. He argued that, prior to the embrace of operationism, psychology had effectively embarrassed itself: having defined validity initially in terms of that which was measured by a test, but then having found itself subsequently unable to provide any good explanation of what it *was* that the most fundamental of psychological tests, the intelligence test, actually measured. Therefore, intelligence testing was tantamount to 'measurement without definition' (Rogers, 1995: 242). Operationism, Rogers argued, was appropriated as a post-hoc justification of extant practice – a convenient response to mounting discontent over the struggle to define intelligence – which helped to explain why it was accepted so quickly, and with so little dissent. In short, it seemed to provide a respectable, indeed high-status, philosophical justification for not being able to define what intelligence tests actually measured, other than operationally in terms of the measurement procedure.

This analysis provides an interesting perspective from which to consider the degradation of the classic definition during the 1930s. Rather than seeing the reduction of validity to the validity coefficient as an explicit theoretical decision – prompted by recognition of operationism as the new philosophical foundation for psychology – it might be seen more as an implicit atheoretical degeneration, which happened to be consistent with the new zeitgeist. (In light of the account provided in Chapter 2, this seems plausible.)

Purely empirical validation was consistent with the zeitgeist to the extent that it deflected attention from the need for a conceptual definition of that which was supposed to be measured, either by the predictor test or by the criterion measure. The criterion measure could be treated as an operational definition in itself and, by extension, as the operational definition of that which was supposed to be measured (or simply predicted) by the predictor test. Purely logical validation was consistent with the zeitgeist to the extent that a test comprised a representative sample from the population of appropriate questions that operationally defined the attribute that was supposed to be measured. In effect, the content of the questions operationalized components of the attribute, such that a test which sampled those questions representatively would constitute an operational definition of the attribute. This was 'validity by definition' in the sense discussed by Mosier (1947). Therefore, the embrace of operationist thinking within mainstream psychology is likely to have prolonged the confusion between pragmatic and conceptual definitions, even in the face of mounting concern over the criterion problem in relation to both aptitude testing and achievement testing.

The explicit conceptualization of validity from an operationist perspective seems to have been more evident during the 1950s to the 1970s than during the early years. Perhaps this is not surprising, because the invention of construct validity constituted a challenge to operationism, and therefore would have shone new light on it. Construct validity constituted a *challenge* in the sense of going beyond operationism in an attempt to remedy its defects. In fact, Rogers (1995) argued that construct validity was intended explicitly to *replace* operationism. However, equally, the papers by Mac-Corquodale and Meehl (1948) and Cronbach and Meehl (1955) can be read as attempts to *salvage* operationism (Green, 1992). The roots of construct validity lay in a version of logical positivism which emphasized the importance of grounding theoretical terms firmly in observational statements. It permitted science to voyage beyond straightforward observation and operationism, but in an important sense it remained firmly rooted in it. Moreover, Cronbach and Meehl proposed construct validity as an *addition* to validity theory, otherwise conceived operationally, for example:

> Criterion-oriented validity, as Bechtoldt emphasizes (3, p. 1245), 'involves the *acceptance* of a set of operations as an adequate definition of whatever is to be measured.' When an investigator believes that no criterion available to him is fully valid, he perforce becomes interested in construct validity because this is the only way to avoid the 'infinite frustration' of relating every criterion to some more ultimate standard. (Cronbach and Meehl, 1955: 282, italics in original)

However, construct validity soon began to be seen as a potential *antidote* to operationist thinking, and in response, a number of validity theorists made the counter-argument in favour of operationism increasingly explicit, including Bechtoldt (1959) and Ebel (1961). Cronbach was later to describe this as 'a last-ditch defense of "operationalism," which nearly all the philosophers were rejecting in the 1950s' (1989a: 160), although the debate between Ebel and Cronbach actually continued for some years. Ebel argued for an operationist alternative to empirical validity – at least in relation to achievement tests. In fact, he went further still, claiming that the concept of validity itself was appropriate only for empirical validation; conversely, that 'if the test we propose to use provides in itself the best available operational definition, the concept of validity does not apply' (Ebel, 1961: 643). Interestingly, in staking this claim, he argued that predictive validity was actually inconsistent with operationism, that the concept of validity itself was inconsistent with operationism, and that overgeneralization of the concept of predictive validity had prevented operationism from being recognized more widely as the solution to the problem of meaning in measurement. Anyhow, reflecting on this quotation from Ebel, Cronbach responded as follows:

> But this language gives the game away, for the 'best available' definition is presumably not the best conceivable, and How good is the operation? remains a meaningful question. (1971: 481)

At least by the early 1970s, the need to invoke meaning beyond the measurement procedure (appropriate 'surplus' meaning) was self-evident to Cronbach, even as far as achievement tests were concerned. As the influence of operationism began to peter out, this realization became increasingly evident to the majority of scientists and practitioners comprising the educational and psychological measurement communities of the 1970s and 1980s. It paved the way to a gradual embrace of construct validity as all of validity.

The entrenchment of fragmented thinking

In Chapter 2 we explored early conceptions of validity and validation with a particular focus on achievement tests, general intelligence tests and special aptitude tests. Originally, and for many throughout the early years, empirical approaches were preferred over logical ones when trying to establish validity. This preference would seem to have been consistent with the classic definition of validity (as mentioned previously, the degree to which a test measured what it was supposed to measure), and its translation in terms of the coefficient of validity (the degree to which a test correlated with its criterion). Thus, during the early years, the more conceptual interpretation of concurrent validation (correlation against a more definitive criterion measure) often was presumed to be the gold standard for *all* tests. However, the very idea of a more definitive criterion measure was questioned increasingly and found wanting. As far as achievement tests were concerned, the alternative idea that validity might be established logically on the basis of judgemental analysis of test content, therefore might have become correspondingly more attractive. Indeed, the new backdrop of operationism would have been receptive to the idea that *only* logical approaches to validation were relevant in these circumstances. As far as aptitude tests were concerned, which were being simply used to predict future competence, it was not even clear that they were supposed to measure anything at all. Therefore it was not unreasonable to treat the results from aptitude tests as *mere* predictions, which suggested that *only* empirical approaches to validation were relevant in these circumstances. However, this was not the more conceptual interpretation of concurrent validity employed to establish measurement (albeit 'measurement lite' in many instances), but the more practical interpretation employed to establish association. In short, the stage was set for the fragmentation of validity even during the early years.

Having said that, the practice of classifying validity into different kinds, which became popular during the 1940s, was more about categorizing different methods for investigating validity (e.g. Greene et al., 1943) or different approaches to validation (e.g. Cronbach, 1949) than about identifying different kinds of validity per se. In fact, it was actually quite hard to conceptualize validity for aptitude tests, since validity was supposed to involve measurement, and aptitude tests were concerned primarily with prediction. From this perspective, sole reliance upon the approach that was to become known as predictive validity made some sense. Conversely, for achievement tests, although it was entirely possible to adopt the more conceptual interpretation of the empirical approach that was to become known as concurrent validity, often it was impractical or implausible to do so. So from this perspective, sole reliance upon the approach that was to become known as content validity also made some sense. Having said that, because it was typically impractical to develop tests that could satisfy the strict sampling requirements of content validity, often additional empirical concerns were elevated. Thus, even within achievement testing, many came to treat item-test correlation as a surrogate for concurrent validation. Finally, as far as general intelligence tests were concerned, both logical and empirical approaches made some sense, although neither was able to furnish especially good evidence. Factor analysis came to be seen as the preferred validation technique: an approach that, in retrospect, we might locate somewhere between a surrogate for concurrent validity and true construct validity.

The first edition of the *Standards* was written to make sense of the landscape of the early years, in which both theory and practice showed elements of both holistic thinking and fragmented thinking. Validity in the main was still defined in terms of the degree to which a test measured what it was supposed to measure: a general, holistic conception of validity. Yet for certain tests, it was not even clear whether they could or should be presumed to measure anything. In terms of validation practice, there was already a large amount of specialization, reflecting preferences for particular kinds of approaches; although in terms of validity theory, it was not uncommon for the approaches to be conceived as complementary. Therefore, it is perhaps unsurprising that the first edition of the *Standards* – indeed, the first three editions – presented inherently mixed messages concerning the nature of validity. In the face of such mixed messages, it seems that many practitioners chose to follow a path of least resistance, treating validity more as a specialized-fragmented concept than a general-holistic one. After all, if there was to be a choice between having to fund a programme of research rather than a one-off study, it should not be surprising if many preferred to think in specialized-fragmented terms which implicitly supported the latter. However, the entrenchment of separatist thinking was not simply a matter of economic opportunity. There were important advances in two major branches of educational and psychological measurement during the 1960s and 1970s that further disposed measurement specialists towards fragmented thinking.

In educational measurement, the entrenchment of fragmented thinking was exacerbated by the rise of criterion-referenced testing. Popham and Husek (1969) insisted that this new emphasis on the criterion, which meant ensuring that test results could be interpreted directly in terms of the mastery of specified learning objectives, substantially elevated the significance of content validity. Furthermore, a new emphasis on ensuring that all students mastered all content substantially lowered the significance of criterion validity: if all students were expected to master all content, then it made little sense to explore validity using correlation, which relied upon being able to discriminate between students on the basis of their end-of-course achievement levels. Moreover, those who believed that carefully specified learning objectives (behavioural outcomes) constituted criteria in their own right apparently needed no recourse to abstract notions of constructs, let alone to construct validity. Sentiments such as these cemented a belief that the only kind of validity of relevance to achievement testing was content validity (e.g. Osburn, 1968).

Fragmented thinking became equally established in personnel psychology, albeit for slightly different reasons. The Civil Rights Act of 1964 in the USA imposed a new responsibility on employers not to discriminate (on the basis of ethnicity, colour, religion, gender or national origin) through their use of psychological tests. In its wake came publications from the Equal Employment Opportunity Commission (EEOC, 1966) and the Office of Federal Contract Compliance (OFCC, 1968) regulating the use of such tests. These documents were not always warmly received, stimulating a controversy that forced personnel psychologists to re-examine their orthodoxies and, in particular, their understanding of validity (Guion, 1976). The subsequent EEOC Guidelines (EEOC, 1970) and the OFCC Order (OFCC, 1971) identified predictive validity as the general model for personnel settings, accepting that, for example, owing to small sample sizes, this might not always be possible, and therefore that content validity or construct validity might be considered a legitimate substitute (Guion, 1977b; Novick, 1981).

Subsequent court cases also influenced attitudes towards validation. For example, the *Griggs* v. *Duke Power Co.* case (401 U.S. 424 (1971)) stressed the importance of job-relatedness between predictors and the criteria that they were supposed to predict (Guion, 1976). This further elevated the significance of content concerns in personnel settings, in contrast with the traditional focus on prediction. Indeed, since the EEOC and OFCC had sanctioned the substitution of content validity for predictive validity, this potentially opened the door to a 'runaway use' of content validity in employment testing (Guion, 1977b: 8). The situation was not improved by publication of the 1978 Uniform Guidelines (EEOC et al., 1978), which allowed all three approaches to validation, but which also reinforced a bias toward content and criterion concerns to the detriment of construct validation (Barrett, 1992). The impact of legislation on conceptions of validity and validation was considered by many to be lamentable. Barrett (1992), for example, observed that the Uniform Guidelines was the product of a single committee comprised mainly of attorneys, that it had not been peer-reviewed, and that it was outdated by the time it was published. The law, he argued, ought not to be considered a bible for professional or scientific practice.

The idea that different kinds of validity could substitute for each other was less extreme than the idea that certain kinds of validity were necessary and sufficient for certain kinds of test interpretation. However, both were premised on the idea of *specialization*: in educational settings, it was assumed often that nothing other than content validity was relevant for achievement tests; in personnel settings, it was assumed often that predictive validity was the gold standard for aptitude tests, but that other forms of validity could be relied on as substitutes if predictive validation proved to be impractical. As mentioned previously, Guion (1980) was soon to characterize the fragmented thinking of the 1970s as embodying a trinitarian conception of validity (three kinds of validity) in contrast to the conception that he preferred, a unitarian one (a single kind).

Although content validity was being increasingly viewed as the specialized type for achievement testing, there was also evidence of a different kind of fragmentation within educational settings: a tendency for test developers and publishers of educational tests to rely exclusively upon empirical evidence. Thus, the 1966 revision explained that it was very risky to rely upon carefully standardized educational achievement tests, supported by a wealth of statistical information, in the absence of any logical analysis of their relation to specified learning outcomes. In fact, this edition included a brand new standard, marked as an 'essential' requirement (see also E1.4 from the 1974 *Standards*):

> C2. Item-test correlations should not be presented in the manual as evidence of criterion-related validity, and they should be referred to as item-discrimination indices, not as item-validity coefficients. (APA et al., 1966: 15)

Many test developers and publishers, it seemed, had been relying upon item-test correlations as a surrogate for concurrent validity, and presenting this information as though it were sufficient to establish validity. This kind of evidence would have been typically generated as a product of test development. If it could be rebranded subsequently as evidence of validity, indeed *sufficient* evidence of validity, then the need to fund additional validation research would disappear. The *Standards* explicitly challenged this presumption. In fact, standard D3.1 (1966) added that measures of reliability in general should not be presented as though they provided evidence of criterion-related validity. Reliability was a necessary condition for validity, it added, but not a sufficient one.

Of course, the entrenchment of fragmented thinking was not universal. On the one hand, it is worth noting how Cronbach reverted to emphasizing 'types of validation' in the third edition of his *Essentials of Psychological Testing* (1970: 121), as opposed to 'types of validity' in the second (1960: 103). This helped to discourage separatist ideas. On the other hand, even some of the most authoritative textbooks of the 1960s and 1970s did appear to interpret the message of the *Standards* in a more fragmented than holistic sense. The discussion of validity in Anastasi's *Psychological Testing* seemed to become more clear-cut over successive editions by becoming more fragmented. For example, the third edition introduced a very useful table which illustrated how a single arithmetic test should be validated differently, according to how its results were to be used (Anastasi, 1968). It had one row for achievement, linked to content validity; one for aptitude, linked to predictive criterion-related validity; one for diagnosing brain damage, linked to diagnostic criterion-related validity; and one for logical reasoning, linked to construct validity. Although Anastasi acknowledged that the categories were not entirely logically distinct, her presentation tended to emphasize their distinctiveness, and hence a fragmented account of validity:

> This example highlights the fact that the choice of validation procedure depends on the use to be made of the test scores. The same test, when employed for different purposes, should be validated in different ways. If an achievement test is used to predict subsequent performance at a higher educational level ... it needs to be evaluated against the criterion of subsequent college performance rather than in terms of its content validity. (Anastasi, 1968: 120–1)

The word to dwell on here is 'rather', because it suggests a fragmented account. It is not the same as the impression given by the first three editions of the *Standards*, when they emphasized that construct, content and criterion validity should all be considered relevant to a test used for predictive purposes.

Seeds of discontent

The publication of the first edition of the *Standards* helped to establish a new consensus over how to characterize quality within educational and psychological measurement – albeit a fairly nebulous consensus. This held that there were different kinds of validity corresponding to a small number of primary interpretations or uses of test scores, and that these were associated with different approaches to validation. However, some interpreted this more strictly than others, and an important variant of the consensus was the idea of substitutability, which held that certain approaches to validation were more suited to specific interpretations or uses; if it was not possible to implement the best approach to validation, then it would be legitimate to fall back on the next best, because a less suitable form of validation would be better than no validation at all. Again, this implied that it was quite legitimate to rely upon a single approach to validation, or even a single validation study, as long as it was the appropriate approach or a legitimate substitute.

As this kind of fragmented thinking became increasingly entrenched, pockets of resistance began to form. A number of key papers were published which began to lay a foundation for the return to a more general, holistic conception of validity, which was to be realised during the Messick years. These papers all emphasized the importance of adopting a more sophisticated, nuanced and complex view of validity and validation. Perhaps the most important paper in this respect was the state-of-the-art review provided by Cronbach (1971), which we discuss in the following section. Also extremely important were contributions from Roger Lennon, Paul Wernimont and John Campbell, and Jane Loevinger, which we discuss below.

Soon after the publication of the very first *Standards* document, a landmark article by Lennon (1956) sought to unpick exactly what it might have meant by 'content validity'. Noting that the *Standards* had not explicitly defined the term, he defined it as follows, in the sense that he believed had been intended:

> [T]he extent to which a subject's responses to the items of a test may be considered to be a representative sample of his responses to a real or hypothetical universe of situations which together constitute the area of concern to the person interpreting the test. (Lennon, 1956: 295)

Lennon crafted this definition carefully to underline his conviction that content validation needed to investigate not simply the content of test questions, but the 'process' (1956: 296) by which they were responded to – echoing sentiments that had been expressed decades earlier by Tyler (e.g. Tyler, 1932b). Ultimately, then, the sample of interest was not a sample of items, but a sample of behaviours elicited by items. This meant that content validity was ultimately a property of *responses* to questions, rather than of the questions per se. Thus, an 'item may function as a measure of reasoning or generalization for one examinee, but measure merely recall for another' (Lennon, 1956: 296), and validity could be claimed only when the intended process had been elicited. As such, even though the items of a test were constant, content validity could differ from one examinee to the next.

Lennon appreciated that defining validity as a property of examinee responses, as well as of test content, was problematic. He claimed that it required a more fundamental kind of representativeness than had been traditionally associated with content validation, although he did not actually explain in any detail how this could be established. Even to the present day it is not entirely clear how this more fundamental kind of representativeness ought to be established. If it is true that we are interested ultimately in the representativeness of cognitive processes used to respond to questions, yet different examinees are likely to respond to the same set of questions using different cognitive processes, then how exactly should representativeness be theorized, let alone investigated? However, Lennon did emphasize how the purpose of validation was to support the interpretation of test scores, and to justify attributing variance in test scores 'to the same sources, and in the same proportion' as variance in the criterion behaviour (Lennon, 1956: 302). Although he did not actually go so far as to conclude that content validity, inter- preted this broadly, morphed into construct validity, he clearly seemed to be mov- ing in this direction.

As noted above, the potential for boundaries to blur became apparent to the authors of the third edition of the *Standards*, who responded by insisting that content validity was purely a matter of test content representativeness, and not also of response process representativeness, since the latter was a matter of con- struct validity. In short, rather than dissolving the distinction between content validity and construct validity – a distinction that was becoming increasingly hard to maintain – they chose to defend it. Yet in doing so, they insisted on an account of content validity that was clearly half-baked: an account that could not be con- sidered in any sense to represent an independent, free-standing kind. Messick was later to locate this at the heart of his critique of content validity: the logical analysis of test content, by subject matter experts, could be considered in no way sufficient to stake a claim to high-quality measurement.

As Lennon was beginning to make clear how the validation of achievement tests required more than traditional content validation, others were beginning to make clear how the validation of aptitude tests required more than traditional predictive validation. Very influential in this respect were Dunnette (e.g. 1963, 1966) and Guion (e.g. 1974, 1976). Guion was later to produce a series of papers that devel- oped Lennon's thesis towards its logical conclusion: that the distinction between content validity and construct validity was artificial and misleading (e.g. Guion, 1977a, 1977b, 1978a, 1978b; see also Tenopyr, 1977 for a similar argument). Particu- larly influential during this period was a paper by Wernimont and Campbell (1968), 'Signs, samples, and criteria'.

The mid- to late 1960s was a period of general dissatisfaction with traditional procedures for predicting job performance. The zeitgeist was captured in the con- clusion of a prominent overview of findings from validation research which had been published during a period spanning many decades:

> [W]hile the general predictive power of aptitude tests in forecasting occupational success is by no means zero, it is far from impressive. For all tests and jobs as a whole, a coefficient in the order of .30 describes the general validity of tests for training criteria, and one of the order of .20 gives the value for proficiency criteria. (Ghiselli, 1966: 125)

Wernimont and Campbell (1968) attributed this outcome to an unfortunate union between the classical conception (empirical validity), and the use of tests as mere signs. The traditional approach to test construction, they observed, involved feeding as many signs as possible into regression equations in the hope of uncovering some-thing useful. This blindly empirical approach needed to be rejected, they argued, in favour of a new emphasis on sampling. Just as content sampling was fundamental to the development and validation of achievement tests, so too ought it to be funda-mental to the development and validation of aptitude tests. Yet Wernimont and Campbell were not simply recommending that applied psychologists should switch from traditional predictive validity to traditional content validity. Like Lennon, they were proposing something far more fundamental: rather than theorizing aptitude testing purely in terms of prediction, applied psychologists ought to theorize it in terms of measurement. Their emphasis, which foreshadowed convictions expressed by Guion and Messick, was on the meaning of predictor measures. With a clearer understanding of what aptitude tests actually measured, many of the established problems of prediction might be overcome. Ensuring the relevance of a predictor measure to its criterion should not only improve accuracy of decision-making, but also transparency and defensibility, since the relationship between predictor and criterion would be obvious for all to see. Wernimont and Campbell concluded their paper by noting that they were attacking predictive and concurrent validity, but not construct validity. Indeed, their paper can be read as a manifesto for construct validation.[5]

The most important and fundamental rejection of the fragmented conception of validity was published shortly after the first edition of the *Standards*. It was a trea-tise on 'Objective tests as instruments of psychological theory', written by Jane Loevinger (1957), and presented as a more radical reformulation of validity theory than even Cronbach and Meehl (1955) had achieved. Loevinger made some impor-tant observations in this paper which undoubtedly stood the test of time, including her critique of content validity. She followed Lennon in observing that there was more to representing the criterion than a simple analysis of test content could ever reveal. However – and more importantly – she explained how, strictly speaking, behaviour in the test situation could never be considered a direct sample of crite-rion behaviour. The idea of *directly sampling* the attribute in question gave the impression of *directly measuring* it, as though a test that sampled rigorously was essentially infallible and obviously valid. By way of contrast, she insisted that the 'psychodynamics of testing' could never be ignored when inferences were to be drawn from test responses:

> Test behavior is always utilized as a sign of non-test behavior ... The very fact that one set of behaviors occurs in a test situation and the other outside the test situation introduces an instrument error which is ignored by the concept of content validity. (Loevinger, 1957: 565)

Thus, considerations of content alone were insufficient to establish validity, even when the test content was highly authentic to the attribute that supposedly was being measured, and the distinction between signs and samples had been over-interpreted. Loevinger similarly criticized predictive validity, observing that the dangers of blind empiricism should not be underestimated. She set herself against the narrowness of classical prediction theory, which prioritized decision-making over measurement, and which therefore valued decision-specific validities at the expense of overall validity (see Lord, 1955 for a defence of classical prediction theory and a rejection of overall validity). Quoting the economist Jacob Marschak (1954), Loevinger emphasized the importance of theory in providing solutions that were potentially useful for a large class of decisions. Classical predictive validity was ad hoc, inherently restricted and therefore of minimal significance. Only one kind of validity, construct validity, elevated the general above the specific, and therefore promised true significance.

From a scientific point of view, Loevinger concluded, construct validity was the whole of validity, and she identified three 'mutually exclusive, exhaustive and mandatory' criteria for construct validation:

1 the substance or content of items should be consistent with the proposed interpretation of test scores
2 structural relations between test items should be consistent with structural relations between non-test behaviours
3 external correlations should be consistent with predictions from what is known about the to-be-measured trait. (Loevinger, 1957: 686)

Adopting a working stance that was more explicitly realist than Cronbach and Meehl's appeared to be, Loevinger drew a distinction between traits and constructs: a trait was what the psychologist aimed to understand, while a construct represented the psychologist's current best understanding of it. The test itself could be viewed as a representation of the current best understanding of the trait, and from this perspective, Loevinger defined the two fundamental questions of construct validity as follows:

1 To what extent does the test measure a trait that 'really' exists – that is, to what extent does it measure anything?
2 How well does the proposed interpretation (framed in terms of the trait) correspond to what is measured by the test?

Cronbach on validation

Although during the 1990s Samuel Messick came to be seen as the new champion of validity theory, much of the groundwork had been laid already by Lee Cronbach. Cronbach was undoubtedly the most influential author of the period between 1950 and 1980, and his advocacy of the validity argument during the 1980s continued to influence thinking on validation into the 21st century. In addition, he not only chaired the APA Committee on Test Standards, which was responsible for the first draft of the *Standards*, but also sat on the Joint Committee for its revision, and was acknowledged with special gratitude in the third edition. He authored multiple editions of the *Essentials of Psychological Testing*, one of a small number of author-itative textbooks on educational and psychological measurement, which would have influenced countless numbers of students during this period. Moreover, not only did he jointly author one of the most creative contributions of all time to the literature on validity theory, Cronbach and Meehl (1955), he was invited subse-quently to write the validity chapter in the second edition of the classic, if not definitive, textbook, *Educational Measurement* (Thorndike, 1971a).[6]

It was not incidental that we headed this section 'Cronbach on validation'. Over the decades, Cronbach focused his analysis more on practical recommendations for validation, and less on theoretical conceptions of validity. That is, his analyses are better characterized as contributing to validation theory or even evaluation theory, than validity theory. Having said that, although Cronbach theorized educational and psychological measurement very much as an applied technology, a social technol-ogy, he by no means over-simplified it to make it accessible to the practising valida-tor. In fact, if anything, he over-complicated it by characterizing validation as a never-ending process of scientific discovery, the responsibility of a scientific com-munity rather than an individual evaluator (Cronbach, 1971). However, he compli-cated it with very good reason, and we conclude this section by exploring the subtlety of his position as it was presented in 1971, and how this influenced future thinking on validity and validation, particularly the work of Samuel Messick.

If a legacy of the 1954 *Standards* was the idea that different tests needed to be validated in different ways, harbouring a fragmented conception of validity and the one-off study approach to validation, then the legacy of Cronbach (1971) was its antithesis. It was as close to a rejection of the trinitarian account as it was possible to come without explicitly rejecting it. However, it was not *quite* an explicit rejec-tion, any more than it was an explicit adoption of a unitarian account: that step was left for Messick to take in 1975. It seems likely that one of the reasons why Cron-bach (1971) did not go quite so far as to propose a unitary account was that he approached validity from the perspective of validation, whereas Messick (1975) was to approach validation from the perspective of validity. In other words, what was important to Cronbach was to argue *in favour* of a multiplicity of *approaches* to validation; whereas what was to prove important to Messick was to argue *against* a multiplicity of *kinds* of validity. They almost met in the middle from their different perspectives, but not quite. The following quotation captures Cronbach's general thesis and its relationship to earlier accounts:

> Validation of an instrument calls for an integration of many types of evidence. The varieties of investigation are not alternatives, any one of which would be adequate. The investigations supplement one another. The person validating a test should give thought to all questions suggested under the three rubrics listed by the committee, though the relative importance of the questions varies from test to test. For purposes of exposition, it is necessary to subdivide *what in the end must be a comprehensive, integrated evaluation of the test*. (Cronbach, 1971: 445; emphasis in original)

The similarities between the sentiments expressed here and those that were to be expressed by Messick are striking. There is a clear indication that the one-off study approach to validation is misplaced, and that all three approaches ought to be considered. Indeed, the idea of a comprehensive integrated evaluation was fundamental to the definition of validity with which Messick opened his classic chapter (Messick, 1989a). Yet it is fair to say that Cronbach (1971) still valued the trinitarian rhetoric to the extent that it highlighted how certain approaches to validation were somehow more fundamental than others to certain kinds of test. In particular, he still drew a significant distinction between the use of tests for making *decisions* about people, and the use of tests for *describing* people, noting that the 'decision maker is particularly concerned with criterion-oriented validation' (Cronbach, 1971: 445).

He amplified this distinction by suggesting that the interpretations underlying tests used for decision-making were far narrower than the interpretations underlying tests used for description. Decisions concerned what to do in a specific situation at a specific point in time for a specific purpose; whereas descriptions were inherently general, which meant that they could be extrapolated across situations, times and purposes. Thus, descriptions (cf. predictions) stored surplus information, which provided the warrant for using test scores in a variety of situations. This difference seemed to be captured well in the distinction that he drew between a predictive interpretation which made no reference to constructs, 'This test indicates that you will do well as an assembler in this camera factory', and a descriptive interpretation framed in terms of a situational construct, 'You will do well at fine manual work' (Cronbach, 1971: 462). Although he did not make the point explicitly, this seemed to suggest that criterion-oriented validation might be sufficient to justify the first interpretation, while the second would require construct validation.

The thrust of the position adopted by Cronbach (1971) seemed to be as follows: if and only if, you are prepared to restrict your interpretation substantially, then you are at liberty to rely exclusively upon either criterion-related validation or content validation, depending on the nature of that interpretation.[7] However, he also seemed to believe that this almost always would be inappropriate, since interpretations thus restricted would prove to be insufficiently useful. So, on the one hand, Cronbach did appear to leave some conceptual space for fragmented and specialized thinking, but only a very small amount of space. For example, content categories 'almost always *are* constructs' (1971: 464, italics in original). More strikingly, although he seemed to imply that there might still be a role for context-bound interpretations supported only by criterion-oriented studies, he also explained very clearly that empirical validation is inevitably retrospective (based on evidence from the past), while the use of a test to make decisions is inevitably prospective (involving predictions about the future). For this reason, decision-making always will involve extrapolation, even if this is simply a matter of extrapolating from historical evidence to the present day. According to Cronbach, the kind of extrapolation required for decision-making was made with the aid of constructs and plausible inference. Put as starkly as this, it would seem legitimate to question whether in fact there could be *any* remaining conceptual space for decisions supported only by criterion-oriented validation. Yet Cronbach did seem to be prepared to allow for this possibility, just as long as situations remained 'sufficiently stable' (1971: 485).

Just as Cronbach (1971) prefigured Messick in his elevation of constructs and construct validation, he also prefigured him in acknowledging the significance of considering values and social consequences as an element of validation. Having recently made a significant contribution to theorizing decision-making (Cronbach and Gleser, 1957, 1965), he was well-aware that it was not simply a technical matter of accuracy, but also an ethical issue of value. He explained how the utility of testing was essentially a matter of the value added by using the test to make decisions, as opposed to making decisions without the test. He also observed how the evaluation of educational tests was ultimately a matter of values, and not simply a matter of alignment, since the aims of education were best understood as constructs that would differ across educators, guided by their respective value-bases. Finally, he stressed the central role of 'plausible counterinterpretations' in structuring validation inquiry (Cronbach, 1971: 465), thus rectifying an implicit confirmationist bias evident within Cronbach and Meehl (1955). This, too, became a central principle for Messick. Ultimately, the similarities between the perspectives adopted by these two giants of educational and psychological measurement are such that the opening sentence of Cronbach's final paragraph can be understood metaphorically as a baton handed to Messick: 'Everything said in this chapter has returned to a concern with understanding' (Cronbach, 1971: 503).

Validity and validation by the mid-1970s

In relation to conceptions of validity and validation, the period between 1952 and 1974 was very much the era of Cronbach and the *Standards*. For the first time an official consensus existed on the characteristics of quality in educational and psychological measurement, and on validity and validation more specifically. Of course, it was not a foregone conclusion that measurement scientists and professionals would buy into the official position statement. Indeed, it is important to recognize that even members of the committees responsible for producing the *Standards* sometimes disagreed substantially. Robert Ebel, for example, was Chair of the Committee on Test Standards for NCMUE, and took a lead in producing the *Technical Recommendations for Achievement Tests* (AERA and NCMUE, 1955). Reflecting on his influence, Cronbach (1983) explained that he managed to persuade the committee of the importance of careful content specifications, and the limitations of criterion-related validity, but not of his view of construct validity. Ebel was never a fan of construct validity, especially in educational settings, despite the importance that ultimately was attached to it within the 1955 document.

Tensions such as these lingered on in the literature of the 1950s to 1970s. Even many of the 'big hitters' were resistant, at least initially, to buying into the new consensus wholesale (e.g. Ebel, 1961; Cattell, 1964; Cureton, 1965; Lord and Novick, 1968). However, as time went by, the official consensus position did begin to be appropriated widely, being adopted increasingly by authors of leading textbooks and, ultimately, influencing conceptions of validity and validation internationally.

Possibly as a consequence of having established consensus by committee, the official position was actually quite confused. In particular, it is just not clear whether the *Standards* promoted a general-holistic view of validity, or a specialized-fragmented one. Neither was this clarified from the first edition to the third, which underscores the subtlety of the confusion. Despite explicit statements to the contrary, the nomenclature of the *Standards* conveyed an impression of independent kinds of validity, which implied that certain approaches to validation were better suited to certain testing contexts. Therefore, for many who were subsequently influenced by this work, it came to embody and cement a fragmented view of validity and validation.

It is interesting to note that the literature during this period tended towards even greater fragmentation of the concept of validity than was evident from the official position statement. In the first edition of the *Standards* there were four basic kinds of validity, although they were reduced to three in the second, and remained at three for the third. Yet all sorts of different kinds of validity either were being used in the literature already, or were introduced into the literature post-1954, for example:

- synthetic validity, generalized validity, situational validity (Lawshe, 1952)
- internal validity, substantive validity, structural validity, external validity (Loevinger, 1957)
- domain validity (Tryon, 1957a, 1957b)
- convergent validity, discriminant validity (Campbell and Fiske, 1959)
- trait validity, nomological validity (Campbell, 1960)
- common sense validity (Shaw and Linden, 1964, from English and English, 1958)
- raw validity, true validity, intrinsic validity (Cureton, 1965)
- empirical validity, theoretical validity (Lord and Novick, 1968)
- occupational validity (Bemis, 1968)
- cash validity (Dick and Hagerty, 1971)
- single-group validity (Boehm, 1972).

These examples – and this list is far from exhaustive – illustrate:

- alternative conceptual schemes for classifying validity – e.g. Loevinger (1957), Lord and Novick (1968);
- sub-divisions of the basic kinds presented in the *Standards* – e.g. Campbell (1960), which subdivided construct validity, and Lawshe (1952), which subdivided predictive validity; and
- entirely new kinds of validity – e.g. Dick and Hagerty (1971).

Yet none of these alternatives, elaborations or additions made any impact whatsoever on the account of validity presented in the *Standards*. So, while officially there were only three or four different kinds between 1952 and 1974, the unofficial number of different kinds increased markedly during this period (Newton and Shaw, 2013). However, not all of them caught on; in fact, most of these unofficial validities made little or no lasting impact. Yet it is interesting to note how the development of an official consensus position did not inhibit the proliferation of new kinds of validity, and how the official consensus position was not at all affected by this pro-liferation. This lack of impact on the *Standards* ought not to be surprising, if its account of validity was intended originally as an antidote to the unhelpful prolif-eration of validity types, as suggested by an introductory passage from Cronbach and Meehl:

> Writers on validity during the preceding decade had shown a great deal of dissatisfaction with conventional notions of validity, and introduced new terms and ideas, but the resulting aggregation of types of validity seems only to have stirred the muddy waters. (Cronbach and Meehl, 1955: 281)

The period between 1952 and 1974 also witnessed the birth and development of construct validity. This was construct validity 'mark 1' (the 'caterpillar'), which was narrower and more philosophically grounded than construct validity 'mark 2' (the 'butterfly') which was to emerge during the Messick years. Initially, as mentioned previously, it was the validity of last resort, when neither logical nor empirical approaches could be relied upon as a gold standard; the 'weak sister' of the valid-ity family (Shepard, 1993: 416). However, construct validity gradually became more significant, while content validity and criterion-related validity became less significant.

With the benefit of hindsight, what is most interesting and now seems most odd about the invention of construct validity was how it initially left traditional approaches to validation largely unquestioned. Not only were they largely unques-tioned within the *Standards*, but the report of the Joint Committee sometimes appeared to adopt a far more extreme stance on their distinctiveness and inde-pendence than many accounts from the early years. Content validity, it might be assumed, was now officially the specialized validity for achievement inferences; predictive validity for aptitude inferences; and concurrent validity for diagnostic inferences. Each required its own definitive criterion: a logical criterion, in the case of content validity; or an empirical criterion, in the case of predictive and concur-rent validity.

The idea that in 1950 it was still plausible to place such reliance on external crite-ria was surprising, given the clarity with which the criterion problem had been recently articulated (e.g. Toops, 1944; Jenkins, 1946; Cronbach, 1949; Thorndike, 1949). If by the end of the 1940s criterion measures were widely acknowledged to be inherently vulnerable – as the individual standards for predictive validity actually explained in some detail – then why was construct validity not introduced as a general solution to the problem of validation, as Loevinger (1957) was later to recommend? After all, the Joint Committee *did* acknowledge that construct validation embraced all of the other approaches, and it acknowledged that construct validation had the poten-tial to inform the validation of any test interpretation. Yet the Joint Committee failed to take these considerations to their apparent logical conclusion: that all validation ought to be conceptualized and practised as construct validation.

The reasons why the Joint Committee failed to go this far are, undoubtedly, manifold. First, it probably would have been beyond the ability of any committee to reformulate validity theory so radically on the basis of such a novel idea as construct validity. After all, the Joint Committee's remit was to develop practical recommendations, rather than to reconceptualize validity and validation per se. Furthermore, if there is a natural tendency for committee products to be conservative (Kane, 2012), then this would have naturally acted as a brake on too radical a statement. In this light, it is perhaps surprising that the Joint Committee's statement was as radical as it was. Rogers (1988) went so far as to claim that the whole idea of construct validity was 'imposed upon the field' (1988: 241) by the committee, 'with no formal, open debate' in the literature (1988: 237). Inevitably, reformulating validity theory for psychological tests constituted an implicit challenge to the defensibility of psychological tests that were already widely in use, such as the Strong Vocational Interest Blank, and which had been developed and validated using largely empirical approaches (Rogers, 1995). If the new concept of construct validity had been presumed to embrace all existing tests – not simply a subset of psychological tests – then the repercussions in the world of testing would have been very much greater, and potentially highly destabilizing. To question the adequacy of well-established logical and empirical approaches, even in the limited context of personality testing, must have been challenging enough for the Joint Committee.

Second, construct validation was heavily theoretical. Indeed, it was grounded in theory testing. To make such a laborious process of scientific inquiry the rule for validation rather than its exception would have been very challenging for test developers and publishers, and it seems unlikely that it would have been received well, particularly in a period during which operationism remained influential. Third, against this background of respect for operationism, it would have seemed odd to argue that all of the attributes of educational and psychological measurement needed to be treated as hypothetical constructs: that is, postulated attributes. Many measurement scientists and professionals of the 1950s still treated criterion measures as though they constituted operational definitions. Although the very idea of the criterion problem cast doubt on this kind of operationist thinking (for all tests, not just for personality tests), it was still fairly engrained in psychology and education. In short, the idea that content validity, predictive validity and concurrent validity could be considered a gold standard each in their own right, still seemed to present itself as a plausible, if somewhat over-simplistic, thesis.

In some ways, construct validity was not a new idea. Campbell insisted that a 'good half of the validation efforts for personality tests since the 1920s' were best described as investigations into construct validity (Campbell, 1960: 547). However, the older investigations tended not to involve testing relationships given by nomological networks, and tended to focus more on hypothetical syndromes, traits or personality dimensions in isolation. This kind of construct validity, Campbell suggested, might be called 'trait validity'. He distinguished trait validity from the more theoretically grounded construct validity described by Cronbach and Meehl (1955), which he called 'nomological validity'. Campbell proposed that when the Taylor

Manifest Anxiety Scale was validated against psychologists' ratings, this was an example of the more constrained kind of construct validation – an example of trait validation. This idea is similar to what we have been referring to throughout this chapter as the more conceptual interpretation of concurrent validation. However, Campbell distinguished trait validity from concurrent validity on the basis that there was no way in which the judgement of psychologists, for example, could really be described as an *a priori* defining criterion. Trait validity, cf. concurrent validity, simply sought an *independent* way of measuring the trait – not necessarily even a better way, and certainly not a definitive way – simply an alternative way. The validity of both measures, he argued, was increased by their agreement or convergence. Not only was evidence of convergence important, between tests assumed to measure the same trait, but also evidence of divergence between tests assumed to measure dissimilar traits. This was to recommend the multitrait-multimethod (MTMM) technique from Campbell and Fiske (1959) as central to trait validation.

Like Lennon (1956) and Loevinger (1957) before him, and Wernimont and Campbell (1968) subsequently, Campbell (1960) helped to sow seeds of discontent with the presentation of validity within the *Standards*, illustrating the more general significance of construct validity. However, at this point in time, and even for those such as Cronbach (1971), who stressed the interrelatedness of different approaches to validation, emphasized the importance of 'ongoing investigation' as opposed to 'one-off study' and understood the general relevance of construct thinking, the unification of the concept of validity – through construct validity – still did not present itself as the logical conclusion. In fact, Cronbach observed that Loevinger's recommendation to elevate construct validity and relegate claims of content validity was too sweeping (Cronbach, 1971: 454–5). There were still important differences to preserve. Perhaps the most important distinction for Cronbach (e.g. 1971: 445) was between validation for decision-making and validation for description:

- How valid is the test for the decision I wish to make?
- How valid is the interpretation I propose for the test?

This is how he framed the distinction in the third edition of *Essentials of Psychological Testing* (see Cronbach, 1970: 122), and exactly the same distinction was drawn in his subsequent chapter, 'Test validation' (see Cronbach, 1971: 445). Decisions and descriptions were somehow fundamentally different for Cronbach. Indeed, occasionally his discussion of decision-making could still seem very crude. For example, Cronbach (1970) contrasted predictive validity and construct validity by explaining that the former was examined in a single study, while the latter involved an ongoing interplay between observation, reasoning and imagination (1970: 142). Similarly, while a single predictive study did little to clarify the psychological meaning of a test, he observed, it did still indicate the test's usefulness for a particular decision (1970: 127).

In thus describing predictive validity, he seemed to side more with Lord than with Loevinger, at least as far as decision-making was concerned. After all, a test did not need to support accurate measurement of a trait in order to improve decision-making: validity coefficients as low as 0.30 were still of 'definite practical value' (Cronbach, 1970: 429). Cronbach was certainly not alone among the leading figures in wishing to differentiate between measurement and decision-making. Nunnally, for example, distinguished sharply between 'assessments' and 'predictors' (e.g. Nunnally, 1959: 58). By 1967 he had adopted the 'tripartite' classification from the 1966 *Standards*, but he still drew his boundaries sharply:

> Predictive validity is determined by, and only by, the degree of correspondence between the two measures involved. If the correlation is high, no other standards are necessary. Thus if it were found that accuracy in horseshoe pitching correlated highly with success in college, horseshoe pitching would be a valid measure for predicting success in college. This is not meant to imply that sound theory and common sense are not useful in selecting predictor instruments for investigation, but after all the investigations are done, the entire proof of the pudding is in the correlations. (Nunnally, 1967: 77)

It was not until the late 1970s and into the 1980s that those boundaries began to be broken down, test score meaning began to command centre stage, and validity returned to being a unified concept.

Notes

1   Cronbach and Meehl (1955) tended to use the term 'attribute' and 'construct' synonymously. Despite our general preference for the term 'attribute' (see Chapter 1), we will use both in this chapter without intending to mark a particular distinction.

2   Cronbach (1989a) later acknowledged that the original formulation was framed largely in terms of accumulating confirmatory results. The idea of explicitly questioning the proposed interpretation, which was to become a central principle of construct validation, was less prominent. Cronbach (1989a) credited Campbell (1957) with the insight that validation needed to be guided by plausible rival hypotheses. Cronbach (1988) observed that the first two editions of the *Standards* described a weaker programme of construct validation, while the third and fourth began to lean towards a stronger programme, with a little more emphasis on rigorous theory-testing.

3   Construct validity is not easy to understand. If you are still struggling but want to know more, we can recommend the following accounts: Orton (1986, 1987), Rogers (1995) and Slaney and Maraun (2008).

4   Interestingly, the 1999 edition opened with a definition that secured a *rapprochement* between the 1966 and 1974 versions, emphasizing both interpretation and use: 'Validity refers to the degree to which evidence and theory support the interpretations of test scores entailed by proposed uses of tests' (AERA et al., 1999: 9).

5   The paper by Wernimont and Campbell (1968) has not always been read in this manner. Barrett (1992), for example, construed it as a rejection of construct thinking, which promoted an atheoretical reliance on the methodology of matching current behaviour to future behaviour. To be fair, this may well have been its substantial legacy. Yet with a thesis grounded so firmly on a foundation of measurement, it is hard not to see their paper as a direct precursor to Guion, Messick and the unitarian thesis.

6   Cronbach made so many seminal contributions during this period that we feel at liberty not to discuss all of them in depth. If more space were available, we would do more justice to the contribution that he made to validity theory through his extension of reliability theory to generalizability theory (e.g. Cronbach et al., 1972), ideas that were developed further by Kane (e.g. 1982). An important insight from Cronbach (1971), linked to the idea of generalizability, was that the procedure to be validated is more than just an instrument: extending, for example, to those who score responses, and to the interaction between raters and those being rated.

7   Incidentally, this kind of thinking resonates to some extent with the distinction that Kane has drawn between ambitious and unambitious interpretations (see Kane, 2006, 2013a, and Chapter 5).

CHAPTER 4

THE (RE)UNIFICATION OF VALIDITY: 1975–1999

This chapter aims to capture the spirit of the period between 1975 and 1999 through an extended discussion of the influence of Samuel Messick, whose ideas on validity increasingly came to dominate the landscape during this phase, ultimately becoming the very zeitgeist of late 20th-century thinking on validity. There are two aspects to this discussion: his triumph and his tribulation.

As we have outlined previously, the classic definition of validity – the degree to which a test measures what it is supposed to measure – presented a unitary conception focused squarely on score meaning. As theorists elaborated this definition, it became more complicated and distinctions began to be drawn, in particular between validity of measurement and validity of prediction (e.g. Cronbach, 1949: 48). With the publication of the first edition of the *Standards* (APA et al., 1954), the concept of validity was fragmented further through the identification and elevation of three or four different kinds of validity. During the 1970s and 1980s, this fragmented conception was transformed back into a unitary one through the concerted efforts of theorists such as Robert Guion, and especially Messick. The unification of validity, based on the principle of validation as scientific inquiry into score meaning, was Messick's triumph.

Even during the early years, measurement professionals were attuned to the consequences of testing, both positive and negative. Researchers such as Monroe and Tyler were early ambassadors for evaluating testing policies from an ethical perspective, arguing that assessment should have a positive impact on education. Messick sought to raise the profile of values, social consequences and ethical evaluation more generally by giving them a more prominent position in the conceptual landscape of educational and psychological measurement. Lee Cronbach (1971) had raised the profile of consequences already through the importance that he attached to investigating utility in addition to validity, emphasizing an area of research in which he had been heavily involved (e.g. Cronbach and Gleser, 1957, 1965). Messick wanted to take this one step further by locating consequences right at the very heart of validity theory. In doing so, he undoubtedly raised their profile to another level. However, in light of the emotive debate that followed, and the confusion that his writing engendered, it is fair to say that his mission was not entirely successful. The extension of validity theory to embrace both scientific and ethical concerns proved to be Messick's tribulation.

The Messick years: triumph and tribulation

Of course, Messick was not the only person to have been writing authoritatively on validity and validation during the period between 1975 and 1999. Cronbach continued to contribute landmark papers (e.g. Cronbach, 1980a, 1988, 1989a). This was also the period during which Michael Kane developed his argument-based approach to validation (e.g. Kane, 1982, 1990, 1992), and many other significant papers were published along the way, including Schmidt and Hunter (1977), Tenopyr (1977), Linn (1978, 1980), Rozeboom (1978), Hambleton (1980), Ebel (1983), Embretson (1983), Norris (1983), Mossholder and Arvey (1984), Lawshe (1985), Haertel (1985), contributions to Wainer and Braun (1988), Frederiksen and Collins (1989), Linn et al. (1991), Moss (1992, 1994), Hubley and Zumbo (1996), Jonson and Plake (1998) and Sireci (1998a, 1998b) to name but a few – as well as many other articles that are discussed in more detail below.

Yet the zeitgeist of the period was not simply captured in the body of work produced by Messick; between the mid-1970s and the late 1990s it was stimulated, moulded and sustained by his thinking. The Messick years took root with the publication of a landmark paper, 'The standard problem: meaning and values in measurement and evaluation' (Messick, 1975), and culminated in the publication of the fifth edition of the *Standards* (AERA et al., 1999). The section on validity within the *Standards* was not actually written by Messick; it was a consensus product of the North American educational and psychological measurement communities. Yet not only did it epitomize his substantive thesis, it also mirrored his confusing discussion of the role of consequences in validation (Newton, 2012a). Therefore, it can be seen as a distillation of the Messick years, published in the year following his death.

The idea of triumph and tribulation is meant to capture the premise of this chapter: that Messick's unification of validity theory was only partly successful. He undoubtedly succeeded in unifying the science of validity, following the lead of Loevinger (1957), but his attempt to unify science and ethics within a broad validity framework ultimately failed.

The Messick years prefigured

Messick's *magnum opus* was his chapter in *Educational Measurement*, 'Validity' (Messick, 1989a). This was a vast, sophisticated, all-embracing account of his position as it had evolved by the end of the 1980s. In a prefatory note, he explained that it was written in honour of Harold Gulliksen, with particular credit given to his paper entitled 'Intrinsic validity' (Gulliksen, 1950). The twin pillars of Messick's thesis were prefigured clearly in this article: both the scientific approach to validity, which goes beyond surface appearances and simplistic conclusions; and the ethical approach to validity, which recognizes the consequences of testing. Indeed, Gulliksen (1950) had illustrated what was to become a central tenet of Messick's thesis: that what might appear at first to be the consequences of merely social or ethical significance (e.g. coaching students to pass tests, with a negative impact on teaching and learning) are also often of technical or scientific significance (e.g. when they exploit a weakness of test design, thereby rendering inferences from test scores invalid).

The Messick years were prefigured also in two reports that he published a decade before his landmark paper (Messick, 1964, 1965). Both papers, written in a climate of severe criticism of educational and psychological testing (e.g. Hoffman, 1962) and growing threat of external regulation of the testing industry, began by acknowledging the importance of both scientific and ethical evaluation:

> The two major criticisms discussed earlier, that some tests are poor in quality and that tests are often misused, parallel two major questions that arise in evaluating the appropriateness of a particular test administration: (a) Is the test any good as a measure of the characteristic it purports to assess? (b) Should the test be used for its present purpose? (Messick, 1965: 138)

Messick presented essentially the same analysis in a paper that was published nearly a decade later. Using almost the same words that he had used a decade earlier, he added:

> The first question is a scientific one; it may be answered by appraising the test's psychometric properties, especially its construct validity. The second question is an ethical one; it must be answered by evaluating the potential consequences of the testing in terms of human values. Both questions must be addressed whenever testing is considered. (Messick and Anderson, 1974: 22)

This belief was voiced in the context of increasing public debate over the defensibility of testing (e.g. following the publication of Jensen, 1969), and a demand from the Association of Black Psychologists for a moratorium on all testing of black people. Messick insisted that the debate engendered by this critique confused scientific questions concerning the adequacy of tests with ethical questions concerning the inadequacy of much testing practice. The two issues, he insisted, were not only 'separable but must be separated' (Messick and Anderson, 1974: 22).

To separate or not to separate? This really is the question that sets the scene for the Messick years. Within his first major contribution to validity theory, Messick (1975) indeed did treat the two issues fairly separately, albeit emphasizing their interrelatedness. However, within his second contribution, Messick (1980) intentionally fused them within a four-way progressive matrix representing a unified conception of test validity built on the foundation of a unified conception of construct validity. The *fusion* of ethical and scientific concerns was to prove a site of tension, and even Messick seemed to roll back from this new liberal position on the scope of validity to a more traditional one. The following sections of this chapter explore the new science of validity, according to Messick, his progressive matrix, and the apparent ebb-and-flow of his thinking on social consequences in validity and validation. It concludes by considering how his thinking impacted on the fourth and fifth edition of the *Standards*.

The new science of validity

The second edition of *Educational Measurement* (Thorndike, 1971a) contained a chapter entitled 'Test validation', written by the academic champion of validity and validation of his time, Lee Cronbach (Cronbach, 1971). Nearly two decades had passed since Cronbach had led work on the first edition of the *Standards*, which spawned his classic treatise on construct validity (Cronbach and Meehl, 1955). During that period, as Messick (1975) observed, Cronbach had come to stress the more general relevance of construct-thinking: constructs were not simply relevant to clinicians and counsellors, for whom construct validity had been originally invented, but to scientists and professionals across all of the sub-domains of educational and psychological measurement. Indeed, because one validated interpretations of test scores, not tests per se, this located constructs firmly at the heart of *all* educational and psychological measurement as the concepts through which attributes were defined and interpreted. In principle, this opened the door to a more embracing account of validation built on a foundation of construct validity. However, in practice, this door remained largely shut until at least the middle of the 1970s, when Messick, Guion and others turned their efforts to wedging it firmly open.

Deeply entrenched fragmentation

When Cronbach and Meehl (1955) developed the idea of construct validation, they readily acknowledged that it would be desirable to determine the psychological constructs that accounted for almost any test (1955: 282). However, they presented their thesis as if they were introducing a particular kind of validity to be used in a specific kind of setting. It was especially suitable for clinicians, counsellors and any other practitioner who was unable to fall back on either the logical gold standard of content validity, or the empirical gold standard of criterion validity. Consequently, as a new wave of clinicians, counsellors and academic researchers began to explore the potential of construct validation, the majority of educational and psychological measurement professionals fell back on what they considered to be their respective gold standards.

In Chapter 3 we saw how fragmented, separatist views of validity and validation became entrenched during the 1960s and early 1970s. In education, this was influenced by the criterion-referenced testing movement. In personnel psychology, it was influenced by the civil rights movement and subsequent employment guidelines and orders. At a more theoretical level, even experts such as Cronbach still drew a fundamental distinction between description and decision-making.

Messick's mission

Messick (1975) sought to eliminate separatist thinking. His two-pronged attack insisted not simply that construct validation was the only defensible approach for evaluating descriptions, but also that construct validation was the only defensible foundation for evaluating decision-making. Thus, following Lennon (1956) and Loevinger (1957), he dismissed the belief that content-related evidence on its own was sufficient to judge measurement quality, particularly the quality of measurement in educational settings. In addition, he dismissed the belief that criterion-related evidence on its own was sufficient to judge the quality of decision-making, particularly the quality of predictions made in personnel contexts.

In staking this claim, he rejected any lingering vestige of the idea that prediction could be evaluated independently of measurement. In short, Messick (1975) went even further than Cronbach (1971) and Loevinger (1957) by emphasizing that construct validity was the rational basis for evaluating both measurement quality and decision-making quality. As far as validity was concerned, the distinction between measurement (description) and prediction (decision) was artificial, since the rational basis for defending prediction was a prior defence of measurement. This necessarily required construct validation: that is, scientific inquiry into score meaning.

Therefore, Messick's primary mission was to rebut this deeply entrenched fragmentation by emphasizing that construct validity was at the heart of all validity. This required not one-off validation studies, but extensive research programmes: the collation of 'a mosaic of research evidence' (Messick, 1980: 1019) comprising content-related evidence, criterion-related evidence and all sorts of additional evidence. Indeed, he challenged the very idea of 'content validity' and 'criterion validity' – as independently existing *kinds* of validity – on the basis that validity comes in only one flavour: construct validity (Messick, 1980).

Messick, who spent his career at the Educational Testing Service, becoming a vice president and then distinguished research scientist, found an ally in Guion, an academic from Bowling Green State University, who specialized in personnel psychology (see Guion, 1974, 1976, 1977a, 1977b, 1978a, 1978b, 1980). Each inspired the other, and they developed similar conclusions on the importance of unification. Into the 1980s, Messick developed his position with more breadth and depth, and ultimately with more influence. This is why we refer to this period as the 'Messick years', and why we present this chapter largely from his perspective.

Why 'content validity' is insufficient

Messick (1975) observed that content validity was understood generally in a manner consistent with the first edition of the *Standards*:

> Content validity is evaluated by showing how well the content of the test samples the class of situations or subject matter about which conclusions are to be drawn. Content validity is especially important in the case of achievement and proficiency measures. (APA et al., 1954: 13)

According to Messick, this characterization risked giving the impression that content validity was basically about the content of a test – that is, how well the content of a test sampled the content of its domain. It risked giving the impression that this was the appropriate kind of validity to establish for achievement or proficiency tests: that content-related evidence was sufficient for establishing the validity (or invalidity) of tests such as this. Content validation typically involved a one-off-study conducted by a panel of expert judges who engaged in a process of logical analysis of the relationship between test content and the specification of content for a domain. Across a series of publications, from Messick (1975) to Messick (1992), this conception of validity and validation was condemned repeatedly.

At least part of the reason for the lingering emphasis on content (as a foundation for validity) and logical analysis (as a foundation for validation) was the persistence of operationist thinking in certain quarters. As we discussed in Chapter 3, operationism was the legacy of a philosophical movement which believed that real science had no place for metaphysical attributes such as intelligence, ability or even proficiency. Strictly speaking, the test did not measure proficiency; it measured simply the content that it measured, and this, so the story went, could be verified by a straightforward process of observation. Messick (1975) argued forcefully that while strict operationist thinking required test scores to be interpreted in terms of content alone, ultimately it was impossible to avoid interpreting results at a higher level: that is, in terms of psychological attributes such as achievement, proficiency or ability. For example, a test that required students to spell a random sample of all of the English words which ended in 'ugh' was, ultimately and unavoidably, a test of their *ability* to spell words ending in 'ugh'.

There are two dimensions to this interpretation: generalization and extrapolation. Generalization takes us from observed performance on the test content to hypothetical performance on the content domain: for example, from 19 out of 20 words correct to 95 per cent of all words ending in 'ugh' correct. Extrapolation takes us from hypothetical performance on the content domain to a more general statement about student ability, proficiency or suchlike: for example, to a very high level of ability to spell words ending in 'ugh'.[1] The idea of operationism might recommend the dictum: 'generalize but do not extrapolate'. Yet generalization is a very curious fiction in the absence of extrapolation. The student did not actually answer 95 per cent of all words ending in 'ugh' correctly, so it is not a report of *actual performance*. And it is hard to see how the idea of a *hypothetical performance* could make sense if claims concerning ability, proficiency, or suchlike, were intentionally withheld. In short, generalization is of no significance in its own right, other than as a launch pad for extrapolation.

Why might such an arcane debate be of any interest to anyone, especially to educational practitioners with a remit for validation and with little interest in philosophy? Well, when discussed naturally in terms of psychological attributes such as ability, it becomes obvious that the traditional method of content validation – the logical analysis of test content – offers nothing more than a partial warrant for generalization and extrapolation. All that it helps to establish is the relevance and representativeness of the content of the test items in relation to the content of a well-defined domain. This is not at all the same thing as establishing the relevance and representativeness of *responses* to the content of test items (Lennon, 1956). Ultimately, of course, we are not interested in tests, but in responses; since responses are the evidence base for educational and psychological measurement: that is, the basis for drawing inferences concerning those who are tested. This recognition entails a variety of related implications for validity and validation, which Messick repeatedly teased out.

First, irrespective of whether the sample of test content is relevant, representative and large enough, it might still fail to elicit the responses that it should. Respondents might fail to demonstrate their true level of ability for all sorts of irrelevant reasons. They might lack motivation to perform optimally, and therefore fail to exert sufficient effort in completing the test. Or they might be motivated to perform optimally, but be prevented from doing so by the way in which the demands of the task are presented: for example, confusingly worded questions or instructions that require an inappropriately high level of reading proficiency. Alternatively, students might produce high-quality responses without actually engaging the processes supposedly associated with the sampled content, as when content intended to elicit a process of reasoning actually engages a process of recall: a classic consequence of test coaching. Problems such as these – *construct-irrelevant easiness* (leading to artificially high scores) and *construct-irrelevant difficulty* (leading to artificially low scores) – mean that a test which has satisfied a group of expert judges on the basis of *a priori* logical analysis still might fall short when actually administered.

Second, even when test content remains identical from one administration to the next, if the population differs or the context of administration differs, the likelihood of appropriate responding might change. Indeed, following exactly the same logic, the likelihood of appropriate responding might differ across different sub-groups of the population during a single administration. For example, a science test that presented no reading comprehension barrier to high-achieving students might present a substantial barrier to low-achieving ones. Once again, a test that appears to be satisfactory in a general sense might fall short under specific conditions of administration or for specific groups.

Third, for all of these reasons, empirical evidence becomes a necessary component of validation in addition to logical analysis. Such evidence might come from 'think aloud' studies, in which respondents are asked to verbalize the cognitive processes in which they engage when answering questions. Or it might come from statistical analyses of response consistency, undertaken to investigate whether items which are assumed to elicit similar responses are actually responded to similarly.

Fourth, judgements of content relevance and representativeness can carry little weight if the scoring of test responses is demonstrably inconsistent or biased. Therefore, it is not only the interpretation of responses that matters, but also the interpretation of scores assigned to those responses. Logical and empirical evidence on scoring quality is also a necessary component of validation.

Concern for the process of responding to test items (which goes beyond concern for item content per se) takes us from the kind of *logical* analysis that had been traditionally associated with content validation, to a kind of *psychological* analysis that was characteristic of construct validation (Messick, 1975). In particular, Messick insisted that content validation provided an entirely insufficient basis for interpreting low scores since, in order to interpret a low score as indicative of low achievement, a range of plausible alternative explanations for poor performance would need to be discounted, such as low motivation, poor reading comprehension, test anxiety, fatigue, sensory impairment, etc. Messick considered the discounting of plausible rival hypotheses to be the 'hallmark' of construct validation (Messick, 1989a: 24). As traditionally conceived, content validation was concerned purely with tests. According to Messick, proper validation – that is, construct validation – was concerned with tests as well as with justifying the interpretation of test responses and test scores.

Why 'criterion validity' is insufficient

Early editions of the *Standards* seemed equally over-simplistic in their discussion of criterion validity, for example:

> Criterion-related validity is demonstrated by comparing the test scores with one or more external variables considered to provide a direct measure of the characteristic or behavior in question. (APA et al., 1966: 13)

According to Messick, this characterization risked giving the impression that criterion validity was tantamount to a coefficient of correlation, derived from a one-off study into the statistical relationship between test scores and criterion scores. The *Standards* also risked giving the impression that only certain kinds of test, e.g. aptitude tests, were the proper subject of criterion validation exercises and, indeed, that criterion-related evidence might be considered sufficient for establishing the validity (or invalidity) of such tests. Once more, across a series of publications, Messick repeatedly condemned this conception of validity and validation.

Again, the superficial plausibility of this over-simplistic conception was explained partly by the persistence of operationist thinking in certain quarters. Those who assumed that each criterion measure constituted an operational definition of 'that which was to be predicted', thereby furnished themselves with an excuse to ignore the criterion problem that had been widely debated since the 1940s (see Chapter 2). By treating the idea of a 'direct measure' (APA et al., 1966: 13) too literally, they blurred a critical distinction between criterion measures and criterion constructs.

Messick put the criterion problem at the heart of his critique of criterion validity. In fact, he observed that the challenge faced in personnel and guidance contexts typically involved two separate criterion problems. Thus, when predicting future job proficiency on the basis of current aptitude, two distinct questions were raised:

1   To what extent is it possible for us to measure aptitude (defined by our predic-
    tor construct) with our aptitude test (the predictor measure)?
2   To what extent is it possible for us to measure job proficiency (defined by our
    criterion construct) with our job proficiency evaluation (the criterion measure)?

Historically, criterion validity often had been defined purely in terms of the correlation between a predictor measure and a criterion measure. However, by the end of
the 1940s, the error of this over-simplification had become very apparent to aptitude
researchers (e.g. Toops, 1944; Thorndike, 1949). They had come to appreciate that
often, everyday criterion measures were seriously inadequate when judged against
idealized criterion constructs: that is, when they were judged against that which the
criterion measure was supposed to measure (see Austin and Villanova, 1992 for an
excellent discussion of the history of the criterion problem). Therefore, the need to
demonstrate the validity of criterion measures became increasingly apparent.

    Messick, with due credit to Guion (1976) and Gulliksen (1950), extended this
line of reasoning by emphasizing that beyond the criterion problem lay the *predictor problem*. This was an important watershed move, since it indicated that
prediction and measurement were not two distinct enterprises, since prediction
ought to be premised on measurement. Traditionally, predictors had been developed to predict, whereas measures had been developed to measure. This is how
Cronbach (1949) and many others presented it, observing that the proof of pud-
ding is in the eating as far as prediction is concerned: if we know that it predicts,
then we know that it predicts; we do not also need to know what, if anything, a
predictor actually measures. Messick rejected this presumption, arguing that predictors should be treated as measures, and therefore should be evaluated in relation to predictor constructs: 'Harold Gulliksen ... made it clear that if you do not
know what predictor and criterion scores mean, you do not know much of anything in applied measurement' (Messick, 1989a: 13). As such, aptitude testing
involved a double duty of construct validation: evaluating the construct validity
of the predictor measure in relation to the predictor construct; and evaluating the
construct validity of the criterion measure in relation to the criterion construct.
This line of thinking has been developed in recent years by Binning and Barrett
(1989) and Guion (2011).

    In expressing validity in terms of the (hypothetical) relationship between predic-
tor measure and criterion construct, Messick re-theorized the role of predictive
evidence in validation practice. He thereby assimilated from Guion (1976) the idea
of validity as the hypothesis of a substantive relationship between predictor measure
and criterion construct. According to this principle, evidence from correlational studies could not be assumed to provide a direct *empirical* justification for the predictive
use of test scores. Instead, it provided support for the hypothesis of a substantive
relationship between predictor measure and criterion construct. That is, it provided
empirical support for a logical or *rational* justification for the predictive use of test
scores. Thus, Messick dismissed the legitimacy of blindly empiricist approaches to
test development.

In summary, Messick put measurement at the heart of prediction, believing that there needed to be a rational basis for prediction, not simply an empirical one. This required empirical evidence and logical analysis to support three separate claims:

1   the attribute defined by the predictor construct can effectively be measured using the predictor measure
2   the attribute defined by the criterion construct can effectively be measured using the criterion measure
3   there is a substantive relationship between the predictor construct and the criterion construct, which justifies the use of test results for predicting criterion values.

Empirical evidence of correlation often provided the principal warrant for claim 3, although Messick followed Guion (1974) in observing that it need not do so, for example, if small sample sizes prohibited the collection of evidence such as this. In the absence of any empirical evidence of a substantive relationship, we might instead rely upon logical analysis – of the relatedness of the predictor to the criterion, e.g. job-relatedness – bolstered by construct validity evidence relating to each of the measures in isolation.

The general relevance of nomological networks

As Messick challenged the insufficiency of content validity and criterion validity, he also began to explain the general relevance of nomological network thinking, which was fundamental to construct validity. His reconceptualization of prediction provides a good example of this. Typically, predictive relationships had been viewed as little more than empirical evidence in support of decision-making. In fact, it had often been assumed that nothing more than empirical evidence of correlation was required in order to justify a decision-making procedure. This is why traditionally, aptitude tests were developed purely to maximize efficient prediction, with relatively little attention given to item content – hence the idea of blind empiricism.

In stark contrast, Messick (1980) argued that prediction was just one of many relationships that established the meaning of a measure. This invoked the idea from construct validity of a nomological network: a network of relationships between constructs. The nomological network provided a useful way of thinking about the relationship between predictor constructs and criterion constructs. This particular predictive relationship that criterion validity had prioritized was just one of many relationships in the nomological network of the predictor construct. In other words, criterion validity was nothing more than a special case of construct validity. Thus, criterion validation was to be subsumed within construct validation, which involved putting such hypothesized relationships to the test.

The idea of a nomological network of relationships also helped to explain the significance of social consequences to validation. Of course, criterion validation was nothing more than an investigation into one kind of social consequence. Understood from this perspective, *any* construct-relevant social consequence (desirable or undesirable) could be considered as a node or strand within a nomological network. Messick referred to consequences within the nomological network as 'action inferences' as opposed to 'interpretive inferences' (e.g. Messick, 1989b: 6).[2] This implied that a person with a certain level of attribute x would, *by definition*, be likely to behave in certain ways: that is, the definition of the attribute itself contained implications for future behaviour. The inference of a certain level of attribute x was the interpretive inference, while corresponding inferences concerning likely behaviour were action inferences. Importantly, where action inferences followed from the interpretive inference, consequential evidence would constitute post-hoc evidence of validity of the interpretive inference.

In order to appreciate the significance of this claim, imagine that we wish to measure a certain level of 'readiness' for a particular educational setting: for example, to decide whether or not children of a certain age should be admitted to the first year of primary education. If so, then the very definition of the attribute 'readiness' would contain a host of action inferences. These action inferences would specify the likely consequences of placing students in one setting as opposed to another: for example, we would predict that students who were judged to be 'ready to progress' ought to make better progress when placed in that setting, and that students who were judged to be 'not ready to progress' ought to make worse progress. As such, evidence of the consequences from decision-making (whether or not students actually did make the progress that they were predicted to make) would contribute to the scientific inquiry into score meaning. Messick was insistent that consideration of consequences such as these was fundamental to the science of validity.

From this perspective, both score-based interpretations and score-based actions were integral to score meaning, and both led to testable inferences. This was the whole point of the nomological network. It provided a framework for generating and testing theoretically grounded hypotheses, emphasizing that validation was quintessentially both data-driven and theory-driven. He described validation as scientific inquiry into score meaning, which involved testing interpretive inferences and action inferences derived from nomological networks, framed in terms of constructs, through which attributes and their implications were understood. Thus, validation involved empirical evaluation of both the meaning and consequences of measurement (Messick, 1992).

The ethical imperative underpinning construct validity

It is worth noting that Messick's justification for putting measurement (i.e. score meaning) at the heart of prediction – indeed, at the heart of all applied uses of test scores – was as much ethical as scientific. It was not only scientifically remiss to overlook construct validity but also ethically irresponsible, since a thorough understanding of score meaning was essential in order to be able to foresee the likely social consequences of testing (Messick, 1964). Consider the converse: imagine, for example, a test for predicting success at university which has been developed on blindly empirical principles, using the final university grade as the criterion measure. Assuming that there is evidence of a strong statistical relationship between results on the predictor test and final grade achieved, why might there be reason to question the use of predictions thus obtained?

One reason is that we might have failed to have noticed a disjunction between our criterion measure and the criterion construct that we *really ought* to have been predicting: e.g. career success, rather than success at university. If so, then we would have rejected students who might well have performed only moderately at university but who would have blossomed in later life, potentially depriving them of their opportunity to make it onto their career ladder in the first place. Alternatively, we might have failed to notice that we were actually measuring an attribute that merely correlated with success at university, and for somewhat questionable reasons, e.g. social conformity. If so, we would have rejected students who might well have performed excellently at university and in their subsequent career, simply due to their unconventional status. Therefore, construct validation – rigorous scientific inquiry into score meaning – was fundamental to Messick for scientific respectability *and* ethical defensibility.

Not only was there an ethical imperative to be able to explain the rational basis for test use, but rigorous scientific inquiry into score meaning also would provide crucial insight into where to look for the possible consequences of test use: in particular, unanticipated negative side-effects. In the absence of this insight, unfortunate consequences might well remain unnoticed. This is what Messick meant when he insisted that 'the meaning of the measure must also be pondered in order to evaluate responsibly the possible consequences of the proposed use' (1975: 956). His reasoning went something like this. First, there always will be consequences arising from test use. Some of them will be construct-relevant and intended: for example, when the best candidate for a job is selected on the basis of an accurate assessment. Others will be construct-irrelevant and unintended: for example, when a poor candidate happens to be selected on the basis of an inaccurate assessment. Second, since all tests are (inevitably) imperfect, there always will be a certain amount of construct-irrelevant variance in test scores, and therefore always some likelihood of construct-irrelevant unintended consequence. Third, we have a duty to understand as fully as possible the nature and prevalence of construct-irrelevant variance in test scores, in order to be in a position to judge whether the construct-relevant intended consequences are likely on balance to outweigh the construct-irrelevant unintended ones. In short, the full meaning of the measure – setting out the reasons why scores vary, including unintended reasons – always needs to be understood in order to be able to evaluate test use responsibly.

All validity is construct validity

By the middle of the 1980s, the impact of equality legislation in personnel settings had resulted in much dissatisfaction with formulaic and over-simplistic interpretations of validity and validation. Landy (1986) mocked current practice, characterizing it as little more than stamp collecting: if your test measures achievement, then consult the content validation checklist and paste your evidence in the content validity space; if your test measures a construct, then consult the construct validation checklist, and paste your evidence in the construct validity space, and so on. Validation, he believed, ought not to be so formulaic. Guion (1980) identified an even more extreme tendency resulting from opportunistic interpretation of the 1978 revision of the Equal Employment Opportunity Commission Guidelines. For example, if a researcher had failed to demonstrate criterion validity, then they might fall back on content validity; and if they then failed to demonstrate content validity, they subsequently might fall back on construct validity. This way of thinking about validation was perverse, Guion observed: it gives the researcher not one, but three different roads to psychometric salvation. According to Messick and Guion, the antidote to formulaic and opportunistic interpretation was to treat validity as a unitary concept, where:

> The unifying nature of the validity of measurement is found in the degree to which the results of measurement (the numbers or scores) represent magnitudes of the intended attribute. (Guion, 1980: 385)

Thus, a fragmented, trinitarian conception of validity was to be transformed into a synoptic unitarian one. Construct validity, it seemed, held the key to this transformation. As Loevinger (1957) had observed more than two decades previously, construct validity was now to be understood as *all* of validity. From a personnel context, Guion had demonstrated forcefully that constructs were central to the validation of aptitude tests. From an educational context, Messick had demonstrated forcefully that constructs were central to the validation of achievement tests. Both agreed that validity was unified through construct validation, which established score meaning, and which therefore provided the rational basis for score use. Neither content validity nor criterion validity could be considered a gold standard any longer – there were no gold standards anymore, just rigorous scientific inquiry into score meaning.

According to Messick, the error underlying both content validity and criterion validity was to foreclose debate too early. The concepts failed to encourage evaluators to explore *plausible counter-hypotheses*, thereby implicitly discouraging them from conducting additional logical analysis or collecting additional empirical evidence that might threaten the claim to validity. The scientific approach embodied within construct validation championed an opposing view which was encapsulated in the image of 'a mosaic of convergent and discriminant findings supportive of score meaning' (Messick, 1992: 1492).

The principle of seeking both *convergent* and *discriminant* evidence was fundamental for Messick. This was not in the sense of advocating sole or even primary reliance upon the multitrait-multimethod (MTMM) methodology developed by Campbell and Fiske (1959). It was in the sense of adopting an open-minded stance to the interpretation of score meaning, actively exploring alternative explanations whenever feasible. Evaluators ought to adopt a rigorous and thorough approach to validation, and should attempt to marshal as much logical analysis and empirical evidence as was possible. Messick conceived of construct validation as a never-ending process of accumulating and synthesizing empirical evidence and logical analysis – just like science itself – in a quest to provide the very best possible account of score meaning. Moreover, like science itself, Messick considered validation to be grounded in theory-testing. It required both a *theory of the attribute* (with general implications for behaviour in non-test situations), and a *theory of the testing process* (with specific implications for behaviour in test situations). The central tenets of Messick's validity theory – the new science of construct validation – can be summarized as follows:

1   'One validates, not a test, *but an interpretation of outcomes from a measurement procedure*' (Cronbach, 1971: 447). This insight is often traced to Cronbach's 'Educational Measurement' chapter (hence this quotation), but in an important sense it always has been at the heart of educational and psychological measurement, to the extent that different uses have been traditionally assumed to imply different interpretations of test results (e.g. Lindquist, 1936; APA et al., 1954; Cronbach and Meehl, 1955). Indeed, as Lindquist and others before him observed, it might be valid to interpret results in terms of a particular attribute for one group but not for another group, or in one context of administration but not another. In short, the claim to validity is *conditional* and *specific* to a particular interpretation and use of results. This is the first pillar of Messick's validity theory, because test results are interpreted in terms of the construct that defines the particular attribute that supposedly is being measured.

2   Validity is premised on measurement. As mentioned previously, the classic definition of validity – the extent to which a test measures what it is supposed to measure – was proposed as early as the 1920s. However, the centrality of measurement was displaced by the idea that prediction implied a somewhat different kind of validity, and was obscured further by the fragmentation of validity from the mid-1950s. Messick firmly quashed the suggestion that validity of prediction was logically distinct from validity of measurement, arguing that demonstrating measurement quality through construct validation provided the rational basis for prediction and the predictive uses of results. Indeed, score meaning provided the rational basis for each and every applied use of results. Therefore, Messick can be credited with reinstating the centrality of measurement to validity theory.

3   All validity is construct validity. Loevinger (1957) was quick to spot the error of the first edition of the *Standards*, which was to establish construct validity as though it were somehow complementary to content and criterion approaches, rather than a superordinate category. Although the idea of construct validity at the heart of Messick's validity theory was essentially that of Cronbach and Meehl (1955), it was presented without much of the philosophical baggage. Construct validity, according to Messick, concerned score meaning. Yet the constructs that defined score meaning did not need to be conceived as unobservable, theoretical postulates in the way that Cronbach and Meehl (1955) seemed to imply.

4   Validity is a faceted concept. Although there was to be only one kind of validity – construct validity – it was still useful to cut and combine validity evidence. Messick chose to do so using a progressive matrix representing two interconnected facets: the source of justification of the testing (evidential basis vs. consequential basis); and the function or outcome of the testing (test interpretation vs. test use). This is discussed in some detail below.

5   Validation is scientific inquiry. In the introduction to his seminal chapter (Messick, 1989a), Messick explained that it was intended to amplify two principles: validity as a unitary but faceted concept, and validation as scientific inquiry. Therefore, construct validation was no more nor less than scientific inquiry into score meaning, which involved testing hypotheses derived from interpretive theories of score meaning. Thus, validation 'embraces all of the experimental, statistical, and philosophical means by which hypotheses and scientific theories are evaluated' (Messick, 1989b: 6).

6   Discounting plausible rival hypotheses is the hallmark of construct validation. This tenet is related to Messick's view of validation as scientific inquiry, and his respect for the principle of falsification within the philosophy of science. Both content validity and criterion validity shared a bias towards confirmation, seeking evidence that might support a desired interpretation, but not evidence that might challenge it. In contrast, at the heart of construct validation was the search for convergent and discriminant evidence: convergent evidence supporting a purported score interpretation; and discriminant evidence discounting plausible alternative interpretations (Messick, 1992). Messick (1989a: 34) emphasized that there were two principal threats to valid interpretation that needed to be addressed: 'construct under-representation', a failure to assess all aspects of the focal attribute in their correct proportion; and 'construct-irrelevant test variance', whereby factors other than the focal attribute cause test scores to vary for irrelevant reasons.[3] Messick (1989a: 24) traced the argument for testing plausible rival hypotheses from Popper (1959[1935]), through Campbell (1957), and then to Cronbach (1971). Wiliam (personal email communication, 16 April 2013) has emphasized to us its synergy with the epistemology of Churchman (1971), whose work on inquiry systems influenced Messick greatly.

7   Validity is a matter of degree. Despite warnings to the contrary in all editions of the *Standards*, the temptation to declare tests either valid or invalid remains strong, as though validity were an all-or-nothing concept. In fact, the contrary principle – that validity comes in degrees – was explicit even during the early years, and embodied in the idea of a validity coefficient. Although Messick cast validity in terms of an overall evaluative judgement, which might encourage all-or-nothing thinking, he emphasized that validity was always a matter of degree.

8   Validation is a never-ending process. If neither content validity nor criterion validity could provide a gold standard for validation research, this raised a fundamental question concerning the relevance and necessity of each of a range of potential sources of empirical evidence and logical analysis. How much of what

kind of evidence and analysis was required in order to establish a claim to validity? Early on, Messick (1980) explained that talk of necessary and sufficient requirements for validation over-simplified what was now a complex and holistic concept. Since at any point new evidence could cast doubt on previous interpretations, it was difficult to claim sufficiency for any particular source of evidence. Similarly, since construct validation envisaged a dense mosaic of evidence, it was difficult to claim that any particular source of evidence was necessary. More fundamentally, Messick saw validation as a never-ending process: not simply because new evidence could threaten established conclusions; but also because new evaluators could reach different conclusions on the basis of the same evidence.

These principles represented a new, scientific approach, and the idea of validation as a one-off study no longer had any currency. Validity was more complicated than that, and validation was much harder work.

The new practice of validation

Validation was much harder work because it necessarily involved the integration of empirical evidence and logical analysis from multiple sources. Throughout the 1980s, Messick tended to categorize these sources within one of the four cells of his progressive matrix. However, for reasons explained below, his matrix proved to be unpopular. During the 1990s he downplayed the matrix, perhaps as a consequence of this, instead grouping the sources within six categories (e.g. Messick, 1995b, 1996):

1 the content aspect
2 the substantive aspect
3 the structural aspect
4 the generalizability aspect
5 the external aspect
6 the consequential aspect.

These categories did feature in Messick (1989a), although the chapter was structured primarily in terms of the matrix, so the categories featured in relation to specific cells, with some (such as content) featuring significantly in more than one cell. The first five categories featured most heavily in his discussion of cell 1, which Messick described as the 'evidential basis of test interpretation' and constituted the heart of his science of validity. He discussed the consequential aspect in other cells, notably cell 4, which he described as the 'consequential basis of test use'. (We too leave the discussion of consequences until later.)

The *content* aspect concerned content relevance and representativeness. First, the boundaries of the attribute needed to be defined, specifying what to include in or exclude from the domain. This would involve developing at least a rudimentary theory of the attribute, in order to enable the sources of construct-relevant difficulty to be understood as the basis for test design and evaluation. In addition to establishing the relevance of tasks to the domain, their representativeness would need to be established to counter the ever-present threat of construct under-representation. Messick (1995a) observed that content relevance and representativeness were established typically using expert judgement on the basis of a logical analysis of test content.

The *substantive* aspect concerned substantive theories, process models and process engagement. In addition to establishing the adequacy of content sampling, the adequacy of process sampling needed to be assured. Moreover, it needed to be established that the processes that were assumed to be engaged in when responding to tasks, actually were engaged in by respondents. Statistical analysis of inter-item consistency might help to indicate whether the same processes were being engaged when responding to items that supposedly engaged the same processes. Qualitative analysis of verbal protocols might help to indicate whether the anticipated processes were engaged for each item. Many other empirical techniques might be employed to explore the same issue.

The *structural* aspect concerned scoring models as reflective of task and domain structure. The quality of test construction provided no reassurance of measurement quality in the absence of evidence concerning the adequacy and appropriateness of procedures for scoring responses. Just as a theory of the attribute should guide the design and evaluation of the test, so too should it guide the design and evaluation of scoring procedures, including procedures for aggregating scores across tasks that comprised the test, as well as for establishing comparability across test forms.

The *generalizability* aspect concerned the boundaries of score meaning. Although the definition of boundaries was covered within the content aspect, providing a foundation for design and evaluation, the fact that testing is a time-limited technology means that neither adequate sampling nor generalization can be taken for granted. Empirical investigation of generalization across occasions, tasks, raters, etc. is always desirable.

Finally, the *external* aspect concerned convergent and discriminant correlations with external variables. Once again, this put the theory of the attribute to the test, in order to establish that relationships predicted to exist were observed in practice; not just evidence of high correlation with variables assumed to be related to the attribute, but evidence of low correlation with variables assumed to be unrelated to the attribute.

Without wanting to be too definitive about the precise number of categories, Messick was clear that 'there are only a half-dozen or so distinct sorts' (1989a: 16). All of these categories bore on the valid interpretation and use of test scores. Therefore, all of these categories were *relevant* to any validation exercise – but was each of these categories of evidence or analysis actually *required* in order to demonstrate validity? Although, as noted above, Messick was reticent to speak of any necessary or sufficient requirements, he did tend to give the impression that all bases really ought to be covered (Moss, 1995). The following passage, which appeared in a very similar form in a number of different publications (e.g. Messick, 1995a, 2000), set out his position quite clearly:

> From the discussion thus far, it should be clear that *test validity cannot rely on any one of the supplementary forms of evidence* just discussed. But neither does *validity require any one form*, as long as there is defensible convergent and discriminant evidence supporting test meaning. To the extent that some form of evidence cannot be developed – as when criterion-related studies must be forgone because of small sample sizes, unreliable or contaminated criteria, and highly restricted score ranges – heightened emphasis can be placed on other evidence, especially on the construct validity of the predictor tests and the relevance of the construct to the criterion domain (Guion, 1976; Messick, 1989). What is required is a compelling argument that the available evidence justifies the test interpretation and use, even though some pertinent evidence had to be forgone. (Messick, 1998a: 70–71, italics in original)

The acknowledgement that a certain source of relevant evidence might have to be forgone, if it really cannot be developed, does seem to give the impression that all categories of evidence should feature in a validation programme if at all possible. However, Messick did state quite explicitly that no one form of evidence was necessarily required, assuming that the argument established on the basis of pre-existing evidence or analysis was sufficiently strong.

The progressive matrix

The progressive matrix was introduced by Messick (1980) to illustrate how the evaluation of scientific and ethical questions could be integrated within a common validity framework, based on a foundation of construct validity. It multiplied his original two questions of science and of ethics into four (Messick, 1981). At the same time, apparently *contra* Messick and Anderson (1974), it stressed that those two questions ought not to be separated.

The progressive matrix is reproduced in Figure 4.1, adapted from a range of alternative versions (e.g. Messick, 1980: 1023; 1988: 42; 1989a: 20; 1992: 1494; 1995a: 748). The cell numbers have been added to clarify our discussion. Messick never actually added numbers to his cells, although in discussing his matrix as progressive, this gave the impression of validation proceeding in some general order from one cell to the next. He explained this by using a flow diagram (see Messick, 1980: 1024) which illustrated progression from construct validity to value implications, to relevance/utility, to social implications. It also illustrated how evidence and conclusions from later stages fed back into earlier ones; so this was not a straightforward progressive matrix per se, but a more complex feedback model for test validity.

The matrix combined two facets:

1   what the assessment culminated in – an *interpretation* versus a *use*; and
2   how the assessment was justified – on the basis of (traditional) *evidence* versus on the basis of (evidence concerning) *values* and *consequences*.

	Test interpretation	Test use
Evidential basis	1 Construct validity (CV)	3 CV + Relevance/utility (R/U)
Consequential basis	2 CV + Value implications (VI)	4 CV + VI + R/U + Social consequences

Figure 4.1   The progressive matrix

The logic of the matrix

The logic of the progressive matrix goes something like this. In cell 1 we have construct validity, the scientific evaluation of score meaning. Construct validity would be established on the basis of the various sources of empirical evidence and logical analysis that were traditionally associated with validity and validation. As such, Messick initially located the first five of his six categories of evidence, described above, within this cell. Therefore, note that even cell 1 in isolation represents a unified conception of construct validity.

Messick illustrated cell 2 in terms of the need to appraise the value implications of score meaning. What he meant by this was that the very act of defining the attribute that was supposed to be measured by a test involved value judgements, and these value judgements needed to be made explicit and interrogated. Any such judgement would need to be articulated through formal construct specification and choosing a name to label the attribute. This process of articulation itself introduced threats to validity: for example, how well did the label reflect the original judgement as to what the test was supposed to measure? Imagine a scale that had been labelled in terms of 'flexibility versus rigidity', rather than 'confusion versus consistency' (Messick, 1989a: 60). Labels such as these would elicit very different value implications, so which value implications were the best match to those originally intended? Therefore, cell 2 required an appraisal of consistency between trait implications (that followed from the construct specification), and evaluative implications (that appeared to follow from the label). Here, the guiding principle was the minimization of inappropriate surplus meaning – implications drawn from the label that ought not to be drawn – especially the minimization of inappropriate evaluative connotations.

The distinction between cell 1 and cell 3 is similar to the distinction that Cronbach (1971) had drawn between assessments that culminated in *descriptions*, and assessments that culminated in *decisions*. However, the motivation for the new progressive matrix was unification, not division. Construct validity was not only unified in its own right, it also provided the glue that would unify the entire matrix. Thus cell 1, test score meaning, provided the rational basis for understanding, and therefore for evaluating test score use. The progressive matrix unified the evaluation of test score interpretation (i.e. description) and test score use (i.e. decision-making) in a manner that departed significantly from Cronbach (1971) and earlier thinking. Clearly, Cronbach (1971) was more sophisticated than earlier thinking, recognizing how description and decision-making were intertwined intimately. Yet in presenting them separately, as though they were somehow logically distinct, this confused matters. Messick believed that his progressive matrix solved the apparent paradox of separate-but-intertwined, thereby straightening out the untidiness of Cronbach's characterization (see Messick, 1989a: 21).

Messick differentiated cell 1 from cell 3 by characterizing them as 'general' versus 'specific'. This implied that it was possible to establish construct validity, in a general sense, yet there was still a need to undertake additional validation research to establish construct validity in a particular local setting for a particular applied use. This was reminiscent of the argument from Guion that a predictor test might have construct validity in terms of whatever it was supposed to be measuring, yet still not be job-related. Job-relatedness would need to be established independently – through the comparison of predictor and criterion constructs – in an attempt to furnish the *specific evidence* (cell 3) that was necessary for buttressing or enhancing the existing *general evidence* (cell 1).

Therefore, the logic of the progressive matrix stood in stark contrast to the logic of earlier fragmented accounts in which, for example, cell 3 evidence (e.g. traditional criterion validity evidence) would have stood independently. According to the new unified account, cell 3 evidence – for example, evidence of a predictive relationship – could never stand independently but only on the foundation of cell 1: a solid understanding of score meaning.

Another way to understand the distinction between cell 1 and cell 3 is in terms of the common practice in the USA of developing achievement tests to reflect the generality of curricula across many different states. Therefore, a test publisher might be able to claim construct validity, in a general sense, at a national level in relation to a generic curriculum. Yet, the use of that test in a particular state would require additional evidence: evidence of construct validity, in a specific sense, at a local level in relation to a specific curriculum (Messick, 1989a: 65).

Finally, cell 4 extended validity to the consideration of social consequences. As the final cell in the progressive matrix, it combined aspects of all three of the cells that preceded it. It was, and has remained, the most controversial of Messick's contributions, and therefore will be discussed in a separate section below on 'The confusing role of social consequences' in validity and validation.

The illogic of the matrix

The progressive matrix was supposed to help readers to cut and combine validity evidence in a manner that not only brought content and criterion considerations under the same umbrella but also embraced values and consequences. Unfortunately, it was presented in a manner that was extremely confusing – if not ultimately confused – as the following observations demonstrate. They extend concerns raised by Shepard (1993, 1997), Markus (1998) and Cizek (2012). First, although the progressive matrix drew a primary distinction between evidential and consequential bases, consequences were still a form of evidence.

Second, Messick characterized cell 2 in terms of the value implications of score meaning, arguing that value implications were not ancillary to score meaning, but central. Yet it is hard to reconcile the idea that value implications are central to score meaning with the fact that they were located in a separate cell labelled 'construct validity *plus* value implications'. Surely cell 2 ought to be the point of departure for both test design and evaluation, not simply a destination along the way? Reckase (1998a) and Wiliam (2010) both made similar points. If value judgements are made clear at the outset, defining the nature and boundaries of the attribute in some detail, then subsequent validation becomes more scientific than ethical concerning the relationship between intended and actual score meaning. Or, to put it more extremely, there can be no validation until the attribute has been characterized in terms of a construct specification. Thus, values are exercised and specified from the outset, and therefore must constitute a reference point for cell 1. Even if values change over time, or if values differ across stakeholders, this simply means changing the construct specification accordingly to provide an alternative yardstick for comparison.

Third, Messick located his discussion of values in the ethical row of his matrix. Yet an important part of his argument was that ultimately, even scientific evaluation was grounded in value judgement (Messick, 1989a: 62). Ironically, much of his discussion of cell 2 was more scientific in essence than ethical, in the sense of seeking consensus rather than dealing with conflict. Thus, he emphasized the importance of supporting value judgements empirically and justifying them rationally (1989a: 63), debating the value implications of construct interpretation in order to edit the kinds of statements that *should* be made (1989a: 60), striving for consistency or commensurability between the trait implications and evaluative implications of construct labels (1989a: 60), and so on. To be fair, he followed Churchman in emphasizing that consensus is the decision rule of science, while conflict is the decision rule of ethics, thus encouraging a genuinely ethical perspective (1989a: 63). Nonetheless, his discussion of implications for validation within cell 2 – within the ethical row – still seemed far more heavily weighted towards scientific concerns and the *appropriate* or *rational* interpretation of test scores.

Fourth, cell 3, which we have characterized so far in terms of relevance, also included aspects of utility and fairness. Considerations such as these take us considerably beyond score meaning and the rational foundation for test use, by emphasizing the costs and benefits of different kinds of decision. They are the very essence of values, consequences and ethical evaluation, which are supposedly represented within the second row of the matrix, not the first.

Fifth, both cell 3 and cell 4 contribute evidence which can and ought to be used in the justification of test interpretation. This was fundamental to Messick's conception of validity; yet they were conceptually separated from test interpretation in a column entitled 'test use'.

Sixth, it is unclear exactly what Messick meant by the concept of progression across the matrix. Did he mean that each new cell embraced an additional aspect of validity? For example, it was explicit that cell 4 was intended to embrace all of the other cells; but it was not at all clear whether cell 3 was supposed to embrace cell 2 (see Table 1 from Messick, 1992 in particular). This was complicated further by the fact that his earliest account discussed value implications second (e.g. Messick, 1980: 1023 and Figure 2), while his later accounts tended to discuss relevance/utility second (e.g. Messick, 1992, 1995a).

In fact, Messick readily acknowledged that the distinctions between cells were fuzzy, overlapping and messy, specifically highlighting certain of the concerns raised above (e.g. Messick, 1989a: 21). He claimed that this was an inevitable consequence of subdividing what was inherently a unitary concept, insisting that the subdivision was useful all the same to highlight a full range of significant concerns. An alternative (and perhaps more parsimonious) reading is that the subdivision simply failed to cut validity at plausible joints.

Finally, consider the most fundamental of questions begged by the matrix: where, exactly, is construct validity supposed to reside? There are at least three candidate answers:

1   cell 1 – pure score meaning
2   cells 1 and 2 – test interpretation
3   cells 1 to 4 combined – validity unified.

Messick often spoke of construct validity in terms of establishing score meaning, which would seem to imply that construct validity resides in the combination of cells 1 and 2: i.e. test interpretation. Conversely, the matrix explicitly represented construct validity in cell 1, and Messick explicitly stated that the other cells involved construct validity *plus* something else. Ultimately, if construct validity was supposed to be all of validity, then surely the whole point of the progressive matrix ought to be that all cells contribute to an overall evaluation of construct validity as a unified concept? (We will return to this dilemma shortly, because it is fundamental to understanding and misunderstanding Messick.)

In conclusion, the idea of the progressive matrix which lies at the heart of the unified theory of validity is extremely confusing. Is this because the complexity of the concept means that any visual representation would be inevitably messy and fuzzy, as Messick claimed? Or is it because the very idea of the matrix was a mistake, as argued most explicitly by Shepard (e.g. 1997: 6)? The following section, which concludes our discussion of the Messick years, culminates in the conclusion that indeed the matrix was a mistake. It not only confused a generation of students of validity, but it may even have confused their teacher: Samuel Messick. If validity somehow needed to integrate the evaluation of both scientific and ethical questions, the progressive matrix failed to illustrate how this was to be achieved.

The confusing role of social consequences

Although cells 2 and 4 were presumed by Messick to comprise the ethical dimension, the majority of debate has focused simply on cell 4: the attempt to introduce evaluation of social consequences into mainstream validity theory. Unfortunately, even limiting our discussion to the consideration of social consequences in cell 4 is confusing enough. For one thing, Messick freely admitted that evidence from social consequences could be equally located in any of the other cells. For another thing, even Messick was unclear as to whether the kind of evaluation that he discussed within cell 4 was essentially ethical or scientific, as will soon become clear.

In Chapter 6 we explore in detail the many ways in which social consequences are relevant to both scientific and ethical evaluation, so we will not labour the point here. However, before discussing how Messick understood their relevance to validity theory, we should clarify exactly what we mean by two of the concepts at the heart of this debate. First, by *social consequence* we mean any impact or side-effect on anyone or anything that somehow is caused by the implementation of a testing policy. Conceived thus broadly, the prefix 'social' is actually superfluous.[4] By *ethical evaluation* we mean an appraisal of the value or worth of consequences arising from implementation of the testing policy. Ethical evaluation is guided by the principle that on balance, benefits ought to outweigh costs. If not, then we would be forced to conclude that implementing the testing policy was worse than not implementing it. (We discuss cost–benefit analyses at length in Chapter 6.)

There is no doubt that Messick considered consequences arising from the implementation of a testing policy to be relevant to the *scientific* evaluation of test score interpretation. However, his reasons are not obvious, and benefit from illustration. Consequences play an important role in the scientific evaluation of measurement quality by providing post-hoc evidence of validity or invalidity. That is, consequences provide evidence to support or challenge a prior claim to validity, gathered after the testing policy has been implemented. Teaching to the test provides a useful illustration. After a few years of administering a high-stakes test, it might be observed that teachers are no longer teaching the full set of learning objectives associated with the curriculum that they are supposed to be following. On further investigation, it might come to light that the objectives no longer taught are those which have been particularly poorly sampled by the test. Of course, no test could sample all learning objectives, but a central tenet of testing is that it is possible to generalize from proficiency evident across the sampled content to proficiency evident across the full content domain. The very fact of teaching to restricted learning objectives undermines this assumption of generalizability, since it implies that scores on the test cannot be interpreted to reflect proficiency across the full content domain. In short, post-hoc evidence from the impact of testing on teaching practice a few years down the line has the potential to undermine any prior claim to high-quality measurement (Koretz, 2005).

Ironically, what *is* in doubt is whether Messick ultimately considered consequences arising from implementation of a testing policy to be relevant to the *ethical* evaluation of test score use. This is ironic, because we began by explaining that the whole point of the progressive matrix was to integrate scientific and ethical evaluation. We now explain our grounds for doubt.

Consequences and the scope of validity theory

> [T]est validity is viewed as an overall evaluative judgment of both the adequacy and the appropriateness of both inferences and actions derived from test scores. (Messick, 1981: 9)

Decades before the Messick years, Loevinger (1957) recognized that construct validity was fundamental to the scientific evaluation of interpretations derived from test scores. During the 1970s and into the 1980s, Messick went further still by arguing that construct validity was fundamental also to the ethical evaluation of actions derived from test scores, because it provided the rational basis for test use and predicting social consequences. As mentioned previously, much of his early work on validity emphasized the importance of considering ethical questions (the justification of test score use) alongside scientific ones (the justification of test score meaning). Indeed, the whole point of the progressive matrix supposedly was to combine ethical and scientific considerations within a unified validity framework, but how far did Messick actually go in extending the scope of validity theory to embrace social consequences? Was his account ultimately scientific, such that validity was about *understanding* the full implications (consequences) of score meaning? Or was his account ultimately ethical, such that validity was about understanding *and valuing* the full implications (consequences) of score meaning *and score use*, including misuse and adverse side-effects?

We believe that Messick shifted his emphasis – or perhaps even unwittingly changed his mind – on this central issue. He appeared to move from a liberal position in which validity ultimately required an overall ethical judgement, to a traditional position in which validity ultimately required an overall scientific judgement. This transition was gradual, it was not made explicit, and both earlier and later accounts were confusing, if not confused. However, the clarity with which his particular positions were argued during the earlier years and later years is sufficient for us to conclude that the transition was real. It involved moving from an intellectual position in which construct validity was just one part of validity, to an intellectual position in which construct validity was all of validity.

Earlier years   In the paper that launched the progressive matrix, Messick (1980) drew an explicit and clear distinction between *test validity* and construct validity. The entire matrix represented the full scope of test validity. Construct validity, by contrast, was located firmly within cell 1, albeit with tentacles reaching out into the remaining cells or (alternatively) with pillars supporting the remaining cells. Whatever the analogy, the cells were distinct in the original version of the matrix because there were aspects of test validity in cells 2 to 4 that went *beyond* construct validity. Messick stated this explicitly and clearly, stopping short 'of equating construct validity with [test] validity [because test] validity entails an evaluation of the value implications of both test interpretation and test use. These implications ... go beyond construct meaning per se' (Messick, 1980: 1015).

Construct validity, Messick argued, was not the narrow alternative to criterion validity or content validity (as Cronbach and Meehl had proposed), but the broad encompassing concept envisaged by Loevinger (1957). Therefore, construct validity was the concept that unified validity scientifically. Conversely, test validity unified validity both scientifically *and* ethically as 'the overall degree of justification for test interpretation and use' (Messick, 1980: 1020). Presented thus, ultimately the overall judgement of test validity was ethical. It concerned the overall worth of a testing programme, judged against alternatives that might well include not operating the programme at all. At the heart of this ethical evaluation was 'the balancing of the instrumental value of the test in accomplishing its intended purpose with the instrumental value of any negative side effects and positive by-products of the testing' (Messick, 1980: 1025). By the time that an evaluator had progressed around the matrix from cell 1 to cell 4, they would have covered all of the test validity bases and be in a position to make this overall evaluative judgement. This same distinction between test validity and construct validity was respected in Messick (1981). Construct validity, he explained, might be fully adequate to support score interpretation, yet 'still not cover all of the validity bases' (1981: 9). It was 'the heart' of validity, but not 'the whole' (1981: 10).

Interestingly, in the first outing of the progressive matrix, Messick (1980) discussed utility modelling and fairness within cell 4 (ethics/consequences), and *not* in cell 3 (science/decisions), where he was later to locate them (see 1980: 1020–1). This would seem to be entirely consistent with an account that originally was attempting to distinguish clearly between scientific and ethical evaluation questions. However, even at this stage, ambiguity was beginning to become apparent, as the Figure 1 illustration of the matrix *did* locate utility in cell 3 (see 1980: 1023). Having said that, his intention may simply have been to highlight the cell 3 technical analysis of utility (as 'usefulness') more than the cell 4 social analysis of utility (as 'valuableness').

Transitional years Messick subsequently appeared to change his emphasis. In a paper discussing findings from a National Academy of Sciences investigation into placing children in special education (of which he was the vice-chair), Messick (1984) stressed the need to distinguish two separate issues:

1 the validity of referral decisions – the validity of the assessment of students' functional needs; and
2 the quality of instruction subsequently received in special education programmes.

He argued that we need to allow conceptual headroom for the possibility that a valid placement decision might be followed by an ineffective intervention, thereby preventing the intended outcome of the decision-making from being achieved. The implications of this position appeared to be twofold. First, a lack of evidence of positive consequences from special education placement does not necessarily challenge the validity of the placement decision, since the failure might be attributable to the quality of the intervention, not to the validity of the assessment. Second, validity relates to the technical quality of assessment and decision-making. Messick explicitly stated that the value of the programme (supported by the assessment-based decision-making procedure) was a separate matter, and one that lay beyond validity.

Interestingly, the term 'test validity' did not appear in Messick (1984), and 'construct validity' appeared only once in passing. Therefore, although his discussion of validity clearly implied the narrow concept of construct validity, it could be argued that he had left conceptual headroom for the broad concept of test validity. After all, even four years later he still accepted that 'construct-related evidence may not be the whole of validity' (Messick, 1988: 35). It is perhaps unclear whether the broad concept of test validity was indeed broad enough to encompass the 'value of the program', which he had distinguished from 'the validity of the placement' (see Messick, 1984: 7 for this distinction). Indeed, maybe this is precisely why he chose not to muddy the water with talk of 'test validity' in this paper.

It is interesting to note how the definition that opened his *magnum opus* failed to distinguish between test validity and construct validity:

> Validity is an integrated evaluative judgment of the degree to which empirical evidence and theoretical rationales support the *adequacy* and *appropriateness* of *inferences* and *actions* based on test scores or other modes of assessment. (Messick, 1989a: 13, italics in original)

Within this chapter, more generally, Messick was actually quite ambiguous over the scope of his new theory of validity. On the one hand, his discussion of cell 1, the essence of construct validity, excluded reference to values and consequences, in line with his earlier view (see Messick, 1989a: 34–58). This seemed to leave conceptual headroom for test validity beyond construct validity; it also seemed to leave space for genuinely ethical evaluation in cell 4, the culmination of the progressive matrix. On the other hand, he now emphasized the pervasive and overarching nature of construct validity, explaining that since all of the cells contributed to the evaluation of score meaning, 'construct validity may ultimately be taken to be the whole of validity in the final analysis' (Messick, 1989a: 21).

This hint of change seemed to be echoed in the summary account of his chapter that he presented in Messick (1989b). This stated explicitly that the appraisal of social consequences was to be subsumed as an aspect of construct validity, adding that all validation is construct validation 'in the sense that all validity evidence contributes to (or undercuts) the empirical grounding or trustworthiness of the score interpretation' (1989b: 8). In the same paper, he also pointed out a further implication, that construct-relevant negative impacts – negative impacts arising from accurate assessment – ought not to result in a judgement of invalidity:

> In particular, it is not that adverse social consequences of test use render the use invalid but, rather, that adverse social consequences should not be attributable to any source of test invalidity such as construct-irrelevant variance. (1989b: 11)

Now, it seemed, Messick was using 'test invalidity' to indicate a narrow, scientific evaluation of score meaning. The implication of this usage was that no construct-relevant adverse consequence, however substantial it might be, could ever be considered a threat to validity, since validity was essentially a matter of score meaning. In fact, evidence of construct-relevant adverse consequences actually would support a judgement of *valid-ity*, not invalidity. Having adopted this perspective, there no longer appeared to be any conceptual headroom left for test validity beyond construct validity. It now seemed that values and consequences were *only* relevant to validity in so far as they contributed to an understanding of construct validity: that is, in so far as they contributed to the scientific evaluation of score meaning.

The account of validity theory presented in Messick (1989a) seems to be balanced precariously between a liberal and traditional outlook. For example, he began his most extensive description of cell 4 by emphasizing that indeed, ethical cost–benefit analyses were a crucial element of validation:

> Thus, although appraisal of the intended ends of testing is a matter of social policy, it is not only a matter of policy formulation but also of policy evaluation that weighs all of the outcomes and side effects of policy implementation by means of test scores. Such evaluation of the consequences and side effects of testing is a key aspect of the validation of test use. (Messick, 1989a: 85)

Indeed, he had included discussion of both utility and fairness in cell 3, indicating that they broached the topic of cell 4 (1989a: 81). Moreover, although the cost–benefit notion of utility was a relatively small component of cell 3, Messick still described it as an 'aspect of validity' (1989a: 78). This seemed to imply a conception in which the judgement of validity was at least partly ethical. Conversely, just a few paragraphs on from the above quotation, he insisted again that construct-relevant adverse consequences were not matters of invalidity, but of validity. This kind of adverse impact presented a threat to the functional worth of the test, and therefore was of relevance to the evaluation of the testing policy, but it did not present a threat to validity. Here, the implication seemed to be that validity was essentially a matter of score meaning, and that impacts that did not threaten score meaning were issues beyond validity in the realm of 'political or social *policy*' (1989a: 85, italics in original). Thus, Messick appeared to switch between a liberal perspective and a traditional one, even within the same chapter. He developed a similarly traditional line of reasoning just a few pages later, at the end of his section on the consequential basis of test use.

Later years   By the middle of the 1990s, Messick had begun to give far more prominence to his half-dozen or so categories of validity evidence, presenting them alongside the progressive matrix, and indeed often foregrounding them at the expense of his matrix. More significantly, he began to focus squarely on construct validity as the whole of the new unified concept of validity. He now routinely presented consequences as a primary source of evidence within this new, more comprehensive theory of construct validity. In Messick (1995a) he took this to its inevitable conclusion, claiming that the entire progressive matrix now represented construct validity. In the same paper, he insisted once again that construct-irrelevant adverse consequences needed to be investigated in the validation process, but that construct-relevant adverse consequences represented a different kind of problem: a problem of social policy. His emphasis no longer seemed to be on the integration of ethical evaluation in the way that it originally had been; in fact, the term 'ethics' appeared only once in Messick (1995a), and not at all in Messick (1995b).

By the late 1990s, Messick seemed to be very much on the defensive, explicitly criticizing liberal interpretations of his work: notably, the suggestion that performance assessment could be justified on the basis of an overall ethical evaluation. For example, in Messick (1996) he insisted that validity could not be claimed on the basis of positive washback alone – a view that was being promoted within the language testing community, particularly in the UK. He singled out a number of offenders, including Morrow (1986), who had claimed that traditional aspects of validity were of little interest to the evaluation of tests of communicative performance. Instead, Morrow claimed, the single overriding concern of examining was to ensure a powerful and positive washback on teaching and learning, which led him to introduce the concept of 'washback validity' as the foundation of all validity for tests of communicative performance. Messick (1996) argued forcefully against this kind of thinking, insisting that positive washback could not be relied upon to establish test validity. Consequential evidence was certainly relevant to any investigation into validity, but in no way could it be considered a sufficient basis for claiming validity.

Finally, in a paper published just before he died, Messick took this anti-liberalism to its logical conclusion: 'In contrast, the consequences of test misuse are irrelevant to the nomological network, to score meaning and to the validation process' (Messick, 1998b: 41). Indeed, quoting a passage from Popham (1997), who had expressed concern that advocates of the liberal position were motivated by a desire to draw attention to the unsound uses of test results, Messick responded that: 'I, for one, had no such motive' (1998b: 40). Having re-read his earliest papers (e.g. Messick, 1965; Messick and Anderson, 1974; Messick, 1975; including quotations cited above in 'The Messick years prefigured' section), this claim seems extraordinary. The misuse of test results was highly significant in his earlier writing, yet now Messick seemed to be claiming that consequences arising from misuse were entirely irrelevant to his thesis. The entire progressive matrix seemed to have been reduced to a scientific evaluation of score meaning, with no room left for genuinely ethical evaluation.

Admittedly, this was now a very comprehensive scientific evaluation: one in which values and social consequences played their part. However, the evaluation of *validity*, of *construct validity*, seemed now to be almost entirely scientific. To be fair, references to the cost–benefit notion of utility still appeared in his later articles, notably under the external aspect of construct validity, and fairness appeared too under the consequential aspect; but these ethical concerns were not emphasized at all, and simply appeared to be mentioned in passing. Reading the later Messick in this way suggests a very traditional account of validity in which the judgement of validity is influenced primarily by scientific considerations and rarely, if at all, by ethical ones. Although we are not alone in reading the later Messick this way – others from Shepard (1997) to Hubley and Zumbo (2011) have provided similar accounts – it does seem to be a fairly extreme reading. Can it really be true that Samuel Messick, once the arch advocate of ethical evaluation, ultimately squeezed it out of his theory of validity?

In response to a critique by Markus (1998), Messick (1998b) criticized those of his critics who preferred to restrict construct validity to the accuracy of score inferences. Because *his* version of construct validity involved considerations of appropriateness, meaningfulness and usefulness in addition to the accuracy of score inferences, this implied ethical judgements of worth as well as scientific judgements of truth. Does this not constitute a direct refutation of our non-ethical reading of the later Messick? Well, within a couple of paragraphs, he had explained that the reason why it was impossible to separate score meaning from the consequences (that *he* considered to be of significance), was that those consequences were an inherent part of score meaning. Therefore, he explained the relevance of values to validity in terms of scientific evaluation, but not in terms of ethical evaluation. Once again, although Messick clearly wanted to embrace ethical evaluation, it is not at all clear that his account of validity theory during his later years could accommodate it easily. He returned repeatedly to an analysis that was primarily technical and scientific (emphasizing consistency and consensus), rather than social and ethical (emphasizing inconsistency and dispute).

The transition   Here, we are left with a dilemma. In his earlier years, Messick presented an account of validity that seemed to be liberal and broad. Construct validity, concerned with the scientific evaluation of test score interpretation, was just one part of a broader theory of test validity, concerned with the ethical evaluation of test score use. In his later years, Messick appeared to present an account of validity that was traditional and narrow: construct validity was now all of validity. Because he still theorized construct validity in terms of score meaning, this meant that all validation was now little more than scientific evaluation, albeit informed by debates over values and evidence involving certain kinds of consequences. Genuinely ethical evaluation concerning the social value of impacts and side-effects from testing certainly would be *informed* by score meaning and its implications, but it was ultimately a matter of social policy, and not within the scope of validity theory. What happened between the earlier and later years? Did Messick simply shift his emphasis and the way that he presented his theory of validity, or did he actually change his mind? We think that Messick ultimately did change his position on the scope of validity, although gradually and subtly, and perhaps without even noticing that he had done so.

In Figures 4.2 and 4.3, we have attempted to capture the change that we detect from our reading of the earlier Messick who presented a more liberal view of (test) validity, and the later Messick who presented a more traditional view of (construct) validity. The liberal matrix represents test validity, broadly interpreted, and locates construct validity primarily in cell 1. The traditional matrix represents construct validity: that is, the whole matrix is now focused on construct validity, which means that genuinely ethical analysis (involving cost–benefit value judgement) has been squeezed out. In the liberal matrix, the arrows radiate out from cell 1 into the other cells, and then back into cell 1. This emphasizes the nomological net, whereby test score meaning has broader implications (i.e. predictable consequences) which support (or undermine) the broader case for the ethical defensibility of test score use; and whereby evidence from implementing the testing policy (i.e. observed consequences) helps to support (or undermine) the narrower case for the scientific defensibility of test score meaning. However, in the traditional matrix the arrows only feed into cell 1, which indicates that the focus is now on the evaluation of test score meaning, albeit informed by evidence from consequences of implementing the testing policy.

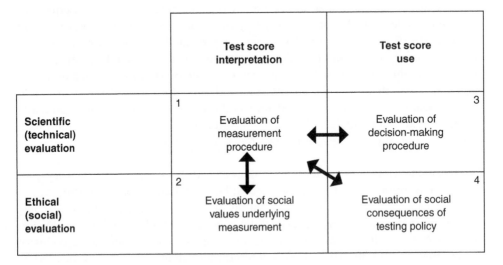

Figure 4.2   Our interpretation of the earlier, more liberal matrix: test validity

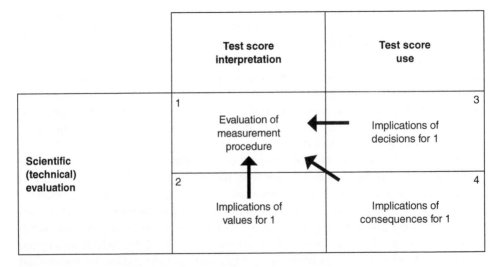

Figure 4.3   Our interpretation of the later, more traditional matrix: construct validity

Messick's attempt to integrate ethical considerations within validity theory – represented by the cells of his progressive matrix – is so confusing that Hubley and Zumbo went so far as to claim that most of those who know about it 'do not understand, or have misinterpreted' it (Hubley and Zumbo, 2011: 220). Their reframing of Messick's matrix is quite similar to the one that we offer in Figure 4.3. However, although we agree that this does seem to be the most appropriate reading of his later work, we are not so sure that it fits his earlier work, which did seem to aspire to genuine integration. Interestingly, McNamara (2001) also responded to what he perceived to be misinterpretation of the progressive matrix. However, he seemed to emphasize the conception implied by Figure 4.2, using the metaphor of 'an ever more encompassing circle' (2001: 336) to highlight the claim that ultimately, validity is social rather than technical. Both clarifications are plausible, we believe, because one emphasizes Messick's later account, while the other emphasizes his earlier one.

Messick never achieved a clear and coherent integration of scientific and ethical evaluation. In fact, during his later years, he seemed to retreat from this aspiration. Part of the reason for this may well have been the way in which his work on consequences was received and, to some extent, subverted. It was subverted by those who used the idea of 'consequential validity' to promote the uptake of 'direct' and 'authentic' assessments, without giving sufficient attention to the technical quality of those measurement-based decision-making procedures. They presented arguments that went like this:

Premise 1: performance assessment has good consequences.
Premise 2: good consequences mean high (consequential) validity.
Conclusion: performance assessment has high validity.

As a measurement professional, first and foremost, this would have undoubtedly vexed Messick. Ironically, it may well have been consequential evidence like this – evidence of adverse impact on the quality of professional debate – that ultimately dissuaded him from embracing a more liberal conception of validity, and instead persuaded him to retreat to the more traditional one.

Professional standards: editions 4 and 5

No discussion of validity theory during the period between 1975 and 1999 would be complete without reference to the fourth and fifth edition of the *Standards*. Not only are they are fundamental in their own right, they are also central to completing the story of the Messick years.

The preface to the 1985 *Standards* explained that the third edition was recognized as having become outdated as early as 1977, and work had begun on a revision by the end of the 1970s. Consequently, the revised edition of the *Standards* was developed largely in parallel with promulgation of the unified theory of validity by Guion and Messick. Therefore, it is perhaps unsurprising that while the

1985 *Standards* presented a view of validity that differed significantly from that presented in 1974, in sympathy with the unitarian conception, the transition was not entirely completed.

However, the 1985 *Standards* was definitely an important milestone. In particular, although all previous editions had explained that the three (or four) aspects of validity were not discrete, and that a complete evaluation of a test was likely to involve information about all aspects, the 1985 edition went further still by stating explicitly that validity 'is a unitary concept' (AERA et al., 1985: 9). Following a recommendation from Messick (1980), it recognized this by no longer describing the categories as *kinds* of validity. Instead, it re-described them as alternative forms of *evidence* of validity:

- construct-related evidence
- content-related evidence
- criterion-related evidence.

Nonetheless, in retaining the traditional three categories, the authors of the new *Standards* were not prepared to follow Messick in claiming that construct validity provided the unifying force. Instead, the authors were more circumspect, suggesting merely that evidence regarding the psychological meaning of the construct is '*usually* relevant and *may* become the central issue' (1980: 9; emphasis added). Neither were the authors prepared to follow Messick in integrating ethical and scientific concerns. Instead, their discussion of validity remained predominantly scientific, albeit with occasional reference to value judgements: for example, the fact that selection decisions always involved them, if only implicitly (1980: 11).

The authors of the new *Standards* were clearly very sympathetic to the unified view of validity, although they were somewhat half-hearted in following through its implications, at least partly as a consequence of political compromise in response to feedback from successive reviewers (see Messick, 1989a: 92). In response, Messick ended his classic chapter by lamenting the partial nature of the conversion represented within the 1985 *Standards*, explaining how it left the door open for the trinitarian view that circumstances might exist in which one kind of validity evidence could be considered sufficient to stake a claim to validity. This, he explained, was tantamount to assuming that there were circumstances in which one kind of validity could constitute the whole of validity: a view that the unitarian account firmly rejected.

A revision of the 1985 *Standards* was initiated in 1991, and the fifth edition was published in 1999. As far as validity was concerned, it completed the conversion begun in 1985, adopting the new theory of validity wholesale. In fact, it promoted a perspective extremely similar to Messick's (Newton, 2012a). In particular, it no longer implied that only certain tests needed to be characterized in terms of constructs, using the term 'construct' more broadly to mean 'the concept or characteristic that a test is designed to measure' (AERA et al., 1999: 5). This provided a foundation for claiming that the 'validity argument establishes the construct validity of a test' (AERA et al., 1999: 174). Just as significantly, the 1999 *Standards* dropped the traditional three categories of evidence in favour of five sources of evidence of construct validity:

1   evidence based on test content
2   evidence based on response processes
3   evidence based on internal structure
4   evidence based on relations to other variables
5   evidence based on consequences of testing.

Although these categories diverged slightly from the six proposed by Messick, clearly they were derived from them and related closely to them.[5] Most important was the addition of consequential evidence and its recognition as a fundamental source of evidence of construct validity. Interestingly, the role of consequences within validity theory was just as unclear within the 1999 *Standards* as it was within Messick's body of work (Newton, 2012a). Adopting a position that very closely resembled that of the later Messick, the authors of the *Standards* defined validity in terms of the *interpretations* of test scores entailed by proposed uses of results: that is, in terms of the scientific question of score meaning (see AERA et al., 1999: 9). Yet, the 1999 *Standards* also suggested that impacts which had nothing to do with score meaning ought to be dealt with as 'part of the validity argument for test use' (AERA et al., 1999: 23). In short, the section on validity within the 1999 *Standards* reflected both Messick's triumph – the unification of validity theory through construct validity – and his tribulation: the obfuscation of validity theory through the attempt to integrate ethical and scientific questions within a single concept.

Validity and validation by the end of the 1990s

In retrospect, it seems hard to disagree with the conclusion that the progressive matrix was a mistake (Shepard, 1997). Having said that, we believe that the intention underlying the original matrix was an excellent one. It was an attempt to emphasize that the following two questions were crucial to any thorough evaluation, and inherently interrelated:

1   Is the test any good as a measure of the characteristic that it purports to assess?
2   Should the test be used for its present purpose?

The matrix was supposed to explain the relationship between these two questions and their relation to the concept of validity, but it was muddled. Over the years, as Messick helped readers to find their way through the ambiguity of the matrix, his presentation became clearer. However, it also became narrower, as scientific questions of test score meaning began to take precedence, while ethical questions of test score use were obscured.

The suggestion that Messick came to promote a traditional view, with an emphasis on scientific evaluation and score meaning, should not be taken to mean that he rejected the significance of values and social consequences – far from it. As explained earlier, he absolutely embraced evidence from social consequences *when they had something to say, positive or negative, about score meaning*. More importantly, it was no accident that he ended his *magnum opus* by emphasizing that validity and values are one imperative, not two. This was fundamental to his thinking. The question that we would ask (and that others have asked) is whether recognition of the centrality of values necessarily forces one to reject any distinction between scientific and ethical questions, or whether it still allows a useful distinction to be drawn, as long as those values are subjected to scrutiny in both cases. Cizek (2012), for example, has insisted on rebuilding these barriers, while recognizing that both kinds of question are grounded in values. Markus (1998) and the commentaries on his article provide an important, albeit challenging, resource on this issue.

We have argued that the intention to integrate scientific and ethical concerns seemed far less apparent in Messick's later work than it had seemed in his earlier accounts. Perhaps, as Cizek (2012) has claimed, a genuine integration of science and ethics was always an impossible dream? We think differently. Is it not the case that the decision to implement any testing policy necessitates an overall, integrated evaluative judgement in which both scientific and ethical concerns must feature? We believe that the early matrix (Figure 4.1) still has a lot of potential to illuminate the ingredients of thorough evaluation as far as testing policy is concerned. Therefore, in Chapter 6 we present a modified version of the early matrix as a framework for scaffolding the evaluation of testing policy.

Messick's triumph was his success in convincing the educational and psychological measurement communities that measurement-based decision-making procedures (i.e. tests) needed to be evaluated holistically on the basis of a scientific evaluation into score meaning. His tribulation was his failure to convince the educational and psychological measurement communities that ethical and scientific evaluation could be straightforwardly integrated. In fact, his attempt to do so led to one of the most notorious debates of all time concerning the scope of validity theory. The field is now genuinely split as to whether, and if so, how evidence from consequences ought to be considered part of validity theory (as we will see in Chapter 5).

It would be wrong to conclude that Messick's quest to integrate ethical and scientific evaluation was a complete failure. After all, he did succeed in raising the profile of ethical questions among measurement specialists. Indeed, the literature on the consequential aspects of testing continues to grow, as the following references illustrate (Mehrens, 1998; Bailey, 1999; Cheng and Watanabe, 2004; Herman and Haertel, 2005; Phelps, 2005, 2012; Green, 2007; Mansell, 2007; Taylor and Weir, 2009; Polesel et al., 2012), and numerous special issues of journals (e.g. Rea-Dickens and Scott, 2007; Merki, 2011; Banerjee, 2012). However, there is also little doubt that the debate on the relationship between consequences and validity has resulted in substantial confusion. A persistent gulf remains between validity theory and validation practice (e.g. Jonson and Plake, 1998; Hogan and Agnello, 2004; Cizek et al., 2008; Wolming and Wikstrom, 2010), with the integration of consequential evidence proving to be a particular cause for concern (Cizek, 2011).

If many within the educational and psychological measurement professions have misunderstand Messick on the values, consequences and ethical dimensions of validity, this should come as no surprise. Messick seemed to change his position significantly over time, with no explicit recognition of this fact; although at no point in time was his position entirely clear and coherent.

Notes

1   Technically speaking, extrapolation takes us both from performance to ability, and from the test situation to non-test situations: that is, from test-specific performance to non-test-specific ability. As Loevinger (1957) explained, the extrapolation from test situation to non-test situation is not trivial, since the process of assessment itself can impact differently across different students, thereby introducing irrelevant variance into a set of scores. As a straightforward example, test anxiety might have an inflationary impact on the scores of a certain kind of student, but a deflationary impact on the scores of another kind. Yet we would not expect these impacts – the impacts of being tested – to generalize to non-test situations.

2   Note once again how this broke down the traditional distinction between description and measurement (interpretive inference), and decision and prediction (action inference). Decisions were now on a par with descriptions. Both were embodied in the nomological network, and therefore both were integral to score meaning.

3   These terms came from Cook and Campbell (1979: 64), although the second was actually an adaptation of 'surplus construct irrelevancies'. However, the concepts can be found in much earlier writings, e.g. Cronbach (1949) and Monroe (1923). They were neatly encapsulated in a quotation from E.L. Thorndike: 'The ideal should be to sample all of intellect [i.e. to avoid construct under-representation] and nothing but intellect [i.e. to avoid construct-irrelevant variance]' (Thorndike, 1925: 6–7).

4   Our broad conception of social consequence includes: consequences for individuals (e.g. personal learning gain from having been placed in an appropriate stream or set), and consequences for institutions (e.g. national economic gain from having channelled students through effective qualification routes into appropriate professions); consequences from accurate assessment (e.g. higher productivity for a company from having selected the right candidate for a job, and a regular salary for the candidate thus selected), and consequences from inaccurate assessment (e.g. the death of patients within a hospital that selected the wrong candidate for a job, and imprisonment for the candidate thus selected); consequences that may

have been anticipated before the testing policy was implemented, both welcomed positive and unwelcomed negative (e.g. the elimination of an historical gender bias in science test results), and consequences that may not have been unanticipated, both positive and negative (e.g. a fall in the number of male students opting to take science); consequences that arise immediately on implementation (e.g. increased reliability of teacher assessment, due to the introduction of centrally-devised coursework projects and marking schemes), and consequences that do not emerge until long after (e.g. decreased discrimination between students due to widespread copying of exemplar projects from the internet); consequences that bear close relation to score meaning (e.g. decreased motivation to study a particular element of the curriculum, resulting from knowledge that it is generally omitted from the test), and consequences that bear little or no relation to score meaning at all (e.g. increased motivation to study the entire curriculum, resulting from knowledge that it is to be tested and that results are to be published).

5   The similarity between the breadth of evidence deemed relevant by the 1999 *Standards* and by Monroe (1923) is interesting to note. It has taken a long time to return to a broad, unitary conception of validity.

CHAPTER 5

THE DECONSTRUCTION OF VALIDITY: 2000–2012

The earliest definition of validity seemed fairly straightforward: the degree to which a test measured what it was supposed to measure. From the mid-1950s, three main kinds of validity were recognized: content, criterion and construct. Content validity and criterion validity still seemed fairly straightforward; if anything, they now seemed more straightforward than their parent concepts, logical validity and empirical validity. Construct validity was the exception, having been invented to deal with exceptional circumstances (when neither content validity nor criterion validity could be relied upon as a gold standard), and having been grounded in (as then) state-of-the-art philosophical thinking. From the mid-1970s, it was acknowledged increasingly that both content validity and criterion validity were over-simplistic, and that neither constituted a gold standard of any sort. In due course, the exception became the rule, as construct validity was crowned all of validity – that is, all of the *science* of validity – since it still remained unclear how to accommodate *ethical* concerns.

At the turn of the millennium, it seemed to many that the field of educational and psychological measurement had embraced wholeheartedly the new unified conception of validity. This was acknowledged officially in the fifth edition of the *Standards* (AERA et al., 1999: 11) and, less officially, in widespread expressions of veneration for the account of validity provided in Samuel Messick's *magnum opus* (Messick, 1989a). This new 'consensus' was affirmed far and wide (Angoff, 1988; Cronbach, 1989a; Dunnette, 1992; Shepard, 1993; Kane, 2001; Downing, 2003; Sireci, 2009). Moss went so far as to describe it as 'a close to universal consensus among validity theorists' (Moss, 1995: 6).

Yet cracks were beginning to show. On the one hand, validity theory was becoming so big that it was increasingly unclear how to translate it into validation practice, particularly if it was supposed to embrace both scientific and ethical concerns. On the other hand, it was unclear whether the concept of construct validity, with its complex philosophical heritage, was actually the best way to unify validity theory after all. It seemed that an element of *deconstruction* might be in order, not only to break down the concept into more manageable components, but also potentially to remove (or at least to reposition) the construct concept. In short, there was a growing sense that both validation practice and validity theory needed to be simplified.

In order to understand this phase, it is important to recognize that there were actually two reasonably distinct debates developing. The first concerned the *nature and significance of construct validity*: a debate over the relatively narrow, scientific issue of score meaning. Although it seemed clear that modern construct validity theory was somewhat different from traditional construct validity theory, distinctions between the two were blurred, and the modern version appeared to be weighed down with philosophical baggage from the traditional one. The second concerned the *scope of validity*: a debate over whether the concept ought to be expanded beyond the relatively narrow, scientific issue of score meaning to embrace broader ethical issues concerning the consequences of testing.

Although this period was characterized by mounting concern over aspects of validity *theory*, it was characterized equally by growing appreciation of the value of a new *methodology* for guiding validation practice: argumentation. The following section discusses the desire to simplify validation practice during this phase, epitomized in the *argument-based approach* to validation. It is followed by an account of the desire to simplify validity theory, evident in the two major debates identified above.

Once again, this chapter is necessarily selective in its coverage of material. Further insights into the spirit of critical reappraisal that characterized this phase can be gleaned from the plethora of special issues that were published during the period.[1]

Finally, it would have been presumptuous for us to have attempted to provide an authoritative historical account of the post-millennial phase, which is far from over as we write. Instead, we have attempted to provide a more nuanced account of validity in the making as we currently see it, as well as to offer our own small contribution to this process. This means that we will engage more actively than in previous chapters with the issues that we introduce. In doing so, we hope to paint the broad landscape of contemporary ideas on validity and validation, and to provide some clues as to how lines of thinking might develop.

The desire to simplify validation practice

Although this chapter concerns developments during the 21st century, the argument-based approach to validation was developed by Michael Kane during the last two decades of the 20th century. In extending ideas from House (1977), Lee Cronbach had invited validators to think in terms of 'validity argument', rather than 'validity research' (Cronbach, 1988: 4). Kane, in turn, extended ideas from Cronbach, enabling measurement specialists to see what this might look like in practice. However, the argument-based approach took a long time to take root, and only began to have a significant impact well into the new millennium. In fact, even having begun to take root, it still proved surprisingly resistant to propagation.

The methodology in principle

Cronbach was invited to address the 1979 Educational Testing Service invitational conference with an update on the account of test validation that he had presented in his 1971 *Educational Measurement* chapter (Cronbach, 1980a). He endorsed the maxim that was soon to become commonplace – that all validation was construct validation – simultaneously admitting that his original account of construct validity had been more suited to the seminar room than to the public arena. For the public arena, it was clear that validation needed to be understood as a *rhetorical* process, involving the convergence of arguments in favour and the refutation of arguments against. In a subsequent article, he diagnosed a fundamental problem with construct validation as it was being currently practised:

> For only a few tests, embedded in major programs of theoretical research, has full-blown construct validation been reported. The great run of test developers have treated construct validity as a wastebasket category. In a test manual, the section with that heading is likely to be an unordered array of correlations with miscellaneous other tests and demographic variables. Some of these facts bear on construct validity, but a coordinating argument is missing. (Cronbach, 1980b: 44)

Admitting that, for many readers, his earlier account had rendered construct validation unduly esoteric and unobtainable, he insisted that it was actually neither: validation involved little more than argument, and arguments do not need to be watertight – they simply need to be sufficiently strong. In a series of papers from the early 1990s onwards, Michael Kane developed this line of reasoning into what became known as the argument-based approach to validation (e.g. Kane, 1990, 1992, 2001, 2002, 2004, 2006, 2009, 2013a). Kane was not the only writer during this period to emphasize the importance of argumentation. Approaches with slightly different emphases were developed by Robert Mislevy (e.g. Mislevy, 2003a, 2003b, 2009; Mislevy et al., 2003); Lyle Bachman (e.g. Bachman, 2005), and with a schema that focused primarily on intended test use, Lorrie Shepard (e.g. Shepard, 1993). Yet Kane's approach became the most familiar during this phase, which is why it is the focus for our chapter.

Kane borrowed a conception of argumentation suitable for analysing everyday arguments from Toulmin (1958). From this perspective, an argument could be understood as an inference from *datum* to *claim*, with the inference supported by a *warrant*, and the warrant justified by *backing*. The concepts of claim, datum, warrant and backing provided tools for deconstructing the 'big question' of validity into manageable chunks. The concept of *inference* was an important organizing principle in this account, and it became clear from Kane's examples that certain inferences were common to almost all measurement arguments: namely, the scoring inference, generalization inference and extrapolation inference.

For example, imagine a test that is supposed to measure achievement in arithmetic. We can divide the testing procedure hypothetically into three distinct inferential steps. In the first step, the datum comprises performance on individual questions, and the claim is that these performances can be legitimately interpreted in terms of an overall test score. Thus, the first step from datum to claim – from *test performance* to *test score* – is the *scoring inference*. Warrants and backing for assumptions such as the following would need to be marshalled:

- rubrics (i.e. marking schemes) effectively identify and reward features of performance associated with different levels of the attribute
- raters (i.e. markers) consistently recognize those features in the elements of performance that they observe, and consistently reward them in accordance with the rubrics
- aggregation rules combine item scores to reflect the relative importance of each element of performance, as defined by the test specification.

The particular form of the test that happened to have been constructed and administered would have been just one of many possible tests that, in principle, might have been employed to measure achievement in arithmetic. Understood in terms of classical test theory, any particular test involves just one sample of questions from the universe of arithmetic questions that might have been asked. Indeed, the testing procedure equally might have involved just one sample of raters from the universe of arithmetic raters that might have been trained. This takes us into the territory of generalizability theory. Here, the issue is essentially one of reliability and unsystematic (random) error. What is the warrant for generalizing from the datum of *test score* to a claim concerning the true score or, more generally, the *universe score*? The second step is the *generalization inference*. Warrants and backing for assumptions such as the following would need to be marshalled:

- elements of performance elicited by the test occur with sufficient frequency to control for sampling error
- linking procedures ensure comparability across test forms
- elements of performance elicited by the test represent (to the extent possible) the full breadth of the test domain.

Scoring and generalization inferences only take us so far; additional bases need to be covered before it is safe to claim validity. In particular, it needs to be established that it is safe to extrapolate from performance in the testing situation to the competence (i.e. the attribute) that is supposedly being measured. Here, an important issue is that attributes are always inferred indirectly rather than apprehended directly (Guilford, 1936; Loevinger, 1957; Messick, 1994), and this inferential process is susceptible to error. One potential source of error is the artificiality of the test situation itself. For example, if students are poorly motivated when being tested, then they are likely to underperform, and this is likely to be true whenever they might happen to be tested, with whichever particular form of the test they happen to be tested. The same might be true for students who find themselves crippled by anxiety in test situations. Another potential source of error is due to a mismatch between the test domain (the universe of tasks consistent with the test specification) and the attribute domain (the full range of real-world behaviours consistent with the definition of the attribute). The test specification operationalizes the attribute by specifying relevant content, processes, contexts, etc., for possible inclusion in the test. Consequently, any inadequacy in the test specification will be mirrored in the design of each test form. Moreover, because a test specification could never be as rich and broad as the attribute that it is supposed to represent, there always will be an inferential gap to be bridged. Bearing these threats in mind, what are the warrants for extrapolating from the datum of a *universe score*, regarding performance in test situations, to a claim concerning an *attribute level*, regarding competence in non-test, real-world situations? The third step is the *extrapolation inference*. Warrants and backing for assumptions such as the following would need to be marshalled:

- the test domain represents (to the extent possible) the full breadth and richness of the attribute domain
- differences in performance quality:

    o are attributable to processes constitutive of the attribute
    o are not attributable to processes beyond the attribute
    o are not attributable to the artificiality of the testing situation.

Taken together, these three inferences – scoring, generalization and extrapolation – constitute the backbone of any measurement argument: they explain why it is legitimate to interpret evidence from test performance in terms of the attribute that supposedly is being measured. According to Kane (e.g. 2013a), the adequacy of this argument will depend on its *coherence* and *completeness*, and on the *plausibility* of the warrants and backing for each of the inferences and their assumptions. If the argument is judged to be sufficiently strong, then the interpretation of test scores (in terms of the attribute) would be valid. It is worth noting that there are no universal criteria for establishing the adequacy or strength of an argument. Shaw and Crisp (2012) found the following criteria from Blair and Johnson (1987) to be useful in conceptualizing the strength of an argument:

- acceptability – the truth status of the premises;
- relevance – whether the assumptions warrant the conclusion; and
- sufficiency – whether the assumptions provide enough evidence, considering everything known.

The argument-based approach to validation can be likened to construction of a *bridge* over a river: on one bank is evidence of test performance; on the other bank is the claim that it represents a certain level of a particular attribute. The bridge spanning the river is likely to comprise at least three arches – scoring, generalization and extrapolation – each of which needs to be robust in its own right. If any arch collapses, then the bridge fails. In one of two very accessible accounts of the argument-based approach, Kane et al. (1999) adopted this bridge metaphor. In the other, Crooks et al. (1996) adopted a different metaphor, of a *chain*. The idea of a chain, perhaps even more vividly than the idea of a bridge, reminds us that an argument is only as good as its weakest link. Moreover, spending time and effort soldering a link that is already strong is not only wasteful but might even be harmful, because it detracts attention from the vulnerability of weaker links.

From a methodological viewpoint, the argument-based approach to validation is neat because it foregrounds the issue of where to begin, how to proceed and when to stop. According to Kane, all validation must begin with a coherent and complete specification of the *interpretive argument*. The interpretive argument is simply an overall structure including essential inferences, assumptions and warrants, but excluding much of the backing from empirical evidence and logical analysis that would be required in order to judge its strength. Crucially, the interpretive argument makes explicit the claim that the exercise is intended to culminate in, as well as the inferential path that leads to it. The foundation on which any interpretive argument is built is the use to which test scores will be put, because that use will indicate the way in which test scores will need to be interpreted (see Chapter 1).

Once the overall structure appears to be complete and coherent, the evaluator then can proceed by constructing a *validity argument*. Backing from empirical evidence and logical analysis is gathered through validation studies to fill in the gaps in the interpretive argument. Once sufficient evidence and analysis have been marshalled, the strength of the overall argument can be judged. Validation stops when the validity argument is judged to be sufficiently strong, or else fundamentally flawed. If the validity argument is not judged to be strong in a global sense, then *conditions of rebuttal* might be specified which restrict the parameters of valid interpretation: for example, to members of one group but not another. Alternatively, the nature of the interpretation itself might be revisited. Thus, even if an ambitious interpretation (defined in terms of a complex attribute) is judged to be invalid, it still might be possible to declare a less ambitious interpretation (defined in terms of a less complex attribute) valid. (We will explain what we mean by ambitious and unambitious interpretations later.)

In 2013, Kane decided to abandon the label 'interpretive argument' in favour of *interpretation and use arguments* (IUAs) because the old formulation had given insufficient weight to uses. The new formulation also usefully allows us to distinguish between interpretation and use arguments. (In the following sections we adopt the new formulation, often referring simply to the 'interpretation argument' when we have restricted our discussion thus.) Note that Kane retained his distinction between IUA and the validity argument (Kane, 2013a).

There are two very useful features of the argument-based approach which further help to explain how to proceed when undertaking validation. The first is the heuristic, from the bridge or chain metaphors, that arches or links that seem to be particularly weak are especially demanding of attention. In the same vein, warrants that are highly plausible *a priori* may not require any backing at all. This resonates strongly with the idea that validation ought to proceed by discounting plausible rival hypotheses: that is, there is no point wasting time and effort on hypotheses that are highly plausible, or on rival hypotheses that are highly implausible. The second is the received wisdom from the literature on argumentation concerning common fallacies that ought to be avoided. One such fallacy is known as *begging the question*: failing to provide the necessary support for a claim. This might occur when a partial justification is provided: a justification that might well support a less ambitious interpretation, but not the more ambitious interpretation that is actually intended. As observed by so many over the years, from Tyler to Lennon to Messick, traditional analysis of test content begged the question of what response processes were actually elicited. Another fallacy is known as *gilding the lily*: amassing a wealth of evidence for claims that are already sufficiently well established. Kane (e.g. 2013a) noted that it is very tempting to marshal a wealth of evidence of a kind that is relatively easy to gather (related, for example, to the generalization inference), thereby distracting attention from the lack of evidence of a kind that is far trickier to gather (related, for example, to the extrapolation inference). The argument-based approach is particularly useful for highlighting problems such as this.

The methodology in practice

Although Kane was intent on making validation far more tractable than it may have appeared under Messick, and although he went to considerable lengths to illustrate the use of his approach, the uptake of his new methodology seemed very limited, even two decades after the publication of his 1992 landmark paper (Schilling, 2007; Goldstein and Behuniak, 2011). An interesting exception is the research that was carried out by Chapelle and colleagues into the revision of the Educational Testing Service's Test of English as a Foreign Language (TOEFL®) (New Generation Test of English as a Foreign Language) between 1990 and 2005 (Chapelle et al., 2008). This study was particularly interesting because it amassed a considerable body of information in relation to categories of evidence presented in the fourth and fifth editions of the *Standards*, yet it ultimately adopted Kane's argument-based approach in order to structure and judge that information. This provided an excellent case study for examining whether the argument-based approach made a difference (Chapelle et al., 2010).

Chapelle et al. (2010) contrasted recommendations from the *Standards* with recommendations from the argument-based approach. According to the *Standards*, any validation ought to begin by specifying a list of propositions that supported the proposed interpretation of test scores (AERA et al., 1999: 9–10). It then ought to proceed by testing each of those propositions against empirical evidence and/or logical analysis. Following this advice, they identified 13 propositions for the revised Test of English as a Foreign Language before deciding that – without knowing exactly how to formulate such propositions, or how many a good validation argument ought to contain – they might carry on doing so indefinitely. They also observed that those 13 propositions were focused more on rationalizing the research that they had already completed, than on illuminating the research that they still needed to do. In short, they felt dissatisfied with the guidance provided by the *Standards*, and turned to Kane instead. Chapelle and colleagues concluded that the argument-based approach *did* make a difference – a very positive one. Whereas the *Standards* lacked the structure required to move forward with decisiveness, the argument-based approach helped them to frame the intended score interpretation, outline the essential research, structure research results into a validity argument and challenge the validity argument. In other words, it helped them to work out where to begin, how to proceed and when to stop.

Other research teams have found the argument-based approach to be very useful, including Schilling and Hill (2007), who evaluated measures of mathematical knowledge for teachers; Wools et al. (2010), who evaluated the driver performance assessment; Goldstein and Behuniak (2011), who evaluated the Connecticut Mastery Test/ Connecticut Academic Performance Test (CMT/CAPT) Skills Checklist; and Shaw and colleagues (Crisp and Shaw, 2012; Shaw and Crisp, 2012; Shaw et al., 2012) who evaluated two international A levels offered by Cambridge International Examinations (general educational qualifications in geography and physics for 16–19-year-olds). However, as we have mentioned previously, examples of successful implementation of the argument-based approach were few and far between, even by the end of the first decade of the new millennium. This raises the obvious question of why such an intuitively useful methodology had not been adopted on a larger scale.

Part of the answer to this question may be that the argument-based approach underlines the fact that validation is not simply a one-off-study but a programme: potentially, a very intensive programme. Of course, the very purpose of adopting this approach is to shine light into the darkest corners of validation practice, and to direct the evaluator to evidence and analysis that they might have neglected otherwise. Yet in doing so, it risks making the task of validation seem daunting. Shaw and Crisp (2012) observed that collecting certain kinds of evidence was very time-consuming and required extensive analysis. It would not be feasible *routinely* to undertake validation research on a scale like this, they argued, even for a major international assessment agency such as Cambridge International Examinations, which is able to draw on scores of dedicated researchers from its umbrella organization, Cambridge Assessment.

Part of the answer also might relate to certain features of Kane's account, which make it a little confusing to understand and apply (Newton, 2013a; Sireci, 2013). One such feature is his distinction between IUAs and validity arguments: a distinction that he claims to be fundamental to the argument-based approach (Kane, 2004). We have struggled to understand what this difference might amount to in practice: two different *kinds* of argument, two arguments or just one argument in different phases? If this distinction is genuinely fundamental to the argument-based approach, then any ambiguity over its interpretation is problematic, possibly even discouraging those new to the methodology from adopting it. Clearly, two requirements *are* fundamental to the argument-based approach. First, it is crucial to begin by specifying the claim that the argument eventually will terminate in, which typically takes the following form: a test score of x can be interpreted as a certain level of attribute y. Second, it is crucial to proceed by specifying, in skeletal form, the logic of the argument that leads to this conclusion, including the assumptions that it entails. We believe that these two requirements comprise the essence of the interpretation argument. However, what of the validity argument? Is it a different *kind* of argument from this? Is it a second argument that runs alongside the interpretation argument? Or is it simply the interpretation argument at a later phase of validation, supported by a much larger body of validation research? We assume that it is simply the latter: the validity argument is just the interpretation argument at the end of validation, rather than at the beginning. On this basis, we wonder whether there is really any need to distinguish between interpretation and validity arguments, or whether the term 'validity argument' is sufficient to cover both (Newton, 2013a).

Another confusing feature, which is positively endorsed by Kane, is the premise that IUAs need to be tailored to each individual validation programme. If different tests are to be interpreted differently and used for different purposes, then there is a strong case for bespoke IUAs. Furthermore, Kane is reticent to recommend anything that looks like a simple checklist, being acutely aware of the folly of the 'toolkit' approach to validation that was widespread between the early 1950s and the late 1970s (see Kane, 2001: 323). Yet this very lack of prescription might begin to dissuade those new to the methodology from adopting it. After all, the validation researcher might well have turned to the argument-based approach (from the *Standards*) in search of clear-cut guidance. Incidentally, it is worth noting that the published examples of its adoption have tended to develop quite different argument structures. Consider, for example, the structures developed by Shaw and colleagues (1) versus Chapelle and colleagues (2):

1   Construct representation → Scoring → Generalization → Extrapolation
2   Domain description → Evaluation → Generalization → Explanation → Extrapolation

Although certain of the inferences were nominally the same, the first two were quite different, and the second argument contained an explanation inference (separating generalization and extrapolation) which was entirely missing from the first. Whether such differences are to be celebrated as indicative of important differences between focal attributes, or to be mourned as a source of unhelpful confusion for the reader, would seem to be a moot point. Interestingly, both saw the need for an additional inference prior to the scoring/evaluation inference; an inference for which Kane (at least post-2006) saw no need. This surely begs an important question concerning the extent to which the scoring–generalization–extrapolation framework captures most of what needs to be captured within any measurement argument.

It is actually quite tricky to decide which assumptions are associated with which inferences, and therefore to judge the completeness of the scoring–generalization–extrapolation framework. For example, when describing the extrapolation inference above, we included the assumption that differences in performance quality are attributable to processes constitutive of the attribute, and not to anything else. However, is this really what the extrapolation inference is all about? On the one hand, the inference that concerns mismatch between test domain and attribute domain (the extrapolation inference) would seem to be a natural home for assumptions concerning the construct-relevance of test score variance. On the other hand, as Shaw and Crisp (2012) proposed, one could argue that a better way to construct the interpretation argument would be to begin by scrutinizing assumptions concerning test performance, not simply test scoring. They referred to the first arch of their bridge as the 'construct representation inference', although it equally might have been called the 'performance inference'. From this perspective, the first arch spans a gap between the person on the bank, and their performance on the first pillar. The basic assumption of this inference is that test-taker performance faithfully represents test-taker attribute; which it might not if, for example, test-takers were simply unmotivated to perform optimally on the test. From this perspective, then, construct-irrelevant variance assumptions might be located towards the beginning of the argument rather than towards the end.

We imagine that Kane would respond that the whole point of the IUA is to get validation researchers thinking *for themselves* about the kind of assumptions that *they* need to investigate. In fact, he made this point explicitly, arguing that validators need to 'slow down a bit' (Kane, 2007: 182) and work out exactly what they need to achieve before embarking on a programme of validation research. From this perspective, it would not actually matter where in the overall argument structure they located their assumptions, just as long as they located them somewhere. However, our concern is that this lack of prescription, combined with the complexity of the task of constructing IUAs, increases the likelihood that researchers new to the methodology may fail to recognize when their IUAs are incomplete and/or incoherent. Certainly, Kane (2007) has acknowledged that this is a serious risk. The converse, he explained, is the risk that greater prescription will result in frameworks that fail to apply equally well across all contexts. Whether greater prescription might prove, on balance, to be more constructive than destructive would seem to be an open question, particularly if greater prescription might encourage a greater number of practitioners to adopt the argument-based approach.

We have explained how this approach is useful in foregrounding where to begin, how to proceed and when to stop. Kane has made a particular virtue of the argument-based approach in helping evaluators to judge when 'enough is enough' as far as validation research is concerned. In doing so, he has challenged the well-worn maxim that validation is a never-ending process. Kane (2013a) attributed this way of thinking to Cronbach (1971, 1989a) and to Anastasi (1986), although he could have equally associated it with Messick (1989a). This brings us back to the central question that we introduced in Chapter 1: how much of what kind of logical analysis and empirical evidence is required in order to substantiate a claim to validity? In a very real sense, Cronbach, Anastasi and Messick had no good answer to this question, because they argued that almost any kind of validation evidence or analysis might be considered *relevant* to any validation programme; and that no mosaic of evidence and analysis could ever be considered absolutely *sufficient*, if only because the same body of evidence and analysis might be judged differently by different evaluators.

The way out of this dilemma, according to Kane, is only to evaluate those claims that actually *need* to be evaluated: that is, only those claims specifically stated in the IUA. Not only will this kind of restraint help to distinguish between that which is required and that which is not, but it also might reveal that certain kinds of evidence and analysis are entirely irrelevant. Ultimately, sufficiency of evidence and analysis would be judged in relation to general criteria for establishing the strength of any informal argument: coherence, completeness and plausibility. Indeed, Kane has argued that 'many inferences and assumptions are sufficiently plausible *a priori* to be accepted without additional evidence, unless there is some reason to doubt them in a particular case' (Kane, 2013a: 15). Therefore, the image presented by Kane is one of tractability, if not simplicity. Yet, plenty of questions remain:

- How many inferences and assumptions are really so innocuous and trivial as to require no backing whatsoever, and how should we decide this?
- When an inference or assumption requires backing, how should we decide how much backing is enough?
- How robust does any evidence or analysis need to be in order to bridge an argumentation gap?
- How is the overall strength of the argument to be judged, and by whom?

Questions such as these are symptomatic of the challenges that would be faced when trying to evaluate any everyday argument. Whereas Kane's pragmatism represents a welcome riposte to the idealism of Cronbach, Anastasi and Messick, we would be mistaken in assuming that argumentation theory per se can furnish a satisfactory answer to the 'how much of what kind...?' question. As Cronbach explained, we are in the territory of 'reasonable argument based on incomplete information' (Cronbach, 1988: 5), rather than perfect argument based on complete information. So, how reasonable is reasonable enough, and how should we make that call? In short, although the argument-based approach is very helpful in explaining how to begin and proceed, it is slightly less helpful in explaining when to stop a validity argument.

To conclude this section, there is a sense in which the argument-based approach to validation is up there – to use a North American idiom – with motherhood and apple pie: after all, every validity claim requires a validity argument, so guidance on how to construct and appraise one surely must be welcomed? However, there is another sense in which the new methodology can be surprisingly hard to implement. As Brennan (2013) observed in his commentary on Kane (2013a), validation practice is still impoverished, and relatively few testing programmes give validation the attention that it deserves. It remains to be seen whether the argument-based approach can fulfil its potential and revolutionize validation practice on a large scale.

The desire to simplify validity theory

Between 2000 and 2012, two related (although distinguishable) debates on the complexity of validity theory flourished. The first was more blatant, and perhaps more emotional. It questioned the scope of validity theory: in particular, whether validity ought to be concerned not only with the evaluation of measurement procedures, but also with the evaluation of decision-making procedures, and ultimately with the overall evaluation of testing policy. This debate was staged in various fora during the 1990s (e.g. two special issues of *Educational Measurement: Issues and Practice*, 16 (2) and 17 (2)), but remained unresolved, and continued to develop into the new millennium. The second was more subtle and sometimes highly abstract. It questioned the nature and significance of construct validity theory: in particular, whether modern construct validity theory needed to be quite so complicated and involved as traditional construct validity theory had seemed. Indeed, some critics went further still by questioning whether the very idea of construct validity deserved the respect that the educational and psychological measurement communities had accorded it. We will explore the second of these debates first.

The nature and significance of construct validity

The maxim 'all validity is construct validity' has a nice ring to it – but just how informative is it? Is modern construct validity theory (à la Messick, 1989a) essentially the same as traditional construct validity theory (à la Cronbach and Meehl, 1955), albeit with a few tweaks here and there? Or is it substantially different, sharing only certain core features? Indeed, should any version of construct validity theory really be considered fundamental to 21st-century validation practice? Questions such as these motivated the post-millennium critical reappraisal of construct validity. In order to appreciate the force of this critique, we need to begin with a brief recap of the traditional version.

The construction of construct validity theory

Construct validity was proposed originally as an alternative to content validity and criterion validity: a specialized type of validity for tests of attributes that were the stock in trade of clinicians, notably personality tests. It was proposed that attributes such as delinquency, psychopathic deviancy and shyness derived their meaning from theories that explained how they related to each other, and how they related to other attributes. Such theories generated predictions about behaviour: for example, a psychopathic deviant who was otherwise quite rational, would be likely to try to conceal their deviancy during a clinical interview. This theory, which provided structure for a whole network of related attributes, specified how certain attributes would be inter-correlated, how other attributes would be unrelated, and so on. The theory was known as a nomological network, and the attributes that it defined were characterized as hypothetical constructs. The attributes were hypothetical because they were not directly observable; as hypothetical postulates, they were constructed by the theorist: that is, they were theoretical constructs.

Classically, the attributes to be measured by achievement tests and aptitude tests often were presumed rather than interrogated: validation interrogated the measurement procedure, but largely took the attribute for granted. However, when construct validity came to the fore, both the measurement procedure and the theoretical construct were under interrogation. In fact, not only was the theoretical construct to be evaluated, but the entire theory – the nomological network – was to be evaluated (Orton, 1987). Therefore, problematic validation evidence might not simply question the test but also the construct itself, as well as the theory within which it was located. Conceived thus, the very idea of validation begins to assume epic proportions.

An important presumption was that test performance would not be influenced by the focal attribute in isolation, and might well be influenced by complex interactions of attributes. Thus, performance on a personality test might be influenced not simply by psychopathic deviancy but also by the respondent's current level of motivation, or by a 'response style' such as acquiescence (the tendency to acquiesce to heterogeneous or neutral item content) or desirability (the tendency to respond desirably). Conceivably, even when the content of a test appeared entirely suited to measuring the focal attribute, consistency observed in test performances actually might have *more* to do with response style than the focal attribute (Jackson and Messick, 1962). Reasoning with a nomological network enabled constructs such as these to be represented, and enabled their interaction during test performance to be theorized.

Only through a scientific programme of research was construct validation possible, the argument went. This required evidence to support predicted consistencies within and between tests, and evidence to counter plausible alternative explanations for observed consistencies. The logic of construct validation was embodied most eloquently in the multitrait-multimethod (MTMM) technique developed by Campbell and Fiske (1959). It required that a variety of attributes (traits) be measured using a variety of methods. Construct validity required evidence of high correlation when the same trait was measured using different methods (convergent evidence), and evidence of low correlation when different traits were measured using the same method (discriminant evidence). Patterns of evidence such as this provided reason to believe that the test was effective in measuring the attribute, and that the attribute and its relation to other attributes was correctly understood. The MTMM came to be seen as the archetypal approach to construct validation; yet it is important to remember that construct validation, as theorized by Cronbach and Meehl, was intended to be informed by *any* kind of evidence and analysis (empirical, logical, experimental, etc.), with the potential to inform the interpretation of test scores.

Deconstructions and reconstructions of construct validity

From the turn of the millennium, dissatisfaction with the idea of construct validity became increasingly explicit, and the general consensus over its supremacy began to be questioned. In addition, significant differences between the accounts of those who considered themselves to be construct validity theorists became more apparent. The following sections provide insight into some of the most important debates of this period.

Borsboom (part 1): tests are valid, not interpretations   Denny Borsboom and colleagues (e.g. Borsboom et al., 2004, 2009; Borsboom, 2005) forcefully criticized the consensus belief, embodied in the fifth edition of the *Standards*, that all validity was construct validity. At the heart of their critique was the claim that the very idea of construct validity was misguided in suggesting that interpretations, i.e. constructs, are what need to be validated. Tests need to be validated, they claimed, not constructs, and they insisted on a very narrow definition of 'test':

> We submit, therefore, that what really matters in validity is *how the test works*, and this is certainly *not* a property of test score interpretations, or even of test scores, but of *the measurement instrument itself* (i.e., of the concrete, physical thing that you can drop on your feet, rather than of a linguistic entity, set-theoretical object, or statistical construction). (Borsboom et al., 2009: 149, italics in original)

Put simply, what mattered was whether the instrument had the capacity to pick up variation in the focal attribute; or whether the test measured what it was supposed to measure, as the classic definition of validity had insisted nearly 100 years earlier. Their intention was to deconstruct validity, to render it a more useful and meaningful concept.

The claim that validity was a property of tests, not interpretations, seemed bizarre to many measurement professionals. After all, it had been recognized since the early years that measurement *instruments* were not the kind of things that could be valid or invalid. As Lindquist put it:

> If a test is 'valid,' it is valid for *a given purpose*, with a given group of pupils, and it is valid only to the degree that it accomplishes that specific purpose for that specific group. It is meaningless to speak of any given test as being valid or invalid apart from any consideration of the purpose it is intended to serve or of the group to which it is to be given. (Lindquist, 1936: 21, italics in original)

The received wisdom insisted that it was simply wrong to talk of 'test validity', because there could be no such thing as a valid or invalid *test* (to suggest otherwise would be tantamount to heresy!). According to the orthodox position, the way to avoid anomalous talk was to refer to a specific interpretation of test scores, because the necessary caveats then could be included in that interpretation. Rather than saying 'this reading comprehension test is valid', we ought to say 'the interpretation of this set of test scores, from this group of test-takers, to be used for this purpose, as measures of reading comprehension, is valid'. This might be laborious, but at least it is correct. Moreover, stating the claim as explicitly as this should help to ensure that anyone who subsequently used that test was made aware of the potential boundaries between appropriate and inappropriate use. The very first validity standard in the first edition of the *Standards* stated clearly that: 'No manual should report that "this test is valid"' (APA et al., 1954: 19), and each subsequent edition of the *Standards* repeated this warning (Newton and Shaw, 2013).

However, this was not really the debate that Borsboom and colleagues had intended to provoke. They had no problem with the idea that validity might differ across groups or situations (e.g. Borsboom and Mellenbergh, 2007: 104–5). They simply assumed that any claim to validity was made against a 'background of regularity conditions' (Borsboom, 2012: 40). In short, they insisted that the conditions under which validity claims do or do not hold are background presumptions, and do not need to be stated explicitly. If so, then it is not incorrect to speak of valid tests after all. The debate that Borsboom and colleagues had intended to provoke was more subtle than this, and we shall explore their arguments in more detail shortly. For now, we turn to a debate that emerged from a similar desire to strip validity down to its bare essentials.

Lissitz and Samuelsen: no need for nomological networks   In a focal paper published in the journal *Educational Researcher*, Lissitz and Samuelsen (2007a) echoed the claim that validity is a property of tests, not interpretations – yet they reached this conclusion on the basis of a quite different argument. As they saw it, the concept of validity had been fabricated into something too large and impractical, and was in need of deconstruction. Specifically, what needed to be dismantled was the notion of a nomological network, and the associated principle that instruments and nomological networks are validated simultaneously. This made no sense in many educational contexts, they believed, because the meaning of an achievement attribute was not defined in relation to other achievement attributes, but was constituted independently of them. Construct definition was undoubtedly critical, they acknowledged, and the foundation for any validation exercise. Yet, *construct definition* was not the same as *theory building*, in the sense envisaged by Cronbach and Meehl (1955). It was largely irrelevant, they claimed, how scores from a mathematics test correlated with scores from an English test. What the test measured was essentially a straightforward, logical inference from its content, rather than a complex, theoretically-mediated inference from its relation to other tests. At best, predictive validity and the use of the MTMM technique to investigate external relationships were secondary concerns; at worst, they were entirely irrelevant. What mattered to Lissitz and Samuelsen was the content of the test and its reliability. These comprised the essence of validity.

The ideas presented in Lissitz and Samuelsen (2007a) were responded to by a number of leading validity theorists who were generally dismissive of their proposals. In particular, it was observed that the manner in which Lissitz and Samuelsen described content validity rendered it suspiciously similar to how they, the respondents, understood construct validity (e.g. Embretson, 2007; Gorin,

2007; Mislevy, 2007). By allowing validation to include analyses of theoretical latent processes, along the lines of Embretson (1983), it seemed that they wished to have their cake and eat it. The respondents also felt that the role of theory in validation should not be underestimated (e.g. Moss, 2007; Sireci, 2007). Validation is, quintessentially, about theory-based hypothesis testing. *Normally* it will be possible to identify plausible rival hypotheses for the patterns of behaviour exhibited in test situations – for example, low motivation as an explanation for poor performance – and these always ought to be considered and ruled out whenever possible.

Although their alternative account was far from watertight, it would be wrong to deny that Lissitz and Samuelsen (2007a) raised an important question concerning the nature and significance of modern construct validity theory. Working with constructs, they claimed, was not the same as engaging in construct validation, where construct validation is presumed to involve, not only evaluating an instrument, nor even evaluating an instrument and its construct in isolation, but evaluating an instrument, its construct and the entire psychological theory in which that construct is embedded (Lissitz and Samuelsen, 2007b). This was the essence of construct validation as portrayed by Cronbach and Meehl (1955). It is why they emphasized that validation is a never-ending process of constructing, testing and revising both instruments and theories of mind. If modern construct validity theorists still considered theory-testing to be the hallmark of construct validation, then was this theory-testing in the grand sense of construct validation, à la Cronbach and Meehl? If so, then how relevant was this conception to present-day validation practice, particularly for educational measurement?

Embretson, Pellegrino and Gorin: the cognitive approach   Asking this question so forthrightly was very effective in flushing out alternative perspectives. In fact, according to Embretson and Gorin, this conception was not at all relevant to present-day validation practice: construct validity theory had evolved significantly since the days of Cronbach and Meehl. According to Gorin (2007), theories were still at the heart of modern construct validation. However, they no longer tended to be *external* to constructs (concerning relationships between attributes within nomological networks); rather, they tended to be *internal* to constructs (concerning the cognitive processes, skills, strategies and knowledge structures required to perform successfully on test items):

> For example, the construct measured by a cognitive test can be described in terms of the cognitive and metacognitive strategies, and multiple alternative paths to correct answers that include sequencing and execution of cognitive subprocesses. These formulations are internal theories that define test constructs and therefore, even within Lissitz and Samuelsen's framework, are relevant for validity examinations. Although they briefly acknowledge the existence of such theories, they fail to grasp the fact that it is the internal theories of the construct (i.e., the relationships among subprocesses and dimensions comprised by the construct), not those of the nomological network, that are the focus of construct validity in contemporary measurement. (Gorin, 2007: 457)

Thus, the pendulum had swung from external to internal. Although Gorin envisaged a role for correlation within validation, and a role for the examination of external structure – to reveal 'patterns that support conclusions regarding what is actually measured' (Gorin, 2007: 459) – her suggestion that attributes are defined internally greatly minimized this role. Indeed, she concluded by stating explicitly that the role of the nomological network had been minimized in current theory. Not surprisingly, given their history of collaboration, Embretson (2007) made essentially the same points. The correlation between scores from a mathematics test and those from an English test were not *irrelevant* to score meaning, she argued, in contrast to Lissitz and Samuelsen. Yet, she added, this kind of evidence 'is not given a major role' (2007: 454) within modern construct validity theory, and is little more than a 'needed safeguard' (2007: 452). Modern theorists minimized the role of external evidence and strongly emphasized the role of internal evidence. In fact, Embretson opened her response by agreeing with Lissitz and Samuelsen that 'internal evidence establishes test meaning' (2007: 449).

The foundations of this position had been laid much earlier by Embretson (1983) in her distinction between two types of validation research:

1   research into *construct representation*, the identification of theoretical mechanisms underlying item responses (internal evidence); and
2   research into *nomothetic span*, the identification of network relationships between test scores and other variables (external evidence).

Although there was still a place for nomothetic span research in construct validation, it was not definitive of score *meaning*, so it was not the same as nomological network research in the sense of Cronbach and Meehl. It was merely indicative of score *significance*, which seemed to imply that it was a more practical concept, mapping out relationships between scores on the test and other measures. The new approach to construct validation, which Embretson termed 'construct modelling', was consistent with a shift in psychological thinking from functionalism to structuralism, and with the widespread embrace of information processing modelling within psychology from the 1980s onwards.

Central to construct representation is the idea of *decomposition*: of tasks into component stimulus features, and of task performance into the exercise of component cognitive resources – i.e. cognitive processes, skills, strategies and knowledge structures. This process of decomposition is heavily theory-driven, requiring postulation of a 'theory of cognitive components' and a 'theory of problem types' (Pellegrino, 1988: 49), and hypotheses linking the two. Here, the goal is to be able to specify the relationship between the features of an item and the component cognitive resources required to answer that item correctly: that is, the goal is to be able to define the specific set of processes, skills, strategies and knowledge structures required for successful performance on the item. Therefore, from the cognitive components approach, validity is very much an item-level concept as opposed to a test-level concept. Embretson and Gorin (2001) argued that this was entirely appropriate, because you need to establish validity *during* the process of item development: that is, *before* test assembly. The nomological network approach was inherently unsatisfactory, they argued, because the idea that score meaning can only be established post hoc renders the test development process unduly hit-and-miss.[2]

The focus on cognition was useful also in reminding measurement professionals that individual differences are not everything when it comes to validation research. The fact that a cognitive process is essential to task performance is fundamental to score meaning (construct representation) without there being any presumption that test-takers ought to differ in terms of their ability to apply this process to the task. In effect, Embretson (1983) turned construct validation on its head. The old approach conceptualized attributes from the outside-in: the meaning of the attribute was given traditionally by the location of a theoretical construct within an external network of constructs. The new approach conceptualized attributes from the inside-out: now, the meaning of the attribute was given by the configuration of an internal network of theoretical constructs.

The shift in focus associated with the cognitive approach is worth emphasizing. It suggests that the concepts of relevance to construct validity are less the *macro constructs* of nomological network theory (attributes such as achievement, aptitude, etc.), and more the *micro constructs* of cognitive theory (resources such as working memory, declarative knowledge, procedural knowledge, planning, attention, encoding, text mapping, abstraction capacity, simultaneous processing, sequential processing, processing speed, etc.). Having said that, these are still deeply theoretical constructs, which suggests that the cognitive approach may not be that far removed from the nomological network approach in the sense of casting validation in terms of theory-testing on a grand scale. However, importantly, the cognitive approach shifts attention from the wood to the trees that comprise it. The theoretical constructs under investigation are the micro constructs (which represent the competencies embodied in successful item performance), rather than the macro construct (which represents the competence embodied in successful test performance). It is almost as though the macro construct is validated, by definition, if all of the micro constructs that constitute it have been validated; or perhaps even that macro constructs are relatively uninteresting or superfluous once score meaning has been effectively defined in terms of micro constructs. Here, there would seem to be room for further explication of the relationship between these two levels of analysis.

While the cognitive approach to validity, test development and validation may have considerable potential, even its advocates admit that actual applications have been lagging (e.g. Embretson and Gorin, 2001). In addition, in placing almost exclusive emphasis on internal evidence for establishing score meaning, it adopts an extreme position that would not be universally accepted. Indeed, although internal evidence is given considerable prominence in the 1999 *Standards*, it does not seem to be prioritized in a manner consistent with the cognitive approach. The pendulum may well have swung, but it is not entirely clear how far.

Kane: not all attributes are hypothetical   Kane (e.g. 2001, 2008, 2011, 2013a) consistently has acknowledged the contribution that traditional construct validity has made to the identification and elevation of three fundamental principles for effective validation:

1   the need for an extended research programme, as opposed to a one-off-study
2   the need to specify in detail the proposed interpretation that is to be validated (before attempting to do so)
3   the need to test assumptions underlying the proposed interpretation, either logically or empirically, and to test them against plausible rival hypotheses.

However, it is tricky to work out whether Kane is ultimately a proponent of modern construct validity theory, or a critic. A particular problem with construct validity, he has observed repeatedly, is that it can be interpreted in a variety of different ways. This was the tenor of his own response to Lissitz and Samuelsen (2007a), which was published in a subsequent edition of *Educational Researcher* (Kane, 2008).

The first interpretation can be attributed to Cronbach and Meehl (1955). As mentioned previously, it concerns the strong programme of construct validation grounded in a philosophy of science that was popular at the time, and which implied the simultaneous evaluation of instruments, constructs and the theories in which they are embedded. Even Cronbach came to reject this strong programme, and suggested that Meehl did too (Cronbach, 1980a, 1980b). Cronbach (1988) contrasted the strong programme of construct validation with a weak one. Kane (2008) identified this as his second interpretation. Whereas the strong programme entailed focused theory-testing, the weak programme entailed little more than 'exploratory empiricism' in which any old correlation was welcomed (Cronbach, 1988: 12). This trivialized the idea of robust inquiry into score meaning. Kane (2008) concluded that Lissitz and Samuelsen (2007a) had criticized this second interpretation of construct validity and, since there was little, if any, support for the weak programme anymore, they were guilty of 'beating a dead horse' (Kane, 2008: 79).

The third interpretation identified by Kane (2008) was the basis of modern construct validity theory, as he understood it. This interpretation was not really a theory as such, but a distillation of the three principles identified above. It was more of a recipe for good evaluation: limited in scope, but sufficient to elevate validation beyond sheer exploratory empiricism to genuine scientific inquiry. Importantly, this science was not premised on the construction of a grand theory or nomological network, in the sense of Cronbach and Meehl (1955). A grand theory was unnecessary, he claimed, because interpretive arguments (IUAs) were sufficient to structure validation research. This was a good thing, he believed, because education and the social sciences have few, if any, grand networks (Kane, 2001: 325).

The IUA not only provides structure, but focus – and this is where Kane's contribution to validation methodology morphed into a contribution to validity theory. Different kinds of interpretation, he claimed, required different kinds of argument; and the nature of the interpretation was critical in determining how much of what kind of empirical evidence or logical analysis was relevant to, or required for, any validation programme. The most fundamental of distinctions that he drew was between interpretations framed in terms of *observable attributes* and *theoretical constructs* (e.g. Kane, 2001, 2006, 2009, 2013a). Observable attributes were far less ambitious and theory-laden than theoretical constructs, and therefore required far less evidence and analysis to substantiate. Theoretical constructs were so ambitious as to invoke the strong programme of construct validation.

By characterizing IUAs in this manner, Kane acknowledged the potential legitimacy of the strong programme while insisting that it was not necessary for all interpretations. In fact, he has referred to all sorts of attributes as though they were observable: 'literacy or proficiency in algebra', 'vocabulary knowledge', 'aptitudes or skills', 'achievement in arithmetic', 'map reading' and 'skill in solving quadratic equations' (Kane, 2013a). The suggestion that such a wide variety of attributes can be considered observable would seem to sideline the strong programme of construct validation within Kane's account. Indeed, as noted earlier, Kane also sidelined the spirit of never-ending inquiry that it engendered, and the idea that most (if not all) kinds of evidence would be relevant to most (if not all) validation studies. This served to distance Kane from one of the central tenets of modern construct validity theory according to Messick. Interestingly, quotations such as the following resonate strongly with Lissitz and Samuelsen (2007a):

> Under the argument-based approach, if the scores are interpreted in terms of an observable attribute, correlations with other variables generally would be irrelevant to their validation. (Kane, 2013a: 35)

> The validation of simple interpretations (e.g., in terms of observable attributes) would require a very limited range of evidence. (Kane, 2013a: 64)

These are exactly the kind of claims that Lissitz and Samuelsen were trying to defend, even though they were judged to have done so inadequately. Kane (2008) argued that following recommendations from Lissitz and Samuelsen would risk transporting validity theory back into the bad old days of the 1950s to the 1970s, when different interpretations were assumed to require different kinds of validation. Ironically, a similar risk might arise in relation to his own account, if it were to be over-interpreted. After all, it is premised specifically on the principle that unambitious interpretations, such as those framed in terms of observable attributes, require only a limited range of evidence.

The very idea of an observable attribute is worth unpacking, because its meaning is not at all obvious. Is it meant to imply that it is possible to observe certain attributes directly; more specifically, that it is possible to observe how much of an attribute a person has? That would *seem* to be the implication. Yet we know that competence is notoriously tricky to infer from performance. Observing a performance directly is not the same as observing an attribute directly. Ultimately, the assessment of attributes always involves a non-trivial process of *indirect inference* from observations of behaviour. The same would be just as true in everyday life as it is in the test situation. Attributes are never actually observed, and measurement is always indirect (Guilford, 1936; Loevinger, 1957; Messick, 1994).

If this is true, then it might bring us back to the idea of a nomological network. Within this network would reside the unobservable – attributes such as proficiency in algebra, motivation, or response styles such as desirability – and beyond it would lie the observable, the instances of behaviour. The nomological network – our theory of mind, if you like – provides a conceptual framework for formulating hypotheses concerning measurement quality. Thus, before we can infer a low level of proficiency from evidence of poor performance on our algebra test, we also need good reason to infer sufficient motivation to have performed optimally – and so on for a range of plausible rival hypotheses involving a variety of alternative unobservable attributes. As such, any inference concerning a focal attribute will be scaffolded by inferences concerning a variety of non-focal attributes within the nomological network.

If nomological network thinking were to prove fundamental to validation, after all, would that render construct validation tantamount to theory-testing on a grand scale, à la Cronbach and Meehl? Not necessarily. If we were to treat the nomological network as a fairly robust system of folk psychological concepts that could be taken for granted, then it could function as a useful *tool for* validation without also necessarily being the *subject of* validation. From this perspective, the attributes of educational and psychological measurement might best be described as neither observable nor theoretical, but as conceptual in the sense discussed by Dennett (1987, 1998).

An interesting feature of the argument-based approach is that Kane could respond to this debate over the nature of attributes (observable vs. theoretical vs. conceptual) by claiming that he is not committed to any theory of mind at all. Indeed, he might add, the whole point of the argument-based approach is that it is up to the *validator* to import *their* theory of mind to the IUA, and to test it out accordingly. If, on the one hand, their theory were to be populated purely by observable attributes, then the IUA would be framed in terms of relatively unambitious interpretations, and validation would be fairly straightforward. If, on the other hand, their theory were to be populated exclusively by theoretical constructs which represented underlying causal entities, then the IUA would be framed in terms of very ambitious interpretations, and validation would be very complex. From this perspective, we might consider Kane's contribution to validity theory not in terms of provision of a new theory of validity per se, but in terms of provision of a new structure for accommodating any number of theories.

Borsboom (part 2): validity is ontological, not epistemological   In a paper entitled 'The concept of validity', Borsboom et al. (2004) set out to challenge currently endorsed conceptions of validity. Their specific target was construct validity, which they characterized as a loose coalescence of ideas stemming from logical positivist thinking on nomological networks, as initially proposed by Cronbach and Meehl (1955), and as subsequently embraced by many theorists in their wake including Messick (1989a) and, according to Borsboom et al. (2009), Kane (2006). Their paper was aptly titled because it focused squarely on the definition of validity and how the term ought to be used. Construct validity theorists, they argued, had misrepresented validity as a matter of epistemology (how we know things), rather than as a matter of ontology (how things are). The correct way to think about validity, they insisted, was ontologically, by treating validity as 'a concept like truth' (Borsboom et al., 2004: 1063).

More specifically, Borsboom et al. (2004) claimed that the correct way to think about validity was as a particular kind of measurement concept: one that represented the essence of measurement, and which provided a foundation for all other measurement concepts. In short, to claim validity was to claim that it was true that the test measured the attribute that it was supposed to measure. Accordingly, they identified two basic conditions as necessary in order to apply the term 'validity' correctly:

1 the attribute must *exist*; and
2 variation in the test scores must be *caused by* variation in the attribute.

Causation was fundamental to their account: the only way to make sense of measurement, they claimed, was in terms of causation; so validity (which by their definition was inherently a measurement concept) also must be framed in terms of causation. This contrasted sharply, they believed, with the concept of construct validity which, given its roots in operationism and logical positivism, did its best to shun talk of things really existing and, therefore, of things really causing.

It is important to emphasize how radical a departure from mainstream validity theory this was. Borsboom et al. (2004) presented their argument as though they were returning to the classic definition of validity (the degree to which a test measures what it is supposed to measure), but they actually went much further than this. By stripping validity 'of all excess baggage' (2004: 1070), they intentionally rendered it independent of other measurement concepts such as reliability, unidimensionality and measurement invariance. In other words, *their* concept of validity allowed that a test could be valid but not reliable: it could be valid to the extent that examinees' scores were genuinely caused by the attribute in question; but it also might be unreliable to the extent that those scores were affected by factors in addition to the attribute. Theirs was a narrower concept than often was (and still is) associated with the classic definition. Even during the early years it was not uncommon for validity to be understood as an umbrella concept for describing overall measurement quality, thereby subsuming other measurement concepts such as reliability within it (Ruch and Stoddard, 1927; Odell, 1928). Conversely, according to Borsboom and colleagues, a test could be valid, but still far from 'optimal' (2004: 1070).

There seemed to be two major motivations underlying Borsboom and colleagues' desire to deconstruct modern construct validity theory. The first was to strip validity back to its essence, which they argued on the basis that treating both social and technical issues under the banner of validity had rendered the concept confusing and impractical (we will return to this motivation shortly when we discuss the scope of validity and the debate between broad and narrow conceptions). The second was to help free the concept of validity from the foundations laid in outdated conceptions of operationism and logical positivism. The foundations of validity, they believed, were far more sensibly laid in *realism*. Whereas construct validity was framed inherently in terms of *interpretation* and aspired to little more than *plausibility*, realism was framed inherently in terms of the *facts* and aspired to the *truth*. Validity was a concept like truth, and therefore ought to be concerned with the facts, not simply with interpretations.

Borsboom and colleagues developed their argument in various ways, two of which we will consider here. The first was an attempt to undermine construct validity theory by claiming that it led to absurd conclusions. We are not convinced by this attack, and feel that it misrepresents the essence of construct validity. The second was an attempt to promote validity as an ontological concept rather than an epistemological one, which elevates fact and true belief above interpretation and justified belief. This is a much more complicated argument to unravel, but we will attempt to do so and explore alternatives to their conclusion.

Borsboom et al. (2009) began their boldly entitled chapter 'The end of construct validity' by claiming that the very idea of validity as a property of test score interpretations, which reflects the strength of evidence for those interpretations, had absurd consequences. It meant that every possible interpretation of test scores could be legitimately framed in terms of construct validity, even interpretations that denied measurement. What should be concluded, they asked, if a programme of research resulted in a strong argument in favour of the following interpretation: the test does *not* measure the intended attribute, or any attribute at all? The construct validity theorist would be forced to accept that this interpretation (the conclusion of the validity argument) had a high level of construct validity, despite the test measuring nothing at all. This, they suggested, was absurd – as was the very idea that validity is a property of a validity argument, which characterizes its adequacy or strength.

The absurdity of this conclusion rests on the premise that validity is a property of a validity argument and, therefore, that *every possible* interpretation of validation evidence must be framed in terms of construct validity. We believe that this misrepresents a theory that was designed to handle *very specific* interpretations: measurement interpretations. Borsboom and colleagues were right that modern definitions of validity, especially the definition in the first sentence of Messick (1989a), do *seem* to focus squarely on interpretation per se, almost as though the idea of a measurement interpretation was not fundamental after all. However, as we discussed in Chapter 4, appearances can be deceptive: the whole point of Messick's reunification of validity theory was to identify measurement as the central focus for all validation. From this perspective, validity is what is claimed on the basis of a strong validity argument, but *validity is not the strength of the validity argument* per se – it is simply what is claimed on the basis of a strong argument.

Validity is what is claimed when there is strong evidence of sufficient measurement quality; invalidity is what is claimed when there is strong evidence of insufficient measurement quality. In short, construct validity is not a concept that applies to any old interpretation; it applies to very specific interpretations – that is, to measurement interpretations.

Even Kane, who has explicitly theorized validation in terms of argumentation, tends not speak of the validity of the validity argument. Instead, he refers to its adequacy, coherence, completeness and plausibility, for example:

> The IUA provides a template for validation and a basis for evaluating the adequacy of the validity argument. If the IUA is coherent and complete and if all of its inferences and assumptions are plausible given the evidence, the proposed interpretations and uses can be considered valid. (Kane, 2013a: 65)

All validity arguments need to be judged in these terms, so these concepts *do* apply to all interpretations (i.e. to all validity arguments and, consequently, to the conclusion of any validity argument), even if the validity argument concludes that there is strong evidence of insufficient measurement quality. However, the concept of validity *only* applies when there is strong evidence of sufficient measurement quality; and it applies to the specific interpretation of outcomes from the measurement procedure as measures of the attribute in question. In other words, to claim that the interpretation is valid is to make a claim like this: 'the scores can be interpreted as a measure of competence in some domain' (Kane, 2012: 69). In effect, this is a claim about a measurement procedure, and so even from the validity argument perspective validity can be legitimately conceived as a *property of a measurement procedure* (Newton, 2012a). Just to hammer the point home, Cronbach and Meehl's seminal paper was entitled 'Construct validity in psychological tests' (1955), and referred repeatedly to the construct validity *of the test*, by which they meant the degree to which the test measured the construct (i.e. postulated attribute) that it was supposed to measure. (Remember that both Kane and Messick extended validity to embrace the interpretation *and use* of test scores, but this is a separable issue that we will discuss later, retaining a tight focus on interpretation and measurement for now.)

The second (albeit related) challenge concerned whether validity is a concept that ought to be restricted to the ontological realm. Borsboom and colleagues argued that validity ought to focus on ontology (and facts) to the exclusion of epistemology (and interpretations):

> [T]here are no universal characteristics of measurement except the ontological claim involved. The only thing that all measurement procedures have in common is the either implicit or explicit assumption that there is an attribute out there that, somewhere in the long and complicated chain of events leading to the measurement outcome, is playing a causal role in determining what values the measurements will take. (Borsboom et al., 2004: 1062–3)

In other words, validity ought to concern whatever it is that makes it true that a test measures what it is supposed to measure. According to Borsboom and colleagues, there are only two things that all measurement procedures have in common, so these must constitute the essential truth conditions for validity: the attribute supposedly being measured must exist; and the attribute must affect the outcomes of the measurement procedure. We can summarize these truth conditions as follows:

1   It is true that:

  i. the attribute exists
  ii. variation (or lack of variation) in the attribute causes variation (or lack of variation) in measurement outcomes.

From this perspective, validity is equivalent to the truth of the existence claim (1.i.) alongside the truth of the causal claim (1.ii.). Validity is not a matter of whether we have grounds for believing these claims: it is not an epistemological concept. Validity is simply whether these claims are true: it is an ontological concept. Indeed, if these claims are true, then they are true, period – which suggests that validity is not a matter of degree but an all-or-nothing concept. However, remember that validity is necessary but not sufficient for optimal measurement, according to the position advocated by Borsboom and colleagues. Thus, measurement outcome variation might be caused by the attribute (reflecting a true signal), but at the same time contaminated by other factors (reflecting noise), rendering the test simultaneously valid and unreliable.

Although this might appear to be an intuitively straightforward and appealing way of framing the definitional question, it does beg two very fundamental questions concerning what it might mean for an attribute to exist, and more complex still, what it might mean for an attribute to cause. Without clear answers to these questions (and we certainly have no clear answers), the implications for validation research remain correspondingly unclear. However, even framing the definitional question like this, we might question whether 1.i. and 1.ii. are the *only* things that successful measurement procedures have in common. Indeed, one might prefer a more subtle and more idealistic definition along the following lines:

2   It is true that:

  i. the attribute exists
  ii. variation (or lack of variation) in the components of the attribute causes variation (or lack of variation) in measurement outcomes – in proportion to how those components comprise the attribute – and variation (or lack of variation) in measurement outcomes is not caused by components of other attributes nor influenced by any other factors.

This is effectively a definition of perfect measurement (from a causal perspective), in which 2.ii. is framed in terms of the twin threats to valid interpretation that Messick emphasized so strongly: construct underrepresentation and construct-irrelevant variance. It treats the attribute more as a composite than a whole, in a manner reminiscent of the cognitive approach, thereby referring more to the causal efficacy of the components than to the causal efficacy of the attribute.[3] Interestingly, by defining perfect measurement, this would appear to render validity a matter of degree after all. Of course, the attribute will still either exist or not exist. However, clearly there will be degrees to which measurement outcomes are caused by the attribute components, as opposed to components of other attributes and degrees to which the components impact on measurement outcomes in proportion to their significance as elements of the attribute. Another interesting feature according to this definition is that other measurement concepts such as reliability and bias are no longer orthogonal to validity, as Borsboom and colleagues proposed. Unreliability results from the unsystematic impact of attribute-irrelevant causes; while bias results from the systematic impact of attribute-irrelevant causes, or from the systematic impact of attribute component underrepresentation. From this perspective, indices of unreliability and bias merely provide *evidence* of invalidity: partial and fallible evidence.

Finally, in staking their claim to definition 1, Borsboom and colleagues failed to acknowledge that all measurement procedures have something else in common that is extremely important: they all terminate in interpretations – measurement interpretations. In the absence of interpretation, there simply is no measurement; there are only long and complicated chains of events. Without interpretation there is nothing more than mercury rising and falling in a tube, a shadow moving around a sundial, or a distribution of marks from a school achievement examination. Without interpretation, there is nothing more than a person sitting on a couch describing an inkblot. Again, there is no measurement without interpretation. Measurement is the endpoint of an interpretive procedure: an interpretive measurement procedure.

When this is appreciated, the very idea of 'a test measuring' begins to sound like a category mistake. Tests are not the kind of thing that can measure; people measure using tests. This is not a trivial point if we are interested in establishing validity in relation to measurement. If what ultimately constitutes measurement is the causal reaction of the measurement instrument under the influence of the attribute, then it seems reasonable to speak of the validity of the measurement instrument. However, if what ultimately constitutes measurement is the *interpretation* of that causal reaction, then it would seem more reasonable to speak of the validity of the interpretation of outcomes from the measurement instrument. There are two different kinds of claim here, that:

- the test measures the attribute – the formulation that Borsboom and colleagues prefer
- outcomes from the test can be interpreted as measures of the attribute – the formulation that construct validity theorists tend to prefer.

Incidentally, both can be framed in terms of the validity of the measurement procedure, although definition of the measurement procedure becomes far broader according to the second alternative, embracing the interpretation itself. This is to suggest yet another potential set of truth conditions for measurement, and a third potential definition of validity:

3   It is true that:

    i. the attribute exists

    ii. variation (or lack of variation) in the components of the attribute causes variation (or lack of variation) in measurement outcomes – in proportion to how those components comprise the attribute – and variation (or lack of variation) in measurement outcomes is not caused by components of other attributes nor influenced by any other factors

    iii. the attribute specification accurately represents the attribute, its components and its relation to measurement outcomes.

This definition adds an interpretation claim to the existence claim and causal claim, as the culmination of the truth about successful measurement. In order for it to be true that an attribute has been measured, the person doing the measuring must be in possession of true beliefs concerning the nature of the attribute, and of how variations in the attribute relate to variations in measurement outcomes. Here, rather than referring to particular beliefs of particular measurers, it seems more reasonable to refer to the collective belief of a measurement community – the product of scientific investigation into the attribute and its measurement – which we might refer to as the *attribute specification:* the explicit construction of the attribute by the scientific community. This extension of definition 1 would seem to be a realist definition of construct validity. It embraces both the validity of the test (3.i. and 3.ii.), and the validity of the construction of the attribute by the measurement community (3.iii.) and, in toto, defines the validity of the measurement procedure.

Definition 3 leads us to the question of how we might pick up the gauntlet thrown down to Kane (2013a) by Borsboom and Markus (2013), developing a theme from Borsboom et al. (2009). Once again, according to Borsboom and colleagues, validity ought to be conceived as a concept like *the truth of* the claim that the test measures the attribute that it is supposed to measure. Yet Kane seemed to want to treat validity as a concept like *justified belief in* the claim that the test measures the attribute that it is supposed to measure. Borsboom et al. illustrated their discomfort with the justified-belief definition with a graph of the 'construct validity of phlogiston measures as a function of time' (2009: 142). According to construct validity theory, they argued, phlogiston measures would be valid just prior to 1775, given strong evidence in favour of phlogiston theory, but invalid just after 1775 in the wake of the strong refutation of phlogiston theory by Lavoisier. Once again, they believed this to be an absurd conclusion. How could a test be valid in one year, yet invalid the next? Surely the test is just an instrument that reacts to changes in its environment, which there must be a truth about as to whether or not it measures, independent of what anyone believes about it or why they believe that?

For Borsboom and colleagues, a measurement procedure is valid if *it is true* that it is possible to measure the attribute that it is supposed to measure. For Kane, apparently, a measurement procedure is valid if *we are justified in believing* that it is possible to measure the attribute that it is supposed to measure, for example:

> The validity of a proposed interpretation or use of test scores at any point in time can be defined in terms of the plausibility and appropriateness of the proposed interpretation/use at that time. (Kane, 2013a: 2)

> Validity is a matter of degree, and it may change over time as the interpretations/uses develop and as new evidence accumulates. The plausibility of a proposed IUA will increase if ongoing research supports its inferences and assumptions (especially those that are most questionable a priori). Validity may decrease if new evidence casts doubt on the proposed IUA. (Kane, 2013a: 3)

The issue is whether we should take passages such as these at face value and assume that Kane really does choose to treat validity as a concept like justified belief, rather than the truth; or whether we might reasonably reinterpret passages such as these as though they were not describing validity per se, but were describing *the defensibility of a claim to validity*. To claim that a measurement procedure is valid is to assert justified belief in its validity. So validity *claims* transport us from ontology to epistemology. Validity claims lie at the heart of the argument-based approach. A validity claim requires a validity argument, and the stronger the validity argument, the more defensible the claim to validity will be. Although Borsboom and colleagues objected to the idea that *validity* decreases when new evidence casts doubt on the interpretation argument, presumably they would not object to the idea that *the defensibility of a claim to validity* decreases in the light of evidence like this. This is only a minor change of wording, but it changes the meaning of the expression significantly in a way that responds to the concerns expressed by Borsboom and colleagues, and that does not undermine the argument-based approach.

Although this is not precisely how Kane framed his response to Borsboom and Markus, he did appear to accept a distinction between justified belief and the truth; albeit explaining that he was far more interested in justified belief than in the truth, which he considered to be unknowable, and which therefore he left in the background. He also focused his comments specifically on the legitimacy of validity claims according to each perspective (see Kane, 2013b: 120). So, reading between the lines, there would seem to be some support for the reinterpretation suggested above, which allows for a degree of reconciliation between the two perspectives. Returning to the example provided by Borsboom and colleagues, if the validity argument regarding the phlogiston measure prior to 1775 had been judged to be sufficiently strong, then indeed it would have been defensible to *claim* that the phlogiston measure was valid; and if the validity argument had been subsequently judged to be insufficiently strong post-Lavoisier, then it would not have been defensible to *claim* that the phlogiston measure was valid.

4   We are justified in believing (it is true) that:

  i. the attribute exists
  ii. variation (or lack of variation) in the components of the attribute causes variation (or lack of variation) in measurement outcomes – in proportion to how those components comprise the attribute – and variation (or lack of variation)

in measurement outcomes is not caused by components of other attributes nor influenced by any other factors

iii. the attribute specification accurately represents the attribute, its components and its relation to measurement outcomes.

Formulation 4 is not a measurement *definition*, but a measurement *claim* – a validity claim – which sets out what that claim entails. Therefore, formulation 4 is ultimately epistemological, and requires a validity argument to establish the case supporting the three sub-claims based on empirical evidence and logical analysis. If the validity argument is sufficiently strong, then we are at liberty to claim validity: that is, to claim that the measurement procedure (and thus the measurement interpretation) is valid (under specified conditions, of course). Now, it seems to us that Borsboom and colleagues have criticized Kane for *defining* validity along the lines of formulation 4: validity *is* the degree of justification for believing that the test measures what it is supposed to measure: i.e. validity *is* the strength of the validity argument (and to be fair, sometimes Kane does write like this). However, as we read Kane, validity is what is claimed when the validity argument provides a strong justification for believing that the test measures what it is supposed to measure, which is specified by the interpretation argument. A strong validity argument is what allows you to claim that the test measures what it is supposed to measure: it is what allows you to claim validity; but a strong validity argument certainly does not make it *true* that the test measures what it is supposed to measure. Validity claims are always provisional.

Interpreted thus, there would not seem to be any logical incompatibility between the argument-based approach and any of the realist definitions identified above, which is consistent with the idea that it is capable of accommodating a range of philosophical perspectives. After all, Kane (2013a) contained a section entitled 'Causal interpretations', which did accommodate the realist perspective introduced by Borsboom et al. (2004).[4] This is to propose a *rapprochement* in which the definition of validity, as Borsboom and colleagues would understand this idea – involving identification of the fundamental characteristics of successful measurement procedures – is the very foundation of the interpretation argument. From this perspective, it is not up to Kane to propose a definition of validity; it is up to the *validator* to import *their* definition of validity to the IUA, reflecting their theories of mind, measurement, and so on. Ultimately, the argument-based approach provides a theory of validation, but not a theory of validity.

Although this attempt at reconciliation strikes us as entirely plausible as far as the interpretation argument is concerned, and entirely in keeping with Kane's focus on validation rather than validity, its extension to the use argument becomes a little more cumbersome. Presumably, the validator would need to begin by defining a different *kind* of validity for the use argument – involving identification of the fundamental characteristics of successful *decision-making* procedures. Although this is not entirely implausible, it would seem to render the concept of validity correspondingly less transparent.

The deconstruction of construct validity theory by Borsboom and colleagues has taken us back into complex philosophical territory, but rightly so. Ultimately, anyone who wants to grapple with validity theory must grapple with some extremely thorny issues in the philosophies of science, measurement and mind. Borsboom and colleagues expressed a preference for philosophical realism, which they considered to be the antithesis of construct validity, but the story is not quite that simple. Cronbach, Messick and Kane all presented conceptions of validity and validation which they believed to be compatible with a range of philosophical positions. Indeed, there has been, and still is, a lively debate over exactly which philosophical perspective Cronbach and Meehl actually subscribed to (e.g. Bechtold, 1959; Norris, 1983; Slaney, 2012). The essence of a construct is that it is conceptual, a linguistic tool. So, an important question was whether the constructs of construct validity were meant to refer to 'real' attributes of the mind – underlying causes of behaviour – or whether they were assumed to be nothing more than useful ways of capturing and expressing patterns of behaviour: that is, *nothing more* than theoretical constructs. Cronbach (1989a) explained that Cronbach and Meehl saw no need to choose between realism and instrumentalism, thereby recommending construct validation to researchers of all persuasions. Having said that, he had explained earlier that the position adopted by Cronbach and Meehl (1955) was essentially instrumentalist (Cronbach, 1971). It seems fair to conclude that the principles of construct validity are compatible with a range of philosophical perspectives, and are certainly not incompatible with realism.

Ultimately, even those like Borsboom and colleagues, who consider realism to be the only game in town, have still to deliver a convincing account of exactly *how* the attributes of educational and psychological measurement are supposed to exist. In the absence of a convincing account, the implications of realism for validation research remain correspondingly unclear, since there are no clues as to what might count as evidence of an attribute existing, and what might count as evidence of its causal impact on measurement outcomes. Borsboom and colleagues were right to lead us back to these murky waters, but unfortunately these waters remain very murky indeed.

One final issue worth returning to at this point is the pragmatism embodied in early conceptions of validity, which allowed that a range of different measurement interpretations – relating to precisely the same set of test scores – might all be judged to be valid simultaneously. Remember, from Chapter 3, the example provided by Anastasi (1968), who suggested that results from a single mathematics test might be validated as achievement measures (for one use), as aptitude measures (for another) and so on (for a range of different uses). The pragmatic corollary was that in principle, both achievement *and* aptitude measurement interpretations might be strongly supported. This kind of thinking would be extremely hard to reconcile with a realist perspective on science, measurement and mind. Even from an instrumentalist perspective, this might not be straightforward to reconcile – but how pragmatic a concept do we want or need validity to be? Do we need it to be a precise scientific concept and, if so, what kind of science do we need to invoke? Or do we really just need something far more heuristic, a concept that invokes metaphorical thinking and rules-of-thumb, as a helpful guide to everyday action under conditions of extreme uncertainty?

Michell and Maraun: doubts about measurement   Questions such as these provide a fitting introduction to one of the most challenging deconstructions of recent years: the critique of educational and psychological measurement. For the best part of a century validity has been defined in terms of the plausibility of measurement interpretations: in effect, whether or not the test measures the attribute that it is supposed to measure. Yet this presupposes that the attributes of educational and psychological measurement are measurable. If these attributes do not actually possess the kind of structure that permits measurement, then it simply will not be possible to measure them, no matter how much time and effort may be invested in the test development process. Across a series of contributions from the 1990s onwards, Joel Michell consistently reminded would-be measurement scientists and practitioners that there is no strong evidence that the attributes of educational and psychological measurement possess the additive structure that would warrant talk of measurement (e.g. Michell, 1990, 1999, 2000, 2005, 2009). The invalidity in validity, Michell concluded, is that 'the concept feigns knowledge where such does not yet exist' (2009: 123).

In a sense, Michell's critique was not devastating, since he did not claim that the attributes of educational and psychological measurement are not measurable; simply that their measurability remains an open question. However, he is right to question the presumption of measurability in the absence of sufficient reason, as undoubtedly this would represent an embarrassing hole in any validity argument. Moreover, Michell has not claimed that the attributes of educational and psychological measurement are imaginary or unknowable; only that it is safer to assume that their structure probably is not additive. It still may be possible to 'assess' them – so the concept of validity could have application as long as appropriately reconstructed in terms of a looser concept of 'assessment' – it is just that the idea of 'measuring' these attributes may be far-fetched.[5] Like Borsboom, then, Michell is right to lead us back to the murky waters of philosophical analysis. It is not enough to interrogate our concept of validity; we also need to interrogate our concept of measurement.

Other writers have gone further still in challenging the presumption of measurement. Maraun (1998), for example, argued that the failure to find convincing solutions to measurement problems in psychology is attributable to the fact that measurement has been mistaken for an empirical matter, when it is chiefly a conceptual one. Moreover, the grammar of the everyday folk psychological concepts that psychologists wish to discuss in measurement terms is so notoriously complex and messy that it looks unlikely that it could ever be amenable to formalization in the sense required by measurement talk. That is, the attributes of educational and psychological measurement are not, and are unlikely ever to become, measurable.

Moss: situated validation   One of the most interesting and provocative attempts to reconstruct traditional validity theory has been spearheaded by Pamela Moss (e.g. Moss, 1994, 1996, 2003, 2013; Moss et al., 2005; Moss et al., 2006). She has presented the problem like this: because validity theory has been developed to deal with standardized assessment procedures, the less standardized the assessment that we are interested in evaluating, the less likely it is that traditional conceptions of validity will apply. This challenge is epitomized in the question of how to conceptualize the evaluation of 'on the fly' formative educational assessment interactions. Here, notice that the emphasis is on assessment *interactions*, not assessment *procedures*. Given that there may be no identifiable procedure common across all such interactions, what is it that we ought to be evaluating, and what concepts ought to steer our evaluations? Even during ongoing formative exchanges, our focus is still on evidence-based interpretations, decisions and actions (Moss et al., 2006) – so there are fundamental synergies between standardized and unstandardized assessment contexts – but the unique, situated and dynamic nature of these interactions somehow needs to be accommodated. Moss has introduced a range of possible perspectives from which such situated, social and interactive assessment exchanges might be scrutinized, borrowing ideas from hermeneutics and sociocultural studies in particular.

In many ways, Moss is the successor to Messick in attempting to reconstruct validity as a fundamentally social concept. However, whereas Messick seemed to retreat a little from his original ambition, Moss has embraced it. She may have opened a can of worms for validity theorists, but the questions that she seeks answers to are extremely important ones. Traditional validity theory has tended to focus on hypothetical, intended and idealized interpretations: if the test is used in the right way, with the right people, and under the right conditions, then it will be possible to measure accurately and make better decisions which, with optimal intervention, should result in positive consequences. Moss has challenged validity theorists to get real: to help make sense of the complex and messy world of everyday assessment and decision-making. The inevitable question, of course, is whether the concept of validity is flexible enough to be stretched this far.

Construct validity in the balance

Since the birth of construct validity in the 1954 *Standards* there have been numerous attempts to deconstruct it, scrutinize its principles and procedures and reconstruct it. As it evolved from 'just one kind of validity' to 'validity itself', it adopted a somewhat less formal persona: it became relevant to the evaluation of any kind of attribute or construct, and loosened its ties to a particular philosophical tradition. However, the process of evolution from traditional construct validity theory to the modern version was subtle. Even now, it is not entirely clear what constitutes the modern version as distinct from the original version, neither is it entirely clear which of the original criticisms still have force. So, this final section will attempt to deconstruct construct validity theory, once again, into a number of relatively discrete elements, in order to consider their significance and examine a range of issues arising.

The nature of validation research

A major reason why construct validity caught the imagination of modern theorists was that it corrected a collective delusion, shared by many measurement specialists working in psychology and education, that validity could be established on the basis of a one-off-study. It was always presumed that the attributes of traditional construct validation required an extended validation research programme; but it took some years before this principle was generalized to all of the attributes of educational and psychological measurement, and construct validation became the rule, not the exception.

One of the earliest criticisms targeted at traditional construct validity theory, which is just as pertinent to the modern version, was that – by insisting that all sorts of evidence and analysis were relevant to construct validation, while not requiring that any particular kind or kinds be furnished – it almost encouraged evaluators to select evidence in favour and to overlook evidence against (Campbell, 1960). Even if researchers were not inappropriately selective in their presentation of evidence, the traditional version remained quite vague, essentially confirmationist and risked lapsing into 'haphazard accumulations of data' (Cronbach, 1971: 483). To counter this threat, two further principles of construct validation emerged. The first was to ensure that validation always began with a reasonably definite statement of the proposed interpretation. The second was to ensure that validation progressed both by collecting evidence in favour of the proposed interpretation, and by putting plausible rival interpretations to the test. This was epitomized in the logic of the MTMM matrix.

Together, these three principles represent what Kane has described as the enduring legacy of construct validity theory: the idea that validation is a programme, not a one-off-study; that it requires a clear statement of the proposed interpretation; and that it needs to proceed by exposing and testing presumptions. These principles remain firmly at the heart of modern construct validity theory. However, beyond these principles, the prescriptions of construct validation remain quite vague, even in modern accounts. For example, there is a tendency to claim, on the one hand, that all kinds of validation evidence and analysis are potentially relevant to any validation programme; while on the other hand, accepting that no particular kind of validation evidence or analysis is necessarily required (although cf. Kane).

From the second edition of *Psychological Testing* onwards, Anastasi (1961) repeatedly warned that the breadth and complexity of construct validity meant that it had not always been clearly understood by those who used the term. It seems fair to conclude that the same remains true today. A common misunderstanding is that construct validation is tantamount to adopting the MTMM approach. Although it would seem odd ever to deny the relevance of evidence from this particular technique, there is no reason to assume that it is necessarily always required. Moreover, as insisted by Cronbach (1989a), assessing convergence and divergence, howsoever that might be achieved, is only a first step towards construct validity.[6]

Although many still value the principle from Cronbach and Meehl that all kinds of validation evidence and analysis are potentially relevant to any validation programme, the waters have been muddied a little by the rise of the cognitive approach. Without necessarily completely disagreeing with this principle, researchers from the cognitive tradition place almost exclusive reliance on internal sources of evidence of score meaning. So, this represents a very particular reconstruction of construct validity theory. Quite how widely this perspective is shared is not clear, although its emphasis does not seem to be reflected in the 1999 *Standards*.

In summary, the three methodological principles that were derived from traditional construct validity theory still seem to hold across all versions of modern construct validity theory. They amount to the claim that good validation is no more or less than rigorous scientific inquiry into score meaning. Unfortunately, considerable debate remains over the precise ingredients of scientific inquiry – particularly the kinds of evidence and analysis that are deemed to be required, or even relevant, to any validation programme. This makes construct validation hard to exemplify, and consequently hard to understand.

The nature of constructs/attributes

One of the reasons why Kane has been reticent to pronounce himself a disciple of construct validity – even the modern version – seems to be that he still sees a potential role for the traditional version. For certain kinds of attributes (theoretical constructs) the original version of construct validity theory, with its sophisticated philosophical perspective, still seems appropriate. Yet for other kinds of attributes (observable attributes), nothing quite so sophisticated is required. Theoretical constructs entail more ambitious interpretations, requiring a greater burden of validation; while observable attributes entail less ambitious interpretations. Whereas theoretical constructs might well require a never-ending process of validation and a dense mosaic of evidence of all kinds – which is the image of validation promulgated by Messick – the validation of observable attributes will be far more circumscribed, requiring far less evidence of fewer kinds. Thus, according to Kane, how much of what kind of empirical evidence and logical analysis is either relevant to, or required for, any particular validation programme, is determined by the nature of the interpretation that needs to be validated: the nature of the construct /attribute involved.

Although at face value this appears to provide an attractive solution to the problem of which ingredients to include in any particular scientific inquiry into score meaning, it also seems to presume a theory of mind in which some attributes are essentially observable, while others are essentially theoretical. This is certainly contestable. A plausible alternative is that none of the attributes of educational and psychological measurement is usefully described as either observable or theoretical. Instead, they might be better described as conceptual: concepts that refer neither to surface-level observable entities, nor to underlying unobservable ones (e.g. Dennett, 1987, 1998). Having said that, to describe them as conceptual is not to deny their reality, or the possibility of somehow assessing them.[7]

Here, the point is not to recommend one philosophical stance over another. It is just to illustrate that sooner or later, validity bottoms out in philosophy, and that different philosophical views on the nature of attributes/constructs are likely to have different implications for validation. This is an area of validity theory that is not at all well developed, unfortunately. There are potentially quite different bases for modern construct validity theory, and their implications are still to be effectively theorized.

The nomological network

The idea of a nomological network was fundamental to the account of modern construct validity theory presented by Messick. It was his organizing principle. The focal construct lay at the centre of the network, with decisions and consequences cast as network nodes. Various constructs were related to the focal construct in various ways, and this kind of network thinking enabled Messick to represent the interaction between construct-relevance and construct-irrelevance across task performances. As such, it provided a theoretical framework for representing both the intended interpretation of test scores (variance attributable to the focal construct, e.g. critical thinking ability), and plausible rival hypotheses (variance attributable to alternative constructs, e.g. general knowledge). To the extent that the nomological network was an organizing principle, for Messick, it provided a conceptual tool with which to structure validation. As a *tool for* validation, there is much to recommend network thinking.

However, as the *subject of* validation, the nomological network is more controversial. As Orton (1987) reminded us, the logic of construct validation as it was originally conceived meant that what was at stake was not only the validity of the measurement procedure, but the validity of the construct and, ultimately, the validity of the entire nomological network. This really is theory-testing on a grand scale. It is not unreasonable to ask, along with Lissitz and Samuelsen (2007a, 2007b), whether this is the best way to conceptualize validation, particularly as practised in many applied contexts such as education. Campbell (1960) had asked essentially the same question nearly 50 years earlier. He claimed that there was a useful distinction to be drawn between two kinds of construct validity: nomological validity, theory-testing on a grand scale; and trait validity, a more restricted notion that focused primarily on traits and their measurement in relative isolation. As far as commercially published tests were concerned, he suggested, nomological validation was 'apt to be rare for some time to come' (Campbell, 1960: 547) – a prediction that would appear to have stood the test of time. Even Cronbach came to acknowledge the potentially repressive effect on research of the very idea of nomological validation. He observed that in the two decades before Cronbach and Meehl (1955), a great deal of research into novel personality measures had been published. Yet after 1955, hardly any such research continued; to the extent that construct validation now seemed to be more like a lifetime of study than a one-off investigation, it had become correspondingly less attractive a proposition (Cronbach, 1986).

Kane, too, has been sceptical of the general relevance of construct validity *qua* theory-testing on a grand scale. Although, like Campbell, he allowed that there might be a relatively small role for it, he did not see it as central, and has largely rejected talk of nomological networks. The conceptual tool that Kane has employed instead of the network is the IUA (Kane, 2013a). Although Kane claims that the IUA plays the same role as the nomological network, albeit in a more general way, it is fair to say that it does so far less graphically: that is, there is nothing about argument structure per se that conjures images of relatedness between focal constructs, non-focal constructs, decisions, consequences and suchlike – the kind of imagery that Messick found so useful.

In addition, nomological networks have been downplayed by those who stress the importance of cognitive psychology to construct validation. Rather than focusing on theories of mind, they focus on theories of cognition. Emphasizing the need to study the anatomy of attributes and the cognitive ingredients of test performance, they imply that this kind of psychological theorizing is fundamental to all validation. This approach also evokes the idea of theory-testing on a grand scale, albeit with a focus on the micro constructs of academic psychology (working memory, encoding, etc.), rather than the macro constructs of folk psychology (aptitude, achievement, etc.).

To summarize, there is still considerable ambiguity over whether nomological network thinking is of value to the majority of measurement professionals, and to modern construct validity theory in general. From one perspective, the network provides a neat conceptual framework for representing both the intended interpretation of test scores and plausible rival hypotheses. From another perspective, measurement professionals tend not to consider themselves to be in the business of theory-testing on a grand scale; they work with folk psychological principles that are largely taken for granted (see Cronbach, 1989a: 160, from Campbell), and are interested primarily in validating measures rather than theories. There does seem to be a general consensus that validation involves the testing of plausible hypotheses concerning score meaning, but to what extent does validation also imply theory-testing on a grand scale?

The label 'construct validity'

Cronbach (1989a) began his review of construct validation (after 30 years) by observing that almost every psychologist who writes about it describes it as confusing. Kane (2012) explained that he was reticent to use the term 'construct', because it had been used in so many different ways over the years that it was no longer clear what it meant. Bramley (2012) presented a similar argument. As a case in point, nowadays Kane tends to reserve the term 'construct' for talk of 'theoretical constructs', while many modern construct validity theorists, as well as the 1999 *Standards*, use 'construct' to mean nothing more specific than score meaning: that is, whatever the test is supposed to measure (Messick, 1992: 1488). This divergence of usage is problematic. For example, we get into muddy waters when we ask questions such as: 'Can the term *validity* be used in a general sense without invoking the notion of a construct?' (Sireci, 2007: 478). If we were to take 'construct' to mean 'theoretical construct', as distinct from 'observable attribute', then we might agree with Kane that there are plenty of examples of construct-free validation. However, if we were to take 'construct' to mean 'whatever the test is supposed to measure', then we would be forced to conclude that there could be no such examples.

A strong case can be made for discarding the modifier 'construct' and referring simply to 'validity'. After all, as explained in the glossary of the 1999 *Standards*, if all validity is supposed to be construct validity, then the modifier is actually redundant. Moreover, making explicit reference to construct validity risks confusion between the specialized construct validation of the trinitarian phase, and the generalized construct validation of the unitarian phase. In fact, there are many different ways of conceptualizing construct validity theory, all of which add to confusion over the meaning of the term (see Loevinger, 1957; Bechtoldt, 1959; Messick, 1992; Smith, 2005; Kane, 2008; Borsboom et al., 2009; Maraun et al., 2009; Lovasz and Slaney, 2013; Maraun and Gabriel, 2013). In our experience, the potential for confusion between trinitarian and unitarian accounts of validity is one of the most problematic corollaries of continuing to use the term 'construct validity'. Students often treat construct validity, content validity and criterion validity as though they come as a package deal. The continued use of 'construct validity' seems implicitly to licence continuing reference to the other two 'types' of validity as well.

In the balance

What should we make of construct validity after nearly 60 years? Are we all construct validity theorists now? In one sense, we probably are. The one-off-study approach to validation is no longer acceptable, so we can no longer claim to be content validators or criterion validators. More importantly, it is also generally accepted that the proper approach to validation involves the identification and testing of plausible rival hypotheses for patterns of behaviour in testing situations – conceptualizing validation scientifically rather than purely logically or empirically – which is the principle that Messick described as the hallmark of construct validation.

However, in another sense, there are very many important points of detail over which present-day validity theorists disagree. In particular, the traditional version of construct validity was premised on a philosophy of science that many now consider to be outdated. Differences of opinion over the ontology of attributes, and the extent to which validation ought to be considered theory-testing on a grand scale, suggests that the essence of modern construct validity theory – if, indeed, there is one – is not at all straightforward to pinpoint. Although there was certainly a time and a reason for insisting that 'all validity is construct validity', that time now may have passed.

The scope of validity

Concern with impacts from testing is nothing new. Critics always have questioned its social value, and defenders always have had to respond to those criticisms. However, to what extent should investigation into consequences be considered an essential component of validation practice and validity theory? The inclusion of consequences would seem (at least) to represent a major paradigm shift from the days of the classic definition, when validity was simply the degree to which a test measured whatever it was supposed to measure. It would seem to render modern validity theory very much larger and more cumbersome than anything that ever preceded it. This is the topic of the second major debate over validity theory during the post-millennium phase: should it be required to embrace ethical issues of consequence beyond scientific issues of measurement?

Although it is appropriate to express the question at the heart of the debate like this, there is a subtle twist: consequences are potentially of interest not only to the ethical evaluation of test score use, but also to the scientific evaluation of test score meaning (see Chapters 4 and 6). So, this is not just a straightforward issue of *whether* measurement professionals ought to be interested in consequences; it is also a matter of *how* they ought to be interested in them. It is a debate over the role of consequential evidence in validity arguments. Perspectives on this debate range from those who insist that validity ought to remain a narrow, scientific concept concerned with the technical quality of a testing procedure, to those who insist that validity ought to become a broad, ethical concept concerned with the social value of a testing policy. Pamela Moss summarized the issues at the heart of this debate excellently.

- Should consequences be considered an aspect of validity at all? If yes, how should the concepts be related?

- Are inappropriate consequences relevant to validity only if they can be traced to a source of construct underrepresentation or construct irrelevant variance?

- Or could negative consequences associated with an otherwise valid interpretation call the validity of the test use into question?

- If yes, does that that mean we have expanded the focus of validity from the focus on an assessment-based interpretation to a focus on the larger system of which the assessment is a part?

- On what grounds should these decisions be made? Epistemological? Ethical? Practical? Political? (Moss, 1998: 6)

Emergence of the debate

Debate over the scope of validity began to take off during the early 1980s, under the influence of both Cronbach and Messick. During this period Cronbach was deeply immersed in evaluation theory, and increasingly had come to see validation as evaluation. He argued that as far as testing was concerned, the focus of evaluation should not be on a test in isolation, but on the entire system within which it was being used (Cronbach, 1980a). During a subsequent discussion of perspectives on validity argument, he specifically included consideration of evidence concerning bad consequences arising from tests of high measurement quality, observing that:

> The bottom line is that validators have an obligation to review whether a practice has appropriate consequences for individuals and institutions, and especially to guard against adverse consequences (Messick, 1980). You (like Yalow & Popham, 1983) may prefer to exclude reflection on consequences from the meanings of the word *validation*, but you cannot deny the obligation. (Cronbach, 1988: 6)

Messick spent many years trying to synthesize scientific and ethical concerns within an all-embracing theory of validity. We believe that he genuinely wanted, from the outset, to include the ethical evaluation of social consequences arising from testing policies within the scope of validity theory. If they were included, then there would be a clear obligation on measurement professionals to investigate them. He went further than Cronbach, commenting specifically on the implicit ambivalence in the above quotation:

> But we would prefer a somewhat stronger phrasing, because the meaning of validation should not be considered a preference. On what can the legitimacy of the obligation to appraise social consequences of test interpretation and use be based, we argue, if not on the only genuine imperative in testing, namely, validity? (Messick, 1989b: 11; see also Messick, 1989a: 20)

We take this to mean: if you integrate the ethical evaluation of social consequences within the concept of validity, then validators are likely to translate this into validation practice; if you do not, then there is a serious risk that no one will take responsibility for evaluating them.

Discontent with this broad perspective on validity was soon to be voiced. Wiley (1991: 89) argued that bad consequences arising from tests of high measurement quality ought to be theorized in terms of 'use errors', not validity. To do otherwise would complicate the concept of validity needlessly, and divert attention from what really mattered to the evaluation of measurement quality. Maguire et al. (1994) agreed: they insisted that concern for the evaluation of consequences should be extricated from validity theory, and instead embodied within ethical guidelines for good practice.

As measurement scientists and practitioners began to get to grips with Messick (1989a), an increasing number began to echo these sentiments. In an editorial entitled 'The great validity debate', Crocker (1997) introduced the first of two special issues of *Educational Measurement: Issues and Practice* devoted to what was fast becoming known as 'consequential validity'. She summarized the debate in terms of whether or not the investigation of possible consequences ought to be defined as an integral part of any validation programme. Indeed, this was how the debate began to take shape, with a 'for' camp embracing the evaluation of social consequences (e.g. Linn, 1997; Shepard, 1997), and an 'against' camp rejecting it (e.g. Mehrens, 1997; Popham, 1997).

The arguments for

The first major defence of the incorporation of consequences was presented by Shepard (1997). She adopted a position that was essentially aligned with Messick, arguing that the 'relationship in the nomological net between prerequisite algebra skills and later success in calculus is central to the meaning of the construct, not an add-on social nicety' (Shepard, 1997: 7). However, it is important to emphasize that Shepard was siding with the position adopted by the later Messick (e.g. 1995a), rather than the earlier (e.g. Messick, 1980). Evidence from consequences had a role to play in arbitrating questions of score meaning – even evidence from unintended side-effects – which was why they were of significance to construct validity: 'In a validity investigation, we don't just express a personal preference for consequences that we like or dislike. Consequences are evaluated in terms of the intended construct meaning' (Shepard, 1997: 8). Moreover, she made very clear that examples of test misuse, whatever their consequences, had no bearing at all on validity.

Linn (1997) largely agreed with Shepard, although he hinted at a more liberal stance, closer to the earlier Messick. He reiterated the concern that removing consequences from validity would relegate their evaluation to a lower priority, and explained that the best way to ensure that consequences remained a central evaluation concern was to include them as a central aspect of 'test validation' (1997: 16). Moss (1998) also leaned towards the more liberal position, arguing that testing practices actually change the social reality within which they operate. Because test score users may not interpret scores in ways intended by developers and publishers, and because their interpretations will change how they understand themselves and others, measurement professionals have a duty to investigate these processes and consequences.

Kane (2013a) also seemed to adopt a liberal position. He clearly did not welcome the ejection of consequences from the concept of validity, and argued in favour of including 'the evaluation of at least some major categories of unintended consequences in the validation of the score use' (Kane, 2013a: 60). He believed that consequences had a limited and less direct role in the evaluation of test score meaning (in the sense discussed by Shepard), but a direct and immediate role in the evaluation of test score use. Adverse impact and systemic consequences were of particular significance. Here, the implication was a requirement for ethical judgements of social value beyond scientific judgements of technical quality. If consequences were not included in validity, test users might mistake the validation of score meaning for the validation of score use; and measurement professionals might abdicate responsibility for the validation of score use, assuming that some other community would take it on. Since it is essential to evaluate consequences, and since 'validity is the bottom line in evaluating testing programs' (2013a: 63), Kane concluded that it did not make sense to exclude consequences from validity.

The arguments against

In response to the positions advocated by Shepard and Linn, Popham (1997) argued that burdening validity with consequences would be detrimental to the evaluation of test score meaning *and* to the evaluation of test score use, because it would result in confusion, not clarity. The traditional conception of validity as the accuracy of score-based inferences was crisp, but still hard for educators to understand. The consequences of making it harder still would represent too high a price to pay. In addition, he argued, the evaluation of test score meaning and test score *misuse* were quite separate: even ludicrous test score misuses would not alter prior judgements of test score meaning; that is, they would not alter the prior judgement of validity as traditionally conceived. Notice how Popham *challenged* the incorporation of consequences on the basis of examples that seemed to have nothing to do with score meaning; whereas Shepard *promoted* the incorporation of consequences on the basis of examples that did. However, both ultimately considered validity to be primarily scientific rather than ethical.

Mehrens (1997) also challenged the wisdom of embracing consequences within validity, proposing that it confounded inferences about measurement quality with inferences about treatment efficacy. He believed that accuracy of inference (e.g. diagnosis of prostate cancer) was logically distinct from the efficacy of subsequent intervention (e.g. cancer treatment). The risk that he saw was exactly the opposite of that later voiced by Kane (2013a): that test users might mistake invalidation of test score use for invalidation of test score meaning. An even bigger threat was that: 'If validity is everything, then validity is nothing' (Mehrens, 1997: 18) – part of the utility of the concept is its precision, and we should not want to lose that. Borsboom and colleagues argued similarly that including everything relevant to the evaluation of testing within validity spoilt the concept for scientist and practitioner alike. Accordingly, the theoretically-oriented would 'get lost in the intricate subtleties', while the practically-oriented would be 'unlikely to derive a workable conceptual scheme with practical implications from it', such that the concept of validity could no longer offer a sense of direction (Borsboom et al., 2004: 1061).

In the second of the two special issues, Reckase (1998b) identified numerous practical problems for test developers with the embrace of consequences. Timing is a particular challenge: given that it is logically impossible to evaluate unanticipated consequences before administering a test live, how rigorous can we expect any prospective evaluation of consequences to be? In addition, because evidence concerning the actual consequences of test use cannot be collected until some time after the test has been administered live, how long should a test developer be given before being required to provide a retrospective evaluation? Most significantly, given the significant challenge of inferring cause–effect relationships from naturalistic (non-experimental) studies, how definitive could we ever expect an evaluation of consequences to be? Green (1998) added that often, publishers of popular tests are not in a position to obtain decent evidence concerning social consequences, particularly given the wide differences in how customers have used those tests; neither did publishers actually have any control over how their tests were used and interpreted. Finally, he observed that the embrace of consequences often resulted in obfuscation and myth, owing to an overreliance on opinion as opposed to evidence: for example, claims that norm-referenced tests necessarily narrow the curriculum, performance assessments necessarily improve learning, and multiple choice tests necessarily inhibit learning.

Lissitz and Samuelsen (2007a) suggested that the concept of consequential validity could be taken to elevate evidence of impact unduly, as though tantamount to the idea that the ends justify the means. Thus understood, bad impacts would invalidate even good tests, and good impacts would validate bad tests. They rejected this position. As we discussed in Chapter 4, Messick (1996) did too.

Finally, numerous authors have insisted that the scientific evaluation of technical quality and the ethical evaluation of social value are entirely different concerns, and therefore ought to be dealt with separately (e.g. Norris, 1995; Lees-Haley, 1996; Orton, 1998; Borsboom and Mellenbergh, 2007; Cizek, 2012). Cizek (2012) has made a particular issue of this, arguing that the two kinds of evaluation are incommensurable. He argued that Messick (1989a) was wrong to define validity in terms of an integrated evaluative judgement of inferences and actions, because it is logically impossible to integrate scientific and ethical analyses. Instead, evidence bearing on measurement ought to be characterized as the *validation* of inferences from test scores; whereas evidence bearing on consequences ought to be characterized as the *justification* of actions based on test scores.

The various camps

In her editorial, Crocker (1997) observed that the prevailing argument would shape the nature of measurement practice for years to come. More than 15 years later, neither side in this debate seems to have prevailed. Part of the reason for this lack of resolution is no doubt due to fact that while the debate appears to be simple and dichotomous, it is actually complex and multifarious. As we noted above, both scientific and ethical issues are potentially involved across the spectrum of evaluation concerns (as we discuss further in Chapter 6). The evaluation of a measurement procedure is not exclusively scientific, and the evaluation of a testing policy is not exclusively ethical. In addition, as noted in Chapter 4, evidence from consequences can be used to elucidate both scientific issues of measurement quality and ethical issues of policy value. However, glossing over some of this complexity, it is still possible to identify at least four broad camps in the debate over the scope of validity theory:

1 liberals – those who are prepared to extend validity to the overall evaluation of testing policy (covering measurement aims, decision-making aims and secondary policy aims from both a scientific perspective and an ethical one)

2 moderates – those who are prepared to extend validity to the technical evaluation of testing policy (covering measurement aims, decision-making aims and secondary policy aims, but only from a scientific perspective)

3 traditionalists – those who are prepared to extend validity to the technical
   evaluation of measurement-based decision-making procedures (covering measurement aims and decision-making aims, but only from a scientific perspective)
4 conservatives – those who are prepared only to extend validity to the technical
   evaluation of measurement procedures (covering measurement aims alone, and
   only from a scientific perspective).

The most obvious example of a *liberal* is Cronbach (e.g. 1988), although the earlier
Messick (e.g. 1980) also seemed to be fairly liberal (see Chapter 4). Moss (e.g. 2007)
suggested that she might align herself with the liberal camp, and Kane (e.g. 2013a)
appeared to suggest likewise.

Like Messick, the *Standards* can be read in different ways. Having said that, the
1999 edition did not seem to go quite so far as the liberal Messick, and perhaps its
'more liberal' interpretation might be better classified as *moderate*. Unlike the earlier
Messick, the 1999 edition tended not to emphasize ethical or social evaluation in the
sense of genuine cost–benefit analyses. However, unlike the later Messick, it did seem
to include within its concept of validity the evaluation of impacts associated with testing policies in the sense of evaluating them in their own right, rather than in terms of
their implications for score meaning. For example, on p.17, the *Standards* referred to
secondary policy aims such as motivating students and achieving positive washback
on teaching, insisting that any claim to this effect also needed to be evaluated. This
seems to imply a technical evaluation of the potential to achieve the policy aim rather
than an ethical evaluation, along the lines discussed in Bennett et al. (2011).

The later Messick (e.g. 1998b) is probably best read as a *traditionalist* (see
Chapter 4). He seemed wedded to the idea that validity was quintessentially about
score meaning, and roundly criticized those who misunderstood his position as
more liberal than this. Messick also insisted that test score meaning and test score
use were inseparable – which is why he explained that nomological networks
supported both interpretive inferences and action inferences – and this broke
down what he considered to be an artificial distinction between measurement and
decision-making. In short, like even the earliest editions of the *Standards*, Messick
included both measurement *and* decision-making within the scope of validity
theory. Shepard (1997) also seemed to advocate this position.

In recent years, *conservatives* have come to the fore. They include Wiley (1991),
Scriven (2002), Borsboom and Mellenbergh (2007), Lissitz and Samuelsen (2007a),
Cizek (2012) and others. They all make essentially the same points: that validity
should be restricted to the evaluation of measurement quality, and that even measurement-based decision-making falls beyond this scope. This is conservative in the
sense that it adopts a highly restricted conception, even ejecting the traditional
concern for criterion validation from the concept of validity. Scriven (2002) and
Lissitz and Samuelsen (2007a) classified criterion validation under an alternative
heading, 'utility'. Scriven explained his motivation as wanting to stop the cheapening
of the notion of validity, while Lissitz and Samuelsen explained theirs as wishing to
propose a more understandable and useable model.

Borsboom and colleagues have transcended conservatism, occupying a position which perhaps is best described as *hyper-conservative* (e.g. Borsboom et al., 2004, 2009; Borsboom, 2005; Borsboom and Mellenbergh, 2007). Rather than treating validity as an umbrella concept with which to characterize overall measurement quality, they preferred to refer to the umbrella concept as 'overall quality' (Borsboom et al., 2004: 1070). They defined validity as just one element of overall quality and independent of other measurement concepts. Borsboom and Mellenbergh (2007) distinguished between measurement concepts (e.g. validity, invariance, precision and unidimensionality); decision concepts (e.g. predictive accuracy, optimality); and impact concepts (the acceptability of the test procedure to institutional users, the people tested and society at large).

The ongoing debate

There are no signs that debate over the scope of validity is likely to be resolved one way or the other in the near future. Ultimately, this is not a technical matter concerning the *proper* use of the term 'validity'. It is simply a matter of how we, the educational and psychological measurement supra-community, decide to use it. It is a matter of convention.

Having said that, some theorists have argued their case as though the debate *could* be resolved on largely technical grounds. For example, on the one hand, Cizek has claimed that validity cannot involve the integration of scientific and ethical evaluative judgements, because it is logically impossible to synthesize the two. On the other hand, he has argued also that evidence 'of the validity of score inferences is a necessary but insufficient condition for recommending or sustaining a justification for test use' (Cizek, 2012: 37). The implication of this concession is that the evaluation of test score meaning is a subset of the evaluation of test score use. If so, then this suggests that scientific judgements of test score meaning need to be *integrated within* ethical judgements of test score use. Therefore, the overall integrated evaluative judgement is ultimately an ethical judgement. Moreover, there is no compelling technical reason why this should not be described as a judgement of validity.

Shepard also sought to resolve the debate on largely technical grounds. She explained how consequential evidence was logically relevant to the evaluation of test score meaning, and therefore was of significance to judgements of construct validity. As such, the 'for' argument presented by Shepard (1997) is entirely compatible with the 'against' argument from Cizek (2012). This is because Shepard's emphasis was on the role of consequences within scientific evaluation, whereas Cizek emphasized the role of consequences within ethical evaluation.

Most arguments concerning the scope of validity have been framed in terms of the potential impacts from narrow versus broad conceptions. The most liberal protagonists have insisted that if we exclude ethical evaluation from validity, then we risk the possibility that no one will take responsibility for it. The most conservative protagonists have insisted that if we include ethical evaluation within validity, then the concept will become too complicated to understand, and will give no useful direction to validation research. Liberals argue that using 'validity' narrowly may fool people (who share their own proclivity) into thinking that the social value of the testing policy has been established, although it has not (yet). Conservatives argue that using 'invalidity' broadly may fool people (who share their own proclivity) into thinking that the technical quality of the testing procedure has been challenged, although it has not (necessarily). Given that the arguments for and against seem so evenly matched, it is not surprising that consensus remains so elusive.

Validity and validation into the 21st century

At the turn of the millennium, it appeared to many that Messick (1989a) had more or less cracked it. He had managed to unify the science of validity and appropriately elevated the importance of ethical evaluation, even if he had not quite managed to synthesize these two dimensions within a single concept. However, less than a decade into the new millennium, things began to seem substantially less clear. Thus, following a period of reconstruction during which the concept of validity was unified on a complex foundation of construct validity, we entered a period of deconstruction reflecting a strong desire to simplify.

The desire to simplify validation practice was epitomized in the argument-based approach, which became increasingly salient during this phase. It appeared, almost unquestionably, to be a good thing, but its uptake appears to have been limited. Whether this is due to ambiguity in the way in which it has been presented, or simply due to the fact that robust validity arguments represent a massive undertaking, is unclear – it may be a bit of both.

The desire to simplify validity theory was epitomized in the many deconstructions and reconstructions of the concept of construct validity, which became increasingly explicit during this phase. As criticisms were being voiced more explicitly, so too were philosophical commitments coming to the fore once again. Different stances are being adopted now on the philosophies of science, measurement and mind. Although this may well be a positive sign, from a measurement science perspective it also threatens to distance the concept of validity even further from the everyday measurement practitioner. Frankly, this stuff is hard enough for even the most accomplished of measurement scientists.

The desire to simplify validity theory was epitomized also in the backlash against the extension of validity to the realm of ethics. The arguments for and against this extension are essentially social rather than technical. As yet, they seem fairly evenly matched, and the jury is definitely still out.

One thing that everyone might possibly agree on is that we are still a long way from having effectively theorized the overall evaluation of testing policy. Over the past century we have made good progress in understanding the evaluation of measurement – although there is still a long way to go. We have made some progress in understanding the evaluation of decision-making – and we have come to appreciate that it is far more complicated than we once thought. In addition, we have made fledgling attempts to understand the evaluation of secondary policy objectives and side-effects, although we have found it hard to disentangle ethical and scientific concerns. When it comes to bringing all of this together within an overarching theory of the evaluation of testing policy, we appear not to have progressed far from the starting blocks. In our final chapter, we will explore foundations for the evaluation of testing policy in an attempt to help map out the territory. The framework that we will outline represents our synthesis of major insights from the literature on validity and validation from the past 100 years.

Notes

1   For example, *Psychological Assessment* (2003), 15 (4), on incremental validity and utility in clinical assessment; *Psychological Assessment* (2005), 17 (4), on construct validity; *Journal of Personality Assessment* (2005), 85 (2), on construct validity; *Industrial and Organizational Psychology* (2009), 2 (4), on content validation; *Industrial and Organizational Psychology* (2010), 3 (3), on synthetic validation; *Social Indicators Research* (2011), 103 (2), on the validation of population-level measures of children's development, well-being and school readiness; *Measurement: Interdisciplinary Research and Perspectives* (2012), 10 (1–2), on the consensus definition of validity; *New Ideas In Psychology* (2013), 31 (1), on constructs; and *Journal of Educational Measurement* (2013), 50 (1), on validity.

2   Although the imperative to design validity into tests has been associated with the cognitive approach (e.g. Embretson, 1998; Embretson and Gorin, 2001; Gorin, 2006; Mislevy, 2007), it is worth mentioning that this sentiment is not new. The same principle has been advocated by many validity theorists across the decades (e.g. Huddlestone, 1956; Cronbach, 1971; Ebel, 1983; Anastasi, 1986).

3   This could have been framed holistically, of course, thereby dispensing with the construct representation element: variation (or lack of variation) in the attribute causes of variation (or lack of variation) in measurement outcomes, and variation (or lack of variation) in measurement outcomes is not caused by other attributes nor influenced by any other factors. Framing it in terms of components simply opened the doors to defining measurement in terms of the classic twin threats.

4   Hood (2009) developed a similar line of reasoning in relation to the critique of Messick (1989a) by Borsboom et al. (2004), suggesting that the two approaches are potentially complementary. Messick provided insight into the epistemology of psychological measurement; Borsboom and colleagues provided insight into the semantic and ontological components. Hood (2009) also illustrated how even Messick (1989a) failed to provide a clear and consistent *definition* of validity, appearing to define it in quite different ways, even on a single page.

5   In fact, Michell claimed that it made little sense to reconstruct the concept of validity in the service of 'assessment' rather than 'measurement'. He seemed to suggest

that validation really ought to be considered unnecessary for an adequately designed test. We find this position hard to understand, given the critique of 'obviously valid tests' and the omnipresent need to test out plausible rival hypotheses for test score consistencies (see Chapter 4).

6   Cronbach noted that, most often, the MTMM technique is applied in a manner that is 'mindless and mechanical' (1989a: 156). Fiske and Campbell (1992), reflecting on the many citations of their classic 1959 paper, claimed that they had yet to see a really good matrix: 'one that is based on fairly similar concepts and plausibly independent methods and shows high convergent and discriminant validation by all standards' (1992: 393). They wondered whether it was even possible to obtain such a matrix, speculating that methods and traits might be so intertwined that their interaction could not be realistically analysed.

7   Although his various accounts do give (us) the impression that Kane promotes a theory of mind in which some attributes are straightforwardly observable, while others are deeply theoretical, he might respond by saying that he is not actually committed to this position, and that his intention is simply to demonstrate how the argument-based approach can accommodate *any* theory of mind – whether more to the observable attribute end of the spectrum, or more to the theoretical construct end.

CHAPTER 6

TWENTY-FIRST-CENTURY EVALUATION

We have shown how the concept of validity has assumed a pivotal role across decades of debate on the characteristics of quality in educational and psychological measurement; also, how it has proven extremely resistant to definition. In our final chapter we attempt to sidestep the lexical dispute over what the term 'validity' ought to apply to, by choosing not to affiliate with any of the camps described toward the end of Chapter 5: that is, by choosing not to define validity either broadly or narrowly. Instead, we focus squarely on the overall *evaluation* of testing policy, and attempt to explain how the various dimensions of evaluation can be related to each other.

This way of ending the book is a response to concerns expressed in recent years by many measurement professionals, that the closer our use of the term 'validation' comes to implying an overall evaluation of testing policy, the harder it becomes to understand, and the more out of reach it seems as a goal (e.g. Fremer, 2000). The problem of conceptualizing evaluation on this scale is a very serious one. Note that neither the 'for' nor the 'against' camps actually deny the importance of comprehensive evaluation on this scale. Their debate is really just about whether the word 'validation' should be used to refer to full-scale comprehensive evaluation, or to just one component of it, contingent on how they choose to define 'validity'. So there is no reason *not* to be concerned about the lack of an overarching theory of the evaluation of testing policy, whatever your perspective on the scope of validity theory might be. We hope to stimulate further thinking on this issue with the aid of a new framework for the evaluation of testing policy, which we use to synthesize many of the major insights from the literature on validity and validation from the past century, thereby ending our book in a fitting manner.

A framework for the evaluation of testing policy

Over the decades, very many frameworks have been proposed for classifying dimensions of quality in educational and psychological measurement. In recent years, resonating with the debate over the scope of validity, many of these have advocated a particular view on which dimensions are properly described in terms of validity, for example:

- *usefulness* – reliability, construct validity, authenticity, interactiveness, impact, practicality (Bachman and Palmer, 1996)
- *internal factors*, aka validity – content, reliability, latent process; versus *external factors* – utility, impact, nomological network (Lissitz and Samuelsen, 2007a)
- *test quality* – theoretical basis of the test, quality of the test materials, comprehensiveness of the manual, norms, reliability, construct validity, criterion validity (Evers et al., 2010)
- *validation* of score inference, aka validity; versus *justification* of intended use (Cizek, 2012).

These represent no more than a selection of frameworks, all of which contrast validity with alternative characteristics of quality. There are many other frameworks to be found in the recent literature, including those which subdivide a broad conception of validity or validation into constituent elements (e.g. Cronbach, 1988; Frederiksen and Collins, 1989; Linn et al., 1991; Moss, 1992; Foster and Cone, 1995; Allen, 2004; Trochim, 2006; Shaw and Weir, 2007; Slaney and Maraun, 2008; Brookhart, 2009; Stobart, 2009; Zumbo, 2009; Guion, 2011; Hubley and Zumbo, 2011).

Given that a stated purpose of the *Standards* is to provide a basis for evaluating the quality of testing practices, it would seem legitimate to ask whether there is any need at all for frameworks such as these. After all, should we not expect the very structure of the *Standards* to provide a useful framework for understanding characteristics of quality? Part I of the 1999 edition, for example, is broken down as follows (in a manner that resembles the original structure of the 1954 edition):

1 Validity
2 Reliability and errors of measurement
3 Test development and revision
4 Scales, norms and score comparability
5 Test administration, scoring and reporting
6 Supporting documentation for tests.

A significant feature of the *Standards* is that it is not written as an academic thesis: it does not cite the literature, its perspective is not associated with a particular paradigm, and it is unashamedly pragmatic. This makes the *Standards* strong as a guide for measurement practice, but weak as a basis for measurement science. In particular, it is unclear how the various chapters of the *Standards* relate to each other conceptually: for example, the relationship that is supposed to obtain between what it describes under the heading of reliability and what it describes under the heading of validity. Admittedly, a paragraph within the validity chapter does state that 'the validity of an intended interpretation of test scores relies on all the available evidence relevant to the technical quality of a testing system' (AERA et al., 1999: 17), including 'adequate score reliability'. Yet the same list that includes reliability also includes 'careful attention to fairness for all examinees', and it is not clear whether it presumes that fairness is relevant to validity in the same way that reliability is relevant to validity. In short, it seems unwise (and probably inappropriate) to rely on the *Standards* for the kind of framework that we need: a cogent framework that is capable of embracing a comprehensive range of evaluation concerns, of cutting the concept of evaluation at conceptually significant joints, and which evaluators may find useful in planning and undertaking evaluation.

On the back of the research for this book, we have concluded that a cogent framework for the evaluation of testing policy ought to demonstrate the following characteristics. First, any framework ought to be able to accommodate the evaluation of *any* use that is to be made of test scores, and *any* impact that is consequent on their use. Second, we agree with Cizek (2012) that Messick (1975) was absolutely right in distinguishing between scientific/technical evaluation questions and ethical/social ones. Therefore, any robust framework should be capable of respecting this distinction. Third, we agree with Borsboom and Mellenbergh (2007) that there are three fundamental evaluation foci for educational and psychological measurement relating to measurement concepts, decision concepts and impact concepts (see also Newton, 2007). However, these distinctions need to be sharpened a little. In particular, any cogent framework needs to be capable of accommodating the fact that consequential evidence has the potential to inform the evaluation of measurement *and* decision-making *and* impacts.

So, where does this analysis leave us? We are not convinced that any of the existing frameworks do justice to all of these concerns, which is why we now propose a new one. Actually, we prefer to think of it as a revision of an old framework: a reinterpretation of the original progressive matrix. In Chapter 4, we were unable to disagree with Shepard (1997) that the progressive matrix was a mistake, although we acknowledged that the underlying intention was an excellent one. Our new matrix is intended to lessen the confusion caused by the way in which the original was presented. In proposing it, we move in the opposite direction from Cizek (2012), who retreated from the four questions of Messick (1980) to the two questions of Messick (1975). We believe that greater clarity can be achieved by adding cells rather than by taking them away. Our neo-Messickian framework for the evaluation of testing policy is presented in Figure 6.1. Robust evaluation, we believe, requires a thorough interrogation of the questions in each of the cells.

Figure 6.1 represents the three core evaluation foci as column headings. *Measurement objectives* concern the test and the attribute (or attributes) that the test is intended to measure. *Decision-making objectives* concern the use (or uses) to which

	Foci for the evaluation of testing policy		
	Mechanism for achieving the primary measurement objective(s)	**Mechanism for achieving the primary decision-making objective(s)**	**Mechanism for achieving secondary policy objectives**
Technical evaluation (technical quality of mechanism)	Is it possible to measure the desired attribute(s) using the test? **1**	It is possible to make more accurate decisions by incorporating test scores into the decision-making process? **2**	Is it possible to achieve a range of secondary impacts by implementing the testing policy? **3**
Social evaluation (social value of mechanism, expenses, pay-offs, impacts, and side-effects)	Have all of the primary measurement expenses been considered? **4a**	Have all of the primary decision-making expenses, pay-offs, impacts and side-effects been considered? **4b**	Have all of the secondary and incidental expenses, pay-offs, impacts and side-effects been considered? **4c**
	Is it acceptable to implement (or continue implementing) the testing policy? **OJ**		

Figure 6.1   Key questions within a neo-Messickian framework for the evaluation of testing policy

Note: OJ (Overall Judgement) embraces the entire matrix.

test scores are intended to be put: the decisions that are supposed to be made on their basis. *Secondary policy objectives* concern the impacts that are supposed to follow from the implementation of the testing policy. This is to draw a distinction between impacts directly associated with the primary decision-making objective (i.e. more accurate decisions attributable to the use of test scores), and impacts which go beyond this (e.g. greater motivation among teachers and students attributable to the requirement on students to sit a test).

The three objectives need to be evaluated initially from a technical perspective, and subsequently from a social one. This culminates in an overall evaluative judgement concerning the social acceptability of the testing policy. Whereas Messick tended to foreground the scientific versus ethical contrast, we prefer *technical versus social* because it is slightly broader and therefore more encompassing. We believe that the new matrix is true to the spirit of Messick's early work (e.g. 1980), as distinct from his later work (e.g. 1995a), reflecting a framework for the overall evaluation of testing policy.

It is helpful to think of these two perspectives in terms of a contrast between *technical quality* (cells 1 to 3) and *social value* (cells 4a to 4c, plus the Overall

Judgement). This is to draw a distinction between different kinds of evaluation criteria: for cells 1 to 3, the criterion is whether it is *technically possible* to achieve the intended objectives by implementing the specified mechanisms; for cells 4a to 4c and the Overall Judgement, the criterion is whether it is *socially acceptable* to do so. Social value is ultimately a matter of trading costs against benefits. Some of these costs will be purely financial, while many will reflect costs that cannot even be translated into a monetary value.

The distinction between technical and social can be clarified, not only with respect to the nature of the evaluation criteria, but also with respect to those from whose perspective the evaluation is to be conducted. If the criterion for cells 1 to 3 is whether it is technically possible to achieve the intended objective through the specified mechanism, this presumes that it is possible to identify a person or institution with ultimate responsibility for that objective. That person or institution is the one with overall responsibility for the decision to implement, or to continue implementing, the testing policy. The technical evaluation is primarily relative to their perspective and their intended objectives. We refer to this person or institution as the *policy owner*. We have decided to use 'policy owner' rather than 'policymaker' because the latter often implies a sponsoring agency or official. From our perspective, the policy owner might be an agency or official; however, equally, they might be a clinical psychologist who chooses to use an off-the-shelf test with a particular client, a large organization whose personnel managers implement a range of occupational tests, or a classroom teacher who designs and uses their own test. The policy owner is where responsibility ultimately lies as to whether the test is implemented or not. In certain circumstances the policy owner might be a secondary user of scores from a test implemented by a different policy owner for a different purpose. In such cases, the secondary user would be responsible for the 'decision policy', rather than the entire testing policy. In practice, the role and responsibility that we ascribe to the policy owner might be shared between individuals or institutions, or it might be delegated by the policy owner to others. Therefore, our account is simplified.

Our account is simplified also in relation to the role of *evaluator*. We tend to describe it more idealistically than realistically, because it is easiest to think in terms of a grand evaluation programme coordinated by a chief evaluator. In reality, we accept that evaluation responsibilities are often widely distributed, and efforts are not always even coordinated. Moreover, we would hope that different teams and stakeholders would bring different talents and perspectives to bear on the overall evaluation of a testing policy (see Haertel, 2013). Having said that, policy owners really do have to make overall decisions concerning whether or not to implement (or to continue implementing) their testing policies. Moreover, these decisions really ought to be based on some kind of rationally structured, overall evaluative judgement of acceptability. It is the logic of this kind of judgement, and the argumentation that supports it, that we hope to clarify. Ultimately though, a plausible account of real-world evaluation practice is beyond the scope of this chapter: it would involve in-depth discussion of many important issues, not least the division of evaluation roles and responsibilities (e.g. Linn, 1998) and conflict of interest issues (e.g. Buck-endahl and Plake, 2006). Incidentally, we draw a conceptual distinction between the role of the evaluator and the role of the policy owner, but it would be possible for the policy owner to adopt both roles.

Technical evaluation concerns whether it is *possible* to achieve the policy owner's objectives by implementing specified mechanisms. This reflects the traditional focus on the *intended* interpretations and uses of test scores. Conversely, social evaluation concerns whether it is *acceptable* to implement the specified mechanisms. It is important to note that the matrix has a role for both discrete *all-or-nothing* judgements (possible, acceptable), and continuous *matter-of-degree* judgements (quality, value). Discrete judgements are implied in the yes/no questions that guide evaluation, and which are located in the main cells of the Figure 6.1 matrix. They sanction all-or-nothing thinking because the decision that ultimately needs to be taken is binary: whether or not to implement the policy. (Of course, policy owners are at liberty to re-evaluate at any point in time, so even all-or-nothing judgements are inherently provisional.) Conversely, continuous judgements are implied in the technical and social evaluative criteria which are located in the row headings of the Figure 6.1 matrix: the quality of the technical mechanisms; and the value of those mechanisms and their consequences. Judgements of *quality* and *value* are continuous. We treat quality as unidirectional: ranging from high quality through low quality, to no quality. We treat value as bidirectional: ranging from high positive value through low positive value, to no value; then through low negative value to high negative value. Messick began his seminal work by emphasizing that it is 'important to note that validity is a matter of degree, not all or none' (Messick, 1989a: 13). Although we appreciate the risks associated with 'thumbs-up' versus 'thumbs-down' thinking (see Cronbach, 1988; Zumbo, 2007; Markus, 2012; Pollitt, 2012) we believe that the matrix can and ought to support both kinds of evaluative judgement (see Newton, 2012a, 2012b).

While it makes sense to try to answer technical questions as definitively as possible – to seek a rational *consensus* over whether it is possible to achieve the policy owner's objectives by implementing specified mechanisms – the same cannot be said of social questions. Social evaluation involves judgements of value, which we accept may differ from one stakeholder to the next. The issue here is less a matter of consensus and more a matter of reconciliation and compromise, or perhaps simply *conflict*. Therefore, the challenge for the evaluator is to ensure that an appropriate range of perspectives is canvassed, and to take account of a variety of potentially conflicting interests: from individual interests to institutional interests and national interests. Indeed, although the matrix culminates in the Overall Judgement – an overall cost–benefit argument and an overall evaluative judgement – different arguments and judgements could be constructed from a range of different perspectives. If nothing else, the evaluator needs to establish the extent to which a range of stakeholders are prepared to accept the policy owner's objectives, the mechanisms used to achieve them and their consequences.

Finally, we should emphasize that the purpose of the matrix is to help guide the process of evaluation by conjoining concerns that are most cogently combined, and by separating concerns that are most cogently separated. For example, on the one hand, we would argue that the technical quality of a measurement procedure can be sensibly theorized independently of its social value, and that it is useful to do so because it helps to clarify the structure of evaluation. On the other hand, it seems less sensible – if not entirely implausible – to theorize the social value of a measurement procedure independently of its technical quality, and the matrix helps to illustrate this relationship by nesting technical questions within a broader social one. This process of separating and conjoining testing concerns inevitably involves the occasional arbitrary decision on the location of a conceptual boundary. However, we hope that even the more arbitrary conceptual boundaries may help to sharpen debate on the nature of robust evaluation arguments.

Defending the new matrix

In proposing a revision of the progressive matrix, we aim to dispel the confusion engendered by its original presentation. The following points explain how we hope to have achieved this.

First, we would not describe the new matrix as 'progressive', because the image of each new cell subsuming earlier ones is not helpful. However, we would describe the cells as 'interdependent' for a number of reasons, most of which were explained by Messick:

1   the same evaluation evidence may be useful in different ways, in different cells
2   the evaluation of measurement quality in cell 1 is fundamental, and will have ramifications across the entire matrix
3   evaluation within cells 4a to 4c directly targets the mechanisms investigated in cells 1 to 3.

Second, the new matrix continues to foreground the core distinction that Messick drew between technical evaluation, which he described as the appraisal of evidence, and social evaluation, which he described as the appraisal of consequences. However, rather than implying that evidence is the focus for one row and consequences for the other, it acknowledges the relevance of *both* evidence *and* consequences to *all* of the cells. In cells 1 to 3, the evidence from consequences informs the evaluation of technical quality; whereas in cells 4a to 4c and the Overall Judgement, consequences are the principal subject of the evaluation of social value.

Third, in a similar sense, values are relevant to *all* of the cells. In cells 1 to 3, values are built into the mechanism by design. As such, a fundamental evaluation question is the degree of consistency between the design of the mechanism and the value-base that it is supposed to embody. By locating this kind of analysis in the second row of his progressive matrix, Messick characterized it as essentially social. We think that it is essentially technical – a matter of consistency – and therefore locate it in our first row. In cells 4a to 4c and the Overall Judgement, values are obviously the basis on which judgements of acceptability are made. Therefore, the major issue across these cells is not one of consistency and consensus, but of *in*consistency and conflict, since the major challenge is how to accommodate divergent value perspectives.

Fourth, the new matrix draws clearer distinctions between technical questions (matters of quality) and social questions (matters of value). For example, whereas Messick incorporated discussion of relevance, utility and fairness in the third cell of his progressive matrix, the new matrix divides them between cells. Thus, relevance is considered to be of particular significance within cell 2, whereas utility and fairness are located more appropriately within cells 4a to 4c and the Overall Judgement.

Fifth, the addition of a column representing secondary policy objectives emphasizes that incidental impacts and side-effects need to be evaluated from both technical and social perspectives. The growing literature on how theories of action (programme theories) can inform the evaluation of policy objectives is particularly relevant to cell 3. Messick did briefly touch on this kind of evaluation issue: for example, he discussed the curriculum enhancement function of the College Board's Advanced Placement Program, 'where the utility of the writing test benefits from any consequent improvements in the teaching of writing' (Messick, 1989a: 85). However, by locating this in his final cell, reflecting the consequential basis of test use, he highlighted social considerations and obscured technical ones. The new matrix locates the technical evaluation of intended impacts in cell 3, and their social evaluation in cell 4c, thereby shining a light on both of these important concerns.

Sixth, the secondary policy objectives column provides a home for any kind of consequence: not only construct-relevant and construct-irrelevant ones, but also construct-neutral ones. That is, it accommodates the evaluation of consequences that may seem tangential to, or independent of, the evaluation of measurement quality, both anticipated-positive (e.g. higher motivation to achieve among students) and unanticipated-negative (e.g. lower motivation to collaborate across schools). Equally, this column accommodates evidence concerning the misuse of testing, either as evidence with which to challenge a theory of action (cell 3), or as evidence of the social unacceptability of the testing policy (cell 4c and the Overall Judgement).

Seventh, the new matrix avoids labelling any cell as 'validity', or anything to do with validity. It is ultimately a framework for the evaluation of testing policy which incorporates a range of disparate concerns. What Messick (1980) originally described as 'construct validity' is still to be found in cell 1. However, to avoid unnecessary terminological quarrelling, we prefer to describe this cell simply in terms of the evaluation of measurement quality. The anticipated level of measurement quality is likely to have implications for all of the other cells – and evidence or analysis undertaken in relation to any of the other cells may contribute additionally to the evaluation of measurement quality – which is why we describe the matrix as interdependent, and evaluation as iterative. However, we see no reason specifically to represent measurement quality within each of the cells in the way that Messick represented construct validity.

Eighth, whereas Kane (e.g. 2013a) has tended to elevate arguments over frameworks, we emphasize the benefit of combining the two. Figure 6.1 hints at the sheer number of distinct arguments that need to be developed in order to evaluate a testing policy: measurement arguments, decision arguments, impact arguments and cost–benefit arguments. For example, for cell 2 alone a separate evaluation argument will be required for each intended use of test scores. In the absence of a structuring framework, it would be easy to forget any number of essential components.

Finally, we should emphasize that *each* of the three columns is described in terms of objectives – that is, purposes – including the intended uses of test scores and the intended impacts from testing. These are the foundation for evaluation across the entire matrix, and for cells 1 to 3 in particular. For example, the use to which test scores are to be put will help to define the attribute that needs to be assessed, and therefore frame the cell 1 evaluation. Exactly the same logic applies for the intended impacts that frame the cell 3 evaluation.

We turn now to a more detailed analysis of technical and social evaluation, before considering evaluation within each of the cells respectively. Figure 6.2 represents Figure 6.1 differently, summarizing the distinguishing features that will be discussed below.

	Foci for the evaluation of testing policy		
	Mechanism for achieving the primary measurement objective(s)	Mechanism for achieving the primary decision-making objective(s)	Mechanism for achieving secondary policy objectives
Technical evaluation Plausibility Viability	Measurement argument 1 Attribute specification Theory of measurement	Decision/ intervention argument 2 Outcome specification Theory of the decision/ intervention	Impact argument 3 Impact specification Theory of impact
Social evaluation Credibility Utility Fairness Legality	Anticipated expenses 4a	Anticipated expenses and pay-offs 4b Intended impacts and anticipated side-effects	Intended impacts and anticipated side-effects 4c Unanticipated expenses, pay-offs, impacts, side-effects
	Overall cost–benefit argument OJ		

Figure 6.2   Core concepts within a neo-Messickian framework for the evaluation of testing policy

Note: OJ (Overall Judgement) embraces the entire matrix.

Evaluation of technical quality: cells 1 to 3

A high-quality mechanism is one that enables the intended objective(s) to be achieved very effectively. As noted above, evaluation within cells 1 to 3 is guided primarily by the intentions of policy owners, and concerns the extent to which it is possible to achieve their objectives. Any high-quality mechanism will demonstrate two important features:

1   theoretical plausibility
2   practical viability.

Measurement objectives, decision-making objectives and secondary policy objectives all need to be evaluated in these terms. For example, a test developer may claim that it is possible, *in principle*, to measure an attribute using a particular procedure, assuming that the administration guidelines are followed (*theoretical plausibility*). However, if it proved to be beyond the reasonable wit or means of the majority of intended users to follow those guidelines, then *in practice* it might not be possible to measure the attribute using the procedure (*practical viability*). To illustrate this point, it might be possible to train intensively a small number of subject-matter experts to follow a set of complex instructions for marking responses to short-answer constructed-response questions, resulting in a very high level of marking consistency. Yet in practice, it might be impossible to scale up this procedure to an operational level for reasons that might include the availability of a sufficiently large pool of subject-matter experts.

Already, the joint consideration of plausibility and viability has taken cell 1 beyond the modern version of construct validity, which is akin to theoretical plausibility alone. Note that the joint consideration of these two features should not be read as reducing the significance of theoretical plausibility; neither does it mean that theoretical plausibility should not be evaluated independently of practical viability. Reason to believe that a procedure lacks practical viability does not necessarily undermine the procedure; it may just mean that the situation in which the procedure is to be implemented needs to be altered. For example, if it is anticipated that the typical user will not have the skill or understanding to follow administration guidelines, then one solution (if it is not possible to simplify the guidelines) would be to restrict the use of the test to a smaller group of trained and certificated users. Similarly, one solution to the problem of scalability would be to take steps to increase the pool of available subject-matter experts. Here, the point is merely to emphasize that the theoretical plausibility of a mechanism does not *guarantee* its practical viability: that it is insufficient to guarantee the achievement of measurement objectives, decision-making objectives or secondary policy objectives.

As for modern construct validity, cell 1 theoretical plausibility presumes a scientific approach to the evaluation of empirical evidence and logical analysis, including the testing of plausible alternative explanations. As far as the secondary policy objectives of cell 3 are concerned – e.g. positive washback on the experienced curriculum – theoretical plausibility is equally technical, albeit perhaps a little less 'scientific' in a purist sense. Paramount here is the notion of a theory of action or programme theory by which the intended impact is supposed to be brought about: it is the theoretical plausibility of this mechanism that is in question. Decision-making objectives, within cell 2, are evaluated typically in terms of both cell 1 measurement quality and additional theory which clarifies the presumed relation-ship between the measured attribute(s) and subsequent decisions. This introduces the idea of relevance or relatedness between construction of the attribute at the heart of the measurement procedure and construction of the outcome at the heart of the decision-making procedure (Guion, 1976).

By introducing the idea of an interpretation and use argument (IUA, formerly known as an interpretive argument), Kane emphasized that it is essential to begin any evaluation with a detailed statement that specifies the following:

- the intended objective;
- the intended mechanism for achieving that objective; and
- some kind of theory explaining how the intended objective is supposed to be achieved by the mechanism.

The purpose of evaluation within cells 1 to 3 is to construct, and ultimately to appraise, the arguments underlying the claims that it is possible to:

1   measure the desired attribute(s) using the test
2   make more accurate decisions by incorporating test scores into the decision-making process
3   achieve a range of secondary impacts by implementing the testing policy.

As explained in Newton (2012b), these arguments actually involve two kinds of conclusion which historically tended not to have been distinguished: one concern-ing the *strength of the argument*, and the other concerning the *degree of technical quality of the mechanism*. Indeed, the nature of these conclusions can evolve inter-actively throughout the course of an evaluation. For example, presumably the evaluator would begin by attempting to construct an argument with which to claim that it was possible to achieve high-quality measurement of the desired attribute. A subsequent appraisal of that argument might judge it to be weak, in the sense of providing only a small amount of supporting evidence or analysis. In an attempt to strengthen the argument, additional evidence or analysis would be generated. Subsequent appraisal might then reveal not that the revised argument for high-quality measurement was strong, but that it could not be substantiated at all. Even though it might not be possible to construct a strong argument concerning *high-quality* measurement of the desired attribute from this foundation of evidence and analysis, it still might be possible to construct a strong argument concerning *low-quality* measurement. In fact, it even might be possible to construct a strong argument concerning high-quality measurement of a differently specified attribute. So in principle, the evaluation could continue along entirely different lines.

Howsoever the arguments and claims were to be constructed (or reconstructed), ideally the culmination of *any* evaluation within cells 1 to 3 ought to be a *strong* argument, supporting a claim concerning a certain level of technical quality – be that high or low. Following Kane (e.g. 2006), the strength of an argument might be judged in relation to its coherence and completeness, and on the plausibility of the warrants and backing for each of its inferences and their assumptions.

Evaluation of social value: cells 4a to 4c and the Overall Judgement

A high positive value mechanism is one that is judged to be very worthwhile in its own right, and that is associated with a profile of expenses, pay-offs, impacts and side-effects that is also judged (on balance) to be very worthwhile. The terms *expense* and *pay-off* are used to highlight financial costs and benefits, whereas *impact* and *side-effect* are used to highlight broader ones. We use *cost* and *benefit* generically. We use *impact* to highlight positive consequences, and *side-effect* to highlight negative ones. This particular distinction (unlike most of the others that we draw) is purely rhetorical, since we want to emphasize where and when both positive and negative consequences should be considered. Elsewhere, we follow the normal convention of treating 'impact' as value-neutral. Of course, the same consequence can be valued both positively or negatively by different people or the same person on different occasions, so it is actually impossible to draw a conceptual distinction between impact and side-effect in terms of value. So again, our distinction is rhetorical. In fact, the distinction between expense/pay-off and impact/side-effect is more rhetorical than conceptual, since they ultimately need to be valued in a common currency – be that by converting impacts and side-effects into monetary values or some other means.

Acceptability is judged ultimately in relation to the nature and prevalence of identifiable consequences, and in terms of cost–benefit analysis, involving value judgements canvassed from a wide range of stakeholders. High positive value means that the overall benefit substantially outweighs the overall cost. Although traditionally, validity and validation have elevated issues of technical quality, the new matrix elevates issues of social value, identifying the acceptability of the testing policy as the focal point for the entire matrix. Its evaluation argument is constructed on the basis of evidence and analysis collated within cells 4a to 4c, and in the light of the technical arguments developed in cells 1 to 3. Unlike evaluation in the technical row of the matrix, which can be constructed in terms of three relatively discrete evaluation arguments, evaluation in the social row of the matrix is ultimately holistic. As such, cells 1 to 3 provide components of the overall evaluation argument in defence of the testing policy; cells 4a to 4c structure the collation of different kinds of evidence and analysis; while the Overall Judgement cell synthesizes everything into an overall evaluative judgement.

The evaluation of social value encompasses a variety of overlapping concerns, which can be illustrated, if not circumscribed, by the following:

1   credibility
2   utility
3   fairness
4   legality.

Although *credibility* sounds quite technical, it is ultimately social, perhaps even political (with a small 'p'). It is intended to encapsulate evaluation concerns related to the respectability of a policy owner's objective or mechanism for achieving that objective, as judged by a range of stakeholders. As noted above, the objectives laid down by the policy owner will embody a particular value-base. Therefore, part of social evaluation is to consider the admissibility of this value-base to anyone who might be affected by the testing policy. For example, if a policy owner has decreed that attainment in science is primarily a matter of ability to reason scientifically, yet the majority of stakeholders believe that attainment in science ought to be about the mastery of scientific facts, then this might well undermine the credibility, and therefore the currency, of the certificate awarded on the basis of the test. If consequently the testing policy were to be judged unacceptable, this would not be attributable to a lack of measurement quality, but to a lack of measurement value.

Utility is essentially an economic concept, and tools for evaluating utility are well developed within the field of economics. On the cost side of the equation, we need to account for the financial expense – fixed costs and variable costs – of developing and implementing the mechanism. Then on the benefit side of the equation, we need to account for financial pay-off from implementation. For example, we would expect a high-quality procedure for making selection decisions to translate into a significant financial benefit for the organization that implemented it. In addition to the costs and benefits expressed directly in terms of monetary value, there are costs and benefits which can be translated into monetary value terms through the exercise of value judgements. Opportunity costs are important to consider from this perspective: the benefits that could be reaped if the money is not spent on developing and implementing the mechanism. It is fair to conclude that economic analysis has not been well developed within educational and psychological measurement (although for useful insights, see Catterall; 1990, 1997; Monk, 1995; Picus, 1996; Hummel-Rossi and Ashdown, 2002).

However, there is an important body of work concerning utility analysis relating to the use of test results for selection, to which Cronbach contributed significantly (e.g. Cronbach and Gleser, 1957, 1965). This literature has tended to focus on the primary decision-making objective and the expenses and pay-offs associated with alternative selection rules, often judged mainly from the employer's perspective (i.e. the policy owner). As broader perspectives on costs and benefits are adopted, we move from evaluating utility to evaluating *fairness*, and become more moral than economic in outlook. Of course, in neither case is the quantification of values at all straightforward. For example, it is not clear how to value the negative impact on an individual of an incorrect selection decision that results in their being prevented from pursuing their career as a pilot; or more complex still, how to value the negative impact on an employer, or on society at large, of an incorrect selection decision that results in the appointment of a pilot who subsequently crashes a plane.

The concepts of fairness and bias became particularly significant in the USA in the latter half of the 20th century in the wake of 1960s equality legislation, particularly as that legislation impacted on testing for special educational provision, graduation, admission to higher education and employment selection (e.g. Thorndike, 1971b; Cronbach, 1976; Sawyer et al., 1976; Willingham and Cole, 1997; Camilli, 2006). Cole and Moss defined bias as 'differential validity of a given interpretation of a test score for any definable, relevant subgroup of test takers' (1989: 205). In other words, bias exists when it is not possible to measure *in the same way* across all subgroups of the population. At worst, it simply may not be possible to measure the desired attribute when using the test with certain subgroups; at best, the quality of measurement may prove to be lower for those groups. Expressed thus, bias is essentially a technical issue, for consideration within cell 1. It only becomes a social issue, of relevance to row 2, once the interpretation or use of the test scores has had some kind of impact – then it becomes a matter of unfairness. The nature of test fairness and its role in evaluation continue to be debated. In the language testing community, the work of Kunnan has been very influential (e.g. Kunnan, 1997, 2000, 2004) and conceptions continue to evolve (e.g. Xi, 2010).

The basic problem for both utility and fairness analysis is the sheer number of impacts, side-effects and stakeholder perspectives that deserve to be considered. For example, in England, national curriculum tests are administered each year to a large proportion of the national cohort of 11-year-olds. Therefore, for each tested cohort each year, there are around 600,000 individuals with direct consequences: effects that are educational, social, emotional, short-term, long-term, of correct classification and incorrect classification, and so on. Then there are effects from the use of aggregated results: effects on policy owners from the use of national-level results to judge policy making; on families and the structure of education and society from the use of school-level results to inform school choices; on school leaders and teachers from the use of school-level and class-level results for rewarding and sanctioning them, and so on. Genuinely comprehensive social evaluation is simply impossible, even if we were to consider only those costs and benefits that could be reasonably translated into a monetary value. However, equally, it would be immoral to ignore the many impacts and side-effects associated with testing policies. As such, the principal social evaluation threat parallels the idea of construct-underrepresentation: failing to capture a sufficiently comprehensive sample of expenses, pay-offs, impacts and side-effects; and failing to capture a sufficiently comprehensive sample of opinions on those consequences.

Although *legality* has its basis in moral fairness, it is distinct in the sense of being made explicit by the rule of law, with penalties liable to those who break it. Therefore it is the ultimate social evaluation consideration as far as testing policy is concerned.

It is clearly social rather than technical, in the sense that the implementation of a procedure that were to support high-quality measurement could be judged illegal on the basis of adverse impact for protected groups. Thus, the principle that students should have the opportunity to learn the material that ultimately they will be tested on has been the basis for legal rulings, independent of the quality of measurement associated with the testing procedure (see Phillips and Camara, 2006).

The starting point for all social evaluation is a detailed statement that specifies a full profile of potential expenses, pay-offs, impacts and side-effects. For an evaluation that was retrospective rather than simply prospective, this would be accompanied by evidence of actual prevalence to date, as well as judgements concerning the likelihood of future prevalence. Retrospective evaluation would enable the identification of unanticipated expenses, pay-offs, impacts and side-effects as well. In addition to establishing the nature and prevalence of identifiable consequences, a full range of stakeholder perspectives would need to be identified, and their opinions canvassed concerning the costs and benefits associated with impacts and side-effects.

The ultimate purpose of the matrix is to support the construction and appraisal of an argument which concludes that is it acceptable (or unacceptable) to implement the testing policy, or to continue implementing it. However, rather than there being a single evaluation argument, there might well be a range of different arguments constructed from different perspectives (e.g. the policy owner perspective, the perspective of a particular stakeholder group). Again, ideally, the culmination of any such evaluation ought to be a strong argument in favour of the claim that the argument terminates in: be that a claim of high positive value, low positive value, no value or even negative value. Notice once again how these judgements of social value are expressed quantitatively. Conversely, the matrix acknowledges that real-world action requires binary decisions – to do or not to do – which is why the overall evaluation question asks simply whether it is acceptable to implement the testing policy. It is straightforward to judge acceptability one way or another when it has been possible to construct a strong social evaluation argument which terminates in the claim that the testing policy is either high positive value or high negative value. However, when, for example, it is claimed that the testing policy has low positive value, the judgement is far harder to call. Clearly, low positive value is *some* positive value, but it would leave the testing policy vulnerable, since even a small amount of additional negative evidence or analysis might swing the balance.

Finally, the idea of constructing social evaluation arguments from a range of different perspectives, in order to enable them to be compared and contrasted, implies a particular view on the role of the evaluator stemming from a particular value-base. It suggests that the evaluator should adopt the role of social scientist for technical evaluation, but a role perhaps more like that of mediator for social evaluation. Having said that, in both cases the guiding principle tends towards 'objectivity' rather than 'subjectivity'. Within this account, the evaluator is not an active campaigner for a particular perspective. As a social scientist, the evaluator explores claims of plausibility and viability not just from their own perspective, but in relation to positions adopted by established communities of practice, both academic and lay. As mediator, the evaluator attempts to help the policy owner and stakeholder groups to understand their own as well as each others' perspectives. In the words of Cronbach, 'the specialist's proper role is to help nonspecialists reach their own conclusions about tests and test data' (Cronbach, 1983: 11).

Illustrating the framework

The following sections illustrate how the evaluation focus and approaches differ across the cells of the new matrix. Because the framework is meant to be capable of embracing a full range of evaluation concerns, this illustration is necessarily restricted and selective. For example, although we have observed already that practical viability needs to be evaluated alongside theoretical plausibility within cells 1 to 3, viability is more pedestrian than plausibility, and because our intention is to illustrate the more interesting and significant concerns, we will not dwell on it further.

The key to understanding the logic of the matrix is to ask whether the underlying evaluation question is essentially one of possibility or acceptability. The first row, technical evaluation, asks whether it is possible to achieve the policy owner's objectives by implementing the mechanisms in question. The second row, social evaluation, asks whether it is acceptable to achieve the policy owner's objectives in those ways. Whereas the evaluation questions within cells 1 to 3 are relatively discrete, this is not true for cells 4a to 4c, which structure the collation of evidence of expense, pay-off, impact and side-effect. The cost–benefit argument that supports the Overall Judgement synthesizes evidence, analysis and argumentation from all the cells.

Cell 1

There is an obvious similarity between the first cell of the original progressive matrix and cell 1 of the new one. Yet with an explicit focus on practicality as well as plausibility, cell 1 of the new matrix could be said to have a slightly broader focus. Essentially, though, it shares a common foundation: that which Messick (1980) described as 'construct validity', and which the 1999 *Standards* simply called 'validity'.

Specifying the attribute

Evaluation across each of the three columns of the framework begins with a clear specification of the intended objective. For cell 1 this is familiar territory, since the objective is to measure, and therefore the measurement objective is defined in terms of the attribute that is supposed to be measured. We will refer to the explicit construction of the attribute (through definition, description, exemplification, etc.) as the *attribute specification*, although others might prefer to call it the 'construct definition'.

Unfortunately, this step is not always taken, and both test design and test evaluation often commence from shaky foundations, with the measurement objective remaining largely implicit (for a recent recognition of this, see Department for Education, 2011). This often occurs within achievement testing, when curriculum statements or lists of learning objectives are assumed to function as though they specified the attribute with sufficient clarity. Conversely, an effective attribute specification ought to go considerably beyond curriculum objectives: for example, to explain the implications of having more or less of the attribute. Cronbach illustrated this point in the following passage (and illustrated an analogous specification for the attribute 'compulsivity' two pages later):

> These miscellaneous challenges express fragments of a definition or theoretical conception of reading comprehension that, if stated explicitly, might begin: 'The student considered superior in reading comprehension is one who, if acquainted with the words in a paragraph, will be able to derive from the paragraph the same conclusions that other educated readers, previously uninformed on the subject of the paragraph, derive.' Just this one sentence separates superior vocabulary, reading speed, information and other counterhypotheses from the construct, reading comprehension. (Cronbach, 1971: 463)

This represents what might be termed the top-down approach to attribute specification: the macro-construct characterization. Recall, from Chapter 5, how the cognitive approach tends to approach attribute specification from the bottom-up, focusing on the cognitive components of competence: the micro-constructs characterization. Whichever approach or combination of approaches is preferred, the attribute specification ought to be the point of embarkation for evaluating measurement quality.

Assuming that an adequate attribute specification accompanies the test, evaluation can commence effectively from this foundation. If not, then an attribute specification will need to be constructed in collaboration with the policy owner (as will be discussed below). The evaluator then focuses squarely on the potential to achieve high-quality measurement on the basis of the mechanism in question: that is, the measurement procedure. The procedure is more than just the instrument as traditionally conceived; it includes the test, scoring, reporting and *conditions* under which each of these are supposed to be undertaken. Conditions might include: administration in silence at a secure testing centre; training and qualification for those employed to mark constructed responses; marking scripts in a secure environment under the guidance of expert team leaders; inputting item scores onto a bespoke processing system; etc. Conditions also should include a statement of the population for whom the test has been designed, with an indication of subgroups for whom or situations within which it may not be possible to achieve high-quality measurement.

Theoretical plausibility

In cell 1, theoretical plausibility is judged in relation to a *theory of measurement*, investigated on the basis of a variety of sources of empirical evidence and logical analyses: for example, the half-dozen or so sources of evidence identified by Messick (1989a; see Chapter 4), or the five identified by the 1999 *Standards*. The bottom line is whether, based on critical evaluation of the evidence and analysis, there is sufficient reason to believe it possible to measure the specified attribute by implementing the measurement procedure, assuming that the conditions of measurement have been met. It is important to emphasize that this requires an overall judgement based on *any* source of evidence that bears on the question of measurement quality, including evidence of reliability, comparability, and so on.

Certain kinds of evidence from the consequences of testing will bear on the question of measurement quality, as the recent debate over score inflation helpfully illustrates. For example, it is widely accepted that most, if not all, achievement tests will underrepresent their domains to some extent, and sometimes this underrepresentation may be predictable across test forms (e.g. Holcombe et al., 2013). Yet predictable underrepresentation per se is not necessarily a threat to measurement quality, as long as it is not associated also with restricted teaching and learning. However, if there were (consequential) evidence that teachers and/or students were restricting their teaching and learning in response to predictable underrepresentation, then this would demonstrate an inevitable negative impact on measurement quality – it would be wrong to treat the results as high-quality measures of the attribute, since those results would fail to indicate that certain elements of the attribute were not actually being mastered.

Policy owner values and purposes

If the guiding question of cell 1 is whether it is possible to measure the desired attribute using the test, then the account of the previous section has omitted one crucial element of the technical evaluation: an investigation into the degree of consistency between the attribute specification, the *specified attribute*; and that which the policy owner ultimately wants to measure, the *desired attribute*. This is a well-known challenge within educational measurement, particularly in countries where there is no national curriculum. In this context, off-the-shelf achievement tests which have been designed to assess generic learning objectives within a domain will be unlikely to reflect exactly the curriculum followed locally within the schools that use them. For bespoke tests which *are* tailored specifically to the needs of the policy owner, inconsistency is likely to be less of an issue. However, when off-the-shelf tests are used, there might well be a significant gulf between the attribute specified by the test developer, and the attribute desired by the policy owner.

Establishing the degree of consistency between the specified attribute and the desired attribute may require additional effort, since it is quite likely that the policy owner will be unable to articulate their desired attribute without support. So, this will require scaffolding and careful questioning. The starting point for any interrogation of the desired attribute is the use, or uses, to which they wish the test scores to be put. As we saw from Chapter 1, the results from a single test might be used in quite different ways, and those different uses would have different implications for the kind of interpretation to be drawn from the results. For one use of results (e.g. placement) the desired attribute might be constructed in a particular way (in terms of achievement); whereas for another use of results (e.g. selection), the desired attribute might be constructed in a different way (in terms of aptitude). Here, what is at stake is whether uses that are fundamental to the policy owner are consistent with the attribute specification that has informed test development. If we are prepared to accept that a single test might be interpreted in a variety of different ways, reflecting a range of different attributes, then this consistency need not be a tight, one-to-one mapping. However, there might well be occasions when the policy owner value-base is entirely at odds with the original attribute specification, even despite superficial similarity.

An example of this might be an achievement attribute such as 'everyday maths' which could be constructed in a variety of different, albeit equally legitimate, ways. One construction might conceive achievement in everyday mathematics as a continuum along which students are to be ranked. Another might conceive achievement in everyday mathematics as a series of hurdles over which students are required to jump. The hurdles conception might reflect a functional outlook held by a policy owner who believes that life presents a range of different kinds of mathematical challenge, and that learners need to be equipped to deal with all of them. This attribute would be defined in terms of a profile of sub-proficiencies, and would imply a conjunctive approach to aggregation or standard-setting across subdomains (e.g. Haladyna and Hess, 2000). In contrast, the continuum conception might reflect a motivational outlook held by a policy owner who believes that students should be encouraged to excel in the areas in which they are most motivated to achieve, regardless of whether this means that they flounder in some. This attribute might be defined in terms of an overall proficiency and might imply a compensatory approach to aggregation or standard-setting across subdomains (although, conceivably, it even might be defined in terms of proficiency in a particular nominated subdomain). Considerations such as these illustrate the relationship between the policy owner value-base, the purpose to which they wish to put test scores, and therefore the way in which test scores need to be interpreted. Here, what needs to be investigated is the degree to which the value-base embodied in the original attribute specification (the specified attribute) is consistent with the policy owner value-base (the desired attribute).

Reconciling values and the 'real world'

There are two different kinds of explanation for persuasive evidence of low-quality measurement. The first, and most obvious, is that the measurement procedure simply failed to operationalize the attribute specification effectively. In principle, the solution to this kind of problem is straightforward: develop a better procedure. The second is that the attribute specification failed to operationalize the world effectively. This is a far more subtle problem, and casts doubt on the legitimacy of the attribute itself, at least as constructed through the specification. From this perspective, the attribute specification might be entirely consistent with the policy owner value-base and the theory of individual difference that it gives rise to, but that value-base and theory might be entirely inconsistent with the world. For many, the longstanding controversy over the legitimacy of intelligence testing illustrates this conundrum (e.g. Gould, 1981). In cases such as this, often it is very difficult to judge which is more to blame for the evidence of low-quality measurement: the attribute specification (value-base and theory), or the test development process. There might be other cases where the judgement is more straightforward. For example, a policy owner might construct an achievement attribute as the combination of two primary sub-proficiencies. However, if empirical evidence demonstrates convincingly that the two sub-proficiencies were substantially negatively correlated, then this would provide good reason for the policy owner to re-examine the theoretical plausibility of their construction. Similar tensions arise when policy owners define achievement attributes (e.g. achievement in English) in terms of sub-proficiencies that are not necessarily strongly correlated (e.g. reading versus writing).

Finally, to reiterate a point made earlier: an evaluation of theoretical plausibility might result in persuasive evidence of high-quality measurement in relation to the attribute specification; yet if the attribute specification has been demonstrated to depart substantially from the policy owner value-base, then strictly speaking we would be forced to conclude that the measurement objective had not actually been achieved. It might be possible to measure *an* attribute using the test, but not the *desired* attribute. Incidentally, by including an evaluation of consistency between desired attribute and specified attribute within cell 1, we include considerations that Messick would have discussed in his second cell. This brings cell 1 of the new matrix more into line with the first *column* of the original progressive matrix.

Cell 2

Just as cell 1 resonates with the first cell of the original progressive matrix, cell 2 resonates with the third, which concerned the scientific evaluation of test use. However, there is a sense in which cell 2 of the new matrix is less embracing than the third cell of the old one, since it focuses squarely on technical issues, nudging social issues into cells 4b and 4c. The question that guides evaluation in cell 2 is whether it is possible to make more accurate decisions by incorporating test scores into the decision-making process. This reminds us that the goal of testing is generally a pragmatic one: not to make perfectly accurate decisions, but to make more accurate decisions than would be made in the absence of test scores. The objective is framed in terms of the technical question of *accuracy*, in order to distinguish it from social questions of utility and fairness that are considered more appropriately in later cells. As emphasized within the original progressive matrix, *relevance* is fundamental to judging decision-making accuracy: if what is supposed to be measured by the test is highly relevant to the decision that needs to be taken, then higher measurement quality ought to ensure greater decision-making accuracy.

Decision-making versus intervention

A particularly tricky issue to grapple with, as far as decision-making is concerned, is the precise focus for evaluation. The problem is that decisions generally result in actions – and often in targeted *interventions* – and this means that there are potentially two distinct evaluation foci. Which of these – the decision or the intervention that the decision results in – is the proper focus for evaluation, or does cell 2 imply the evaluation of both? This conundrum has caused a lot of confusion in the debate over the scope of validity, so we will be careful to explain it clearly here. We saw in Chapter 5 how Mehrens (1997) considered it to be very unwise to confound inferences concerning measurement quality (e.g. the diagnosis of prostate cancer) with inferences concerning treatment efficacy (a particular medical intervention). In fact, as we saw in Chapter 4, Messick (1984) made the same point a few years earlier, arguing that it was important to distinguish between the validity of assessment of students' functional needs (e.g. the diagnosis of educable mental retardation) and the quality of instruction subsequently received (a special educational programme). Logically, it would seem entirely possible for the decision-making to be accurate, but for the intervention to be ineffective. According to Messick, we can isolate the first of these issues, the technical quality of decision-making, by theorizing it in terms of 'responsiveness to *optimal* future instruction' (Messick, 1984: 6; emphasis added).

From this perspective, an accurate decision is one that would achieve the intended outcome under conditions of optimal intervention. In order to *understand* the potential to improve decision-making accuracy by incorporating test scores into the decision-making process, we require clarity concerning the outcome that is supposed to be achieved by the decision-making and intervention, supplemented by a theoretical analysis of the mechanism by which that outcome is supposed to be achieved. Moreover, in order to *evaluate* this potential, we need to investigate the extent to which those outcomes are actually achieved on the basis of the decision-making and intervention – not on the basis of a hypothetical optimal intervention, but on the basis of an actual, 'warts-and-all' intervention.

Importantly, from the perspective of cell 2, investigation into the outcome of the 'warts-and-all' intervention is not an evaluation of the *social value of the outcome*, but an investigation into the nature of the outcome, in order to inform evaluation of the *technical quality of the decision-making*. Evaluation of the social value of the outcome is a matter for cell 4b. However, what about evaluation of the *technical quality of the intervention* as distinct from the technical quality of the decision-making? Given that we are discussing a framework for the evaluation of testing policy, we might choose to theorize this separately. Conversely, if the whole purpose of the decision-making is to support an intervention, then this would not seem to be very sensible. Moreover, it is hard to see how we could judge the quality of the decision-making effectively without simultaneously judging the quality of the intervention. After all, if the testing policy is not delivering the goods, we need to know where to lay the blame in order to understand how to rectify the situation. However, importantly, they are separable issues and it is useful to separate them.

Specifying the outcome

As in cell 1, evaluation in cell 2 also begins with a clear specification of the intended objective. This is the intended outcome of the decision-making and intervention: the reason why the decision is made. We will refer to explicit construction of the outcome of decision-making (through definition, description, exemplification, etc.) as the *outcome specification*. We introduce the idea of an outcome specification as a direct analogue to the attribute specification. Indeed, we think that there is a useful parallel between the attribute and outcome specification described here and the IUA, described in Kane (2013a). In both cases, we need to begin by making explicit the objective that is supposed to be achieved by implementing the procedure: first, the measurement objective (the interpretation); second, the decision-making and intervention objective (the use).

In order to illustrate the outcome specification and its relation to what the policy owner wants to achieve by implementing the decision-making procedure and intervention, imagine a baseline test of achievement in science that is used to place first-year secondary school students into one of three teaching sets. In terms of measuring achievement in science, measurement quality is defined primarily in terms of the potential for ranking students correctly in terms of the attribute. The decision, however, makes additional requirements, including the location of cut-scores on the achievement continuum. Indeed, if the decision were to be based on more than just the test score, then a rule by which to combine all of the information would be required. To work out how best to locate cut-scores and to identify how best to combine multiple sources of information, we would need to explore in greater detail the rationale for segregating students into teaching sets.

One kind of rationale is that students will have made different levels of progress in primary school and will need to pick up the science curriculum in secondary school from where they left off, even though ultimately all of them will be taught the same content. Therefore, cut-scores might be used to group students in terms of their prior mastery of the science curriculum, and results from the science test alone might be considered sufficient for this purpose. A different kind of rationale is that certain students will be less able than others to master the more demanding content of more advanced courses, and therefore that students should be channelled into different instructional programmes. In this case, cut-scores might be used to discriminate between students on the basis of their potential for mastering different kinds of content in the future, and results from other assessments might be considered useful for supplementing information from the science test. In both cases, the outcome specification would be characterized in terms of the placement of students in groups that best catered for their teaching and learning needs and, therefore, in terms of optimal learning for students in all three sets.

Further insight into how we might characterize an outcome specification derives from a paper by Penfield (2010), who discussed the use of test scores for making grade promotion and retention decisions. Central to the framework that Penfield employed was an evaluation of the effectiveness of the treatment that was contingent on the retention decision. He described this as a kind of placement decision:

a decision to place students back in the grade from which they had come. On the basis of two major evidence bases, Penfield concluded that retention is a poor form of placement: it does not serve to improve academic achievement, and leads to increased school drop-out. In terms of our framework, we might characterize the outcome specification for those students who were retained, in terms of academic achievement during the year following the grade retention decision: our intention is that their achievement, a year after the retention decision, should be higher than it would have been, had they been promoted.

Circumscribing the outcome specification thus would help to render an evaluation into the technical quality of the decision-making procedure more tractable. It specifies the outcome broadly enough to have real-world currency, yet narrowly enough to theorize meaningfully and therefore to investigate. However, note that not all of the evidence that Penfield (2010) identified would be directly relevant to an investigation presented like this. For example, evidence of substantially lower achievement some years down the line and evidence of higher levels of school drop-out would not speak directly to the issue of whether the decision was effective in achieving its outcome, thus specified. In fact, it would be quite possible for the test-based decision-making procedure to achieve its short-term intended objective – higher levels of achievement during the subsequent school year than would have occurred if the students had been promoted – *and* for it to result in unacceptable, long-term side-effects further down the line: for example, higher rates of school drop-out. Clearly, both short-term intended impacts and long-term, unintended side-effects need to be investigated. However, in terms of our evaluation framework we think it is useful to separate them, because they *can* sensibly be separated and, by separating them, we help to make evaluation more tractable and the results of the evaluation more informative. We would locate the technical evaluation of the proximal decision-making objective in cell 2, leaving the social evaluation of both proximal and distal impacts and side-effects for cells 4b and 4c. As mentioned previously, this process of carving up the components of evaluation inevitably requires the occasional arbitrary decision as to what to categorize where; but the rewards from carving the components thus are to be reaped in terms of focus and clarity for the evaluation. These are complicated issues that need to be carefully unpacked.

Theoretical plausibility

Alongside the outcome specification, a more detailed *theory of the decision* is required to explain the mechanism by which the decision is supposed to achieve its outcome. For example, if the rationale were for students to pick up a curriculum where they left off, then the theory of the decision might include assumptions such as: mastery of prior science content is important to mastery of future science content; the score on the science test provides a good indication of a student's location along a trajectory of science learning; and so on. If the assumptions in the theory were not to hold, then the rationale for using the test scores to make placement decisions would be missing, and we would not expect the placement decisions to achieve their intended outcome. The role of the theory of the decision is ultimately to explain the relevance of the attribute specification to the outcome specification: *why* it might be possible to make more accurate decisions by incorporating test scores into the decision-making process, thereby facilitating our intended outcome.

Remember that we have defined an accurate decision as one that would achieve the intended outcome under conditions of optimal intervention. This suggests that we need to supplement our theory of the decision with a *theory of intervention*. Returning to our example of grouping students on the basis of their science test results, if we were to characterize the outcome specification in terms of optimal learning for students placed in the various groups – for example, a year following the placement decision – then the intervention would refer to the teaching received in those groups tailored to the learning needs identified by the measurement and decision-making process. The theory of intervention would explain how the teaching should be tailored to those needs in order to achieve the intended outcomes.

The example of assessment for learning, formative assessment, is useful to introduce here. Central to the definition of assessment for learning, particularly within the tradition that has developed from the UK, has been an emphasis on the use of assessment information to identify *and to close the gap between* where students currently are in their learning, and where they need to go (Black and Wiliam, 1998a; Assessment Reform Group, 2002; Gardner, 2012). This led Stobart (2006) to conclude that there is a fundamental difference between validity for summative assessment, and validity for formative assessment:

- summative is judged primarily in relation to the interpretation of assessment outcomes and measurement quality;
- formative is judged primarily in relation to the use of assessment outcomes and the consequences of their use – the learning that does or does not occur.

An alternative way to think about the difference is by dividing assessment for learning into an assessment (measurement) component, followed by an instructional (intervention) component. Rather than prioritizing the ultimate outcome, we would be giving each component the attention that it deserves. Along exactly these lines, Nichols et al. (2009) distinguished the 'assessment phase' from the 'instructional phase' within a general framework for evaluating the validity of formative claims. This incorporated a theory of measurement within the first phase, and a theory of intervention in the second. We think that even greater clarity could be achieved by bridging the two with a theory of the decision.

These three components correspond to: first, measuring the attribute; second, using the measure to allocate test-takers to an appropriate intervention; and, third, implementing the intervention. Imagine, for example, the use of results from a pre-university science programme to select between applicants who wished to study for a medical degree. During the measurement phase, the objective is to assess mastery of the pre-university science programme. This would be successful if those assessed high (low) were those with highest (lowest) achievement in science. During the decision-making phase, the objective is to use those measurements to allocate students to intervention conditions: that is, to make accurate selection decisions. This would be successful if those selected (rejected) were those who would be most (least) likely to succeed as medics under conditions of optimal training. Finally, during the intervention phase, the objective is to train students to become good medics. This would be successful if indeed all of the selected students were to become good medics. Again, what we are trying to do here is to separate potentially separable components, to help to make evaluation more tractable and the results of the evaluation more informative. Having said that, although we have spoken of a distinct theory of measurement, theory of the decision and theory of intervention, ultimately these theories must shade into each other. After all, the whole point of the exercise is to construct a conceptual bridge between measurement, decision-making and intervention.

The idea of a theory of intervention has not been a dominant feature of the literature on validity and validation, although there is an emerging body of work in relation to formative assessment (e.g. Black and Wiliam, 2012; Stobart, 2012). This is interesting, given that the traditional concept of criterion validity is fundamentally dependent on the nature and quality of the training that is received once successful applicants have started work. Incidentally, in this context, the criterion construct is tantamount to the outcome specification discussed earlier. The criterion problem resonates with the arbitrary decisions that need to be made when establishing parameters for the outcome specification. Although discussion of theories of intervention has tended not to have been as explicit and dominant as perhaps it ought to have been, there has been more attention to the theory of the decision, particularly within personnel settings, so we will end our discussion of cell 2 by considering different ways in which theorists have constructed this concept.

Different ways of constructing a theory of the decision

There is no single, generally accepted approach to developing a theory of the decision, and quite different approaches can be found in the literature. An important distinction can be drawn between approaches that seek to reinterpret the attribute that is supposed to be measured in terms of the decision that is to be made – thereby aiming to theorize decision-making as far as possible in terms of measurement – and those that treat measurement and decision-making as quite distinct.

The principle of integrating as much as possible of the theory of the decision within the theory of measurement has a long pedigree, and seems to be an implicit foundation for the definition of validity within the 1999 *Standards*: the degree to which evidence and theory support the interpretations of test scores entailed by proposed uses of results. The implication of 'entailed by proposed uses' is that test scores may be interpreted in different ways, dependent on the uses to which they will be put. For example, we might use scores from a single mathematics test to measure 'achievement in general mathematics at primary school' in relation to one use of results, or to measure 'aptitude for applied mathematics at secondary school' in relation to another. Although the test most likely will have been designed to represent an achievement-based attribute specification, evaluation (validation) could be equally conducted in relation to an aptitude-based one. The idea is to specify the attribute at the heart of the evaluation in terms that are optimally tailored to the intended use of results: that is, in terms that are 'entailed by' that use, in the terminology of the *Standards*.

Newton (2012a) referred to this practice as *multi-construct interpretation*, and described it in some detail. It implies that the theory of measurement should incorporate as much of the theory of the decision as possible. Ideally, from this perspective, the theory of measurement and the theory of the decision would overlap to such an extent that high measurement quality would be tantamount to (i.e. effectively guarantee) high decision-making quality. Of course, the consequence is that the measurement theory becomes far more complex, and contains far more assumptions than it otherwise might need to have.

Cronbach (1971) opened his classic chapter in *Educational Measurement* with the example of a test that was used to rank students in terms of their 'readiness' for a particular programme of reading instruction. The implication of defining the test in terms of an attribute such as 'readiness' for a certain kind of reading instruction, rather than simply in terms of, for example, 'achievement' in reading, is that the theory of measurement itself will need to incorporate predictions concerning testing consequences. This is exactly what Messick (1989a, 1989b) meant when he insisted that consequences should be understood as action inferences within the nomological network: inferences that needed to be tested out. Thus, evaluating the potential to measure 'readiness' would require comparing each student's actual progress during the year following the decision with predictions from the theory of measurement. The idea of mutli-construct interpretation has been developed by various validity theorists, most notably, Lorrie Shepard (e.g. Shepard, 1990, 1993, 1997).

Readiness can be thought of as an attribute quite like aptitude, in the sense that it is intended to capture something about how an individual will behave in a particular context in the future. Aptitude testing has been the focus of a great deal of work in personnel psychology, and the nature of the aptitude attribute itself has been the subject of much debate. One approach akin to multi-construct interpretation is to evaluate an aptitude test as though it actually *measured* the specific aptitude. For example, a battery of tests used to select between applicants to a medical education programme might be evaluated in terms of the extent to which it measured the attribute 'physician aptitude' (see Tenopyr, 1977 for an account which reads quite like this). A quite different approach is for each test in the battery to be separately evaluated, each in relation to the attribute that it was designed originally to measure. Therefore, the battery would not be assumed to *measure* aptitude in any meaningful sense; it would simply 'measure' the composite of whatever the separate tests measured. Moreover, the use of the battery for selecting between applicants to a medical education programme would require a distinct theory of the decision, in order to establish the relevance of the battery to the decision-making.

By way of summary, the multi-construct interpretation approach defines a new global attribute directly in terms of the intended use of results. By evaluating the quality of measurement of this new attribute, it reduces the gap between evaluation of measurement and evaluation of decision-making. That is, to justify the claim that a test measures readiness is to justify the claim that it can be used to make readiness decisions. However, the alternative approach sticks with the attribute that the test was originally designed to measure: meaning that the evaluation of measurement and decision-making remain quite distinct, and need to be theorized separately.

The way in which Guion (e.g. 1976) theorized the evaluation of aptitude testing epitomized this alternative approach. For Guion, there was a clear distinction between what the predictor test was supposed to measure (the predictor construct), and that which was to be predicted: what the criterion test was supposed to measure (the criterion construct). In construct validation terms, the construct validity of the predictor test needs to be evaluated in terms of the predictor test attribute specification, while the construct validity of the criterion measure needs to be evaluated in terms of the criterion measure attribute specification. In addition, beyond the evaluation of measurement quality we need to evaluate the 'hypothesis of a relationship' (Guion, 1978b: 208) between predictor construct and criterion construct. In personnel settings, this is what would be typically known as the hypothesis of job-relatedness. Again, in the way that Guion conceptualized evaluation, this lay *beyond* construct validity. In effect, he drew a clear distinction between a theory of measurement and a theory of the decision, where the hypothesis of job-relatedness is part of the theory of the decision. Job-relatedness concerned the relevance of the predictor to the criterion, to be established: logically, e.g. based on a logical analysis of structural relationships; and empirically, e.g. based on empirical evidence of the correlational relationship.

Both evaluation approaches have long traditions. In certain contexts, if done well, there might not be much to choose between them. However, since the logic of decision-making is often very dense and complex, the attempt to reduce the gap between the evaluation of measurement and the evaluation of decision-making may not be in the best interests of clarity and transparency. Any step that can be taken to elucidate the many separable stages in the evaluation of decision-making quality is probably worth taking. So, we would recommend treating the evaluation of measurement quality and the evaluation of decision-making quality as two interdependent but conceptually distinguishable phases, and two distinct kinds of argument (the measurement argument and the decision and intervention argument).[1]

Here, the issue is one of complexity and the pay-off from deconstructing large problems into smaller ones. Braun (2012) highlighted the complexity of evaluating value-added models which are employed to identify differential impacts on student learning across teachers. Models such as these make use of all sorts of measures (of differing quality), and involve complex techniques for combining those measures (the quality of which also needs evaluating). To the extent that such models are used to make decisions about teachers, there will be additional issues of how to distinguish teachers at one level of value-added from teachers at another, not to mention the broader issue of the relevance of the value-added model to the specific decisions that are to be taken. Of course, if value-added models are to be used in conjunction with other information to make these decisions, then this increases the complexity of the evaluation process by another level of magnitude. Again, it makes a lot of sense, whenever appropriate, to deconstruct the overall evaluation project into a series of more manageable questions and arguments. This can help to expose the reasoning underlying the claim that the decision-making mechanism can be legitimately employed to achieve the intended objective.

Cell 3

We think that much of the confusion surrounding the original matrix can be attributed to the fact that it only had two columns, regarding measurement and decision-making, when it really ought to have had three. The reason is that there are primary impacts that are related directly to the use of measurement for decision-making (discussed in cell 2), and secondary impacts that may be quite unrelated. Where these secondary impacts are explicitly part of the rationale underpinning the testing policy – for example, the positive impact of testing on effort expended by students and teachers – they need to be evaluated from both social and technical perspectives. As such, column 3 is concerned not with impacts per se, but with impacts that are incidental to the primary decision-making objective(s) of the testing policy. This seems to be precisely what was intended by standard 1.23 of the 1999 *Standards*:

> When a test use or score interpretation is recommended on the grounds that testing or the testing program per se will result in some indirect benefit in addition to the utility of information from the test scores themselves, the rationale for anticipating the indirect benefit should be made explicit. Logical or theoretical arguments and empirical evidence for the indirect benefit should be provided. (AERA et al., 1999: 23)

Specifying the impact

Evaluation within cell 3 begins with a clear specification of the intended objective. In this instance, the objective is to achieve a set of additional positive impacts beyond those captured by the primary decision-making objective(s). We refer to the explicit construction of this set of additional positive impacts (through definition, description, exemplification, etc.) as the *impact specification*. A complete impact specification would need to identify all of the incidental impacts that the policy owner intended to achieve by implementing the testing policy.

The idea of an intended impact implies a positive consequence that is presumed to be contingent on implementation of the testing policy, attributable either to the implementation of the testing policy per se, or to a particular characteristic of its implementation. For example, it is widely assumed that a major positive impact of using test scores to make graduation decisions is that students will be more motivated to acquire intended learning objectives throughout the course of instruction. If there were no graduation test – or more correctly, if there were no graduation decisions – it would be assumed that students would be far less motivated to learn. The motivating impact of the testing policy is presumed to occur largely (although not entirely) independently of the quality of measurement or decision-making. That is, even a low-quality test might have the desired impact (although below a certain level of quality, the obvious unfairness of the system would undermine it). The mechanism underlying this impact might be presumed to operate in terms of what students had to win or lose from studying for the test: for example, the educational or occupational doors that would be opened or closed; or the social kudos or stigma associated with passing or failing.

In addition to intended impacts attributable to the testing policy, there will be intended impacts attributable to particular characteristics of its implementation. For example, when national curriculum assessment was introduced to England in the late 1980s, it was generally accepted that reporting in terms of absolute criteria, rather than in terms of relative scores, would enhance motivation to study, particularly for the least able. Instead of receiving essentially the same norm-referenced certification of failure each year, these low-attaining students would be able to track real progress from one year to the next in terms of what they actually knew, understood and could do. Unfortunately, the impacts from level-based reporting were not as positive as was hoped originally (Oates, 2010).

Earlier, we drew a distinction between construct-relevant impacts, construct-irrelevant impacts and construct-neutral impacts. Construct-relevant impacts were consequences arising from accurate assessment, construct-irrelevant impacts were consequences arising from inaccurate assessment, while construct-neutral impacts were consequences that were largely independent of measurement quality. We have just observed how the positive impact of testing on motivation is presumed typically to occur largely independently of the quality of measurement or decision-making, and therefore might be described as construct-neutral. With this in mind, it would be possible to make a case for locating the technical evaluation of construct-neutral impacts within cell 3, but locating the technical evaluation of construct-relevant and construct-irrelevant impacts within cell 1. If only for the sake of clarity, we would recommend evaluating all secondary impacts, construct-neutral or otherwise, within cell 3: that is, all intended impacts beyond the primary decision-making objective(s). This avoids the need to make subtle and perhaps arbitrary distinctions between what should, or should not, count as construct-neutral. It also means that evaluation within cell 1 remains centrally focused on measurement quality, rather than extending also to the evaluation of impact quality. Thus, intended impacts directly attributable to enhanced construct-relevance – e.g. positive washback on teaching and learning arising from the implementation of a test worth teaching to (e.g. Frederiksen, 1984; Yeh, 2001) – ought to be evaluated from a technical perspective within cell 3.

Theoretical plausibility

The evaluation of theoretical plausibility for cell 3 investigates whether it is possible to achieve the set of positive consequences identified in the impact specification by implementing the testing policy. One way to conduct an evaluation such as this might be to observe the consequences of implementing the policy over an extended period of time, perhaps a decade or so. In fact, this would not be at all advisable for a variety of reasons, the most obvious being that at least some kind of prospective evaluation should be undertaken even before the testing policy is implemented, let alone at intervals more frequent than every decade or so. More importantly, the idea of establishing causation on the basis of observation alone is fanciful (see also Reckase, 1998b; Cizek, 2011). Impacts can be investigated effectively only by adopting a more scientific approach, developing and testing hypotheses on the basis of theoretical models. Therefore, in addition to specification of the objectives, we require a *theory of impact* for each of the intended positive consequences. By exposing the assumptions underlying each theory of impact, it becomes possible to examine them critically in the light of empirical evidence and logical analysis.

Despite nearly 100 years of theorizing validity for measurement and decision-making, it is fair to say that our understanding of how to evaluate broader policy objectives remains very limited. Recent attempts, typically framed in terms of theories of action, represent a step in the right direction (e.g. Hamp-Lyons, 1997; Lane et al., 1998; Baker and Linn, 2002; Forte-Fast and Hebbler, 2004; Haertel and Herman, 2005; Marion and Pellegrino, 2009; Nichols et al., 2009; Bennett et al., 2011). However, there is still a lot of work to be done to establish general principles and robust guidance for evaluating impact arguments.

As for cells 1 and 2, cell 3 is only concerned with the technical evaluation of intended objectives. It is neither concerned with their social evaluation, nor unintended impacts, positive or negative, nor test misuse. All of these are considered within subsequent cells.

Cells 4a to 4c

As explained earlier, we use cells 4a to 4c to structure the collation of evidence and analysis concerning expense, pay-off, impact and side-effect. Our intention is to ensure that a full profile of actual and potential costs and benefits is represented across these cells. In practice, certain kinds of cost and benefit could be located just as easily in any one of the cells, but that is not important. What is important is to ensure that they all appear somewhere. Indeed, the very fact that there are so many potential costs and benefits to consider is the rationale for using the structure created for technical evaluation also to scaffold our social evaluation.

Although it seems reasonable to reach an overall evaluation conclusion for each of cells 1 to 3 respectively, the same cannot be said for cells 4a to 4c. When it comes to judgements of social value, the acceptability of the testing policy only can be judged holistically in relation to the full complement of expenses, pay-offs, impacts and side-effects. As such, cells 4a to 4c provide nothing more than a useful structure for identifying the various components of the cost-benefit profile. The overall evaluation of this profile, in the light of conclusions reached within cells 1 to 3, is the subject of the Overall Judgement.

Cell 4a expenses

We have chosen to locate the evaluation of consequences (*as* consequences, cf. as evidence of technical quality) within the second and third columns: i.e. not within cell 4a. For one thing, consequences traditionally associated with testing tend not to arise directly from the measurement process itself, but from the uses to which measurements are put. For example, a selection test might predict differently across certain subgroups of the population, but differential prediction is merely of academic interest until selection decisions are actually made. It is the selection decision that manifests unfairness when it takes no regard of the evidence of differential prediction. As such, until measurements are acted on, differential prediction, differential item functioning, population invariance and other related concepts remain purely technical issues of measurement rather than social matters of consequence.

Having said that, it would be possible to make a case for locating the evaluation of certain consequences within cell 4a: those which seemed to arise primarily from the measurement process itself, as distinct from subsequent decision-making. For example, a school leaving certificate such as the General Certificate of Secondary Education (GCSE) in England, might serve a gatekeeping function for access to higher level courses, whereby students are accepted as long as they are able to demonstrate a minimum level of proficiency (e.g. five GCSEs at grade C or above). Yet because GCSEs report grades across the entire spectrum of attainment – from exceptional performance (grade A*) to under-performance (ungraded) – there will be additional social consequences that are not contingent on the primary decision-making objective, if only as a result of self-evaluation (e.g. constructing oneself not simply as having failed, but as being 'a failure' or 'stupid'). Once again, although it would be possible to make a case for treating such consequences within cell 4a, we have chosen to deal with the social evaluation of all such side-effects in cell 4c. That is, if only for the sake of clarity, we have decided to exclude the consideration of impacts and side-effects from cell 4a. Again, what matters is that the full complement of costs and benefits associated with implementing the testing policy are represented *somewhere* within cells 4a to 4c; it is not important exactly where.

Within cell 4a, then, we are interested primarily in expenses associated with the measurement process: the cost of purchasing and administering an off-the-shelf test, commissioning and administering a bespoke test, or designing, developing and administering a test in-house. These need to be investigated and recorded as the major contribution of cell 4a to the overall cost–benefit analysis. The financial returns from this investment are presumed to be associated primarily with improved decision-making, which falls into cell 4b, so cell 4a focuses principally on expenses.

Cell 4b primary expenses, pay-offs, impacts and side-effects

To the extent that decision-making incurs additional expenses, whether capital or ongoing, these will need to be investigated and recorded within cell 4b. However, of much more interest is the consideration of broader costs and benefits associated with the primary decision-making objective, particularly those related to utility and fairness. By restricting cell 4b to the consideration of expenses, pay-offs, impacts and side-effects related to the primary objective – i.e. those immediately linked to the use of test scores – we postpone consideration of all secondary impacts and side-effects to cell 4c. Again, these are not watertight distinctions (the idea of primary versus secondary side-effects is particularly fuzzy), so the important consideration is to ensure that all bases are covered somewhere across 4a to 4c.

It is well-known that measurement quality is not the only consideration in determining the social value of a test-based decision-making procedure. In fact, it has long been recognized that even relatively low-quality measurement and low predictor-criterion correlations can be associated with considerable improvements in selection efficiency under certain circumstances (e.g. Taylor and Russell, 1939; Cronbach and Gleser, 1957, 1965). Conclusions such as this gave new confidence to applied psychologists in the post-war period, as evidence mounted that the predictive power of aptitude tests in forecasting occupational success was 'far from impressive' (Ghiselli, 1966: 125). Indeed, Cronbach and Gleser (1957) suggested that many of the utility studies of this period were motivated by the 'public relations' problem of convincing policy owners that the benefits from testing outweighed their considerable expense.

Fundamental to judging the social value of a decision-making procedure is the impact of error. From the employer perspective, error represents a financial cost: reduced productivity and/or the expense of terminating the employee's contract and appointing a new employee. In addition, different kinds of error may be valued differently: for example, false positive (e.g. appointing an applicant who turns out to be incompetent) versus false negative (e.g. letting slip an applicant who would have turned out to be competent). Considerations such as these would influence the judgement of acceptability of the decision-making procedure from the policy owner perspective. Others might judge the acceptability of the same decision-making procedure entirely differently: for example, the false negative applicants who were rejected erroneously.

In a similar way, viewing the same decision-making procedure from different perspectives can result in different perceptions of fairness. Thorndike (1971b) explained how a test that functioned effectively as a predictor (even one that functioned equally effectively across subgroups, i.e. a technically unbiased predictor test) still could result in unfair decision-making when viewed from the perspective of the group rather than the individual. In this situation, potential for unfairness can arise when the mean predictor test score of one (sub)group is substantially lower than that of another; in particular, when the mean score of the first group lies below the predictor cut-score, while the mean score of the second group lies above it. To appreciate the significance of this situation, remember that at both means – as a consequence of prediction error – certain individuals would achieve better than predicted on the criterion (if they were given the chance), while others would achieve worse than predicted. Thorndike explained how the group whose mean lay above the cut-score would over-represent false positive errors (i.e. inappropriate selections); whereas the group whose mean lay below the cut-score would over-represent false negative errors (i.e. inappropriate rejections).

In short, it is quite possible for a high-quality decision-making procedure to select the majority of an already advantaged group (many of whom would not actually make the grade), and to reject the majority of an already disadvantaged group (many of whom otherwise would have made the grade). So, even a decision-making procedure that is not biased in a technical sense still may have the potential to cluster advantage and disadvantage differently across groups. What seems to be fair from the perspective of an individual – using the same cut-score for all applicants – therefore seems to be unfair from the perspective of a group. In this case, the desire for meritocratic selection and the desire to redress social imbalance in the workplace or university would be placed in tension.

Analyses such as these demonstrate the importance of revealing the hidden potential consequences of decision-making procedures, to ensure that they are acceptable to the policy owner and stakeholders. With this aim in mind, Cronbach et al. (1980) presented a model designed to help expose contradictions among different definitions of fairness, commenting in particular on the trade-off between increasing representation of low-scoring minority group members (to ensure a more representative workforce), and maximizing overall quality of the workforce or student body. The point of their model was not to recommend one value-base over the other, but to help make explicit the consequences of alternative strategies, in order to allow those trade-offs to be made intelligently. In fact, analyses such as these can be used to determine whether it is technically possible to operationalize the policy owner value-base using the decision-making procedure. So, in this sense they also might have a role to play in cell 2.

When issues of fairness concern groups that are protected under the law, they have the potential to become legal issues. The 1981 *Debra P.* case (Debra P. v. *Turlington*, 644 F.2d 397, 408, 5th Cir. 1981) is often discussed in the literature (e.g. Phillips and Camara, 2006) as a prime example. The background to this case was evidence of substantially lower graduation rates among African American students in Florida, which had used a basic skills test to award graduation diplomas. The court found that African American students who had attended segregated elementary schools had not been provided with adequate notice of the requirements of the impending test, or provided with adequate opportunity to learn the required skills. To deprive students of graduation diplomas under these circumstances was judged to be unlawful. A later hearing along similar lines, the 1999 *G.I. Forum* case (*G.I. Forum et al.* v. *Texas Education Agency et al.*, U.S. District Court, CA No. SA-97-CA-1278EP), alleged adverse impact on members of ethnic groups in Texas resulting from the use of its graduation test. This time, with adequate notice and adequate opportunity to learn (and with a test judged to be of sufficient technical quality), the adverse impact was *not* judged to be unlawful.

The examples provided above offer no more than an impression of the range of issues that deserve consideration within cell 4b. We certainly have not provided a comprehensive map of the territory. The purpose of evaluation within this cell is to explore in as much detail as possible the nature and prevalence of expenses, pay-offs, impacts and side-effects related to the primary decision-making objective(s):

that is, those immediately linked to the use of test scores. Not only is this task of documentation formidable in itself, but cell 4b is also concerned with canvassing and representing opinions of pay-offs, impacts and side-effects that do not have an obvious monetary value attached to them: views that are likely to differ quite substantially across stakeholders. Cronbach and Gleser (1957: 109) described the assignment of values to outcomes as the Achilles' heel of decision theory, often seeming so arbitrary and subjective as to raise doubt over the very idea of social evaluation. However, as they went on to explain, if there were no attempt to bring the assignment of values to the foreground then they would remain in the background, implicit, unrecognized and unexamined. Dunnette acknowledged similar concerns, suggesting that utility analysis should be viewed 'more as a way of thinking about [decision-making] than as a set of formal rules or prescriptions for attaching numbers or cost figures to evaluations of different outcomes' (Dunnette, 1966: 182). Methodologically, this aspect of the evaluation of testing policy would seem still to be in its infancy.

Cell 4c secondary expenses, pay-offs, impacts and side-effects

Even if it were *possible* to achieve a range of primary and secondary impacts by implementing the testing policy (cells 2 and 3), it still might not be *acceptable* to do so. To judge acceptability, we need to consider the value of those intended impacts *and the value of any other expense, pay-off, impact or side-effect* associated with the policy. Cell 4c attempts to mop up these remaining considerations. The kinds of impact and side-effect that need to be specified and valued within cell 4c will include:

- intended impacts
- anticipated side-effects
- unanticipated expenses, pay-offs, impacts and side-effects.

One especially important kind of side-effect to watch out for stems from maladministration, misuse or subversion: implementing aspects of the testing policy in ways that depart from operational guidelines, particularly when intentional. This might involve:

- test invigilators allowing too much time for test-takers to complete their tests;
- test-takers cheating during the test;
- the test being administered to subgroups for whom it was stated as unsuitable;
- results being interpreted and used in inappropriate ways;
- results being falsified on university applications, and so on.

Even if evaluation within cells 1 to 3 had established that it was possible to achieve the intended policy objectives, the acceptability of the system still might be compromised by the consequences of widespread maladministration, misuse or subversion.

Of course, this need not spell the death of the policy, since this kind of evaluation evidence can be used formatively to identify ways to prevent or overcome such challenges. For example, falsification of personal results on university applications might be overcome by feeding results directly from the testing agency to the universities to which students apply, or by making certificates harder to fake.

As implementation continues across a number of years, the evaluator needs to keep a close eye on ongoing costs, particularly unanticipated expenditure increases. For large-scale assessment, this can occur when contracted agencies renegotiate their contracts. The expenses and risks associated with transferring a large-scale assessment to new contractors, let alone the scarcity of high-quality contractors, tends to weigh the negotiation dice in favour of the contractor. Keeping assessment in step with societal and educational expectations can be financially challenging, particularly as education becomes increasingly technology-driven and decreasingly paper-dependent. Technological change equally has the potential to reduce ongoing expenses, as assessment processes that traditionally relied heavily on expensive human resources become automated: for example, the evaluation of constructed responses.

All sorts of unanticipated impacts and side-effects need to be investigated, in order to highlight the trade-offs and compromises that need to be judged. One of the most important trade-offs to consider concerns testing time, particularly when larger, more 'authentic' assessments are employed. The tension here is between being able to generalize from results, which favours longer assessment, and not burdening test-takers unnecessarily, which favours shorter assessment. For example, there are good motivational reasons for implementing modular assessment systems which allow multiple opportunities for re-sitting an examination throughout the duration of a course of instruction. However, when a side-effect of widespread re-sitting is the disruption of instruction itself, this raises important concerns. Evaluating the introduction of modular assessment within A level examinations in the UK, Eva Scott recorded the observation of a college manager who claimed that 'we basically lose a month of teaching because of resits' (Scott, 2012: 441). Although that particular manager considered the negative side-effect to be worthwhile, others did not; particularly managers working in schools rather than sixth-form colleges. In the UK, increasing the number of assessment opportunities for GCSE and A level examinations (targeted at 16 and 18-year-olds, respectively) has resulted in what might be called 'opportunity to exercise' consequences, since modular examinations take sports halls out of action for long periods during the year. Similar concerns over the costs and burden of assessment have been recently voiced in the USA, where some chief state school officers have resisted early plans for assessing Common Core State Standards, which have proposed the administration of multiple performance tasks over several days (Herman and Linn, 2013).

We noted under cell 1 (and in Chapter 4) that certain kinds of evidence from the consequences of testing will have scientific implications relevant to the evaluation of technical quality. The same consequences also will have ethical implications relevant to the evaluation of social value. This is the sense in which Frederiksen (1984) claimed that the greater financial expense of assessments other than multiple-choice might be justified in terms of their value for instruction: specifically, the positive backwash impact on teaching and learning attributable to increased construct-representation, especially the teaching of higher level cognitive skills. Of course, performance assessment is no panacea, and there are also likely to be negative side-effects to factor into the overall evaluative judgement (e.g. Bond, 1995). Mapping the complex territory of impacts and side-effects is no mean feat, and attaching social value to those consequences is harder still – yet it is fundamental to judging the acceptability of alternative assessment arrangements.

Proponents of school-based assessment, notably Paul Black and Dylan Wiliam, have long argued that external examining cannot be judged purely in terms of its technical quality, but also must be judged in terms of its impact on teaching and learning. One critical impact, they have argued, is teacher disempowerment in relation to assessment, particularly formative assessment (e.g. Wiliam and Black, 1996; Black and Wiliam, 1998b). This could occur either as a consequence of teachers having too much responsibility for summative assessment, which pushes formative concerns into the wings, or as a consequence of having too little responsibility for summative assessment, which encourages them to see assessment as something done to students by external agencies rather than as an integral part of their own professional responsibility. In a similar way, emphasizing the importance of evaluating side-effects that may have nothing to do with technical quality per se, Sireci (2007) used the example of computer-based testing. Although a computer-based test might have been judged entirely satisfactory from a technical perspective, if it resulted in schools turning students away due to a lack of computing resource, then this adverse impact might have implications for the future of the testing policy.

The taxonomy of impacts and side-effects prepared by Abu-Alhija (2007) provides a useful starting point for anyone serious about mapping the territory of impacts and side-effects associated with large-scale educational assessment. The taxonomy in Camara (1997) suggests how this kind of map might be extended into a more comprehensive evaluation methodology. Whatever the process by which evaluation is undertaken, the important thing is that it should rise above what Mehrens described as 'passing pure proselytizing off as if it is research based' (Mehrens, 1998: 3). There is surely a place for passionate criticism of testing policy, even partisan critique that focuses purely on a small number of high negative value side-effects. However, genuine evaluation must be broader and fairer than this, in terms of profiling expenses, pay-offs, impacts and side-effects, and canvassing opinions.

The Overall Judgement

There is no overall evaluative judgement for cells 4a, 4b or 4c individually. Therefore, the Overall Judgement draws together the evidence and analysis collated in cells 4a to 4c to support an overall evaluative judgement of social value of the testing policy as a whole, in the light of prior conclusions from cells 1 to 3. The

Overall Judgement answers the question: is it acceptable to implement (or continue implementing) the testing policy? Not only does this constitute the focal question for the social evaluation row, it also constitutes the focal question for the entire matrix.

It is important to recognize that there could be any number of overall evaluative judgements depending on the perspective: that is, the value-base from which the evaluation was being conducted. Earlier, we suggested that the purpose of the matrix is to support the construction and appraisal of an argument which concludes that is it acceptable (or unacceptable) to implement the testing policy, or to continue implementing it. Now, we emphasize that different arguments may need to be constructed to represent different value-bases, to do justice to a broad range of stakeholder perspectives. This is to propose that the role of the evaluator is to construct an overall cost–benefit argument on behalf of the policy owner – and potentially to construct additional arguments on behalf of *other stakeholder groups* – rather than to construct the overall cost–benefit argument on the basis of their *own* personal value-base. In stressing this point, we support the 'political perspective' on evaluation outlined by Cronbach (1988), despite attaching particular significance to the policy owner perspective.

Admittedly, it is hard to see how the Overall Judgement could be anything other than highly impressionistic, despite there being an obvious responsibility on the evaluator to impose as much structure and rigour on the judgement as possible. Inevitably and appropriately, the final judgement of social value will go way beyond earlier judgements of technical quality concerning the mechanisms of the testing policy. Indeed, there is no necessary relationship between judgements of technical quality and the overall acceptability of the testing policy: in principle, a mechanism judged to be of low technical quality still could be judged to be of high positive value, if it were to generate a large number of high positive value impacts.

This issue, of trade-off between high positive value consequences and low-quality measurement, has been discussed in the language testing community for some time now (e.g. Morrow, 1986; cf. Messick, 1996). At the very least, researchers have recommended a change of perspective by treating impacts as integral considerations within the test development process, rather than as incidental observations following implementation. For example, Fulcher and Davidson (2007) introduced the notion of 'effect-driven testing', whereby design decisions are driven by the evaluation of anticipated impacts (see also Fulcher, 2009; Fulcher and Davidson, 2009). Building on ideas from Bachman and Palmer (1996) and Milanovic and Saville (1996), and from work carried out during the following decade (e.g. Taylor, 2005), Saville developed an analogous principle of 'impact by design' (Saville, 2010), which is now at the heart of Cambridge English examinations (e.g. Cambridge ESOL, 2011).

The idea that a mechanism judged to be of low technical quality still might be judged to be of high positive value brings us back to one of the major tensions in the history of validity theory: the relationship between measurement and decision-making, and in particular, whether it is important for decisions to be based on high-quality measurement. Over the decades, many have argued that there are all sorts of circumstances in which it is entirely acceptable for decisions to be based on low-quality measurement. To think otherwise, argued Gaylord and Stunkel, is to confuse standards for pure and applied research:

> For one thing, validity in the applied research area can be acceptable at a much lower correlational level than 'validity' as used above in the pure science area. Dr. Herbert A. Toops has frequently taken delight in pointing out to his students that a validity of .08 between a very crude index of potential egg-laying ability on the part of pullets and their later egg yield has saved the farmers of his state many millions of dollars each year in culling their flocks. The confusion of the requirement of extremely high 'validity' in the pure research area with usable validity in the applied research area has caused needless waste in the rejection of usable instruments. (Gaylord and Stunkel, 1954: 298)

However, recall how others have constructed the overall cost–benefit argument in terms broader than monetary value alone, most notably Samuel Messick:

> Hence, construct meaning is not only extremely important but essential in applied testing. Granted, empirical test-criterion prediction alone often sustains test use in practice. But this is a strictly pragmatic basis, not necessarily a valid one. It is heavily contingent on acceptable side effects of the testing, because there is no accompanying theoretical rationale for justifying appropriateness of test use in the face of adverse testing consequences. (Messick, 1989a: 77)

Messick argued that there is an obligation on policy owners to be able to establish the credibility of their testing policy on a rational basis, not just a pragmatic one. That is, given the inevitability of decision-making errors and negative consequences, the policy owner has a moral responsibility to be able to explain why it is that more accurate decisions can be made by incorporating test scores into the decision-making process, and thereby to put themselves in a position from which they are able to rebut allegations of unfairness or discrimination. A similar point could be made slightly differently: if all that you can muster is evidence of a 0.08 correlation, then you are going to need to mount a very strong case for implementing the testing policy, especially to those (like the chickens) whose necks are on the line. Pragmatic arguments that weigh judgements of positive social value too heavily are especially vulnerable, because different stakeholder groups are likely to make different judgements of value (the argument that a mechanism saves farmers lots of money, for example, is unlikely to swing the vote in all constituencies – especially the hen house). In the absence of a persuasive rational argument for test use, the implementation of a testing policy represents a hostage to fortune.

There are many perspectives from which the acceptability of the testing policy might be judged, and we conclude this section by considering four particularly important ones: the policy owner, the academy, the public and the law. We use these final subsections to explore a number of outstanding issues, particularly those related to issues of credibility, compromise and trade-off between the value-bases of various stakeholders.

Acceptable to the policy owner

Cronbach (1988) exhorted evaluators to resist pressure to concentrate on what people in power have specified as *their* chief question. Early selection research into utility made this mistake, he explained, only to be corrected later by broader investigations into fairness and legality. Conversely, since it is the policy owner who has the power to decide whether or not to implement (or to continue implementing) the testing policy, there is a duty on the evaluator to help the policy owner to reach an overall evaluative judgement.

Part of this process is to consider whether the various mechanisms of measurement, decision-making and impact have sufficient technical quality to achieve the objectives specified by the policy owner. If this turns out not to be at all true, then subsequent consideration of expense, pay-off, impact and side-effect might be judged to be superfluous. However, even in the light of demonstrably high-quality mechanisms, the policy owner could be swayed by persuasive evidence of negative side-effects or unforeseen expenses, or negative valuations from other stakeholders. Therefore, even when initially helping the policy owner to construct a cost–benefit argument, there is a clear onus of responsibility on the evaluator to ensure that a broad range of perspectives is canvassed. In effect, the obligation that arises from having attached particular significance to the policy owner perspective is to ensure that a wide range of alternative perspectives is represented to the policy owner. What must be resisted is any pressure to bias the collation of evidence and analysis, so it is up to the evaluator to ensure that the basis from which the policy owner reaches their overall evaluative judgement is as robust, broad and fair as possible. However, it is the policy owner who makes the final decision to implement (or to continue implementing) the testing policy, so the overall cost–benefit judgement is ultimately theirs to make.

Acceptable to the academy

Within the cell 1 section entitled 'Reconciling values and the "real world"' we observed that the attribute specification might be entirely as intended by the policy owner, yet entirely inconsistent with the world. A more complex but realistic account would accept that the attribute specification might be consistent with the world from one perspective, but inconsistent with the world from another. Similarly, an argument that persuaded the policy owner of high measurement quality might not persuade another stakeholder. This is the nature of scientific debate, and in the end its resolution (if resolution ever can be claimed) is a matter of how many of the most influential measurement specialists are persuaded by the various arguments at any particular point in time. In short, while it might be possible rationally to defend a particular account of the world – a particular view of attributes to be measured and measurement quality – ultimately, the credibility of this account is a matter of social value: its admissibility within a broad community of practice. As far as testing policies are concerned, admissibility to the scientists and professionals who comprise the educational and psychological measurement supra-community would be of particular significance. Indeed, acceptance from within this broad community of practice might be assumed to diffuse into the wider public consciousness. In speaking of acceptability to the academy, we are allowing intentionally the line between technical and social to blur. Having said that, although we are happy to acknowledge that science eventually bottoms out in value judgement, we still see the benefit in distinguishing between a technical approach to evaluation and a social one.

Acceptable to the public

Scientific and professional consensus may not always be sufficient to establish the credibility of a testing policy. Consensus from the general public may prove to be more important. If an educational policy owner decrees, by intention or unwittingly, the construction of a particular kind of attribute specification, then this will require at least a modicum of consent from the general public. On numerous occasions, policy owners in England have insisted that national assessment systems be redesigned to operate on non-compensatory (conjunctive) principles. In the mid-1980s, a great deal of research was undertaken to establish the feasibility of making O level examinations (for 16-year-olds) strongly criterion-referenced, under the insistence of the then-secretary of state, Keith Joseph (e.g. Joseph, 1984). Ultimately, it was felt that the principal challenges were social rather than technical: it would be possible to award examination grades on the basis of mastery profiles across large numbers of subdomains; however, the inconsistency of performance across subdomains, which was typical of O level examinations of the time, would mean that very few students would ever make the grade unless standards were set so low as to render them worthless. In short, the desired attribute specification could be operationalized from a technical perspective, but it would be unlikely to be considered credible by the general public.

Sometimes professional interpretations and public interpretations are inconsistent, and this can result in a measurement procedure being judged credible from one perspective, but not from the other. For example, Messick (1981) noted how a test of scholastic aptitude might be interpreted in terms of developed abilities by measurement professionals, but in terms of innate capacity by the public at large. The question for the policy owner is how to respond to this tension. It is not simply a matter of siding with the professionals: after all, if the test were to be implemented in the context of widespread misunderstanding, then negative consequences would follow. Moreover, assuming that those to be tested are members of the public, it may not be politically viable to implement it at all. Cronbach confronted this dilemma in the first edition of his classic textbook:

> So important is user acceptability in working with teachers, industrial personnel men, physicians, and others that the psychologist must often use a test which would be his second or third choice. If he is certain that he should wean others from their initial preference, he must undertake a deliberate campaign in favour of the test he advocates. (Cronbach, 1949: 47)

What is often described as 'face validity' is partly a technical issue of measurement quality and partly a matter of measurement value: i.e. public acceptability. On the one hand, it is *not* good for test-takers to be able to spot what personality tests are attempting to measure, because they may be tempted to fake their response (Bornstein, 1996). This is essentially a technical concern, since the test-takers will remain motivated to take the test, but measurement quality may suffer. On the other hand, it *is* good for test-takers to be able to spot what achievement tests are attempting to measure, otherwise the lack of transparency could end up as a technical concern related to construct-irrelevant variance, attributable to lack of understanding of the questions or lack of motivation to engage. However, if it was entirely unclear what a national achievement test was supposed to be measuring, then it probably would not even make it to the implementation stage without significant protest.

A final issue related to public acceptability concerns the openness and transparency of assessment agencies. Historically, many agencies operated behind closed doors and their operating procedures remained shrouded in secrecy (Rhoades and Madaus, 2003; Newton, 2005a). This is changing. Society is now less deferential and less trusting of its institutions. Assessment agencies are being increasingly held to account for their actions and the consequences thereof. This new climate establishes a tension between a desire to be less opaque about procedures and products, and a concern not to expose their fragility, given that inevitably any assessment procedure or product will fall far short of perfection in terms of technical quality. A particular challenge is the publication of evaluation evidence, since it always exposes a significant gulf between measurement perfection and measurement reality. To the extent that assessment agencies have been less than entirely open and transparent about measurement inaccuracy in the past, revelation of its true nature and prevalence now has the potential to destabilize testing policy. In short, the error that has long been known (behind closed doors) to be inevitable and unavoidable may now be seen by the public and its media in a somewhat different light: as unacceptable. This tension between trust and transparency, and the need for greater public understanding of assessment, particularly measurement inaccuracy, has been discussed by Newton (2005a, 2005b, 2013b).

Acceptable under the law

One perspective that cannot be ignored is the rule of law. The introduction of equality legislation across the world has raised important new hurdles for testing policies to clear. Debate stemming from legislation and legal rulings has featured increasingly in the measurement literature of recent decades (e.g. McClung, 1979; Lerner, 1981; Phillips, 1994, 1996; Sireci and Green, 2000; Parkes and Stevens, 2003; Phillips and Camara, 2006; Sireci and Parker, 2006; Cummings, 2008, 2009; Elwood and Lundy, 2010), particularly in relation to selection testing (e.g. Guion, 1976; Landy, 1986; Dunnette, 1992).

Although there are good reasons for the courts and measurement professions to share a common understanding of technical quality (cf. Langenfeld and Crocker, 1994), there is no presumption that they should be expected to share a common understanding of social value. Indeed, the judiciary and measurement professions have clashed on numerous occasions: for example, 'truth in testing' laws were enacted by New York and California in the early 1980s to make admissions tests, papers, scripts and correct answers available to students. The statute was passed despite protests from the Educational Testing Service, which argued that it would violate test security, increase administration costs and disadvantage minorities and the disabled (Bersoff, 1981).

The context of the Overall Judgement

We have mentioned already the problem of how to decide whether it is acceptable to implement a testing policy judged to have low positive value: low positive value is not that far from low negative value, and therefore from unacceptability. A judgement of low positive value is potentially very vulnerable to new evidence.

More complex still is the context against which the testing policy is to be judged. Alternatives to the testing policy somehow need to be factored into the overall cost–benefit argument. They might include:

- implementing a modified testing policy
- implementing an entirely new testing policy
- not implementing any testing policy at all:

  o by making decisions in different ways (e.g. by lottery); or
  o by not making decisions at all (Ebel, 1964; Cole and Moss, 1989).

Conceivably, a testing policy that otherwise might be judged to have low negative value – and therefore to be unacceptable – might be considered preferable to not implementing any testing policy at all, if the anticipated consequences of not implementing a testing policy were judged to be especially dire.

Conclusion

Conceptualizing the comprehensive evaluation of testing policy is extraordinarily complex; actually conducting an evaluation of this kind is even more challenging a prospect. Yet evaluate we must, because in the absence of any attempt at systematic and comprehensive evaluation, partial and anecdotal evaluation will necessarily hold sway. We can be sure that testing policies will continue to be implemented, either on the basis of one or the other. The more steps that are taken toward systematic and comprehensive evaluation, the less any policy owner will need to (or will be able to) rely on the partial and anecdotal. In presenting a framework for the evaluation of testing policy, we have attempted to reinterpret the original progressive matrix from Messick (1980). This is far from a grand theory of the evaluation of testing policy, but we hope that we have helped to steer a course in that direction by mapping out its territory in a manner that seems cogent, comprehensive and useful.

Chapter 1 began by identifying a question that has been central to the literature over the past century: how much of what kind of logical analysis and empirical evidence is required in order to substantiate a claim to validity? We can now extend this question by asking how much of what kind of evidence and analysis is required in order to establish the technical quality of the primary measurement objective(s), the primary decision-making objective(s) and secondary policy objectives; and how much of what kind is required in order to establish the social value of the overall testing policy? Unfortunately, there are no easy answers to these questions, and we still seem to be a long way from being able to answer them satisfactorily. Having said that, it does seem fair to conclude that we are now much clearer than our predecessors concerning *what kinds* of evidence and analysis are relevant to answering each of these questions. Moreover, there is now general agreement that it is appropriate to adopt a scientific approach to generating this evidence and analysis, and ultimately to frame evaluation in terms of the construction of arguments rather than in terms of the production of research. Yet, when it comes to the question of *how much* of this evidence and analysis is required, it is far harder to be definitive. Truly comprehensive evaluation is an impossible ideal against which we will always fall short. So, just how comprehensive is comprehensive enough? How strong does an evaluation argument need to be? When should an evaluation argument stop? How should evaluation priorities be established? Cronbach (1989a) offered a few useful suggestions to get us thinking in the right direction – proposing criteria that included prior uncertainty, information yield, cost and leverage of the evidence and analysis – but there is still much work to be done.

Extending this line of questioning: is it better to be pragmatic or idealistic when it comes to theorizing evaluation for educational and psychological measurement? In Chapter 4 we saw how Messick tended towards idealism. In Chapter 5 we saw how Kane tended towards pragmatism. It is no coincidence that Kane (2006) entitled his classic chapter 'Validation', while Messick (1989a) called his 'Validity'. The tension between these two giants of the literature echoes a debate between two leading lights of an earlier era; between Ebel, who wanted to make sure that validation was practical (Ebel, 1983), and Cronbach, who responded 'what price simplicity?' when life is just not that simple (Cronbach, 1983). Indeed, this tension between pragmatism and idealism has been a constant refrain in our account, as illustrated further by the perspectives adopted by Lindquist and Tyler during the 1930s and 1940s. In fact, Cronbach and Tyler are good examples of theorists who seemed to be pulled in opposite directions by both pragmatic and idealistic tendencies.

Although it seems unlikely that we will have cracked the evaluation of testing policy by the end of the 21st century, it seems equally likely that we will still be striving earnestly to do so, and that we will have made substantial progress along the way. We hope that this book may be able to make some small contribution to that laudable, never-ending enterprise.

Note

1   For anyone who is not convinced, we would refer them to the commentaries on Newton (2012a) by Braun (2012), Borsboom (2012) and Markus (2012), as well as the reply by Newton (2012b).

REFERENCES

Abu-Alhija, F.N. (2007) 'Large-scale testing: benefits and pitfalls', *Studies in Educational Evaluation*, 33 (1): 50–68.

Allen, M.J. (2004) *Assessing Academic Programs in Higher Education*. Boston, MA: Anker Publishing Company Inc.

American Educational Research Association (AERA) and National Council on Measurements Used in Education (NCMUE) (1955) *Technical Recommendations for Achievement Tests*. Washington, DC: National Education Association.

American Educational Research Association (AERA), American Psychological Association (APA) and National Council on Measurement in Education (NCME) (1985) *Standards for Educational and Psychological Testing*. Washington, DC: American Psychological Association.

American Educational Research Association (AERA), American Psychological Association (APA) and National Council on Measurement in Education (NCME) (1999) *Standards for Educational and Psychological Testing*. Washington, DC: American Educational Research Association.

American Psychological Association (APA) (1950) 'Ethical standards for the distribution of psychological tests and diagnostic aids', *American Psychologist*, 4 (11): 495–501.

American Psychological Association (APA) (1952) 'Technical recommendations for psychological tests and diagnostic techniques: preliminary proposal', *American Psychologist*, 7 (8): 461–75.

American Psychological Association (APA), American Educational Research Association (AERA) and National Council on Measurements Used in Education (NCMUE) (1954) 'Technical recommendations for psychological tests and diagnostic techniques', *Psychological Bulletin*, 51 (2) (part 2): 1–38.

American Psychological Association (APA), American Educational Research Association (AERA) and National Council on Measurement in Education (NCME) (1966) *Standards for Educational and Psychological Tests and Manuals*. Washington, DC: American Psychological Association.

American Psychological Association (APA), American Educational Research Association (AERA) and National Council on Measurement in Education (NCME) (1974) *Standards for Educational and Psychological Tests*. Washington, DC: American Psychological Association.

Anastasi, A. (1954) *Psychological Testing*. New York: The Macmillan Company.

Anastasi, A. (1961) *Psychological Testing* (2nd edition). New York: The Macmillan Company.

Anastasi, A. (1963) 'Some current developments in the measurement and interpretation of test validity', in A. Anastasi (ed.), *Testing Problems in Perspective*. Washington, DC: American Council on Education, pp. 307–17.

Anastasi, A. (1968) *Psychological Testing* (3rd edition). New York: The Macmillan Company.

Anastasi, A. (1976) *Psychological Testing* (4th edition). New York: Macmillan Publishing Co. Inc.

Anastasi, A. (1986) 'Evolving concepts of test validation'. *Annual Review of Psychology*, 37, 1–15.

Angoff, W.H. (1988) 'Validity: an evolving concept', in H. Wainer and H.I. Braun (eds), *Test Validity*. Hillsdale, NJ: Lawrence Erlbaum, pp. 19–32.

Assessment Reform Group (2002) 'Assessment for learning: 10 principles. Research-based principles to guide classroom practice. Available at: http://assessmentreformgroup.files.wordpress.com/2012/01/10principles_english.pdf (accessed 1 July 2013).

Austin, J. (1995[1832]) *The Province of Jurisprudence Determined* (ed. W.E. Rumble). Cambridge: Cambridge University Press.

Austin, J.T. and Villanova P. (1992) 'The criterion problem: 1917–1992', *Journal of Applied Psychology*, 77 (6): 836–74.

Bachman, L.F. (2005) 'Building and supporting a case for test use', *Language Assessment Quarterly*, 2 (1): 1–34.

Bachman, L.F. and Palmer, A. (1996) *Language Testing in Practice*. Oxford: Oxford University Press.

Bailey, K.M. (1999) *Washback in Language Testing*. Princeton, NJ: Education Testing Service.

Baker, E.L. and Linn, R.L. (2002) *Validity Issues for Accountability Systems*, CSE Technical Report 585. Los Angeles, CA: National Center for Research on Evaluation, Standards and Student Testing, University of California.

Banerjee, J. (2012) 'Guest editorial', *Research Notes*, 50: 2–3.

Barrett, G.V. (1992) 'Clarifying construct validity: definitions, processes and models', *Human Performance*, 5 (1–2): 13–58.

Bechtoldt, H.P. (1959) 'Construct validity: a critique', *American Psychologist*, 14 (10): 619–29.

Bemis, S. (1968) 'Occupational validity of the general aptitude test battery', *Journal of Applied Psychology*, 52 (3): 240–4.

Bennett, R.E., Kane, M. and Bridgeman, B. (2011) *Theory of Action and Validity Argument in the Context of Through-course Summative Assessment*. Princeton, NJ: Educational Testing Service.

Bersoff, D.N. (1981) 'Testing and the law', *American Psychologist*, 36 (10): 1047–56.

Bingham, W.V.D. (1937) *Aptitudes and Aptitude Testing*. New York: Harper & Brothers Publishers.

Binning, J.F. and Barrett, G.V. (1989) 'Validity of personnel decisions: a conceptual analysis of the inferential and evidential bases', *Journal of Applied Psychology*, 74 (3): 478–94.

Black P. and Wiliam, D. (1998a) *Inside the Black Box: Raising Standards Through Classroom Assessment*. London: King's College London.

Black P. and Wiliam, D. (1998b) 'Assessment and classroom learning', *Assessment in Education: Principles, Policy and Practice*, 5 (1): 7–74.

Black P. and Wiliam, D. (2012) 'Developing a theory of formative assessment', in J. Gardner (ed.) *Assessment and Learning* (2nd edition). London: Sage, pp. 206–29.

Blair, J.A. and Johnson, R.H. (1987) 'Argumentation as dialectical', *Argumentation*, 1 (1): 41–56.

Boehm, V.R. (1972) 'Negro–white differences in validity of employment and training selection procedures', *Journal of Applied Psychology*, 56 (1): 33–9.

Bond, L. (1995) 'Unintended consequences of performance assessment: issues of bias and fairness', *Educational Measurement: Issues and Practice*, 14 (4): 21–4.

Bornstein, R.F. (1996) 'Face validity in psychological assessment: implications for a unified model of validity', *American Psychologist*, 51 (9): 983–4.

Borsboom, D. (2005) *Measuring the Mind: Conceptual Issues in Contemporary Psychometrics*. Cambridge: Cambridge University Press.

Borsboom, D. (2012) 'Whose consensus is it anyway? Scientific versus legalistic conceptions of validity', *Measurement: Interdisciplinary Research and Perspectives*, 10 (1–2): 38–41.

Borsboom, D. and Markus, K. (2013) 'Truth and evidence in validity theory', *Journal of Educational Measurement*, 50 (1): 110–14.

Borsboom, D. and Mellenbergh, G.J. (2007) 'Test validity in cognitive assessment', in J.P. Leighton and M.J. Gierl (eds), *Cognitive Diagnostic Assessment for Education: Theory and Applications*. New York: Cambridge University Press, pp. 85–115.

Borsboom, D., Cramer, A.O.J., Keivit, R.A., Scholten, A.Z. and Franic, S. (2009) 'The end of construct validity', in R.W. Lissitz (ed.), *The Concept of Validity: Revisions, New Directions and Applications*. Charlotte, NC: Information Age Publishing, pp. 135–70.

Borsboom, D., Mellenbergh, G.J. and van Heerden, J. (2004) 'The concept of validity', *Psychological Review*, 111 (4): 1061–71.

Bracht, G.H. and Glass, G.V. (1968) 'The external validity of experiments', *American Educational Research Journal*, 5 (4): 437–74.

Bramley, T. (2012) '"Measurement" and "construct" need to be clarified first. Commentary on Newton, P.E. "Clarifying the consensus definition of validity"', *Measurement: Interdisciplinary Research and Perspectives*, 10 (1–2): 42–5.

Braun, H. (2012) 'Conceptions of validity: the private and the public'. *Measurement: Interdisciplinary Research and Perspectives*, 10 (1–2): 46–9.

Brennan, R.L. (2006) 'Perspectives on the evolution and future of educational measurement', in R.L. Brennan (ed.), *Educational Measurement* (4th edition). Washington, DC: American Council on Education/Praeger, pp. 3–16.

Brennan, R.L. (2013) 'Commentary on "Validating the interpretations and uses of test scores"', *Journal of Educational Measurement*, 50 (1): 74–83.

Bridgman, P.W. (1927) *The Logic of Modern Physics*. New York: Macmillan.

Brookhart, S.M. (2009) 'The many meanings of "multiple measures"', *Educational Leadership*, 67 (3): 6–12.

Brown, T. (2010) 'Construct validity: a unitary concept for occupational therapy assessment and measurement', *Hong Kong Journal of Occupational Therapy*, 20 (1): 30–42.

Buckendahl, C.W. and Plake, B.S. (2006) 'Evaluating tests', in S.M. Downing and T.M. Haladyna (eds), *Handbook of Test Development*. Mahwah, NJ: Lawrence Erlbaum Associates, pp. 725–38.

Buckingham, B.R., McCall, W.A., Otis, A.S., Rugg, H.O., Trabue, M.R. and Courtis, S.A. (1921) 'Report of the Standardization Committee', *Journal of Educational Research*, 4 (1): 78–80.

Buros, O. (1977) 'Fifty years in testing: some reminiscences, criticisms and suggestions', *Educational Researcher*, 6 (7): 9–15.

Burt, C. (1924) 'Historical sketch of the development of psychological tests', in Board of Education (ed.), *Report of the Consultative Committee on Psychological Tests of Educable Capacity and Their Possible Use in the Public System of Education* (Hadow Report). London: HMSO, pp. 1–61.

Cain, P. (1982) *Examination Registers of the University of London, 1838–1889*. London: University of London.

Camara, W.J. (1997) 'Use and consequences of assessments in the USA: professional, ethical and legal issues', *European Journal of Psychological Assessment*, 13 (2): 140–52.

Cambridge ESOL (2011) *Cambridge English: Making an Impact*. Cambridge: Cambridge ESOL.

Camilli, G. (2006) 'Test fairness', in R.L. Brennan (ed.), *Educational Measurement* (4th edition). Washington, DC: American Council on Education/Praeger, pp. 221–56.

Campbell, D.T. (1957) 'Factors relevant to the validity of experiments in social settings', *Psychological Bulletin*, 54 (4): 297–312.

Campbell, D.T. (1960) 'Recommendations for APA test standards regarding construct, trait or discriminant validity', *American Psychologist*, 15 (8): 546–553.

Campbell, J.P. (1976) 'Psychometric theory', in M.D. Dunnette (ed.), *Handbook of Industrial and Organizational Psychology*. Chicago, IL: Rand McNally College Publishing Company, pp. 185–222.

Campbell, D.T. and Fiske, D.W. (1959) 'Convergent and discriminant validation by the multitrait-multimethod matrix', *Psychological Bulletin*, 56 (2): 81–105.

Campbell, D.T. and Stanley, J.C. (1966[1963]) *Experimental and Quasi-experimental Designs for Research*. Chicago: Rand McNally College Publishing Company.

Cattell, J.M. (1890) 'Mental tests and measurements'. *Mind*, 15: 373–80.

Cattell, J.M. and Farrand, L. (1896) 'Physical and mental measurements of the students of Columbia University', *Psychological Review*, 3 (6): 618–48.

Cattell, R.B. (1943) 'The measurement of adult intelligence', *Psychological Bulletin*, 40 (3): 153–93.

Cattell, R.B. (1964) 'Validity and reliability: a proposed more basic set of concepts', *Journal of Educational Psychology*, 55 (1): 1–22.

Catterall, J.S. (1990) *Estimating the Costs and Benefits of Large-Scale Assessments: Lessons from Recent Research*, CSE Technical Report 319. Los Angeles, CA: National Center for Research on Evaluation, Standards and Student Testing, University of California.

Catterall, J.S. (1997) 'Reflections on economic analysis and education policy: introduction'. *Educational Evaluation and Policy Analysis*, 19 (4): 297–99.

Chapelle, C.A., Enright, M.K. and Jamieson, J. (eds) (2008) *Building a Validity Argument for the Test of English as a Foreign Language*. London: Routledge.

Chapelle, C.A., Enright, M.K. and Jamieson, J. (2010) 'Does an argument-based approach to validity make a difference?', *Educational Measurement: Issues and Practice*, 29 (1): 3–13.

Cheng, L. and Watanabe, Y. with Curtis, A. (eds) (2004) *Washback in Language Testing: Research Contexts and Methods*. Mahwah, NJ: Lawrence Erlbaum Associates.

Churchman, C.W. (1971) *The Design of Inquiring Systems: Basic Concepts of Systems and Organization*. New York: Basic Books.

Cizek, G.J. (2011) 'Reconceptualizing validity and the place of consequences', paper presented at the Annual Meeting of the National Council on Measurement in Education. New Orleans, LA, 7–11 April.

Cizek, G.J. (2012) 'Defining and distinguishing validity: interpretations of score meaning and justification of test use', *Psychological Methods*, 17 (1): 31–43.

Cizek, G.J., Rosenberg, S.L. and Koons, H.H. (2008) 'Sources of validity evidence for educational and psychological tests', *Educational and Psychological Measurement*, 68 (3): 397–412.

Cole, N.S. and Moss, P.A. (1989) 'Bias in test use', in R.L. Linn (ed.), *Educational Measurement* (3rd edition). Washington, DC: American Council on Education. pp. 201–19.

College Board (2013a) 'SAT: About the tests'. Available at: http://sat.collegeboard.org/about-tests (accessed 1 March 2013).

College Board (2013b) 'History'. Available at: http://about.collegeboard.org/history (accessed 1 March 2013).

Cook, T.D. and Campbell, D.T. (1979) *Quasi-experimentation: Design and Analysis Issues for Field Settings*. Boston, MA: Houghton Mifflin Company.

Courtis, S.A. (1916) 'Courtis tests in arithmetic: value to superintendents and teachers', in G.M. Whipple (ed.), *The Fifteenth Yearbook of the National Society for the Study of Education. Part I. Standards and Tests for the Measurement of the Efficiency of Schools and School Systems*. Chicago, IL: University of Chicago Press, pp. 91–106.

Crisp, V. and Shaw, S.D. (2012) 'Applying methods to evaluate construct validity in the context of A level assessment', *Educational Studies*, 38 (2): 209–22.

Crocker, L. (1997) 'Editorial: The great validity debate', *Educational Measurement: Issues and Practice*, 16 (2): 4.

Cronbach, L.J. (1946) 'Response sets and test validity'. *Educational and Psychological Measurement*, 6: 475–94.

Cronbach, L.J. (1949) *Essentials of Psychological Testing*. New York: Harper & Brothers.

Cronbach, L.J. (1960) *Essentials of Psychological Testing* (2nd edition) New York: Harper & Brothers.

Cronbach, L.J. (1970) *Essentials of Psychological Testing* (3rd edition) New York: Harper & Row.

Cronbach, L.J. (1971) 'Test validation', in R.L. Thorndike (ed.), *Educational Measurement* (2nd edition), Washington, DC: American Council on Education, pp. 443–507.

Cronbach, L.J. (1974) *Essentials of Psychological Testing* (3rd edition). New York: Harper & Brothers.

Cronbach, L.J. (1976) 'Equity in selection: where psychometrics and political philosophy meet', *Journal of Educational Measurement*, 13 (1): 31–41.

Cronbach, L.J. (1980a) 'Validity on parole: how can we go straight?', in W.B. Schrader (ed.) *Measuring Achievement: Progress Over a Decade. Proceedings of the 1979 Educational Testing Service Invitational Conference*. San Francisco, CA: Jossey-Bass, pp. 99–108.

Cronbach, L.J. (1980b) 'Selection theory for a political world', *Public Personnel Management*, 9 (1): 37–50.

Cronbach, L.J. (1983) 'What price simplicity?', *Educational Measurement: Issues and Practice*, 2 (2): 11–12.

Cronbach, L.J. (1986) 'Social inquiry by and for earthlings', in D.W. Fiske and R.A. Shweder (eds), *Metatheory in Social Science: Pluralisms and Subjectivities*. Chicago, IL: University of Chicago Press, pp. 83–107.

Cronbach, L.J. (1988) 'Five perspectives on validity argument', in H. Wainer and H.I. Braun (eds), *Test Validity*, Hillsdale, NJ: Lawrence Erlbaum, pp. 3–17.

Cronbach, L.J. (1989a) 'Construct validation after thirty years', in R.L. Linn (ed.), *Intelligence: Measurement, Theory and Public Policy*. Urbana, IL: University of Illinois Press, pp. 147–71.

Cronbach, L.J. (1989b) 'Lee J. Cronbach', in G.Lindzey (ed.), *A History of Psychology in Autobiography. Volume III*. Stanford, CA: Stanford University Press, pp. 63–93.

Cronbach, L.J. (1989c) 'Educational Measurement, Third Edition', *Educational Measurement: Issues and Practice*, 8 (4): 22–5.

Cronbach, L.J. (1992) 'Four *Psychological Bulletin* articles in perspective', *Psychological Bulletin*, 112 (3): 389–92.

Cronbach, L.J. and Gleser, G.C. (1957) *Psychological Tests and Personnel Decisions*. Urbana, IL: University of Illinois Press.

Cronbach, L.J. and Gleser, G.C. (1965) *Psychological Tests and Personnel Decisions* (2nd edition) Urbana, IL: University of Illinois Press.

Cronbach, L.J. and Meehl, P.E. (1955) 'Construct validity in psychological tests', *Psychological Bulletin*, 52 (4): 281–302.

Cronbach, L.J., Gleser, G.C., Nanda, H. and Rajaratnam, N. (1972) *The Dependability of Behavioral Measurements: Theory of Generalizability for Scores and Profiles*. New York: Wiley.

Cronbach, L.J., Yalow, E. and Schaeffer, G. (1980) 'A mathematical structure for analyzing fairness in selection', *Personnel Psychology*, 33 (4): 693–704.

Crooks, T.J., Kane, M.T. and Cohen, A.S. (1996) 'Threats to the valid use of assessments', *Assessment in Education: Principles, Policy and Practice*, 3 (3): 265–85.

Cumming, J.J. (2008) 'Legal and educational perspectives of equity in assessment', *Assessment in Education: Principles, Policy and Practice*, 15 (2): 123–35.

Cumming, J.J. (2009) 'Assessment challenges, the law and the future', in C. Wyatt-Smith and J. Cumming (eds), *Educational Assessment in the 21st Century: Connecting Theory and Practice*. Dordrecht: Springer, pp. 157–82.

Cureton, E.E. (1951) Validity, in E.F. Lindquist (ed.) Educational Measurement pp. 621–694) Washington, DC: American Council on Education.

Cureton, E.E. (1965) 'Reliability and validity: basic assumptions and experimental designs', *Educational and Psychological Measurement*, 25 (2): 327–46.

Dennett, D.C. (1987) *The Intentional Stance*. Cambridge, MA: Bradford Book/MIT Press.

Dennett, D.C. (1998) *Brainchildren: Essays on Designing Minds*. London: Penguin Books.

Department for Education (2011) *The Framework for the National Curriculum: A Report by the Expert Panel for the National Curriculum Review*. London: Department for Education.

Dick, W. and Hagerty, N. (1971) *Topics in Measurement: Reliability and Validity*. New York: McGraw-Hill Book Company.

Downing, S.M. (2003) 'Validity: on the meaningful interpretation of assessment data', *Medical Education*, 37 (9): 830–7.

Dunnette, M.D. (1963) 'A modified model for test validation and selection research', *Journal of Applied Psychology*, 47 (5): 317–23.

Dunnette, M.D. (1966) *Personnel Selection and Placement*. Belmont, CA: Wadsworth Publishing Co.

Dunnette, M.D. (1992) 'It was nice to be there: construct validity then and now', *Human Performance*, 5 (1): 157–69.

Dunnette, M.D. and Borman, W.C. (1979) 'Personnel selection and classification systems', *Annual Review of Psychology*, 30: 477–525.

Ebel, R.L. (1961) 'Must all tests be valid?', *American Psychologist*, 16 (10): 640–7.

Ebel, R.L. (1964) 'The social consequences of educational testing', in A.G. Wesman (ed.), *Proceedings of the 1963 Invitational Conference on Testing Problems*. Princeton, NJ: Educational Testing Service, pp. 130–43.

Ebel, R.L. (1983) 'The practical validation of tests of ability', *Educational Measurement: Issues and Practice*, 2 (2): 7–10.

Elwood, J. and Lundy, L. (2010) 'Revisioning assessment through a children's rights approach: implications for policy, process and practice', *Research Papers in Education* 25 (3): 335–53.

Embretson, S.E. (1983) 'Construct validity: Construct representation versus nomothetic span', *Psychological Bulletin*, 93 (1): 179–97.

Embretson, S.E. (1998) 'A cognitive design system approach to generating valid tests: Application to abstract reasoning', *Psychological Methods*, 3 (3): 380–96.

Embretson, S.E. (2007) 'Construct validity: A universal validity system or just another test evaluation procedure?', *Educational Researcher*, 36 (8): 449–55.

Embretson, S.E. and Gorin, J.S. (2001) 'Improving construct validity with cognitive psychology principles', *Journal of Educational Measurement*, 38 (4): 343–68.

English, H. and English, A.A. (1958) *Comprehensive Dictionary of Psychological and Psychoanalytical Terms*. New York: Longmans, Green and Co.

Equal Employment Opportunity Commission (1978) 'Uniform guidelines on employee selection procedures', *Federal Register* 43, 38290–38315. Washington, DC: Equal Employment Opportunity Commission.

Equal Employment Opportunity Commission (1966) 'Guidelines on employment testing procedures', *Federal Register* 31, 6414. Washington, DC: Civil Service Commission, Department of Labor and Department of Justice.

Equal Employment Opportunity Commission (1970) 'Guidelines on employee selection procedures', *Federal Register*, 35, 12333–12336. Washington, DC: Equal Employment Opportunity Commission.

Evers, A., Sijtsma, K., Lucassen, W. and Meijer, R.R. (2010) 'The Dutch review process for evaluating the quality of psychological tests: history, procedure and results', *International Journal of Testing*, 10 (4): 295–317.

Fernberger, S.W. (1932) 'The American Psychological Association: a historical summary, 1892–1930', *Psychological Bulletin*, 29 (1): 1–89.

Fiske, D.W. and Campbell, D.T. (1992) 'Citations do not solve problems', *Psychological Bulletin*, 112 (3): 393–5.

Fogelin, R.J. and Sinnott-Armstrong, W. (2001) *Understanding Arguments: An Introduction to Informal Logic* (6th edition). Fort Worth, TX: Harcourt College Publishers.

Forte-Fast, E. and Hebbler, S. with ASR-CAS Joint Study Group on Validity in Accountability Systems (2004) *A Framework for Examining Validity in State Accountability Systems*. Washington, DC: Council of Chief State School Officers.

Foster, S.L. and Cone, J.D. (1995) 'Validity issues in clinical assessment'. *Psychological Assessment*, 7 (3): 248–60.

Frederiksen, J.R. and Collins, A. (1989) 'A systems approach to educational testing', *Educational Researcher*, 18 (9): 27–32.

Frederiksen, N. (1984) 'The real test bias: Influences of testing on teaching and learning', *American Psychologist*, 39 (3): 193–202.

Freeman, F.N. (1914) 'Tests', *Psychological Bulletin*, 11 (7): 253–56.

Freeman, F.N. (1917) 'Review of "Manual of Mental and Physical Tests"', *Psychological Bulletin*, 14 (3): 105–6.

Fremer, J. (2000) 'Promoting high standards and the "problem" with construct validation', *NCME Newsletter*, 8 (3): 1.

Fulcher, G. (2009) 'Test use and political philosophy', *Annual Review of Applied Linguistics*, 29: 3–20.

Fulcher, G. and Davidson, F. (2007) *Language Testing and Assessment*. London: Routledge.

Fulcher, G. and Davidson, F. (2009) 'Test architecture: Test retrofit', *Language Testing*, 26 (1): 123–44.

Galton, F. (1869) *Hereditary Genius: An Inquiry into its Laws and Consequences*. New York: D. Appleton and Company.

Galton, F. (1890) 'Remarks by Francis Galton, F.R.S.', *Mind*, 15: 380–1.

Gardner, J. (ed.) (2012) *Assessment and Learning* (2nd edition) London: Sage.

Gaylord, R.H. and Stunkel, E.R. (1954) 'Validity and the criterion'. *Educational and Psychological Measurement*, 14 (2): 294–300.

Geisinger, K.F. (1992) 'The metamorphosis of test validation', *Educational Psychologist*, 27 (2): 197–222.

Ghiselli, E.E. (1966) *Occupational Aptitude Tests*. New York: John Wiley and Sons.

Gleser, G.C. and DuBois, P.H. (1951) 'A successive approximation method of maximising test validity', *Psychometrika*, 16 (1): 129–39.

Goldstein, J. and Behuniak, P. (2011) 'Assumptions in alternate assessment: an argument-based approach to validation', *Assessment for Effective Intervention*, 36 (3): 179–91.

Goodenough, F.L. (1950) *Mental Testing: Its History, Principles and Applications*. London: Staples Press.

Gorin, J.S. (2006) 'Test design with cognition in mind', *Educational Measurement: Issues and Practice*, 25 (4): 21–35.

Gorin, J.S. (2007) 'Reconsidering issues in validity theory', *Educational Researcher*, 36 (8): 456–62.

Gould, S.J. (1981) *The Mismeasure of Man*. Harmondsworth: Penguin Books.

Gray, B.T. (1997) 'Controversies regarding the nature of score validity: still crazy after all these years', paper presented at the Annual Meeting of the Southwest Educational Research Association. Austin, TX, 23–25 January.

Green, A. (2007) *IELTS Washback in Context: Preparation for Academic Writing in Higher Education*, Studies in Language Testing 25. Cambridge: University of Cambridge ESOL Examinations.

Green, C.D. (1992) 'Of immortal mythological beasts: operationism in psychology', *Theory and Psychology*, 2 (3): 291–320.

Green, D.R. (1998) 'Consequential aspects of the validity of achievement tests: a publisher's point of view', *Educational Measurement: Issues and Practice*, 17 (2): 16–19.

Greene, H.A., Jorgensen, A.N. and Gerberich, J.R. (1943) *Measurement and Evaluation in the Secondary School*. New York: Longmans, Green and Co.

Guilford, J.P. (1936) *Psychometric Methods*. New York: McGraw-Hill Book Company.

Guilford, J.P. (1946) 'New standards for test evaluation', *Educational and Psychological Measurement*, 6 (4): 427–39.

Guion, R.M. (1974) 'Open a new window: validities and values in psychological measurement', *American Psychologist*, 29 (5): 287–96.

Guion, R.M. (1976) 'Recruiting, selection and job placement', in M.D. Dunnette (ed.), *Handbook of Industrial and Organizational Psychology*. Chicago, IL: Rand McNally College Publishing Co., pp. 777–828.

Guion, R.M. (1977a) 'Content validity: three years of talk – what's the action?', *Public Personnel Management*, 6 (6): 407–14.

Guion, R.M. (1977b) 'Content validity: the source of my discontent', *Applied Psychological Measurement*, 1 (1): 1–10.

Guion, R.M. (1978a) 'Scoring of content domain samples: the problem of fairness', *Journal of Applied Psychology*, 63 (4): 499–506.

Guion, R.M. (1978b) '"Content validity" in moderation', *Personnel Psychology*, 31 (2): 205–13.

Guion, R.M. (1980) 'On trinitarian doctrines of validity', *Professional Psychology*, 11 (3): 385–98.

Guion, R.M. (2011) *Assessment, Measurement and Prediction for Personnel Decisions* (2nd edition). New York: Routledge.

Gulliksen, H. (1950) 'Intrinsic validity', *American Psychologist*, 5 (10): 511–17.

Guttman, L. (1950) 'The problem of attitude and opinion measurement', in S.A. Stouffer, L. Guttman, E.A. Suchman, P.F. Lazarsfeld, S.A. Star and J.A. Clausen (eds), *Measurement and Prediction. Studies in Social Psychology in World War 2, Volume IV*. Princeton, NJ: Princeton University Press, pp. 46–59.

Haertel, E. (1985) 'Construct validity and criterion-referenced testing'. *Review of Educational Research*, 55 (1): 23–46.

Haertel, E. (2013) 'Getting the help we need'. *Journal of Educational Measurement*, 50 (1): 84–90.

Haertel, E.H. and Herman, J.L. (2005) 'A historical perspective on validity arguments for accountability testing', in J.L. Herman and E.H. Haertel (eds), *Uses and Misuses of Data for Educational*

Accountability and Improvement. The 104th Yearbook of the National Society for the Study of Education, Part 2. Malden, MA: Blackwell Publishing, pp. 1–29.

Haladyna, T.M. (2006) 'Roles and importance of validity studies in test development', in S.M. Downing and T.M. Haladyna (eds), *Handbook of Test Development.* Mahwah, NJ: Lawrence Erlbaum Associates, pp. 739–55.

Haladyna, T. and Hess, R. (2000) 'An evaluation of conjunctive and compensatory standard-setting strategies for test decisions', *Educational Assessment,* 6 (2): 129–53.

Halkidi, M., Batistakis, Y. and Vazirgiannis, M. (2002) 'Cluster validity methods: part 1', *SIGMOID Record,* 31 (2): 40–5.

Hambleton, R.K. (1980) 'Test score validity and standard-setting methods', in R.A. Berk (ed.), *Criterion-Referenced Measurement: The State of the Art.* Baltimore, MD: Johns Hopkins University Press, pp. 80–123.

Hamp-Lyons, L. (1997) 'Washback, impact and validity: Ethical concerns', *Language Testing,* 14 (3): 295–303.

Herman, J.L. and Haertel, E.H. (eds) (2005) *Uses and Misuses of Data for Educational Accountability and Improvement.* Chicago, IL: National Society for the Study of Education.

Herman, J. and Linn, R. (2013) *On the Road to Assessing Deeper Learning: The Status of Smarter Balanced and PARCC Assessment Consortia.* California, LA: National Center for Research on Evaluations, Standards, & Student Testing.

Hoffman, B. (1962) *The Tyranny of Testing.* New York: Crowell-Collier Press.

Hogan, T.P. and Agnello, J. (2004) 'An empirical study of reporting practices concerning measurement validity', *Educational and Psychological Measurement,* 64 (4): 802–12.

Holcombe, R.H., Jennings, J.L. and Koretz, D. (2013) 'The roots of score inflation: An examination of opportunities in two states' tests', in G. Sunderman and K. Wong (eds), *Charting Reform: Achieving Equity in a Diverse Nation.* Greenwich, CT: Information Age Publishing, pp. 163–89.

Holtzman, N.A. and Watson, M.S. (eds) (1997) 'Promoting safe and effective genetic testing in the United States', final report of the Task Force on Genetic Testing. Available at: www.genome.gov/10001733 (accessed 1 January 2012)

Hood, S.B. (2009) 'Validity in psychological testing and scientific realism', *Theory and Psychology,* 19 (4): 451–73.

House, E.R. (1977) *The Logic of Evaluative Argument.* Los Angeles: Center for the Study of Evaluation, University of California Los Angeles.

Hubley, A.M. and Zumbo, B.D. (1996) 'A dialectic on validity: where we have been and where we are going', *Journal of General Psychology,* 123 (3): 207–15.

Hubley, A.M. and Zumbo, B.D. (2011) 'Validity and the consequences of test interpretation and use', *Social Indicators Research,* 103, 219–30.

Huddlestone, E.M. (1956) 'Test development on the basis of content validity', *Educational and Psychological Measurement,* 16 (3): 283–93.

Hull, C.L. (1928) *Aptitude Testing.* London: George G. Harrap and Co. Ltd.

Hummel-Rossi, B. and Ashdown, J. (2002) 'The state of cost–benefit and cost-effectiveness analyses in education', *Review of Educational Research,* 72 (1): 1–30.

Jackson, D.N. and Messick, S. (1962) 'Response styles and the assessment of psychopathology', in S. Messick and J. Ross (eds), *Measurement in Personality and Cognition.* New York: John Wiley and Sons, pp. 129–55.

Jenkins, J.G. (1946) 'Validity for what?', *Journal of Consulting Psychology,* 10 (2): 93–8.

Jensen, A.R. (1969) 'How much can we boost IQ and scholastic achievement?', *Harvard Educational Review,* 39 (1): 1–123.

Jonson, J.L. and Plake, B.S. (1998) 'A historical comparison of validity standards and validity practices', *Educational and Psychological Measurement,* 58 (5): 736–53.

Jordan, A.M. (1923a) 'The validation of intelligence tests'. *Journal of Educational Psychology,* 14 (6): 348–66.

Jordan, A.M. (1923b) 'The validation of intelligence tests', *Journal of Educational Psychology,* 14 (7): 414–28.

Joseph, K. (1984) 'Speech by the Rt Hon Sir Keith Joseph, Secretary of State for Education and Science', North of England Education Conference, Sheffield, 6 January.

Kane, M.T. (1982) 'A sampling model for validity', *Applied Psychological Measurement*, 6 (2): 125–60.

Kane, M.T. (1990) *An Argument-Based Approach to Validation*, ACT Research Report Series: 90–13. Iowa City, IA: ACT.

Kane, M.T. (1992) 'An argument-based approach to validity', *Psychological Bulletin*, 112 (3): 527–35.

Kane, M.T. (2001) 'Current concerns in validity theory', *Journal of Educational Measurement*, 38 (4): 319–42.

Kane, M.T. (2002) 'Validating high-stakes testing programs', *Educational Measurement: Issues and Practice*, 21 (1): 31–41.

Kane, M.T. (2004) 'Certification testing as an illustration of argument-based validation', *Measurement: Interdisciplinary Research and Perspectives*, 2 (3): 135–70.

Kane, M.T. (2006) Validation', in R.L. Brennan (ed.) *Educational Measurement* (4th edition). Washington, DC: American Council on Education/Praeger, pp. 17–64.

Kane, M.T. (2007) 'Validating measures of mathematical knowledge for teaching', *Measurement: Interdisciplinary Research and Perspectives*, 5 (2): 180–7.

Kane, M.T. (2008) 'Terminology, emphasis and utility in validation', *Educational Researcher*, 37 (2): 76–82.

Kane, M.T. (2009) 'Validating the interpretations and uses of test scores', in R.W. Lissitz (ed.), *The Concept of Validity: Revisions, New Directions and Applications*. Charlotte, NC: Information Age Publishing, pp. 39–64.

Kane, M.T. (2011) 'Validating score interpretations and uses: Messick Lecture, Language Testing Research Colloquium, Cambridge, April 2010', *Language Testing*, 29 (1): 3–17.

Kane, M.T. (2012) 'All validity Is construct validity. Or is it?', *Measurement: Interdisciplinary Research and Perspectives*, 10 (1–2): 66–70.

Kane, M.T. (2013a) 'Validating the interpretations and uses of test scores', *Journal of Educational Measurement*, 50 (1): 1–73.

Kane, M.T. (2013b) 'Validation as a pragmatic, scientific activity', *Journal of Educational Measurement*, 50 (1): 115–22.

Kane, M.T., Crooks, T.J. and Cohen, A.S. (1999) 'Validating measures of performance', *Educational Measurement: Issues and Practice*, 18 (2): 5–17.

Kelley, T.L. (1927) *Interpretation of Educational Measurements*. New York: World Book Company.

Koretz, D. (2005) 'Alignment, high stakes and the inflation of test scores', in J.L. Herman and E.H. Haertel (eds), *Uses and Misuses of Data for Educational Accountability and Improvement. The 104th Yearbook of the National Society for the Study of Education, Part 2*. Malden, MA: Blackwell Publishing, pp. 99–117.

Koretz, D. (2008) *Measuring Up: What Educational Testing Really Tells Us*. Cambridge, MA: Harvard University Press.

Kral, E.A. (2008) 'Ralph Winfred Tyler: Curriculum, instruction and evaluation reformer ranked among world's fifty modern thinkers on education'. Available at: http://nsea.org.alpha.picker-ingcreative.com/sites/default/files/content_images/Resources/NebraskaProfiles.pdf#page=174 (accessed 1 October 2013).

Kunnan, A.J. (1997) 'Connecting validation and fairness in language testing', in A. Huhta, V. Kohonen, L. Kurki-Suonio and S. Luoma (eds), *Current Developments and Alternatives in Language Assessment*. Jyväskylä: University of Jyväskylä, pp. 85–105.

Kunnan, A.J. (2000) 'Fairness and justice for all', in A.J. Kunnan (ed.), *Fairness and Validation in Language Assessment*. Cambridge: Cambridge University Press, pp. 1–14.

Kunnan, A.J. (2004) 'Test fairness', in M. Milanovic and C. Weir (eds), *European Language Testing in a Global Context*. Cambridge: Cambridge University Press, pp. 27–48.

Kvale, S. (1995) 'The social construction of validity', *Qualitative Inquiry*, 1 (1): 19–40.

Landy, F.L. (1986) 'Stamp collecting versus science: validation as hypothesis testing', *American Psychologist*, 41 (11): 1183–92.

Lane, S., Parke, C.S. and Stone, C.A. (1998) 'A framework for evaluating the consequences of assessment programs, *Educational Measurement: Issues and Practice*, 17 (2): 24–8.

Langenfeld, T.E. and Crocker, L.M. (1994) 'The evolution of validity theory: Public school testing, the courts and incompatible interpretations', *Educational Assessment*, 2 (2): 149–65.

Lather, P. (1986) 'Issues of validity in openly ideological research: between a rock and a hard place', *Interchange*, 17 (4): 63–84.

Lather, P. (1993) 'Fertile obsession: validity after poststructuralism'. *Sociological Quarterly*, 34 (4): 673–93.

Lawshe, C.H. (1952) 'Employee selection', *Personnel Psychology*, 5 (1): 31–4.

Lawshe, C.H. (1985) 'Inferences from personnel test and their validity'. *Journal of Applied Psychology*, 70 (1): 237–8.

Lees-Haley, P.R. (1996) 'Alice in Validityland, or the dangerous consequences of consequential validity', *American Psychologist*, 51 (9): 981–3.

Lennon, R.T. (1956) 'Assumptions underlying the use of content validity', *Educational and Psychological Measurement*, 16 (3): 294–304.

Lerner, B. (1981) 'The minimum competency testing movement: Social, scientific and legal implications', *American Psychologist*, 36 (10): 1057–66.

Linden, K.W. and Linden, J.D. (1968) *Modern Mental Measurement: A Historical Perspective*. New York: Houghton Mifflin Company.

Lindquist, E.F. (1936) 'The theory of test construction', in H.E. Hawkes, E.F. Lindquist and C.R. Mann (eds), *The Construction and Use of Achievement Examinations: A Manual for Secondary School Teachers*. Cambridge, MA: Riverside Press, pp. 17–106.

Lindquist, E.F. (ed.) (1951) *Educational Measurement*. Washington, DC: American Council on Education.

Linn, R.L. (1978) 'Single-group validity, differential validity and differential prediction', *Journal of Applied Psychology*, 63 (4): 507–12.

Linn, R.L. (1980) 'Issues of validity for criterion-referenced measures', *Applied Psychological Measurement*, 4 (4): 547–61.

Linn, R.L. (1997) 'Evaluating the validity of assessments: the consequences of use', *Educational Measurement: Issues and Practice*, 16 (2): 14–16.

Linn, R.L. (1998) 'Partitioning responsibility for the evaluation of the consequences of assessment programs', *Educational Measurement: Issues and Practice*, 17 (2): 28–30.

Linn, R.L., Baker, E.L. and Dunbar, S.B. (1991) 'Complex, performance-based assessment: expectations and validation criteria', *Educational Researcher*, 20 (8): 15–21.

Lissitz, R.W. and Samuelsen, K. (2007a) 'A suggested change in terminology and emphasis regarding validity and education', *Educational Researcher*, 36 (8): 437–48.

Lissitz, R.W. and Samuelsen, K. (2007b) 'Further clarification regarding validity and education', *Educational Researcher*, 36 (8): 482–4.

Loevinger, J. (1947) 'A systematic approach to the construction and evaluation of tests of ability', *Psychological Monographs*, 61 (4): i–49.

Loevinger, J. (1957) 'Objective tests as instruments of psychological theory', *Psychological Reports*, 3 (3): 635–94.

Lord, F.M. (1955) 'Some perspectives on "the attenuation paradox in test theory"', *Psychological Bulletin*, 52 (6): 505–10.

Lord, F.M. and Novick, M.R. (1968) *Statistical Theories of Mental Test Scores*. Reading, MA: Addison-Wesley.

Lovasz, N. and Slaney, K.L. (2013) 'What makes a hypothetical construct "hypothetical"? Tracing the origins and uses of the "hypothetical construct" concept in psychological science', *New Ideas in Psychology*, 31 (1): 22–31.

McCall, W.A. (1922) *How to Measure in Education*. New York: The Macmillan Company.

McClung, M.S. (1979) 'Competency testing programs: Legal and educational issues', *Fordham Law Review*, 47 (5): 651–712.

McNamara, T. (2001) 'Language assessment as social practice: challenges for research', *Language Testing*, 18 (4): 333–349.

MacCorquodale, K. and Meehl, P.E. (1948) On a distinction between hypothetical constructs and intervening variables. *Psychological Review*, 55 (2): 95–107.

MacPhail, F. (1998) 'Moving beyond statistical validity in economics', *Social Indicators Research*, 45 (1–3): 119–49.

Maguire, T., Hattie, J. and Haig, B. (1994) 'Construct validity and achievement assessment', *Alberta Journal of Educational Research*, 40 (2): 109–26.

Mansell, W. (2007) *Education By Numbers: The Tyranny of Testing*. London: Politico's Publishing.

Maraun, M.D. (1998) 'Measurement as a normative practice: implications of Wittgenstein's philosophy for measurement in psychology', *Theory and Psychology*, 8 (4): 435–61.

Maraun, M.D. and Gabriel, S.M. (2013) 'Illegitimate concept equating in the partial fusion of construct validation theory and latent variable modelling', *New Ideas in Psychology*, 31 (1): 32–42.

Maraun, M.D., Slaney, K.L. and Gabriel, S.M. (2009) 'The Augustinian methodological family of psychology', *New Ideas in Psychology*, 27 (2): 148–62.

Marion, S.F. and Pellegrino, J. (2009) 'Validity framework for evaluating the technical quality of alternate assessments based on alternate achievement standards', invited presentation, National Council on Measurement in Education Annual Meeting, San Diego, CA, 14–16 April.

Markus, K.A. (1998) 'Science, measurement and validity: is completion of Samuel Messick's synthesis possible?', *Social Indicators Research*, 45 (1–3): 7–34.

Markus, K.A. (2012) 'Constructs and attributes in test validity: reflections on Newton's account', *Measurement: Interdisciplinary Research and Perspectives*, 10 (1–2): 84–7.

Markus, K.A. and Borsboom, D. (2013) *Frontiers of Test Validity Theory: Measurement, Causation and Meaning*. New York: Routledge.

Markus, M.L. and Robey, D. (1980) *The Organizational Validity of Management Information Systems*. Cambridge, MA: Center for Information Systems Research, MIT.

Marschak, J. (1954) 'Probability in the social sciences', in P.F. Lazarsfeld (ed.), *Mathematical Thinking in the Social Sciences*. Glencoe, IL: The Free Press, pp. 166–215.

Maxwell, J.A. (1992) 'Understanding and validity in qualitative research', *Harvard Educational Review*, 62 (3): 279–300.

Meehl, P.E. (1945) 'The dynamics of "structured" personality tests', *Journal of Clinical Psychology*, 1 (4): 296–303.

Meehl, P.E. (1971[1945]) 'Meehl, P.E. (1945): Reprinted with prefatory comment', in L.D. Goodstein and R.I. Lanyon (eds), *Readings in Personality Assessment*. New York: Wiley, pp. 245–53.

Mehrens, W.A. (1997) 'The consequences of consequential validity', *Educational Measurement: Issues and Practice*, 16 (2): 16–18.

Mehrens, W.A. (1998) 'Consequences of assessment: What is the evidence?', *Education Policy Analysis Archives*, 6 (13): 1–30.

Merki, K.M. (2011) 'Guest editor's introduction. Special issue: Accountability systems and their effects on school processes and student learning', *Studies in Educational Evaluation*, 37 (4): 177–9.

Messick, S. (1964) 'Personality measurement and college performance', in A.G. Wesman (ed.), *Proceedings of the 1963 Invitational Conference on Testing Problems*. Princeton, NJ: Educational Testing Service, pp. 110–29.

Messick, S. (1965) 'Personality measurement and the ethics of assessment', *American Psychologist*, 20 (2): 136–42.

Messick, S. (1975) 'The standard problem: meaning and values in measurement and evaluation', *American Psychologist*, 30 (10): 955–66.

Messick, S. (1980) 'Test validity and the ethics of assessment', *American Psychologist*, 35 (11): 1012–27.

Messick, S. (1981) 'Evidence and ethics in the evaluation of tests', *Educational Researcher*, 10 (9): 9–20.

Messick, S. (1984) 'Assessment in context: appraising student performance in relation to instructional quality', *Educational Researcher*, 13 (3): 3–8.

Messick, S. (1988) 'The once and future issues of validity: assessing the meaning and consequences of measurement', in H. Wainer and H.I. Braun (eds), *Test Validity*. Hillsdale, N.J: Lawrence Erlbaum Associates, pp. 33–45.

Messick, S. (1989a) 'Validity', in R. Linn (ed.) *Educational Measurement* (3rd edition). Washington, DC: American Council on Education, pp. 13–100.

Messick, S. (1989b) 'Meaning and values in test validation: The science and ethics of assessment', *Educational Researcher*, 18 (2): 5–11.

Messick, S. (1992) 'Validity of test interpretation and use', in M.C. Alkin (ed.), *Encyclopedia of Educational Research*, Volume 4 (6th edition). New York: Macmillan Publishing Company, pp. 1487–95.

Messick, S. (1994) 'The interplay of evidence and consequences in the validation of performance assessments', *Educational Researcher*, 23 (2): 13–23.

Messick, S. (1995a) 'Validity of psychological assessment: Validation of inferences from persons' responses and performances as scientific inquiry into score meaning', *American Psychologist*, 50 (9): 741–9.

Messick, S. (1995b) 'Standards of validity and the validity of standards in performance assessment', *Educational Measurement: Issues and Practice*, 14 (4): 5–8.

Messick, S. (1996) 'Validity and washback in language testing', *Language Testing*, 13 (3): 241–56.

Messick, S. (1998a) 'Alternative models of assessment, uniform standards of validity', in M. Hakel (ed.), *Beyond Multiple Choice: Evaluating Alternatives to Traditional Testing for Selection*, pp. 59–74. Mahwah, NJ: Lawrence Erlbaum Associates.

Messick, S. (1998b) 'Test validity: a matter of consequences'. *Social Indicators Research*, 45 (1–3): 35–44.

Messick, S. (2000) 'Consequences of test interpretation and use: the fusion of validity and values in psychological assessment', in R.D. Goffin and E. Helmes (eds), *Problems and Solutions in Human Assessment: Honoring Douglas N. Jackson at Seventy*. Norwell, MA: Kluwer Academic Publishers, pp. 3–20.

Messick, S. and Anderson, S. (1974) 'Educational testing, individual development and social responsibility', in R.W. Tyler and R.M. Wolf (eds), *Crucial Issues in Testing*. Berkeley, CA: McCutchan Publishing Corporation, pp. 21–34.

Meyer, G. (1934) 'An experimental study of the old and new types of examination: I. The effect of the examination set on memory', *Journal of Educational Psychology*, 25 (9): 641–61.

Meyer, G. (1935) 'An experimental study of the old and new types of examination: II. Methods of study', *Journal of Educational Psychology*, 26 (1): 30–40.

Meyer, M. (1908) 'The grading of students', *Science*, 28: 243–50.

Michell, J. (1990) *An Introduction to the Logic of Psychological Measurement*. Hillsdale, NJ: Erlbaum.

Michell, J. (1999) *Measurement in Psychology: A Critical History of a Methodological Concept*. Cambridge: Cambridge University Press.

Michell, J. (2000) 'Normal science, pathological science and psychometrics', *Theory and Psychology*, 10 (5): 639–67.

Michell, J. (2005) 'The logic of measurement: a realist overview', *Measurement*, 38 (4): 285–94.

Michell, J. (2009) 'Invalidity in validity', in R.W. Lissitz (ed.), *The Concept of Validity: Revisions, New Directions and Applications*. Charlotte, NC: Information Age Publishing, pp. 111–33.

Milanovic, M. and Saville, N. (1996) 'Considering the impact of Cambridge EFL Examinations', manuscript internal report. Cambridge: Cambridge ESOL.

Mislevy, R.J. (2003a) *Argument Substance and Argument Structure in Educational Assessment*, CSE Report 605. Los Angeles, CA: National Center for Research on Evaluation, Standards and Student Testing, University of California Los Angeles.

Mislevy, R.J. (2003b) 'Substance and structure in assessment arguments', *Law, Probability and Risk*, 2 (4): 237–58.

Mislevy, R.J. (2007) 'Validity by design', *Educational Researcher*, 36 (8): 463–69.

Mislevy, R.J. (2009) 'Validity from the perspective of model-based reasoning', in R.W. Lissitz (ed.), *The Concept of Validity: Revisions, New Directions and Applications*. Charlotte, NC: Information Age Publishing, pp. 83–108.

Mislevy, R.J., Steinberg, L.S. and Almond, R.G. (2003) 'On the structure of educational assessments', *Measurement: Interdisciplinary Research and Perspectives*, 1 (1): 3–67.

Monk, D.H. (1995) 'The costs of pupil performance assessment: a summary report', *Journal of Education Finance*, 20 (4): 363–71.

Monroe, W.S. (1923) *An Introduction to the Theory of Educational Measurements*. Cambridge, MA: Riverside Press.

Monroe, W.S. (1935) 'Effect of measurement on instruction', *Journal of Educational Research*, 28 (7): 496–7.

Monroe, W.S. (1945) 'Educational measurement in 1920 and in 1945', *Journal of Educational Research*, 38 (5): 334–40.

Montgomery, R.J. (1965) *Examinations: An Account of their Evolution as Administrative Devices in England*. London: Longmans, Green and Co.

Morrow, K. (1986) 'The evaluation of tests of communicative performance', in M. Portal (ed.), *Innovations in Language Testing: Proceedings of the IUS/NFER Conference 1985*. Windsor: NFER-NELSON, pp. 1–13.

Mosier, C.I. (1947) 'A critical examination of the concepts of face validity', *Educational and Psychological Measurement*, 7 (2): 191–205.

Moss, P.A. (1992) 'Shifting conceptions of validity in educational measurement: implications for performance assessment', *Review of Educational Research*, 62 (3): 229–58.

Moss, P.A. (1994) 'Can there be validity without reliability?', *Educational Researcher*, 23 (2): 5–12.

Moss, P.A. (1995) 'Themes and variations in validity theory', *Educational Measurement: Issues and Practice*, 14 (2): 5–13.

Moss, P.A. (1996) 'Enlarging the dialogue in educational measurement: voices from interpretive research traditions', *Educational Researcher*, 25 (1): 20–8.

Moss, P.A. (1998) 'The role of consequences in validity theory', *Educational Measurement: Issues and Practice*, 17 (2): 6–12.

Moss, P.A. (2003) 'Reconceptualizing validity for classroom assessment', *Educational Measurement: Issues and Practice*, 22 (4): 13–25.

Moss, P.A. (2007) 'Reconstructing validity', *Educational Researcher*, 36 (8): 470–6.

Moss, P.A. (2013) 'Validity in action: lessons from studies of data use', *Journal of Educational Measurement*, 50 (1): 91–8.

Moss, P.A., Pullin, D., Gee, J.P. and Haertl, E.H. (2005) 'The idea of testing: psychometric and sociocultural perspectives'. *Measurement: Interdisciplinary Research and Perspectives*, 3 (2): 63–83.

Moss, P.A., Girard, B.J. and Haniford, L.C. (2006) 'Validity in educational assessment', *Review of Research in Education*, 30: 109–62.

Mossholder, K.W. and Arvey, R.D. (1984) 'Synthetic validity: a conceptual and comparative review', *Journal of Applied Psychology*, 69 (2): 322–33.

Newton, P.E. (2005a) 'The public understanding of measurement inaccuracy', *British Educational Research Journal*, 31 (4): 419–42.

Newton, P.E. (2005b) 'Threats to the professional understanding of assessment error', *Journal of Education Policy*, 20 (4): 457–83.

Newton, P.E. (2007) 'Clarifying the purposes of educational assessment', *Assessment in Education: Principles, Policy and Practice*, 14 (2): 149–70.

Newton, P.E. (2010) 'Educational assessment – concepts and issues: the multiple purposes of assessment', in P. Peterson, E. Baker, and B. McGaw (eds), *International Encyclopedia of Education* (3rd edition). Oxford: Elsevier, pp. 392–6.

Newton, P.E. (2012a) 'Clarifying the consensus definition of validity', *Measurement: Interdisciplinary Research and Perspectives*, 10 (1–2): 1–29.

Newton, P.E. (2012b) 'Questioning the consensus definition of validity', *Measurement: Interdisciplinary Research and Perspectives*, 10 (1–2): 110–22.

Newton, P.E. (2013a) 'Two kinds of argument?', *Journal of Educational Measurement*, 50 (1): 105–9.

Newton, P.E. (2013b) 'Ofqual's Reliability Programme: a case study exploring the potential to improve public understanding and confidence', *Oxford Review of Education*, 39 (1): 93–113.

Newton, P.E. and Shaw, S.D. (2013) 'Standards for talking and thinking about validity', *Psychological Methods*, 18 (3): 301–19.

Nichols, P.D., Meyers, J.L. and Burling, K.S. (2009) 'A framework for evaluating and planning assessments intended to improve student achievement', *Educational Measurement: Issues and Practice*, 28 (3): 14–23.

Norris, S.P. (1983) 'The inconsistencies at the foundation of construct validation theory', in E.R. House (ed.), *Philosophy of Evaluation: New Directions for Program Evaluation*, no. 19. San Francisco, CA: Jossey-Bass. pp. 53–74.

Norris, S.P. (1995) 'Measurement by tests and consequences of test use', in *Philosophy of Education*. Urbana, IL: Philosophy of Education Society, pp. 303–6.

Novick, M.R. (1981) 'Federal guidelines and professional standards', *American Psychologist*, 36 (10): 1035–46.

Nunnally, J.C. (1959) *Tests and Measurements: Assessment and Prediction*. New York: McGraw-Hill Book Company.

Nunnally, J.C. (1967) *Psychometric Theory*. New York: McGraw-Hill Book Company.

Oates, T. (2010) *Could Do Better: Using International Comparisons to Refine the National Curriculum in England*. Cambridge: Cambridge Assessment.

Odell, C.W. (1928) *A Glossary of Three Hundred Terms Used in Educational Measurement and Research*. Urbana, IL: University of Illinois.

Office of Federal Contract Compliance (1968) 'Validation of employment tests', *Federal Register*, 33, 14392–14394. Washington, DC: Department of Labor.

Office of Federal Contract Compliance (1971) 'Employee testing and other selection procedures', *Federal Register*, 36, 19307–19310. Washington, DC: Department of Labor.

Orata, P.T. (1940) 'Evaluating evaluation', *Journal of Educational Research*, 33 (9): 641–61.

Orton, R.E. (1986) 'Do tests measure those constructs that people interpret them to measure?', *Educational Theory*, 36 (3): 233–40.

Orton, R.E. (1987) 'The foundations of construct validity: towards an update', *Journal of Research and Development in Education*, 21 (1): 23–35.

Orton, R.E. (1998) 'Samuel Messick's consequential validity', in *Philosophy of Education*. Urbana, IL: Philosophy of Education Society, pp. 538–45.

Osburn, H.G. (1968) 'Item sampling for achievement testing', *Educational and Psychological Measurement*, 28 (1): 95–104.

Osburn, W.J. (1933) 'Educational tests and their uses: the selection of test items', *Review of Research in Education*, 3: 21–32.

Parkes, J. and Stevens, J.J. (2003) 'Legal issues in school accountability systems', *Applied Measurement in Education*, 16 (2): 141–58.

Peak, H. (1953) 'Problems of objective observation', in L. Festinger and D. Katz (eds), *Research Methods in the Behavioral Sciences*. London: Staples Press Limited, pp. 243–99.

Pellegrino, J.W. (1988) 'Mental models and mental tests', in H. Wainer and H.I. Braun (eds), *Test Validity*. Hillsdale, NJ: Lawrence Erlbaum. pp. 49–59.

Penfield, R. (2010) 'Test-based grade retention: does it stand up to professional standards for fair and appropriate test use?', *Educational Researcher*, 39 (2): 110–19.

Phelps, R.P. (ed.) (2005) *Defending Standardized Testing*. Mahwah; NJ: Lawrence Erlbaum.

Phelps, R.P. (2012) 'The effect of testing on student achievement, 1910–2010', *International Journal of Testing*, 12 (1): 21–43.

Phillips, S.E. (1994) 'High-stakes testing accommodations: validity versus disabled rights', *Applied Measurement in Education*, 7 (2): 93–120.

Phillips, S.E. (1996) 'Legal defensibility of standards: issues and policy perspectives', *Educational Measurement: Issues and Practice*, 15 (2): 5–13, 19.

Phillips, S.E. and Camara, W.J. (2006) 'Legal and ethical issues', in R.L. Brennan (ed.), *Educational Measurement* (4th edition). Washington, DC: American Council on Education/Praeger, pp. 733–55.

Picus, L.O. (1996) *Estimating the Costs of Student Assessment in North Carolina and Kentucky: A State-Level Analysis*, CSE Technical Report 408. Los Angeles, CA: National Center for Research on Evaluation, Standards and Student Testing, University of California Los Angeles.

Polesel, J., Dulfer, N. and Turnbull, M. (2012) *The Experience of Education: The Impacts of High Stakes Testing on School Students and Their Families. Literature Review*. Sydney: Whitlam Institute, University of Western Sydney.

Pollitt, A. (2012) 'Validity cannot be created, it can only be lost', *Measurement: Interdisciplinary Research and Perspectives*, 10 (1–2): 100–3.

Popham, W.J. (1997) 'Consequential validity: right concern – wrong concept', *Educational Measurement: Issues and Practice*, 16 (2): 9–13.

Popham, W.J. and Husek, T.R. (1969) 'Implications of criterion-referenced measurement', *Journal of Educational Measurement*, 6 (1): 1–9.

Popper, K. (1959[1935]) *Logik der Forschung [The Logic of Scientific Discovery]*. London: Hutchinson.

Rea-Dickens, P. and Scott, C. (2007) 'Editorial. Washback from language tests on teaching, learning and policy: evidence from diverse settings', *Assessment in Education: Principles, Policy and Practice*, 14 (1): 1–7.

Reckase, M.D. (1998a) 'The interaction of values and validity assessment: does a test's level of validity depend on a researcher's values?', *Social Indicators Research*, 45 (1–3): 45–54.

Reckase, M.D. (1998b) 'Consequential validity from the test developer's perspective', *Educational Measurement: Issues and Practice*, 17 (2): 13–16.

Rhoades, K. and Madaus, G. (2003) *Errors in Standardized Tests: A Systemic Problem. Report of National Board on Educational Testing and Public Policy*. Chestnut Hill, MA: Boston College Center for the Study of Testing.

Richardson, M.W. and Adkins, DC (1938) 'A rapid method for selecting test items', *Journal of Educational Psychology*, 29 (7): 547–52.

Roach, J. (1971) *Public Examinations in England 1850–1900*. Cambridge: Cambridge University Press.

Rogers, T.B. (1988) 'The introduction of construct validity to the assessment field: an historical analysis', in L.P. Mos, H.V. Rappard and H.J. Stam (eds), *Recent Trends in Theoretical Psychology*. New York: Springer-Verlag, pp. 237–46.

Rogers, T.B. (1989) 'Operationism in psychology: a discussion of contextual antecedents and an historical interpretation of its longevity', *Journal of the History of the Behavioral Sciences*, 25 (2): 139–53.

Rogers, T.B. (1995) *The Psychological Testing Enterprise: An Introduction*. Pacific Grove, CA: Brooks/Cole Publishing Company.

Rozeboom, W.W. (1978) 'Domain validity – why care?', *Educational and Psychological Measurement*, 38 (1): 81–8.

Ruch, G.M. (1924) *The Improvement of the Written Examination*. Chicago, IL: Scott, Foresman and Company.

Ruch, G.M. (1925) 'Minimum essentials in reporting data on standard tests', *Journal of Educational Research*, 15 (5): 349–58.

Ruch, G.M. (1929) *The Objective or New-type Examination: An Introduction to Educational Measurement*. Chicago, IL: Scott, Foresman and Company.

Ruch, G.M. (1933) 'Educational tests and their uses: recent developments in statistical prediction', *Review of Research in Education*, 3: 33–40.

Ruch, G.M. and Stoddard, G.D. (1927) *Tests and Measurements in High School Instruction*. New York: World Book Company.

Rulon, P.J. (1946) 'On the validity of educational tests', *Harvard Educational Review*, 16: 290–6.

Ryan, D.G. (1939) 'A note on methods of test validation', *Journal of Educational Psychology*, 30 (4): 315–19.

Saville, N. (2010) 'Developing a model for investigating the impact of language assessment', *Research Notes*, 42: 2–8.

Sawyer, R.L., Cole, N.S. and Cole, J.W.L. (1976) 'Utilities and the issue of fairness in a decision theoretic model for selection', *Journal of Educational Measurement*, 13 (1): 59–76.

Scates, D.E. (1947) 'Fifty years of objective measurement and research in education', *Journal of Educational Research*, 41 (4): 241–64.

Schilling, S.G. (2007) 'Generalizability and specificity of interpretive arguments: observations inspired by the commentaries', *Measurement: Interdisciplinary Research and Perspectives*, 5 (2): 211–16.

Schilling, S.G. and Hill, H.C. (2007) 'Assessing measures of mathematical knowledge for teaching: a validity argument approach', *Measurement: Interdisciplinary Research and Perspectives*, 5 (2): 70–80.

Schmidt, F.L. and Hunter, J.E. (1977) 'Development of a general solution to the problem of validity generalization', *Journal of Applied Psychology*, 62 (5): 529–40.

Schouwstra, S.J. (2000) 'On testing plausible threats to construct validity', PhD thesis, University of Amsterdam. Available at: http://dare.uva.nl/en/record/220482 (accessed 1 January 2012).

Scott, E.P. (2012) 'Short-term gain at long-term cost? How resit policy can affect student learning', *Assessment in Education: Principles Policy and Practice*, 19 (4): 431–49.

Scriven, M. (2002) 'Assessing six assumptions in assessment', in H.I. Braun, D.N. Jackson and D.E. Wiley (eds), *The Role of Constructs in Psychological and Educational Measurement*. Mahwah, NJ: Lawrence Erlbaum Associates, pp. 255–75.

Shaw, D.J. and Linden, J.D. (1964) 'A critique of the Hand test', *Educational and Psychological Measurement*, 24 (2): 283–4.

Shaw, S.D. and Crisp, V. (2012) 'An approach to validation: developing and applying an approach for the validation of general qualifications', *Research Matters* (special issue 3): 1–44.

Shaw, S.D. and Weir, C.J. (2007) *Examining Writing: Research and Practice in Assessing Second Language Writing*. Cambridge: Cambridge University Press.

Shaw, S.D., Crisp, V. and Johnson, N. (2012) 'A framework for evidencing assessment validity in large-scale, high-stakes international examinations', *Assessment in Education: Policy, Principles and Practice*, 19 (2): 159–76.

Shepard, L.A. (1990) 'Readiness testing in local school districts: an analysis of backdoor policies', *Journal of Education Policy*, 5 (5): 159–79.

Shepard, L.A. (1993) 'Evaluating test validity', *Review of Research in Education*, 19: 405–50.

Shepard, L.A. (1997) 'The centrality of test use and consequences for test validity', *Educational Measurement: Issues and Practice*, 16 (2): 5–8.

Sireci, S.G. (1998a) 'Gathering and analysing content validity data', *Educational Assessment*, 5 (4): 299–321.

Sireci, S.G. (1998b) 'The construct of content validity', *Social Indicators Research*, 45 (1–3): 83–117.

Sireci, S.G. (2007) 'On validity theory and test validation', *Educational Researcher*, 36 (8): 477–81.

Sireci, S.G. (2009) 'Packing and unpacking sources of validity evidence: history repeats itself again', in R.W. Lissitz (ed.), *The Concept of Validity: Revisions, New Directions and Applications*. Charlotte, NC: Information Age Publishing, pp. 19–37.

Sireci, S.G. (2013) 'Agreeing on validity arguments', *Journal of Educational Measurement*, 50 (1): 99–104.

Sireci, S.G. and Green, P.C. (2000) 'Legal and psychometric criteria for evaluating teacher certification tests', *Educational Measurement: Issues and Practice*, 19 (1): 22–31, 34.

Sireci, S.G and Parker, P. (2006) 'Validity on trial: psychometric and legal conceptualizations of validity', *Educational Measurement: Issues and Practice*, 25 (3): 27–34.

Slaney, K.L. (2012) 'Laying the cornerstone of construct validity theory: Herbert Feigl's influence on early specifications', *Theory and Psychology*, 22 (3): 290–309.

Slaney, K.L. and Maraun, M. (2008) 'A proposed framework for conducting data-based test analysis', *Psychological Methods*, 13 (4): 376–90.

Smith, G.T. (2005) 'On construct validity: issues of method and measurement', *Psychological Assessment*, 17 (4): 396–408.

Spearman, C. (1904) '"General intelligence": objectively determined and measured', *American Journal of Psychology*, 15: 201–93.

Starch, D. (1916) *Educational Measurements*. New York: The Macmillan Company.

Starch, D. and Elliott, E.C. (1912) 'Reliability of the grading of high-school work in English', *The School Review*, 20 (7): 442–57.

Starch, D. and Elliott, E.C. (1913) 'Reliability of grading work in mathematics', *The School Review*, 21 (4): 254–9.

Stevens, S.S. (1935) 'The operational definition of psychological concepts', *Psychological Review*, 42 (6): 517–27.

Stevens, S.S. (1951) 'Mathematics, measurement and psychophysics', in S.S. Stevens (ed.), *Handbook of Experimental Psychology*. New York: Wiley, pp. 1–49.

Stobart, G. (2006) 'The validity of formative assessment', in J. Gardner (ed.), *Assessment and Learning*. London: Sage, pp. 133–46.

Stobart, G. (2009) 'Determining validity in national curriculum assessments', *Educational Research*, 51 (2): 161–79.

Stobart, G. (2012) 'Validity in formative assessment', in J. Gardner (ed.), *Assessment and Learning* (2nd edition). London: Sage, pp. 233–42.

Sutherland, G. (1984) *Ability, Merit and Measurement: Mental Testing and English Education 1880–1940*. Oxford: Oxford University Press.

Taylor, H.C. and Russell, J.T. (1939) 'The relationship of validity coefficients to the practical effectiveness of tests in selection: discussion and tables', *Journal of Applied Psychology*, 23 (5): 565–78.

Taylor, L. (2005) 'Washback and impact: the view from Cambridge ESOL', *Research Notes*, 20: 2–3.

Taylor, L. and Weir, C.J. (eds) (2009) 'Language testing matters: Investigating the wider social and educational impact of assessment – proceedings of the ALTE Cambridge Conference, April 2008', in *Studies in Language Testing*, 31. Cambridge: University of Cambridge ESOL Examinations.

Tenopyr, M.L. (1977) 'Content-construct confusion', *Personnel Psychology*, 30 (1): 47–54.

Terman, L.M. (1918) 'Tests of general intelligence', *Psychological Bulletin*, 15 (5): 160–7.

Terman, L.M., Lyman, G. Ordahl, G., Ordahl, L., Galbreath, N. and Talbert, W. (1915) 'The Stanford revision of the Binet-Simon scale and some results from its application to 1000 non-selected children', *Journal of Educational Psychology*, 6 (9): 551–62.

Thorndike, E.L. (1903) *Educational Psychology*. New York: Teachers College, Columbia University.

Thorndike, E.L. (1904) *An Introduction to the Theory of Mental and Social Measurements*. New York: Teachers College, Columbia University.

Thorndike, E.L. (1916) *An Introduction to the Theory of Mental and Social Measurements* (2nd edition) New York: Teachers College, Columbia University.

Thorndike, E.L. (1925) 'The improvement of mental measurements', *Journal of Educational Research*, 11 (1): 1–11.

Thorndike, R.L. (1949) *Personnel Selection: Test and Measurement Techniques*. New York: John Wiley and Sons, Inc.

Thorndike, R.L. (ed.) (1971a) *Educational Measurement* (2nd edition) Washington: DC.: American Council on Education.

Thorndike, R.L. (1971b) 'Concepts of culture-fairness', *Journal of Educational Measurement*, 8 (2): 63–70.

Thorndike, R.L. and Hagen, E.P. (1955) *Measurement and Evaluation in Psychology and Education*. New York: John Wiley and Sons Inc.

Thorndike, R.L. and Hagen, E.P. (1961) *Measurement and Evaluation in Psychology and Education* (2nd edition) New York: John Wiley and Sons Inc.

Thorndike, R.L. and Hagen, E.P. (1969) *Measurement and Evaluation in Psychology and Education* (3rd edition) New York: John Wiley and Sons Inc.

Thorndike, R.L. and Hagen, E.P. (1977) *Measurement and Evaluation in Psychology and Education* (4th edition) New York: John Wiley and Sons Inc.

Thurstone, L.L. (1931) *The Reliability and Validity of Tests: Derivation and Interpretation of Fundamental Formulae Concerned with Reliability and Validity of Tests and Illustrative Problems.* Ann Arbor, MI: Edwards Brothers, Inc.

Toops, H.A. (1944) 'The criterion', *Educational and Psychological Measurement*, 4 (1): 271–97.

Toulmin, S. (1958) *The Uses of Argument.* Cambridge: Cambridge University Press.

Travers, R.M.W. (1951) 'Rational hypotheses in the construction of tests', *Educational and Psychological Measurement*, 11 (1): 128–37.

Trochim, W.M. (2006) 'The research methods knowledge base' (2nd edition), Web Center for Social Research Methods. Available at: www.socialresearchmethods.net/kb/ (accessed 1 October 2006).

Tryon, R.C. (1957a) 'Reliability and behavior domain validity: reformulation and historical critique', *Psychological Bulletin*, 54 (3): 229–49.

Tryon, R.C. (1957b) 'Communality of a variable: formulation by cluster analysis', *Psychometrika*, 22 (3): 241–60.

Tyler, R.W. (1931a) 'A generalized technique for conducting achievement tests', *Educational Research Bulletin*, 10 (8): 199–208.

Tyler, R.W. (1931b) 'New tests', *Educational Research Bulletin*, 10 (7): 197–8.

Tyler, R.W. (1932a) 'Improving test materials in the social studies', *Educational Research Bulletin*, 11 (14): 373–9.

Tyler, R.W. (1932b) 'Measuring the results of college instruction', *Educational Research Bulletin*, 11 (10): 253–60.

Tyler, R.W. (1934) 'Techniques for evaluating behavior', *Educational Research Bulletin*, 13 (1): 1–11.

Tyler, R.W. (1936) 'Needed research in the field of tests and examinations', *Educational Research Bulletin*, 15 (6): 151–8.

University of Chicago Library (2008) 'Guide to the Ralph W. Tyler Papers 1932–1988'. Available at: www.lib.uchicago.edu/e/scrc/findingaids/view.php?eadid=ICU.SPCL.TYLER (accessed 1 April 2013).

University of Illinois (2011) 'Walter S. Monroe Papers, 1912–13, 1917–26, 1930–40, 1949–50, 1956', University of Illinois Archives. Available at: http://archives.library.illinois.edu/archon/?p=collections/controlcard&id=500, (accessed 15 May 2013).

von Mayrhauser, R.T. (1992) 'The mental testing community and validity: a prehistory', *American Psychologist*, 47 (2): 244–53.

Wainer, H. and Braun, H.I. (eds) (1988) *Test Validity.* Hillsdale, NJ: Lawrence Erlbaum.

Waluchow, W.J. (2009) 'Four concepts of validity: reflections on inclusive and exclusive positivism', in M. Adler and K. Himma (eds), *The Rule of Recognition and the United States Constitution.* Oxford: Oxford University Press, pp. 123–44.

Wernimont, P.F. and Campbell, J.P. (1968) 'Signs, samples and criteria', *Journal of Applied Psychology*, 52 (5): 372–6.

Whipple, G.M. (1915) *Manual of Mental and Physical Tests.* Baltimore, MD: Warwick and York.

Wikipedia (2013) 'SAT', 18 September. Available at: http://en.wikipedia.org/wiki/SAT (accessed 1 March 2013).

Wiktionary (2013) 'Validus', 28 August. Available at: http://en.wiktionary.org/wiki/validus (accessed 10 May 2013).

Wiley, D.E. (1991) 'Test validity and invalidity reconsidered', in R.E. Snow and D.E. Wiley (eds), *Improving Inquiry in Social Science: A Volume in Honor of Lee J. Cronbach.* Hillsdale, NJ: Lawrence Erlbaum Associates, pp. 75–107.

Wiliam, D. (2008) 'Quality in assessment', in S. Swaffield (ed.), *Unlocking Assessment: Understanding for Reflection and Application.* Oxford: Routledge, pp. 123–37.

Wiliam, D. (2010) 'What counts as evidence of educational achievement? The role of constructs in the pursuit of equity in assessment', *Review of Research in Education*, 34 (1): 254–84.

Wiliam, D. and Black, P. (1996) 'Meanings and consequences: a basis for distinguishing formative and summative functions of assessment', *British Educational Research Journal*, 22 (5): 537–48.

Willingham, W.W. and Cole, N.S. (eds) (1997) *Gender and Fair Assessment*. Mahwah, NJ: Lawrence Erlbaum Associates.

Wolfe, D. (1946) 'The reorganization of the American Psychological Association', *American Psychologist*, 1 (1): 3–6.

Wolming, S. and Wikstrom, C. (2010) 'The concept of validity in theory and practice', *Assessment in Education: Principles, Policy and Practice*, 17 (2): 117–32.

Wood, B.D., Lindquist, E.F. and Anderson, H.R. (1933) 'Educational tests and their uses: basic considerations', *Review of Research in Education*, 3: 5–20.

Woody, C. and Others (1935) 'A symposium on the effects of measurement on instruction', *Journal of Educational Research*, 28 (7): 481–527.

Wools, S., Eggen, T. and Sanders, P. (2010) 'Evaluation of validity and validation by means of the argument-based approach', CADMO, 8: 63–82.

Xi, X. (2010) 'How do we go about investigating test fairness?', *Language Testing*, 27 (2): 147–70.

Yeh, S.S. (2001) 'Tests worth teaching to: constructing state-mandated tests that emphasize critical thinking', *Educational Researcher*, 30 (9): 12–17.

Zumbo, B.D. (2007) 'Validity: foundational issues and statistical methodology', *Handbook of Statistics*, 26: 45–79.

Zumbo, B.D. (2009) 'Validity as contextualized and pragmatic explanation and its implications for validation practice', in R.W. Lissitz (ed.), *The Concept of Validity: Revisions, New Directions and Applications*. Charlotte, NC: Information Age Publishing, pp. 65–82.

INDEX